THE BROKEN BODY

Challenges in Contemporary Theology

Series Editors: Gareth Jones and Lewis Ayres
Ming Hua Theological College, Hong Kong and University of Durham, UK

Challenges in Contemporary Theology is a series aimed at producing clear orientations in, and research on, areas of "challenge" in contemporary theology. These carefully co-ordinated books engage traditional theological concerns with mainstreams in modern thought and culture that challenge those concerns. The "challenges" implied are to be understood in two senses: those presented by society to contemporary theology, and those posed by theology to society.

Published

THE BROKEN BODY

Israel, Christ and Fragmentation

Sarah Coakley

WILEY Blackwell

Registered Offices
John Wiley & Sons, Inc., 111 River Street, Hoboken, NJ 07030, USA
John Wiley & Sons Ltd, The Atrium, Southern Gate, Chichester, West Sussex, PO19 8SQ, UK

For details of our global editorial offices, customer services, and more information about Wiley products visit us at www.wiley.com.

Library of Congress Cataloging-in-Publication Data
Names: Coakley, Sarah, 1951– author.
Title: The broken body : Israel, Christ and fragmentation / Sarah Coakley,
    Harvard University Department of Religion Cambridge, US.
Description: Hoboken, NJ : John Wiley & Sons, Ltd., [2024] | Includes
    index.
Identifiers: LCCN 2024004262 (print) | LCCN 2024004263 (ebook) | ISBN
    9781405189231 (paperback) | ISBN 9781118780824 (adobe pdf) | ISBN
    9781118780800 (epub)
Subjects: LCSH: Jesus Christ–Person and offices. | Jesus Christ–History
    of doctrines.
Classification: LCC BT198 .C538 2024 (print) | LCC BT198 (ebook) | DDC
    232–dc23/eng/20240229
LC record available at https://lccn.loc.gov/2024004262
LC ebook record available at https://lccn.loc.gov/2024004263

Cover Design: Wiley
Cover Illustration: Noyon Missal, French, thirteenth century, MS Typ 120, fol 4 seq 7, illumination of Synagōgē and Ecclēsia, sacrificing the Lamb of God. Houghton Library, Harvard University. Reproduced with permission.

Set in 11.5/13pt Bembo by Straive, Pondicherry, India

Printed and bound by CPI Group (UK) Ltd, Croydon, CR0 4YY

C9781405189231_030424

*For Arthur, Theodore (Teddy) and Simon Claude,
the next generation of seekers for Christ*

Contents

Contents

Preface

This book is a successor to an earlier volume in the *Challenges in Contemporary Theology* series, which was entitled *Powers and Submissions: Spirituality, Philosophy and Gender* (Oxford: Blackwell, 2002).[1] I characterized that earlier book, at the time, as my first volume of *Gesammelte Schriften,* an accompaniment to an emerging project in systematic theology which was, and is, also ongoing.[2] Unlike that earlier volume of essays, however (where the cluster of themes which united its content were only identified retroactively), this current book has been planned for a long time, and the chapters drawn together here were always intended to fit together into a cumulative argument about contemporary Christology and its purviews. The core theme of 'brokenness' (in all its ambiguity and richness), and its relation to various forms of 'apophaticism', in both speech and practice, is explored analytically in the Prologue that follows.

Over the years in which these essays were researched and written, I have accumulated a great number of debts to other scholars and colleagues, discussion partners in Jewish/Christian dialogue (both in Israel and elsewhere), and above all to my former students and research assistants at Harvard and Cambridge. In the last category I must first and foremost thank Philip McCosker, Mark Nussberger, Shai Held, Michon Matthiesen, Timothy Dalrymple, Cameron Partridge, Hjördis Becker-Lindenthal, and (in the very last stages of editorial work), Amanda Bourne in Alexandria, VA. This book simply could not have

---

[1] This is now prospectively planned to be re-published by Wiley-Blackwell in a 2nd edition, with a new authorial essay on critical responses and debate included.

[2] The first volume was published as *God, Sexuality and the Self: An Essay 'On the Trinity'* (Cambridge: C.U.P., 2013), and the second volume, *Sin, Racism and Divine Darkness: An Essay 'On Human Nature'* (Cambridge: C.U.P., 2025) is forthcoming.

taken the shape it has without their extraordinary practical, linguistic and theological assistance of every sort: *gratias ago vobis*.

But I am no less grateful to another 'great cloud of witnesses', some alas no longer living, whose influence and conversation is writ large throughout these pages. Amongst these I must mention especially, with deep appreciation (and in the case of the first names in this list, *in piam memoriam*): †Joseph Blenkinsopp, †Joseph (Jossi) Dan, †David Hartman, †Aaron Lazare, †Robert Murray, S.J., †Krister Stendahl, †John Webster; and Gary A. Anderson, Erik Aurelius, Elitzur Bar-Asher, Anthony Baxter, John Behr, Markus Bockmuehl, John W. Bowker, Brian Britt, Sebastian Brock, Jack Caputo, Andrew Chester, Fr. Maximos (Nicholas) Constas, Richard Cross, Brian E. Daley, S.J., Stephen T. Davis, Paul DeHart, C. Stephen Evans, Michael Fishbane, David F. Ford, Yehuda (Jerome) Gellman, Alon Goshen-Gottstein, Richard B. Hays, Moshe Halbertal, Charles Hefling, William Horbury, Peter Kang, Cleo McNelly Kearns, Ed Kessler, Arthur Kleinman, Martin Laird, O.S.A., Jon Levenson, Andrew Louth, Christoph Markschies, Giulio Maspero, Bruce McCormack, John Milbank, Jeremy Milgrom, R. W. L. Moberly, David Newheiser, David Novak, Gerald O'Collins, S.J., Kimberly C. Patton, Beverly Roberts Gaventa, Eugene Rogers, Christian Schlenker, Jon Schofer, Kate Sonderegger, Carol Steiker, Jesper Svartvik, Richard Swinburne, Kathryn Tanner, Keith Ward, Michael Welker, Merold Westphal, and Rowan Williams.

The second section of this book consists of four hermeneutical investigations of topics that supposedly divide Judaism and Christianity definitively. These essays were originally explored in very rich and deep conversations at the Shalom Hartman Institute, the Tantur Ecumenical Institute, and the Swedish Theological Institute, in Israel; and at conferences supported by the Templeton Foundation in Cambridge, and by the Research Centre of Interdisciplinarity and Theology in Heidelberg. I am greatly indebted to all these places of learning and of scholarly and inter-religious conviviality, and to the remarkable people who lead them.

The last four chapters of this book were originally presented as 'named' lectures in two venues: as the Hensley Henson Lectures at Oxford; and later (in slightly revised form) as the John Albert Hall Lectures at the University of Victoria, British Columbia, Canada. I am most grateful to those who made my sojourns in those two places both memorable personally, and also suggestive of the need for further reflection and revision of my thinking, now at last undertaken.

I must also express my deep gratitude to the editors of this *Challenges* series, Gareth Jones and Lewis Ayres, whose patience with me has been nothing short of heroic; and to the many editors and sub-editors at Wiley-Blackwell over the years who have guided this project to completion, in particular: Rebecca Harkin, Juliet Booker, Clelia Petracca, Laura (Adsett) Matthews, Ed Robinson, Martin Tribe and Madhurima Thapa.

Without the support that my own erstwhile university institutions (Harvard, Cambridge) have provided over the last years, and, more particularly, the generous grants, sabbatical time, and financial backing which have been garnered from the Leverhulme and McDonald Foundations of late, probably even now this book would have not have come to completion. All these forms of generosity and trust remind us that gift and sacrifice are not opposites (as is also discussed in this volume), but coterminous and cooperative undertakings only fully comprehensible in the economy of grace.

Sarah Coakley
Alexandria, VA
Candlemas, 2024

Acknowledgements

With the exception of the 'Prologue' and Chapter 10 ('Sacrifice Re-visited: Blood and Gender'), all the essays in this volume have appeared in earlier settings, but have been included here with either light or more significant revisions. Where the copyright lies with the earlier publisher, I am grateful for permission to reproduce the material. The details of these earlier publications are as follows:

'The Identity of the Risen Jesus: Finding Jesus Christ in the Poor', in eds. Beverly Roberts Gaventa and Richard B. Hays, *Seeking the Identity of Jesus: A Pilgrimage* (Grand Rapids, MI: Eerdmans, 2008), 301–319. Reprinted by permission of the publisher.

'Does Kenōsis Rest on a Mistake? Three Kenotic Models in Patristic Exegesis', in ed C. Stephen Evans, *Exploring Kenotic Christology: The Self-Emptying God* (Oxford: O.U.P., 2006), 246–264. Reproduced with permission of the Licensor through PLSclear.

' "Mingling" in Gregory of Nyssa's Christology: A Reconsideration', in eds. Andreas Schuele and Günter Thomas, *Who is Jesus Christ for Us Today? Pathways to Contemporary Christology* (a Festschrift for Michael Welker) (Louisville KY: Westminster/John Knox, 2009), 72–84. Reproduced by permission of the publisher.

'What Does Chalcedon Solve and What Does it Not? Some Reflections on the Status and Meaning of the Chalcedonian "Definition" ', in eds. Stephen T. Davis, Daniel Kendall, S.J. and Gerald O'Collins, S.J., *The Incarnation: An Interdisciplinary Symposium on the Incarnation of the Son of God* (Oxford: O.U.P., 2002), 143–163. Reproduced with permission of the Licensor through PLSclear.

'Re-Thinking Jewish/Christian Divergence on the "Image of the Divine": the Problem of Intra-Divine Complexity and the Origins of the Doctrine of the Trinity', in eds. Michael Welker and William Schweiker, *Images of the Divine and Cultural Orientations: Jewish, Christian and Islamic Voices* (Leipzig: Evangelische Verlagsanstalt, 2015), 133–149. Reproduced by kind permission of Michael Welker.

'On the Fearfulness of Forgiveness: Psalm 130:4 and its Theological Implications', in eds. Andreas Andreopoulos, Augustine Casiday and Carol Harrison, *Meditations of the Heart: The Psalms in Early Christian Thought and Practice*, a Festschrift for Andrew Louth (Turnhout: Brepols, 2011), 33–51. Reproduced with permission of the publisher.

'On Clouds and Veils: Divine Presence and "Feminine" Secrets in Revelation and Nature', in ed. John W. Bowker, *Knowing the Unknowable: Science and Religions on God and the Universe* (London: I. B. Tauris, 2009), 123–159. Reproduced with permission of the publisher.

'In Defense of Sacrifice: Gender, Selfhood, and the Binding of Isaac', in eds. Linda Martín Alcoff and John D. Caputo, *Feminism, Sexuality and the Return of Religion* (Bloomington: Indiana University Press, 2011), 17–38. Reproduced with permission of the publisher.

'"*In Persona Christi*": Who, or Where, is Christ at the Altar?', in *A Man of Many Parts: Essays in Honor of John Westerdale Bowker on the Occasion of His Eightieth Birthday*, ed. Eugene E. Lemcio with an Introduction by Rowan Williams (Eugene OR: Pickwick Publications, 2015), 95–112. Reproduced by permission of Wipf and Stock Publishers.

'The Woman at the Altar: Cosmological Disturbance or Gender Fluidity?', *The Anglican Theological Review* 86 (2004), 75–93 (a small section of this article appears in Chapter 9: permission granted by the Executive Director and Managing Editor, *The Anglican Theological Review*).

'Why Gift? Gift, Gender, and Trinitarian Relations in Milbank and Tanner', *Scottish Journal of Theology* 16 (2008), 224–235. © 2008 *Scottish Journal of Theology*. Reprinted with permission.

'Transubstantiation and its Contemporary Renditions: Returning Eucharistic Presence to the Body, Gender, and Affect', in *"Yes, Well . . ." Exploring the Past, Present and Future of the Church: Essays in Honor of John W. Coakley*, ed. James Hart Brumm (Grand Rapids, MI: Reformed Church Press [Eerdmans], 2016), 61–81. *Reformed Church Press*, 475 Riverside Drive, New York, NY 10115, USA. All rights reserved. Reproduced with permission.

The quotation in the 'Prologue', n. 39, from Elizabeth Jennings's poem 'Easter', is reproduced from her *The Collected Poems* (Manchester: Carcanet Press, 2012), with kind permission of David Higham Associates Ltd.

The illustrations which appear in this book (on the front cover, and in Chapters 8 and 10), are reproduced with the gracious permission of the following libraries, publishers, and art institutions:

Front cover: Noyon Missal, French, thirteenth century, MS Typ 120, fol 4 seq 7, illumination of *Synagōgē* and *Ecclēsia*, sacrificing the Lamb of God. Houghton Library, Harvard University. Reproduced with permission.

Figure 8.1: Rembrandt van Rijn, 'The Sacrifice of Abraham', 1655, etching. Rijksmuseum, Amsterdam. Reproduced with permission.

Figure 8.2: Rembrandt van Rijn, 'The Sacrifice of Isaac', 1635, oil painting. The State Hermitage Museum, St. Petersburg. Reproduced with permission. Photograph by Vladimir Terebenin, © The State Hermitage Museum.

Figure 8.3: 'Drawing of the *akedah* by a disturbed boy of 14 years, attending a Child Guidance Clinic'. Reproduced from Erich Wellisch, *Isaac and Oedipus: A Study in Biblical Psychology of the Sacrifice of Isaac, The Akedah* (New York: Humanities Press, 1954), facing p. 97, by permission of the Taylor and Francis Group, Academic Books Permissions.

Figure 8.4: George Segal, 'Abraham and Isaac: In Memory of May 4, 1970, Kent State University', 1978–1979, cast bronze. The statue stands on the campus of Princeton University, Princeton, NJ: The John B. Putnam Memorial Collection, Princeton University, partial gift of the Mildred Andrews Fund. Photograph © Getty Images, reproduced with permission.

Figure 10.1: Unknown northwest German Master, 'Eucharistic Man of Sorrows with the Allegorical Figure of *Caritas*', c. 1470. Wallfar-Richartz-Museum & Fondation Corboud. Reproduced by permission. Photograph © Rheinisches Bildarchiv Köln, rba_c010594.

Figure 10.2: Giovanna Bellini, 'Pietà Donà delle Rose', c. 1505, Galleria dell'Accademia, Venice. Photograph © Getty Images, reproduced with permission.

Figure 10.3: Jean Auguste Dominique Ingres, 'Madonna and the Consecrated Wafer', 1865, Metropolitan Museum of Art, New York. In the public domain.

The publishers apologize for any errors or omissions in the above list and would be grateful to be notified of any corrections that should be incorporated in the next edition or reprint of this book.

Prologue: The Broken Body

This book is concerned with how and where Christians *encounter* Jesus Christ and acknowledge his identity, in all its mystery and fulness. It also asks, secondly, how believers can, or should, then best *express* what they believe about him. And finally, and thirdly, it begins to probe how that expression is bound up with what they necessarily *do* to live out that belief and embrace its demands, not only through Christian sacramental and ecclesial practices, but also on the border-lands of the church, and especially in the historic and fraught relationship of Christianity to Judaism. For it is thus, I propose, that they come to 'know' Christ 'more nearly', both through habituation and continual surprise.

These three tasks constitute, as I see it, the fundamental concerns of any attempt at a 'Christology' – that is, any adequate expression of the contours of belief in Christ as the salvific God/Man. But beyond and beneath these initial concerns, and perhaps more challengingly, this book asks in various ways what initial human presumptions or attitudes have to be *broken* in order for any proper response to emerge to these core riddles of Christian faith in relating to Jesus Christ. That issue is my central concern in what follows immediately in this Prologue. The lines of thought about such 'brokenness' may, perforce, not be immediately familiar ones, and certainly they are ones which in some cases could court controversy and critique; and hence the need to explain them anticipatorily. But as I shall argue here, they are vital for any rich and discerning understanding of the christological task.

I should also immediately make it clear at the outset, moreover, that this is therefore a book of essays that should be read as *prolegomena* to any future Christology, rather than as a full and substantial

Christology *per se*.[1] That is, I am engaged in this book in preliminary explorations,[2] which will shape what I finally wish to say about Christ as the fulsome revelatory divine presence in any 'systematic' theology worthy of the name. But these preliminary explorations are necessary steps, because none of them is completely obvious in the current theological terrain, and several of them may even seem surprising or contentious. Let me now explain.

The Christological Question

'Who *is* Christ?' This is a deceptively simple question, and it hides a multitude of possible theoretic 'sins' and differences of opinion only scarcely below the surface of immediate theological consciousness. Dietrich Bonhoeffer, one of the most perspicacious commentators on this topic in the modern period, left only lecture notes on the problem ('the christological question', as he himself called it);[3] but he was one of the few theologians in the twentieth century to have pinpointed with such insight its real richness and its accompanying difficulties. It is not for nothing that his analysis starts with the insistence that 'silence' should precede any attempt to answer this question – since Christ, he says, is essentially inexpressible, whilst at the same time supremely revelatory: thus, 'The silence of the Church is silence before the Word'.[4] A true Lutheran, however, Bonhoeffer goes on immediately to fulminate – contentiously, of course – against the suggestion that this silence might be the silence of what he calls the 'mystics'; for he takes it that *their* 'dumbness' would be both solitary and self-referential. Instead, he says, an essential paradox has to be grasped at the outset of the christological task: 'To speak of Christ means

---

[1] My hope is to supply that fuller account in the fourth and last volume of my ongoing 'systematic theology', as prospectively outlined in my *God, Sexuality and the Self: An Essay 'On the Trinity'* (Cambridge: C.U.P., 2013), at p. xv. I explain there why my Christology is left until last in the systematics, not as 'demotion' but as 'climax'.

[2] This book thus performs a similar function in my writing to that of an earlier volume in this *Challenges* series (*Powers and Submissions: Spirituality, Philosophy and Gender* (Oxford: Blackwell, 2002)), whose contents acted as anticipatory goads, intimations and footnotes to the arguments of the unfolding 'systematic theology', especially to volume 1, *God, Sexuality and the Self*.

[3] Dietrich Bonhoeffer, *Christ The Center*, tr. Edwin H. Robertson (San Francisco: Harper & Row, 1978).

[4] Ibid., 27.

to keep silent; to keep silent about Christ means to speak. When the Church speaks rightly out of a *proper silence*, then Christ is proclaimed'.[5]

Ironically, however, the 'mystic' in the Western tradition who most closely anticipated this paradoxical insight of the Lutheran Bonhoeffer about a 'proper silence' before Christ was the sixteenth century Carmelite friar, John of the Cross, only a slightly later contemporary of Luther himself. As John wrote in one of his most famous aphorisms: 'The Father spoke one Word, which was his Son, and this Word he speaks always in eternal silence, and in silence it must be heard by the soul'.[6]

The essays that follow in this book cannot therefore be said to be straightforwardly 'Bonhoefferian', for – amongst other differences from him – they engage insistently with earlier traditions of 'mystical theology' (patristic and medieval) towards which Bonhoeffer harboured a certain suspicion, and which find a certain climax in John of the Cross himself. But what they do share with Bonhoeffer is an intense interest in *analyzing* what can, and cannot, be said in the task of Christology (out of a 'proper silence'), and what therefore remains the necessary arena of divine revelatory mystery, indeed the unfinished business – at least from our human perspective – in any authentically Spirit-filled response to the crucified and resurrected Jesus. And what goes along with this insight is an attempt to clarify first and afresh, as Bonhoeffer also did so presciently and in his own way, what must thereby be the *relationship* between certain primary elements in any modern christological armoury: the 'Christ' as biblically proclaimed in the New Testament; the 'historical Jesus' as earnestly probed behind the biblical texts by modern critical scholarship; and the patristic tradition of metaphysical speculation as to Christ's 'person' and 'natures'.

Understanding how these three different genres of reflection on Christ relate, or should relate, in our quest for Christ's 'identity' is one of the most complex and subtle questions of contemporary

---

[5] Ibid., my emphasis.

[6] John of the Cross, 'Sayings of Light and Love', 100, in tr. Kieran Kavanaugh, O.C.D. and Otilio Rodriguez, O.C.D., *The Collected Works of John of the Cross* (Washington, DC: Institute of Carmelite Studies, 1991), 92. Rowan Williams, in *The Wound of Knowledge: Christian Spirituality from the New Testament to St John of the Cross* (London: Darton, Longman & Todd, 1979), chs. 7, 8 (on Luther and John of the Cross, to be read in tandem), throws considerable light both on the contiguity and congruence of Luther's and John of the Cross's views on 'proper silence', but also on Luther's (as also Bonhoeffer's) resistance to 'mystical' individualism, in favour instead of the *Deus absconditus* of the cross.

Christology: it is, after all, a special conundrum created by the modern period in its forging of a newly intense appeal to the second element in this triad.[7] I choose to tackle this issue head-on in the opening chapter of this book. Immediately, and out of this initial reflection, an argument of my own starts to emerge about how any proper response to the identity and presence of the risen Christ is *necessarily* 'apophatic' in a particular sense, that is, 'broken open' to the unexpected and the mysterious in the Spirit's brokerage of a form of displacement from our natural expectations and categories.[8] We would – reasonably enough, or so it seems – like to catch and hold what *we* might know and recognize in Christ, to make it our own possession, even express it in purely propositional terms; and the modern 'quest' for Jesus as an

---

[7] I draw attention here to John Webster's insightful comment that Christology in the modern period has seen overall a certain withdrawal from speculative reflection on the 'ontological' Christ, and a correlative and compensatory obsession with the 'economic' Christ (especially as grasped through historical study): see his 'The Place of Christology in Systematic Theology', in ed. Francesca Aran Murphy, *The Oxford Handbook of Christology* (Oxford: O.U.P., 2015), ch. 39, esp. 615–617, 619, 621–625. It will be clear in what follows in this Prologue that I resist this modern disjunction and seek to repair it.

[8] 'Apophasis' technically means 'saying no', or 'unsaying'; but in the context of its classic theological application (e.g., in the influential work of the late-fifth century Dionysius the Areopagite) it does not simply or straightforwardly mean propositional 'denial', let alone an absolute *nescience* about the divine, since the project is undergirded by a progressive contemplative *journey* into the life of God, which is revelatory and participatory in nature. (For a succinct definitional discussion of the meanings of the disputed terms 'mystical theology', 'apophaticism' and 'negative theology', see my earlier essay, 'Dark Contemplation and Epistemic Transformation', in eds. Oliver D. Crisp and Michael C. Rea, *Analytic Theology: New Essays in the Philosophy of Religion* (Oxford: O.U.P., 2009), ch. 14, esp. 280–281.) When fulsome revelation and divine mystery are rightly held together in *Christology*, as I shall argue in this volume, 'apophasis' will involve both a set of strategies for speaking about God-in-Christ to protect that unique combination of factors (and to ward off idolatrous misconstruals), and also a number of attendant spiritual practices that inculcate an openness to the *Spirit's* drawing us into the expanding orbit of Christ's truth from which these very insights can be attained (see 1 Cor 12. 3: 'No one can [even] say "Jesus is Lord" except by the Holy Spirit'). It follows that 'apophaticism', Christology and pneumatology are tightly woven together in the argument I develop through this book, and which is distinctive of it. For a survey of some other renditions of 'apophatic Christology' (a relative neologism) which have appeared of late, see Philip McCosker, 'Sitit Sitiri: Apophatic Christologies of Desire', in eds. Eric Bugyis and David Newheiser, *Desire, Faith, and the Darkness of God: Essays in Honor of Denys Turner* (Notre Dame, IN: University of Notre Dame Press, 2015), 391–413.

object of critical historical investigation inevitably courted, from the start, this ambition to probe to a new level of certainty about what could be verified about his life, teaching and person, as if the mystery that inevitably surrounds God in Godself could somehow be dispelled or moderated in the case of his Son. For often we still presume that getting at the 'historical', or 'human', Jesus will be the proper means of taking hold of what *we* need to know in responding to a more elusive divine revelation.[9]

Worse: the ambition may even be extended to a felt need to *justify*, by historical and empirical means, the very metaphysical claims enshrined in later credal statements about the second Person of the Trinity. But this, I submit, is a vain and misplaced propulsion – a 'category mistake' – as is argued at some length in Chapter 1. Attempting to map the modern 'historical Jesus' directly onto the historic creeds in this way is fraught with confusion,[10] not least because it also sometimes attempts to short-circuit, and even displace, the issue of what it is to encounter the *risen* Jesus – without which the question of the 'identity' of Christ is idolatrously shrunk from the outset, and the historic creeds denuded of all their soteriological power.

---

[9] But this represents a dismaying rendition of John 1. 18 ('No one has ever seen God; the only Son, who is in the bosom of the Father, he has made him known'), since according to the distinctive Johannine theology – which has no inkling, of course, of the modern 'quest for the historical Jesus' – the 'making known' of God by the Logos requires a 'believing *into*' the risen Son which is by no means obvious to a dispassionate observer, let alone lacking in any richness of divine mystery. Yet it is the Son who has made himself *seen* in incarnational space/time, as is insisted here. With this text compare also 1 John 4. 12 ('No one has ever seen God; [but] if we love one another, God abides in us and his love is perfected in us'), a reflection which clearly insists also on certain moral or spiritual preconditions for the appropriate fiduciary response to the divine presence in Christ.

[10] I explain in Chapter 1 that the term 'the historical Jesus' is also unfortunately ambiguous; for it may connote, on the one hand, the human, incarnated, Jesus during his life on earth ('the earthly Jesus'), or, rather differently, the modern attempt to probe and circumscribe this reality via historical–critical means ('the historian's Jesus'). It is the attempt to justify credal claims about the Son of God on the basis of the *latter* that leads to this confusion, both philosophical and theological, since, at best, the 'historian's Jesus' could only display or suggest aspects of his remarkable humanity, not definitively establish him as 'God'. Not that many modern and contemporary theologians do not continue to harbour this essentially empiricist ambition: Joachim Jeremias in Germany, for instance, who was reacting to Bultmann's very different, 'kerygmatic', christological approach; and a line of illustrious British New Testament scholars in the tradition of C.H. Dodd, most especially, in this generation, N.T. Wright.

It follows, as I go on to argue further in Chapter 1, that although the modern 'historian's Jesus' inevitably and rightly retains enormous and enticing interest for all Christians who seek to deepen their understanding of the identity of Christ in his historical manifestation (even though this quest remains fraught with endless scholarly disagreements of interpretation), it cannot be either the justificatory starting point, nor the constraining and final criterion, for his divine reality: this is one of the most significant areas in which an apophatic 'saying no' has to occur in Christology. Yet, in a slightly different sense of 'saying no', this 'historian's Jesus' can indeed have a crucial role, as I also argue in Chapter 1, in being deployed strategically *against* ideological, distorted or idolatrous renditions of that same Jesus. In other words, we must say 'no' to attempts to defuse or ignore his risen mystery, just as we also say 'no' to attempts to hijack his risen reality for falsely political, distorting, or even merely complacent ecclesiastical ends.

It is thus not coincidental that Bonhoeffer was the modern theologian so particularly concerned to locate the (to him, judiciously circumscribed[11]) importance of the 'historian's Jesus', at the same time as he also cautioned against the dangers of an idolatrous rendition of the same project: his own political and social context, we can now see more clearly, was quite crucial here for his perspective and insight.[12] Writing with his 'back up against the wall' (as another great christologian of the late modern period would later call it[13]), Bonhoeffer the Lutheran was

---

[11] In fact, Bonhoeffer rather intriguingly insists that a 'historical Jesus' focus in Christology can easily lead also to a modern form of docetism, where Jesus's ideas become disconnected from his 'person': see *Christ the Center*, 80–82. For Bonhoeffer's stress, in contrast, on the need for a 'critical' or 'negative' Christology, see ibid., 74–75, 100–102.

[12] From a sociological perspective we might therefore characterize Bonhoeffer's Christology as a strident critique of a 'Church-type' (state-mandated) Lutheranism in political collusion with Nazism. For more on social 'typologies' and their relation to Christian doctrine in general, and Christology in particular, see n. 14, below.

[13] Howard Thurman, *Jesus and the Disinherited* (New York: Abingdon, 1949) represents one of the most significant christological works from an Afro-American theologian in the 'Jim Crow' era, and one that used then-current historical-Jesus research (especially on Jesus in his Jewish context) precisely to *resist* a complacent racist christological idolatry. The book memorably begins: 'Many and varied are the interpretations dealing with the teachings and the life of Jesus of Nazareth. But few of these interpretations deal with what the teachings and the life of Jesus have to say to those who stand, at a moment in human history, with their backs against the wall' (ibid., 11).

teaching for a state-church that was at this very time in danger of completely idolatrous corruption by Nazi ideology; and thus he was necessarily expressing his own theological, indeed specifically *christological*, resistance. His 'saying no' was therefore not merely an attention to an appropriate set of semantic rules for Christology, but a lived-out practice of spiritual and political protest. And this was in relation to the very Christ whose Word was speaking to him afresh out of the primordial divine silence to which his teaching and preaching witnessed.

Thus, once the necessary *simultaneity* of dazzling revelation and dark hiddenness in our response to the risen Christ is better understood, we also begin to see that even to restrict our christological reflections to the three sources of reflection already mentioned (the 'biblical Christ', the 'historian's Jesus', and the Christ of conciliar definitions) is itself too constrained an understanding of the christological undertaking and its necessary points of reference; we must attend also and always to the social *context* of our christological utterances,[14] but also at the same time to the sometimes-shattering pervasiveness of the presence of Christ in our midst, at least for those attuned to receive it: for 'Christ plays in ten thousand places', as Gerard Manley Hopkins once expressed this mystery poetically.[15] I go on therefore towards the

---

[14] It was Ernst Troeltsch (1865–1923) who prophetically demonstrated the crucial conditioning dimension of social context for any doctrinal utterance, a thesis expounded especially clearly at the end of his great study of the history of Christian social teachings: tr. Olive Wyon, *The Social Teaching of the Christian Churches* (orig., 1912; London: Allen and Unwin, 1931), see esp. 994–997 ('Christian Thought Dependent on Social Factors'). By clarifying how christological proposals, too, would always correlate to some extent with 'types' of social relationship ('Church', 'Sect' and 'Mystic'), Troeltsch was able to indicate, albeit far too briefly in this particular work, the social and political 'patternings' of different kinds of Christology, and their religious significance. Troeltsch's work, I believe, lies influentially, if mutedly, in the background of Bonhoeffer's christological insights, especially in his stress on 'negative' Christology as a form of ('sectarian') resistance. For comments on the ongoing significance for Christology of Troeltsch's sociological analyses, see my own early monograph, *Christ Without Absolutes: A Study of the Christology of Ernest Troelstch* (Oxford: O.U.P., 1988), esp. 191–197.

[15] See Gerard Manley Hopkins, 'As Kingfishers Catch Fire', which ends:
' ... for Christ plays in ten thousand places,
Lovely in limbs, and lovely in eyes not his
To the Father through the features of men's faces'.

end of Chapter 1 to unfurl an appeal to the patristic tradition of
'spiritual sensation' to account for the epistemological conditions
under which the Spirit can indeed 'break open' our hearts and minds
to the pervasive and transforming reality of Christ's risen presence in
these 'ten thousand places': in Word, in sacrament, in the 'body of
Christ' which is the church, but especially too in moral acts of mercy
and compassion to the oppressed and the poor.

But what exactly, then, does this 'breaking open' to the full reality
of Christ, as so far discussed, actually connote? Is there not a danger
here of mere obfuscation on the one hand (the apophatic 'darkness'
motif as merely blinding, élitist or confusing, as some might cynically
interpret it), or, on the other, of the naïve valorization of multiple
experiential agendas, under the false aegis of 'mystical' appeals to
the presence of Christ? The answer, of course, is that both these spiritual dangers are always and ever on offer (we can never dispel them
completely, and that is why spiritual discernment in this area is so
important). But that does not mean that we cannot do sterling work
in continuing to probe and clarify the epistemological, semantic,
metaphysical, and moral questions which this christological arena
holds up to us. And the rest of this Prologue will now be devoted to
this task.

How to *Speak* of Christ: The Positive and the Negative Poles

So far was have discussed a 'breaking open' of consciousness to the
risen Christ which is the creative starting point of any deep reflection
on his personal identity, brokered in the Spirit. This is a theological
point of essentially *epistemological* (and thus also wider 'spiritual')
significance. But this lesson has immediate consequences, as already
hinted, for a different, this time *semantic*, sense of 'apophaticism' as
applied to all our faltering attempts to describe, define, or comprehend through any kind of linguistic expression, what Christ *is* 'for us'.
In Chapter 4 of this book I make an attempt to unravel this issue in
specific reference to the so-called 'Chalcedonian Definition', the document propounded by a decree of the church in the mid-fifth century
(451 CE) to provide a conciliar norm for any future christological
'orthodoxy'. The immediate political fall-out from this attempt is

well-known,[16] and was profoundly messy and divisive ecclesiastically; but what is less agreed upon, even now, is quite what the 'Definition' was actually attempting to achieve in the first place, and what it therefore should connote now for the Christian faithful. The answer I supply in Chapter 4 is my own response to the question of the spiritual importance of understanding what can, and cannot, be grasped about the reality of Christ in such (rightly)-attempted credal protections against heresy.

This task involves pinpointing another form of 'saying no', in the sense of *linguistically* protecting a unique mystery whilst also 'breaking open' consciousness to further horizons of christological possibility. The word 'horizon' (as opposed to 'definition'), is in fact a less misleading translation of the original Greek term used for this text (*horos*). What it is attempting to do, therefore, as I argue in some detail in Chapter 4, is to indicate the boundaries of what can, and what cannot, be constrained or explained in any formal attempt such as this to protect the unique metaphysical mystery of the God/Man; and at the same time it gestures invitingly beyond the edges of what *can* be said into an encounter with the divine reality itself, displayed incarnationally in Christ. By the same token (utilizing a combination of the 'positive' and the 'negative' modes, linguistically understood), it also deliberately uses key technical terms (*hypostasis, phusis*) that are themselves, in a sense, intentionally 'apophatic' in their minimalism. One can, of course, attempt some basic indication, in explicating the meaning of the 'Definition', of what Christ's 'person' (*hypostasis*) and 'natures' (*phuseis*) denote here, and even – provisionally – how they might be related; but at the time of the writing of the 'Definition' the deeper philosophical aspects of these questions were by no means

---

[16] Classic historical textbooks such as Jaroslav Pelikan, *The Christian Tradition* , vol. 1, *The Emergence of the Catholic Tradition (100–600)* (Chicago: University of Chicago Press, 1971), ch. 5, and vol. 2, *The Spirit of Eastern Christendom (600–1700)* (Chicago: University of Chicago Press, 1974), ch. 2, remain a helpful starting point in charting these lasting and significant reactions to the Chalcedonian 'Definition', and their historic ecclesiastical outcomes. A much more recent, succinct, account of the same resistances and reactions to Chalcedon (which also draws on the work of Alois Grillmeier) may be found in Andrew Louth, 'Christology in the East from the Council of Chalcedon to John Damascene', in ed. Murphy, *The Oxford Handbook of Christology*, ch. 9, esp. 139–148.

fully plumbed, and the use of these key terms was therefore seemingly intended more as a wedge against various forms of error than as a full clarification. However, we should not mistake *this* 'apophatic' strategy (as some moderns influentially have done, under one form of an appeal to Wittgenstein's later philosophy), as merely the creation of linguistic 'rules' in quest of a form of semantic hygiene, as if strong metaphysical assertions were not also being made quite emphatically.[17] This latter presumption, I argue, presents a false disjunction; for we should neither mistake the Chalcedonian 'Definition' for a full propositional explication of the riches of Christ's reality, nor yet for any withdrawal from a profound underlying metaphysical confidence about the irreducible uniqueness of the incarnation itself. Both these aspects of the christological task are fully compatible under a suitably 'apophatic' rendition.

When we then turn back to some of the pre-Chalcedonian christologians with such lessons in mind, it may be a surprise to find that we can now read at least some of them more charitably than heretofore – less as false approximations to a later, 'achieved', conciliar truth, and more as subtle explorations of the relation between given biblical authority, tentative philosophical explication, and necessary divine mystery. I discuss these matters in Chapters 2 and 3 of this volume in relation to two central themes in the Christology of Gregory of Nyssa (c.335–c.395), expositions which I believe to have been gravely misunderstood and misjudged by many in the tradition – at least until recently.[18]

To be sure, Nyssen's christological writings are *ad hoc* and unsystematic; we cannot claim that they represent a finished product, and

---

[17] I contest certain dimensions of Richard A. Norris's influential rendition of Chalcedon along these lines in ch. 4, *intra*. More recently I have been somewhat bemused to find that Bruce Lindley McCormack's reading of me on this point (in *The Humility of the Eternal Son: Reformed Kenoticism and the Repair of Chalcedon* (Cambridge: C.U.P., 2021), 28, n. 4), merely conflates my view with that of Norris, missing the point that I myself continue to insist on the core *metaphysical* assertions made by Chalcedon.

[18] The work of Brian E. Daley, S.J., and of John Behr in the Anglophone literature (as I discuss in chs. 2 and 3, *intra*), already marked an important turning point in the assessments of Nyssen's christological writings; but arguably there still remains much more work to be done.

the full coherence of what he proposes is often – at least at first blush – elusive and unresolved. But what emerges from a closer examination of his treatment of the two controversial christological themes that I examine here ('Kenosis' in ch. 2, and 'Mingling' in ch. 3), is a pattern of christological thinking which further amplifies our understanding of Christology as a 'breaking open' of 'apophatic' consciousness. We should not of course be surprised to find Gregory excelling in this genre, given his foundational contribution to the resolution of the later Arian controversy, and his particularly novel and perspicacious account of the paradoxical relation of trinitarian and 'apophatic' thinking therein.[19] But perhaps what is less well understood is how this same sensibility is present also in his christological treatises. What we see here, I propose, is an implicit christological 'method' (worthy of further reflection and analysis), in which a richly 'semiotic'[20]

---

[19] Two contrasting, but equally influential, accounts of Gregory of Nyssa's 'apophaticism' may be found in Jean Daniélou, *Platonisme et théologie mystique: Essai sur la doctrine spirituelle de saint Grégoire de Nysse* (rev. ed., Paris: Aubier, 1953), and Ekkehard Mühlenberg, *Die Unendlichkeit Gottes bei Gregor von Nyssa: Gregors Kritik am Gottesbegriff der klassischen Metaphysik* (Göttingen: Vandenhoeck and Ruprecht, 1966). The resolution of their differences is key to understanding the complexity of Nyssen's position. A more recent study of Gregory's trinitarian theology in the light of his 'apophaticism' illuminatingly utilizes contemporary linguistic theory to attempt to explain it afresh: Scot R. Douglass, *Theology of the Gap: Cappadocian Language Theory and the Trinitarian Controversy* (New York: Peter Lang, 2005). But amongst the most important current attempts to explicate the relation of Nyssen's 'apophatic' thinking to his particular contributions to trinitarian thought are: Lewis Ayres, 'On Not Three People', in ed. Sarah Coakley, *Re-Thinking Gregory of Nyssa* (Oxford: Blackwell, 2003), 15–44 (see also ibid., *Nicaea and Its Legacy: An Approach to Fourth-Century Trinitarian Theology* (Oxford: O.U.P., 2004), ch. 14); and Giulio Maspero, *Trinity and Man: Gregory of Nyssa's Ad Ablabium* (Leiden: Brill, 2007).

[20] I use the term 'semiotic' here with the intentional overtones of Lacanian psychoanalytic theory, especially as expounded by the French feminist Julia Kristeva (who is discussed especially in ch. 10 of this volume). With these authors the term relates to the pre-linguistic realm of the child's identification with the maternal, and is contrasted with the so-called 'masculine' 'symbolic' arena – of language, distinction, and clarification. Here, by extension, I intend 'semiotic' to connote a means of reasoning that draws richly on the unconscious and on multiple narratives and symbols, without necessarily seeking a definitive propositional conclusion to a developed line of argument.

approach to a variety of relevant biblical texts, symbols and metaphors, which mutually bombard and co-inform one another, is conjoined with an equally rich exploration of pagan philosophical materials of relevance which might supply analytic clarification of the matter in hand. In applying these insights doctrinally, however, the existing philosophical tropes are never allowed by Nyssen simply to control or dominate without some correction, but are brought into new alliance and counterpoint with the vying biblical materials, and in interaction with the undergirding spiritual practice of the theological investigator. Such is the locus, according to Gregory, of a suitably 'apophatic' rendition of christological revelation.[21] In large part, I argue at the end of these chapters, Gregory thereby anticipates the insights of the slightly-later 'mystical' theologian, Dionysius the Areopagite, for whom appropriate theological utterance is always a matter of 'saying yes', 'saying no', and then saying 'no' even to the 'no'.[22] For only thus does one advance on a three-tiered *journey* into God which is not simply a matter of a discerningly 'apophatic' semantic theory (important as that is), but more fundamentally of an extended religious epistemology of personal transformation and insight. The ultimate goal is a *participation* in God, not simply the production of an exacting

---

[21] It is true that Nyssen falls foul of certain Chalcedonian 'rules' retrospectively – at least when his theme of 'mingling' is unsympathetically understood as a 'confusion' of the two natures. But as I shall show in chs. 2 and 3, *intra*, his unique construal of the ecstatic divine 'outpouring' of Phil 2, combined with his understanding of that divine gift for the progressive purification of the human passions in the life of Christ, allows for a narrative understanding of Christ's *human* growth-in-God that is wholly congruent with a modern rendition of the significance of the 'historical Jesus' (*qua* human life of Jesus: 'the earthly Jesus'). It is thus able to confront the challenges that the much later modern 'kenoticists' were concerned with, but without 'trimming' any divine attributes away, however temporarily. Moreover, his concomitant rendition of the 'mingling' of the divinity and humanity of Christ, when sympathetically read and understood, does not obliterate the human but salvifically suffuses it with divine potency.

[22] See Dionysius the Areopagite, 'Mystical Theology', in tr. Colm Luibheid, *Pseudo-Dionysius: The Complete Works* (London: S.P.C.K., 1987), 133–141. (This modern translation is not without its problems, but the core point about the three stages of ascent is made clearly at ibid., 136, 138–140.)

linguistic account of what can, and cannot, be said propositionally about God and the God/Man who is Christ.

Christology and Judaism: What is at Stake?

Up to now I have made no direct mention of the major christological complications raised by the indissoluble – but historically heinous and tragic – relation of Christianity to Judaism, although this theme has necessarily lurked in our earlier discussion of 'the historical Jesus' (Jesus the Jew). In one sense, of course, this christological 'complication' and its core attendant question is obvious: is Jesus the long-expected Jewish 'Messiah', or is he not? And is *any* Christian doctrine of Christ therefore necessarily 'supersessionist', or is it not? Much depends here, as we shall see, on the very definition (and remaining ambiguity) of the term 'supersessionism'.[23] The second section of this volume is devoted to a set of complex hermeneutical explorations which aim to 'break open' this issue afresh – in a yet further sense of that metaphor of 'breaking' already explored; and it argues, cumulatively, through these several essays, that no Christology worthy of the name can duck or evade the matter of Christianity's historic, and ongoing, relation to Israel. Whatever it is that Christians want to say of Christ must therefore be integrally connected to his, and Christianity's, rootedness in Hebrew Scripture and tradition: the theme of ultimate

---

[23] I tackle this problem in detail in ch. 5, *intra.* I argue there that even when the anti-Jewish, exclusivist, form of 'supersessionism' (in which Christianity displaces and rejects Judaism) is replaced with a 'one covenant' view in which Jesus simply fulfils Jewish Messianic expectations, there still remains the problem of the core Christian claim about Jesus precisely *as Messiah*. I am therefore critical of various 'liberal' attempts to defuse this latter 'scandalon' of Christian Christology completely; and I propose an alternative focussed on the Christian doctrine of the Trinity in which the preliminary 'offence' is acknowledged, but the future is kept open to an eschatological convergence, precisely through the Spirit. We should note too that this whole 'supersessionist' problem looks different in the light of a classic patristic/scholastic view of time as participation in divine *eternity*, rather than in a linear trajectory of one religious tradition superseding another *after* it: for astute comments on this point, see Matthew Levering, *Sacrifice and Community: Jewish Offering and Christian Eucharist* (Oxford: Blackwell, 2005), 5–7.

eschatological re-convergence between Judaism and Christianity, unforgettably bequeathed to us by the apostle Paul in Romans 9–11, thus remains as fresh as ever, and necessarily as yet unfinished.[24]

My method, in the four chapters that follow in Part II of this volume, is exploratory and preliminary in relation to this key topic, and by the same token it is also essentially exegetical: I do not attempt here to settle this issue in some more ambitious, analytic, or philosophical mode.[25] And that is entirely advised. Taking four core themes that are normally associated with 'breaking' Judaism and Christianity *apart* (in a negative or exclusionary sense of Christian 'supersessionism'), what is discovered in all four cases is actually an extraordinary hidden nexus of ongoing *shared* theological insight, arguably the harbinger of a deeper unity that is still being worked out through and between the

---

[24] There have of course been many other attempts at this task of *rapprochement*, post-World War II, chief among them being the enormously creative, albeit internally divergent, works of New Testament scholars engaged in the 'New Perspective on Paul' project. In the arena of scholastic thought on Jewish tradition, I have found Matthew Levering's *Christ's Fulfillment of Torah and Temple: Salvation according to Thomas Aquinas* (Notre Dame: University of Notre Dame Press, 2002), particularly illuminating and suggestive. In the realm of modern systematic theology, I have been influenced by those who have both followed, and also critiqued, Karl Barth's paradoxical understanding of Israel's 'election *for rejection*' (see Katherine Sonderegger, *That Jesus Christ was Born a Jew: Karl Barth's Doctrine of Israel* (College Park, PA: Pennsylvania State University Press, 1992), 173, my emphasis); by the extensive work of Paul M. van Buren (see n. 28, below); and more recently by the excellent collection of essays from both Jewish and Christian authors in ed. George Hunsinger, *Kart Barth, the Jews and Judaism* (Grand Rapids, MI: Eerdmans, 2018). To the extent that my own method in this volume witnesses to any originality in this realm of Jewish/Christian understanding, it is by assuming that deep scriptural attention and prayerfulness, along with a willingness to follow the 'golden string' of traditions to their more esoteric and 'mystical' ends, is one, indeed one profound, way to keep the conversation between traditions in creative play, 'up to the end'.

[25] I must acknowledge once more (see too the Preface) how these reflections originally arose from shared Jewish/Christian textual explorations (in *ḥavruta* groups in Israel, and elsewhere). This shared practice, inspired by rabbinical method, involves a discipline of 'staying with the texts' and their receptions – in this case in both traditions – an undertaking that occasions endless surprises and dislocations, ones which I myself would often attribute to the 'interruption' of the Spirit in shared prayer and worship.

two traditions. But this convergence is often manifested most vibrantly, as it turns out, in rather hidden, forgotten, or 'mystical' texts that characteristically disclose their wisdom only through deep and patient practices of spiritual reading and attention. This in itself may once again be significant, as we shall now see.

The first such exploration (Chapter 5) proposes the seemingly strange idea of an incipient *Jewish* proto-'trinitarianism', to be discerned in a number of texts and traditions within Judaism itself; and it thus breaks open the possibility of a deep remaining congruence of Jewish and Christian 'monotheisms' from this surprising perspective. The proposal is that the christological nettle that is so problematic for Judaism in relation to Christianity cannot be grasped without placing it first within its rightfully *trinitarian* context: as in Chapter 1 (above), the Spirit's relational position in the Godhead is crucial for understanding how monotheism is both fully retained yet 'broken open' to Messianic presence.[26] And this involves a subtle exploration of a theme that Judaism and Christianity share in their deepest roots: that our profoundest relation to God explored in prayer and worship already requires a reflexive *conversation* between God-and-God, in which the pray-er, participating in this exchange, is being drawn into an anticipatory longing for, and acknowledgement of, the presence of the Messiah. Moreover, it is not a coincidence here that Judaism itself fully anticipated this theme of reciprocal divine exchange in worship which became so fundamental for early Christianity's understanding of the very recognition of Jesus as God's Son.

Monotheism is not in any sense *abrogated* by these insights, I argue, but is merely complexified by the very practices of prayer (God speaks to God here), and the accompanying desire for the very presence of the longed-for Messiah in this space of worship. However, even as this conjoined sensibility between Judaism and Christianity is aroused and acknowledged, it cannot dispel the problem of the distinctively Christian claim about Jesus's already-achieved Messianic status within Christianity itself. Christianity is inherently and necessarily

---

[26] This is what distinguishes my position from many earlier discussions of the inter-testamental 'inner-complexity' of Jewish thinking about the divine (on which see esp., *inter alia*, Peter Schäfer, *Mirror of His Beauty: Feminine Images of God from the Bible to the Early Kabbalah* (Princeton: Princeton University Press, 2002), and the more extended discussion in ch. 5, *intra*).

'supersessionist' in this one sense, I argue; but the key issue is how the Spirit interrupts any attempt at a settled claim to *replace* the Judaism on which it depends, and to which it is inexorably conjoined. Hence, once again we see that Christology must always be closely tied to pneumatology and to the deep prayer that acknowledges its own impetus within the Godhead:[27] to seek the full reality of the Messiah, I propose, is always to acknowledge the 'not-yet' as well as the 'already'. As Paul van Buren once put it, with deliberate irony, ' The task of a Christian theology of Israel is to help the church hear and learn from Israel's Yes *and No*, its *denial* of the church's Jesus Christ for the sake of faithfulness *to* the church's God and the Father of Jesus Christ'.[28]

---

[27] See Romans 8. 26–27, a passage which forms a major fulcrum of discussion (particularly in relation to its patristic reception) in my *God, Sexuality and the Self: An Essay 'On the Trinity'* (Cambridge: C.U.P., 2013), ch. 3. It is of course once more (see n. 7, above) important to distinguish, at least in principle, between the eternal relations of the Son to the Spirit (and the Father) in the 'ontological' life of the Trinity, and the role of the Spirit in the 'economy' of salvation, in bringing believers into personal union with Christ, and in goading the church overall to a deeper communal union with him. But ultimately the two forms of thinking about the Spirit must constitute a correlated vision.

[28] Paul M. van Buren, *A Theology of the Jewish-Christian Reality*, Part 2: *A Christian Theology of the People Israel* (New York: Seabury Press, 1983), 36, my emphasis. The quotation continues: 'Fundamentally, therefore, a Christian theology of Israel will be christological in ways that may be surprising for traditional Christian theology. If we succeed in hearing the Jewish No positively, indeed explicitly as God's word to his church, and therefore as a word through Jesus Christ (for that is how God has chosen to address his church in bringing it from death to life), it will come to us as Christ's word to his church, delivered through the mouths of his brothers and sisters, the Jewish people. . . . We may learn of him through them of our perpetual flight from incarnation, from the act of the Creator's intimacy with his creatures which was sealed for Israel at Sinai, and for the church in Jesus Christ.' It is not insignificant that at the end of this trilogy on Jewish/Christian relations (see Part 3: *Christ in Context* (San Francisco: Harper & Row, 1988), 269–270), van Buren also avers that it is the Spirit that binds the church to *Israel*, just as it also binds the church together in community to Christ (i.e., in the *totus Christus*). For a fearless retroactive appreciation of the importance of van Buren's – now unjustly neglected – contribution to Jewish/Christian understanding, see Ellen T. Charry, 'Paul M. van Buren's *A Theology of the Jewish-Christian Reality*', *Journal of Ecumenical Studies* 57 (2022), 383–410.

My comparative treatment of Jewish and Christian theologies of 'forgiveness' in Chapter 6 goes on to parallel this set of insights. One should not have to choose between forgiveness as the sole prerogative of God (supposedly the 'Jewish' view), and forgiveness as demanded of all humans (supposedly the 'Christian' one) – as this disjunction is often represented in modern Jewish/Christian discussions.[29] Rather, after a lengthy exegetical examination of some rich and relevant sources, one may see afresh that human forgiveness is only possible in leaning *into* God's forgiveness: that is, one might say, the very meaning of the coming of the 'Son of Man' (who *is* 'God', from the Christian perspective), and who thus has the 'power to forgive sins' (Mark 2.10 and parallels), and who resides in his own open future of forgiveness into what Augustine later termed the *totus Christus*.[30] From this perspective, the Christian church (as the very 'body of Christ') does indeed ever hold out the prospect of true and efficacious sacramental

---

[29] See esp. the memorable volume by Simon Wiesenthal and symposia, *The Sunflower* (New York: Schocken Books, 1976; rev. and expanded ed., 1997), which is discussed at some length in ch. 6, *intra*.

[30] Augustine's understanding of the *totus Christus* is a complex and rich theme, building directly on Paul's idea of the church as the 'body of Christ' (Romans 12. 4–5, I Cor 12. 12), and particularly enunciated in Augustine's commentaries on the psalms (his *Enerrationes in Psalmos*). For a short introduction to this theme in Augustine, see Tarsicius van Bavel, 'The "*Christus Totus*" Idea: A Forgotten Aspect of Augustine's Spirituality', in eds. Thomas Finan and Vincent Twomey, *Studies in Patristic Christology* (Dublin: Four Courts, 1998), 84–94. The reason why this theme has attracted much criticism amongst Protestant commentators of late is that it might appear too complacently to *identify* Christ and his church (even *qua* institution), as if the church were not in need of ongoing redemption from its own sin and blindness, or perhaps indeed as if Christ somehow needed his church in order to be complete in himself. But Augustine himself, as a perceptive recent article by J. David Moser shows ('*Totus Christus*: A Proposal for Protestant Christology and Ecclesiology', *Pro Ecclesia* 29 (2020), 3–30), was aware of these issues, and appeals explicitly to the Holy Spirit (as the 'gift' of love) as that by which the church must be constantly drawn afresh, and purifyingly, into the desired union with Christ: see esp. Augustine, *Sermo* 267. 4 (*PL* 38 col.1231), so too *Sermo* 268. 2 (*PL* 38 col.1232–1233), as cited by Moser (ibid., n. 17). It follows, as is also argued *seriatim* in this Prologue, that a crucial dimension of pneumatology *for* Christology (at the level of the 'economy'), is precisely the Spirit's continuing loving lure in the human heart, and so also in the church at large, to be more fully conformed to Christ, up to the end.

forgiveness, but always in an awareness of its own ecclesiastical frailty as yet still in need of being guided by the Spirit into *full* and perfect union with the divine/human Christ. Again, the story of forgiveness is not yet finished between Judaism and Christianity, any more than it is within the Christian church itself.

The third essay in this section then traces the unfolding of another classic locus of Christian supersessionism: the issue of the 'veil of Moses', and its presumed removal in the event of Christ (so Paul: 2 Cor 3. 7–18). But for Paul himself that did not of course mean the divine *rejection* of Judaism, but rather the promise of an ultimate eschatological convergence with Christianity (see again Romans 9–11). So re-examining how 'veiling', and 'cloud-darkness' (another closely-related Mosaic and wilderness theme in Jewish revelation), work in relation to the later re-engagement with these topics in Jewish and Christian theology is once more crucial here. Again, the deeper one probes into the history of Jewish and Christian reception of these particular themes, the more a surprising convergence appears: 'veiling' and 'clouds' are protective of a divine appearance that is 'dazzling darkness' to the human – revelation and unknowing together. These symbols do not therefore bespeak the much later modernist choice between revelatory erasure as pure nescience (in relation to the Kantian *noumenal* realm), over controlled scientific truth (in relation to the *phenomenal* realm), as comes to be presumed in the post-Kantian turn of critical philosophy.

Finally, in Chapter 8, the biblical *topos* also used fleetingly by Paul to represent the final achievement of Christ's salvation (the 'sacrifice of Isaac'[31]) is creatively re-appropriated along similar lines to these accompanying chapters. But in this chapter there is not a primary concentration, in a modernist vein, on Abraham's psychic ordeal and test of obedience in Genesis 22 (as in the interpretations of Kant and Kierkegaard), but rather (as in the rich medieval rabbinical traditions on the *akedah* emerging from the European persecutions and pogroms) on the ordeal of Isaac himself. Here is the one, Isaac, in whom God 'changes the game', we might say, even for what we might expect of relations within Godself in the matter of sacrifice; and indeed – through the offices of an interventionist angel – once

---

[31] See the allusion in Romans 8. 32 to Genesis 22. 12.

again pneumatologically 'interrupts' what might seem to be a re-condoned arrangement of patriarchal religion, founded in ancestry, obedience and threatened violence.[32] It would indeed be easy to come away from the lessons of Genesis 22, as many modern feminists have exposed, with precisely this latter, violent and patriarchal, interpretation of the story. But once again, a more subtle rendition of the text – which 'plays between the lines' in midrashic mode – allows an alternative rendition, one in which divine intervention not only *undercuts* violence and patriarchalism, but also questions the whole ecology of gender and patriarchalism on which such associations are built.

Indeed, various other surprising concomitant messages about gender are found 'between the lines' in these foregoing essays on Jewish/Christian biblical themes, especially when 'mystical' or esoteric texts are in play.[33] And so by the end of the second section in this volume we begin to see that the 'breaking' of certain classic presumptions about the supersessionism of Christianity over Judaism also brings in its train certain intriguing 'breakings open' beyond patriarchal forms of *both* of these historic religions. What I termed above (in relation to Gregory of Nyssa's early christological method) the 'mutually-bombarding' exegetical approach to problematic theological questions, is here developed more systematically as a means of keeping open the role of the Spirit in its constant interruptive propulsion against any false, idolatrous, or precipitous *identification* of Christ and his church, and especially any false hegemony of Christianity over Judaism. For – to repeat – the story of the church is not yet finished; and the church remains manifestly frail and sinful, not least in its

---

[32] I am here of course already provocatively placing the *akedah* within a Christian trinitarian mode of thinking: see ch. 8, *intra,* for my justification for this playful, and quite free, use of classic texts – both Jewish and Christian – to explore this inexhaustibly rich text afresh. Chapter 8 is indeed deliberately novel exegetically in this volume, and different in style from the other three chapters in Part II, having arisen originally from a conference in which Derridean and post-Derridean forms of philosophical analysis were dominant.

[33] As also seen preliminarily in Chapter 1, in relation to the 'semiotic' evocations of 'spiritual sense' (ch. 1, *intra*), and as explained theoretically in n. 20, above. Various themes which fascinatingly undermine any settled gender 'binary' also emerge in Chapters 7 and 8, especially.

understanding of its ongoing relation to the history of Israel. If we cannot confront this challenge, then – I dare to suggest – we cannot respond to the risen Christ himself.

Christ, the Eucharist and the Broken Body: Sacrifice and Its Moral Demands

So far in this Prologue I have written about various forms of 'breaking', or 'breaking open', which allow a window onto the depth and breadth of Christ's reality, founded on his own 'breaking open' of the gates of death in the resurrection. Without a confrontation with the particular transformations of resurrection life, I have urged, no attempt to give substance to Christ's identity will have proper meaning in the first place. The last section of this volume, however, is devoted to a cluster of themes that arguably should have been enunciated much earlier: the preceding death of Christ himself; his foundational manifestation of salvific and sacrificial divine/human 'brokenness' here, and especially as his sacrifice relates to his own understanding of the traditions of Israel; his institution of the eucharist as an extension of his own 'body' for the future life of the church; the outflowing implications therefrom for any rich Christian theology of the eucharist and its moral efficacy; and the significant final lessons for where we are to *find* the full and encompassing 'identity' of Christ.

But in fact the delay in coming to these climactic themes in this book is advised. For without the preparatory explorations of the earlier two sections of the volume, it would not have been possible to lay out an argument for a very particular set of 'breakings open' as *founded* in the life, death and resurrection of Jesus. The third section of this volume (Chapters 9–12), then, moves to draw some of the lessons of the first two sections into an explicit consideration of the outcomes of Jesus's life, death and resurrection as expressed in the ritual and theology of the Christian eucharist. It expounds and unfolds the eucharist's own relation to Judaism and to Jewish sacrifice; and it explores in some depth (in Chapters 9 and 10, in particular) the further surprising ways in which issues of bodily gender again lap at the edges of these themes; it seems, then, that where due attention to the subtlety of divine interaction with the human occurs, and is pneumatologically received, certain shifts in supposedly-fixed human views of gender invariably also occur. Moreover, the more fundamental anthropological category of 'desire' here also comes to the fore (as it has done already in Chapter 1, and in my earlier 'systematic' theology[34]), as the argument unfolds for a yet further 'breaking open' of human desire to the incorporative logic of *divine* desire in the liturgy of the eucharist. For God's desire for us, always held out to us in the life and death and resurrection of his Son, necessarily challenges and 'breaks' our own sinful desires; and in the eucharist, supremely, it offers an efficacious reformulation of them by participation in his body and bloody. For, when rightly understood, *his* sacrifice – of which the eucharist is a re-presentation and spiritual extension – is no 'patriarchal' sacrifice-as-violence, but precisely its (mysterious) toppling and condemnation, which itself breaks open and exposes patriarchy and abuse for what they are. Often, as is most horribly true, such abuse has been falsely mandated, *and still is*, by 'religious practices' – even by the use of the liturgy of the eucharist itself; but in the authentic searching of the Spirit, I argue here, such a demonic rendition is progressively exposed, brought to light, and condemned. Admittedly, the contemplative, eucharistic, reformulation of desire can also itself at times be deeply and authentically painful and challenging, as it confronts and convicts the exigences of sin *in* us; but this is at base a propulsion of divine grace, a manifestation of pure divine love and gentleness, even if at times it is misleadingly *felt* as judgement and alienation – more truly, in fact, it is a purification, a purgation. This is not the 'shattering' of violence and abuse, then, but as John of the Cross puts it, in his magisterial account of the 'dark nights', the 'light and gentle' touch of God.[35] It follows that the

---

[34] See Coakley, *God, Sexuality and the Self*, esp. 7–11, 13–15, on the nature of desire (as primarily in God – though without *lack* – and only secondarily in the human, made 'in God's image', but besmirched by sin); and ibid., 58–60, for the theory that desire is 'more fundamental than gender', and that the Spirit's purifying invitation into the trinitarian life of God causes the binary of gender to be 'ambushed by three-ness'. In this current volume, ch. 1 already opens up the importance of the topic of desire in relation to the recognition of Christ's resurrection life, and chs. 9–12 ramify this topic further in relation to the eucharistic transformation of desire.

[35] John of the Cross, 'Dark Night', Book II, Chapter 6, *Collected Works*, 403: 'How amazing and pitiful it is that the soul be so utterly weak and impure that the hand of God, though light and gentle, should feel so heavy and contrary. For

Christic 'broken body' (again, when rightly and discerningly understood) is the only broken body that is simultaneously mystically uniting of its followers and at the same time mystically healing of their
wounds.

   These are major and debatable theological claims, to be sure, and
they are worked out in the last section of this volume with due
attention to a number of associated themes and challenges: the place
of the priest at the altar as '*in persona Christi*' (whether male or female:
that divisive debate is once more re-addressed), both summoning
and deflecting human desires to their necessary divine purification
in Christ (Chapter 9); the role of Christ's own intentional sacrifice
in relation to Jewish tradition, and of how this also now plays out in
the church in gendered terms, both in summoning worldly views
of gender and in transforming them (Chapter 10); the importance
of Christ's sacrifice precisely *as* sacramental 'gift', rather than as
any ritualized manipulation, apotropaism, or mandated violence
(Chapter 11); and the long-disputed question of Christ's eucharistic
'presence', and how it relates to sacramental and pneumatological
efficacy in the contemporary lives of believers (Chapter 12). All
along, the continuing theme of the Christian church's necessary
openness to the future, and to the ongoing Jewish tradition alongside
it, provides an inescapably eschatological perspective on Christ's
identity, as his own eucharistic 'fragments' – we might say – remain
as yet 'ungathered' on the mountains.[36] And through these various
discussions, as I have intimated, a final set of evocations of the symbol of 'breaking', or 'breaking open', arise thereby, and are added to
the cumulative force of the thesis that has been developing throughout the book about the nature of Christology, its mode of expressions, its applications and goals, its mysteries and revelations, its
moral and spiritual implications.

   It is time now to re-gather these points in closing.

---

the hand of God does not press down or weigh on the soul, but only touches it; and
this mercifully, for God's aim is to grant it favors and not to chastise it.'

[36] The allusion is to the very early Christian writing, *The Didachē*, 9.4, 'Of the
Eucharist': 'As this broken bread, once dispersed over the hills, was brought together
and made one loaf, so may thy Church be brought together from the ends of the
earth into thy kingdom' (in tr. Maxwell Staniforth, *Early Christian Writings: The
Apostolic Fathers* (London: Penguin, 1968), 231.

Conclusions: Christology, 'Apophasis' and the Broken Body

I wrote at the beginning of this Prologue that some of the themes and arguments in this volume might appear unfamiliar, even contentious, to contemporary theological readers. Perhaps the best way to re-address and clarify that comment further in closing is to provide a succinct recapitulation of the different ways in which the rich and multifaceted trope of 'breaking' has been variously applied throughout this argument, and how that strategy, in turn, bespeaks the particular understanding of 'apophatic' Christology which I have here wished to propose.

The metaphor of 'breaking', or 'breaking open', has in this Prologue been applied quite profligately – indeed almost chaotically, some might object – to a range of 'family resemblance' theological themes that cluster around the topic of the doctrine of Christ and spiral out in various directions. But we are now in a position to see that there is a core point of metaphysical ballast in this exploration of 'brokenness', from which the other, connected, themes then issue forth. The pattern may be explicated thus:

1. Christ's 'broken body' refers primarily to his sacrificial death as the God/Man, which is the only broken body which, *qua* risen and eucharistically distributed, also unites and heals those who are 'broken' by sin. This is the core *metaphysical* claim about 'breaking' in this volume, which simultaneously refers to the mystery of Christ's transcendent, salvific, divine nature and to the fragility of his human nature, 'hypostatically' united in his 'person'. This account, it is also claimed, represents the *inverse* of the 'sacrifice (breakage)-as-patriarchal-abuse' rendition of Christ's death; for it is pure divine self-gift, meeting and 'breaking' the law of sin.[37]

---

[37] It has not, then, been my ambition to deny, in outlining the complex nexus of themes of 'breaking' and 'breaking open' in this book, that the Christian life comes with any guarantee of protection against painful challenge, or psychic or physical suffering, at certain times of our lives, perhaps indeed throughout our lives: such are the inevitable implications of our intrinsic mortal frailty, of our own resistant sinfulness, but more importantly of what Paul describes as the invitation to be drawn by the Spirit ever more deeply into the logic of Christ's own passion and triumph

Moreover, it is in the power of the Holy Spirit (Romans 8. 11, 1 Peter 3. 18) that Christ's own resurrection 'breaks' the power of death, and opens up the possibility of a new human response, the implications of which now follow.

2. The *epistemological* outcome of this metaphysical core has various dimensions, as I have here proposed. I have called it, above, the 'breaking open' of an 'apophatic consciousness', itself 'brokered in the Spirit'.[38] Distinctive to this consciousness is its paradoxical

---

(see again Romans 8. 14–17). Some of these 'breakings', to be sure, involve involuntary sufferings which we can see even at the time as *unavoidable* 'slings and arrows of outrageous fortune' – as simply part of the tragic lot of humanity. But the crucial issue for theological discernment, constant care, and fierce moral resistance, is the potential for the authentic Christian story about 'life and death contending' to be distorted *under this rubric* by those who sinfully abuse power to destructive ends, precisely in order to justify or occlude their own abuse. I hope it will be clear that the christological and pneumatological vision I am outlining in this volume involves no mandate of unnecessary or *avoidable* suffering of any sort in my use of this cluster of 'breaking' themes, let alone a justification of any abusive *infliction* of pain; for the Spirit's 'breaking' is always for the sake of resurrection life and salvation, and that is the acid test of discernment. In this essentially pneumatological understanding of 'breaking' – the 'interruption' of the Spirit that is always on offer, alluring and challenging us – there may indeed be a necessary sense of purifying desolation or transcendent fear (the 'flames of incandescent terror', as T.S. Eliot memorably put it) as our own sins are fully confronted; but underneath lie the 'ah – bright wings' (Gerard Manley Hopkins) of the Spirit's ongoing outreach of divine love and invitation.

[38] It may be important here in closing to clarify further how the pneumatological dimensions of my christological proposal contrast with other forms of 'Spirit Christology', so called. It will be obvious, I trust, that I am not supporting, first, a 'Spirit Christology' of a 'low', 'adoptionist' variety, such as hinted at occasionally in the New Testament itself (e.g., Romans 1. 4, Acts 2. 36), and in some early 'apostolic' writings, and has had modern repristinations in projects by 'liberal' scholars such as G. W. H. Lampe, *God as Spirit* (Oxford: Clarendon, 1977), or Roger Haight, S.J., 'The Case for Spirit Christology', *Theological Studies* 53 (1992), 257–287, and ibid., *Jesus Symbol of God* (Maryknoll: NY: Orbis Books, 1999). But nor do I share the ingenious, but rather eccentric, recent views of Ian A. McFarland, 'Spirit and Incarnation:Towards a Pneumatic Chalcedonianism', *International Journal of Systematic Theology* 16 (2014), 143–158, and ibid., *The Word Made Flesh: A Theology of the Incarnation* (Louisville, KY: Westminster John Knox, 2019) that a 'Chalcedonianism without reserve' is only possible if the humanity of Jesus is solely animated by the

combination of revelatory brightness and enduring dark, divine, mystery: these are not opposites, but inexorably twinned and entwined in Christ's manifestation of his person. This emerging 'apophatic' consciousness also affects our senses over time such that we can respond to the risen Christ through all of them, but in particular by hearing his Word with new surprise and attentiveness, by coming to see him in others, especially in the faces of the poor and the suffering, and by tasting and touching and even smelling him through the medium of eucharistic worship, embodied ritual and prayer. What is also noteworthy about this Spirit-endowed consciousness is its refusal to allow the notion of the resurrected Christ to be *constrained* by human categorizations and projects: the false ambition, for instance, to reduce Christ to the 'historian's Jesus'; the temptation to try and justify Jesus's status as the God's Son by historical research; and the lure of succumbing to idolatrous or politically manipulative accounts of Jesus which do not acknowledge the power of his risen and transformative life.

3. An approach to *speaking* of God then follows from the above, involving forms of linguistic or semantic theory (these are various in the wider Jewish and Christian tradition) about how to 'break open' the horizon of the mystery of the divine, by

---

Spirit (and not in any way 'causally' affected by his divinity). This proposal seems to me to come close to 'dividing the persons' of the Trinity, as well as dividing, rather than uniting, the natures of Christ – by declaring Christ's divinity completely 'invisible' and making the Spirit do the work that would normally be attributed to a properly-developed theory of the *communicatio idiomatum*. In contrast, my pneumatological proposals in this particular volume concentrate mainly on the significance of the Spirit *in the 'economy'*, both in the matter of Jesus's own birth, life and resurrection, but by extension in the crucial *epistemological* responses to Christ in the Christian life in general: in the initial recognition of the risen Christ, in the concomitant response to Jesus as 'Lord', in the 'breaking open' of an 'apophatic' consciousness (described in detail above), and in the ongoing opening up of the church to its fuller Christic identity. For my concomitant understanding of the role of the Spirit in relation to Father and Son in the *eternal* life of God, see my *God, Sexuality and the Self*, ch. 7, and more recently my Duquesne Holy Spirit Lecture, 2016, now reprinted as 'Beyond the *Filioque* Disputes? Re-assessing the Radical Equality of the Spirit through the Ascetic and Mystical Traditions', in ed. Radu Bourdeianu, *It is the Spirit Who Gives Life: New Directions in Pneumatology* (Washington, DC: Catholic University of America Press, 2022), 153–174.

protecting the boundaries of what can properly be said about God, and what should not be attempted at all, but rather lived *into*. And here we reach the core meaning of 'apophasis', which is — after all — first and foremost about saying 'no'; and yet there are *many* strategies for safeguarding the unique mystery of God (and God-in-Christ), which are each of them forms of 'saying' and 'not saying' which deflect us from improper idolatry or *hubris*. We noted above some of the following, in particular: the credal or conciliar protection of Christ's mystery by setting a boundary (*horos*) on attempts to *explain* this unique metaphysical event, and instead 'saying no' to various possible erroneous interpretations; the use of what I earlier called 'minimalist', or abstract, technical terms for the same protective purposes; the use of mutually-bombarding metaphors and symbols and scriptural narratives to evoke Christ's uniqueness, again as a strategy against heresy or over-constraining explanation; the 'saying no' even to '*negative*' statements about Christ, in order to indicate the ecstatic, labile spiritual journey involved in coming to know God-in-Christ 'by acquaintance', which must more fundamentally undergird any linguistic theory about how to speak of him. Such are some of the important 'apophatic' strategies which must accompany any rich Christology which aims to keep 'breaking open' the horizon to divine mystery and presence.

4. By the same token, the historic and tragic tensions and 'brokenness' of the relation of *Judaism and Christianity* must themselves be 'broken open' once more, I argued, to the new possibility of a final eschatological convergence such as foretold by Paul in Romans 9–11. This 'breaking open' mirrors the 'breaking open' of 'apophatic consciousness', described above, in that it allows once more the very possibility of deep spiritual congruence (in the Spirit) between the two traditions, amidst profound and painful division and enmity, and centuries of shameful Christian persecution of the Jewish people. Here the 'saying no' which Judaism has necessarily always said to Christianity's claim that Jesus is the Messiah, must be heard therefore not as a straightforward denial, but as a discerning critique of Christianity's false, displacing, understandings of supersessionism, and a searching moral judgement on Christianity's own failures to manifest Christ's charity and presence in the life of the church and beyond. In short, Christ's body remains 'broken' in a

tragic sense until its salvific 'brokenness' is extended to re-engage the life of Israel from whence it came.

5. And thus likewise, the *eucharistic* meaning of the 'broken body' is here re-conceived in the light of all that has here been proposed. To participate efficaciously in the consuming of Christ's own 'broken body' is to be engaged in a process of life-long sanctification in which the 'brokenness' of sin is itself 'broken': it is challenged, forgiven, transformed into new life and energy. The 'breaking' and mending of sinful desires is predicated on Christ's own salvific sacrifice, and indeed on his own intrinsic relation to the Jewish people and traditions out of which he sprang in his human incarnation. To understand this involves a very sensitive account of how ritualized bodies may, over time, be incorporated into a form of life which evinces this new life, this new energy. It follows that the Christian eucharist, far from breaking Judaism and Christianity apart, far more truly re-confirms their inexorable point of convergent unity. As that consciousness is again 'broken open', so too is the question of sacramental *efficacy* brought once more to the fore with new force: for what is Christ's eucharist if it does not 'break open' a new future, in the Spirit, for his people, and indeed open up a new hope of an eschatological future for the peoples of the world and for the cosmos? The eucharist is not simply a ritual to be repeated, but a demanding life to be lived. But as it is revelatory, it is no less – and simultaneously – a 'dark', albeit 'luminous', mystery which enshrines the divine power of the resurrection.[39]

---

[39] One may recall, in closing, the wonderful poem entitled 'Easter' by Elizabeth Jennings. It begins:

'I was the one who waited in the garden
Doubting the morning and the early light.
I watched the mist lift off its own soft burden,
Permitting not believing my own sight.' ...

The poem ends (my emphasis):

'*It was by negatives I learnt my place.*
The garden went on growing and I sensed
A sudden breeze that blew across my face.
Despair returned but now it danced, it danced.'

6. Finally, a last evocation of 'brokenness' has been implicit in much of the above, but deserves underlining once more in closing. For if Christ's 'broken body', once for all sacrificed for the sins of the world, is nonetheless still, in its anticipatory openness to the eschaton, still pneumatologically 'scattered' and fragmented, it follows that the call of the Spirit in binding us more closely to Christ is also the call of the Spirit to continue to reform the church (*semper reformanda*), to purge and cleanse it, and to re-unite it ever more closely with its other members: this is the final vision of the *totus Christus*, but it remains still unfinished, and in that sense still 'broken', up to the end.

Such, then, is the approach to Christology that animates these pages.

PART 1

Seeking The Identity of Christ

1

On the Identity of the Risen Jesus: In Quest of the 'Apophatic' Christ

Introduction: The Problem of the 'Identity' of Jesus

'*Who, or why, or which or what is the Akond of SWAT?*',[1] wrote Edward Lear in one of his more elusive nonsense poems. No less elusive, however, is the somewhat parallel question: *Who, or why, or which, or what, is the 'risen Jesus'?* The opening chapter of this book will attempt to probe this misleadingly simple theological question afresh. In particular, it will propose a systematic solution to the task of analysing how historical, dogmatic and what we might call 'spiritual', or 'ascetic', approaches to the quest for Jesus's identity might relate, and mutually inform one another. At the same time, I shall begin to ask where the appropriately 'apophatic' dimensions of the task of Christology might also lie. The task is a curiously complicated one, as we shall see. Not only is there still great difficulty, even after 200 years of 'historical Jesus research', in bringing modern historical/critical discussions about the identity of 'Jesus' into clear relation to the older credal, dogmatic

---

[1] Edward Lear, *The Complete Nonsense of Edward Lear*, ed. Holbrook Jackson (London: Faber & Faber, 1947), 257.

The Broken Body: Israel, Christ and Fragmentation, First Edition. Sarah Coakley.
© 2024 John Wiley & Sons Ltd. Published 2024 by John Wiley & Sons Ltd.

reflection on his 'person';[2] but still less is there a consistent confidence manifested in contemporary systematic theology, as I see it, about the means and possibility of a *direct* relation to the 'risen Jesus' now, about what this claim might mean, and about how the probative recognition of him might occur. Indeed, we might say that this last, pressingly existential, question has been all-but occluded – embarrassedly repressed, even – in the era of obsession about the 'historical' identity of Jesus.

Let me take a telling example of this modern trend, by way of introduction. Over 50 years ago, in the heyday of the second 'quest for the historical Jesus', there was a notoriously frustrating debate between Rudolf Bultmann and Ernst Käsemann on the 'continuity', or lack thereof, between the 'historical Jesus' and the 'risen Christ'.[3] After observing awhile the interesting spectacle of these titans in combat, the insightful commentator might have begun to discern that the two giants were apparently arguing at cross-purposes: what Bultmann meant by 'the historical Jesus' (and which he so strenuously denied had any 'continuity' with the risen Christ of Paul and the gospels) was *not* what Käsemann meant by the same term 'Jesus' (which he equally

---

[2] As already mentioned in the 'Prologue', above, the greatest modern counter-example to this 'rule' remains Dietrich Bonhoeffer's (unfinished) lectures on Christology, *Christ The Center*, tr. Edwin H. Robertson (San Francisco: Harper & Row, 1978). Opening with the insistence that 'Teaching about Christ begins in silence' (ibid., 27), Bonhoeffer goes on to explicate in his own distinctive, Lutheran, way the difficult relationship of modern 'historical Jesus' research to classic, conciliar expositions of Christ's 'person' and 'natures', given the perennial Christian propulsion to 'proclamation'. A sensitive and appreciative exposition of the enduring importance of Bonhoeffer's Christology on this score has recently been given in Rowan Williams, *Christ: The Heart of Creation* (London: Bloomsbury, 2018), esp. 169–198. Paul DeHart's *Unspeakable Cults: An Essay in Christology* (Waco, TX: Baylor U.P., 2021), whilst not focusing lengthily on Bonhoeffer's Christology, nonetheless also provides one of the most nuanced and original contemporary accounts of how to relate the 'historical Jesus' to the 'risen Christ' and to the Christ of conciliar and scholastic dogma.

[3] Käsemann conveniently recapitulates the various moments in this debate with Bultmann in 'Sackgassen im Streit um den historischen Jesus', ET in *New Testament Questions of Today* (London: SCM, 1969), 23–65. He is responding to Bultmann's 'Das Verhältnis der urchristlichen Christusbotschaft zum historischen Jesus' (Heidelberg: Carl Winter, [2]1961)

emphatically insisted had to be personally continuous with the risen Christ). But nor did 'continuity' have the same valency for them either: for one (Bultmann), it meant full and complete 'identity' – identity in *all* characteristics, between the prior and latter state ('Jesus' and the 'risen Christ') – and that is what he wanted to deny; for the other (Käsemann) it merely meant a contentful enduring of certain *key* characteristics between the two – and that is why he insisted on it.[4] Untangling these confusions about identity seemed to leave little room, ironically, for serious spiritual analysis of what it could mean to encounter 'Jesus' *now*.[5]

Three lessons appear to me, with hindsight, to have emerged from this rather tortured and exhausting debate of the 1950s; yet I think it is questionable whether these same lessons have been brought forward consciously into today's continuing, and popular, fascination with the 'identity of Jesus' as (purportedly) capable of delivery by New Testament scholarship. New 'quests' for the 'historical Jesus' have, since Bultmann, succeeded older 'quests', in sometimes confusing waves of fashion;[6] yet the analytic, *philosophical*, distinctions that need drawing in order to avoid repeating some of the mistakes about the category of 'identity' implicit in the Bultmann/Käsemann debate are often absent from the empirical rehearsal of the New Testament 'evidences', even now.

In the first section of this chapter, then, I shall rehearse these lessons, but always with an eye to our specific theological goal of clarifying what might be at stake in utilizing historical reconstructions (*one* means of epistemic access) to help identify the '*risen* Jesus'. From here, in the second section of the chapter, I shall turn to the ontological pole and go on to place these (distinctively modern, historiographical) problems in a more robustly *christological* context

---

[4] See *New Testament Questions of Today*, 43–58.

[5] The debate between Bultmann does presume – and contend over – Bultmann's 'eschatological Jesus', and his 'continuity' or otherwise with the 'historical Jesus'; but there is little contentful discussion of what *constitutes* the identity of the post-Easter 'eschatological Jesus'.

[6] We should note that the most recent decades of 'historical Jesus' work have witnessed a fantastic range of hypotheses about Jesus' 'real' identity – from Cynic teacher to 'marginal Jew', from gnostic partner of Mary Magdalene to conscious reformer of Jewish patriarchalism.

of analysis; we shall attempt here the tricky task of mapping what
we have learnt from the modern, historical debates about 'Jesus' onto
the older, dogmatic debates about his 'person' and 'natures'. This
somewhat risky undertaking cannot, however, be effected without
generating some further important distinctions in which analytic
philosophy of 'identity' can also come to our aid. Our continuing
task here will be to clarify quite what meaning of 'identity' we are
after when we inquire about the personal identity of Jesus, and particularly of the risen Jesus. The results of these first two (admittedly
somewhat arduously cerebral) sections will then open us to the substantial proposals of the third, in which the most novel dimension
of my argument will emerge. Here we shall shift back again to the
epistemological pole and discuss one specific way of recognizing this
identity of the 'risen Jesus' in our contemporary lives, in the context
of ministry to the poor and dispossessed. Following leads laid down
in the New Testament, but particularly in the fourth-century
Cappadocian Fathers' theology of donation to the poor, we shall
argue that the Parable of the Sheep and the Goats in Matt. 25. 31–46
presents us with the suggestion of a surprising, indeed we might say
'apophatic', form of epistemic transformation required for the *full*
acknowledgement of the 'identity' of the risen Jesus. We shall close
with some systematic conclusions about the relation of practices to
theory in this proposed account of the meaning of the 'identity of
the risen Jesus' and of our graced access to him.

Cautionary Tales from the Bultmann/Käsemann Debate: The Historical Approach to Jesus's Identity

Let me turn, then, in this first section, to the following three lessons that
I see to have emerged from the Bultmann/Käsemann debates of the late
1950s on the 'historical Jesus', and how the enunciation of them might
help us unpick the knotty question of the risen Jesus's 'identity'.

Firstly, the disjunction between the so-called ('sogenannte')
'historical Jesus' and the 'risen', or 'biblical', Christ was surely now
seen – as Bultmann and Käsemann untangled their convoluted
misunderstanding – to have been a specifically nineteenth-century
product, and one arguably infused from the start, 'from Reimarus to
Wrede', with a false positivism about the capabilities of historical

reconstruction. For according to this disjunction, the 'historical Jesus' had connoted what one could get *hold of* – verify with the scientific tools of modern research; whereas the 'risen Christ' in contrast – if needed at all – was decidedly elusive: he could easily became a sort of gnostic, wafting, idea, or – when rescued to some extent by Bultmann and his ilk – a code for an internal existential *response* by the believer.[7] Käsemann was rightly concerned about being asked to make this (ostensibly false) choice between 'Jesus' and the 'Christ'; yet his own proposals of reconstruction arguably slid back towards the perils of the first, 'historical', alternative (despite the amount of ink he spilled in accusing Joachim Jeremias of a more obvious return to positivistic 19th-century 'historical Jesus' research).[8] So the question remained: how to avoid the false disjunction from the outset? Was it not fuelled precisely by a misleading historical positivism on the one hand, and a pervasive and question-begging coyness about 'supernaturalism' on the other? Had the possibility of a direct encounter with the *risen Jesus* been covertly erased even as the disjunction between the 'historical Jesus' and the 'biblical Christ' had been endlessly rehearsed?

Secondly, the Bultmann/Käsemann debate also underscored the persistent ambiguity of the very term 'historical Jesus'. For Bultmann, it seemingly had the primary meaning of 'historian's Jesus', a product therefore of a fallible, human enterprise and not a proper *basis* for faith; to 'found' belief on such a reconstruction could only, as he argued in *Faith and Understanding*, be a manifestation of 'works right-eousness'.[9] For Käsemann, however, the same term at least sometimes meant the 'earthly [or pre-Easter] Jesus', with which – necessarily, he argued – there had to be some substantial 'continuity' if the 'risen

---

[7] The danger of this aspect of Bultmann's Christology is illuminatingly – but sympathetically – discussed throughout James F. Kay, *Christus Praesens: A Reconsideration of Rudolf Bultmann's Christology* (Grand Rapids: MI, Eerdmans, 1994).

[8] See Käsemann, *New Testament Questions of Today*, 24–35, for his sharp critique of Jeremias, and for what Käsemann calls Jeremias's presumption that 'the historian has an access road to God himself' (p. 34).

[9] See Bultmann, *Faith and Understanding* (London: SCM, 1969), ch. 1, for the clearest enunciation of this point.

Christ' was not to evaporate into a docetic or ghostly visitant.[10]
So here, secondly, the question remained: how *should* one construe
the significance of the 'historical Jesus' (and in which sense) for the
understanding of the 'identity of Jesus'?

And then thirdly, the debate also revealed a connected muddle – or
evasion – that lurked in the same nineteenth-century 'Jesus'/'Christ'
diremption. The fascination of the choice between *two* (and only two)
alternatives in this debate had led the 'biblical Christ' and the 'risen
Christ' to become virtual synonyms (over against the 'historical Jesus').
This caused an insidious blurring that occurred just as the false disjunction was driven home, that is, the blurring between *ontological*
states of Jesus's 'identity' (whether 'earthly' or 'risen'), and *epistemological* forms of response to him (whether through historical research or
decisions of faith). Too often, it seemed, the first and second 'questers'
reduced the former to the latter category: they made the question of
Jesus's identity *either* a matter of (human) historical reconstruction *or*
of (equally human) responses of 'faith' (albeit animated, purportedly,
by prior divine 'grace'). The actual earthly or risen Jesus (*se ipse*)
threatened to disappear from view into a sort of *noumenal* no-man's
land – except, as was notoriously quipped against Bultmann, when he
put in a miraculous appearance between 10 and 11 a.m. on a Sunday
morning at the behest of a gifted Lutheran preacher.[11] Probably, this
last evasion (or reduction) was at least as much the effect of modernistic coyness over 'supernaturalism' as was the initial disjunction
between 'Jesus' and 'Christ' itself. But I suspect that it also arose – as I
have hinted – from an unacknowledged neoKantian presumption that

---

[10] See, for example, *New Testament Questions of Today*, 43: the 'historical Jesus' is
'among the criteria of [the] validity' of the New Testament kerygma; and thus he is
an 'irreplaceable Jesus'. In *Jesus Means Freedom* (Philadelphia: Fortress Press, 1969),
Käsemann gives another reason why the 'historical Jesus' is so crucial to him, viz., as
criterion of judgement against a potentially corrupt or idolatrous view of 'Jesus'
presented by the church: see ibid., 151.

[11] This quip is of course only partly fair to Bultmann's christological position. James
F. Kay concludes his insightful study of Bultmann's Christology by distinguishing
three strands in it which are often not held in perfect balance by Bultmann himself:
the 'mythical (or storied)' Jesus, the pre-Easter historical figure, and the contemporary, 'eschatological' presence of Jesus in the Word of proclamation (see *Christus
Praesens*, 174).

the divine per se was now epistemologically off-limits, except insofar as *we* 'construct' it. The idea, for instance, that one might actually 'see' the 'risen Jesus' himself, today, now, in some important and transforming way that involves response to *his* proffered 'identity', came, implicitly (even if both Bultmann and Käsemann themselves explicitly denied this) to be regarded as fantastic and pre-critical – so much so that the possibility could seemingly not even be mentioned. It is this coyness that this chapter seeks to address and contest.

But meanwhile, today, the idea still endures in some quarters that the question of the 'identity of Jesus' can be *settled* by appeal to historical reconstruction, that is, by reference to what we have just called the 'historian's Jesus'. Why else, one might say, are there the continuing popular *frissons* of excitement occasioned by the Jesus seminar, by Marcus Borg, or by John Dominic Crossan? The idea of *settling* the 'identity' of a past figure in this way, after all, is not obviously stupid; it might be regarded, surely, as relatively uncontentious in historians' circles if applied to some other past figure (Socrates, Genghis Khan, for instance), on whom historical details are relatively scarce, and mediated through texts and traditions with a distinct 'slant' to them. Despite the fact that philosophers might baulk, and inquire much more closely what precisely the quest for 'identity' could entail (a point to which we shall return),[12] historians are generally at ease with the task of an assiduous and critical gathering of evidence for the characterization of a past life – in this loose sense of 'identity'. Yet in the case of Jesus such an historical approach is obviously *pre-theological*. By definition, it shrinks what can be said of Jesus to what the secular historian regards as appropriate to her task and duty, and as such it necessarily consigns him to the past.[13] Yet if this secular reduction is to

---

[12] Modern analytic philosophy distinguishes i. discussion of the problem of 'identity' as 'sameness' between items with identical characteristics (the issue of the so-called 'identity of indiscernibles'), and ii. discussion of the problem of 'personal identity' through time and change.

[13] To be sure, according to a specifically *idealist* view of the historical task, it is deemed possible to reconstruct and even 're-enact' the life of a past figure by appropriate historiographical skills (see, for example, R. G. Collingwood, *The Idea of History* (Oxford: Clarendon Press, 1946), esp. Part V). But clearly even this is distinctively different from claiming to encounter a living and resurrected 'Son of God'.

be avoided, what are the alternatives open to us in the matter of the 'identity of Jesus'?

The rest of this chapter will be devoted to sketching *one* such alternative, one in which the 'historian's Jesus', as we have defined it, can indeed continue to play a certain significant role (although not a primary or decisive one) in answer to the question of 'Jesus'' human 'identity', and in which a certain boldness about a claimed access to the 'risen Jesus' *himself* will be a salient feature of the discussion. But to arrive at this alternative we first have to renounce the modern dualism (as it still bedevilled Bultmann and Käsemann) between 'the historical Jesus' and the 'Christ of faith', *tout court* – at least as it appears to apply *ontologically* to the 'identity of Jesus'; and we have to probe both through and behind the disjunction. It appears, then (and this is the conclusion of this first part of my reflections), that we need to be dealing with *four* items for discussion and analysis rather than two: the 'historian's Jesus' and the 'response of faith to "Christ"' at the epistemological level, and the 'earthly Jesus' and the 'risen Jesus' at the ontological level. Whereas the first two items are clearly distinct forms of human analysis and response (though maybe not as cleanly disjunct as some would have it: more on that shortly), the latter two items are arguably *personally* 'identical': they constitute descriptions of the 'same' 'person' at different times – an issue which we must now explore. For it is here that we hit distinctive christological and philosophical issues that require much further explication.

Christological Identity as 'Hypostasis': The Ontological Approach to Jesus's Person

We have noted up to now how tempting it is to impose the modern template of a 'Jesus/Christ' disjunction onto the issue of the 'person' of Jesus himself. But in this way, modern debates about the identity of the Jesus of '*history*' can become confusingly entangled with premodern debates about the 'person' (*hypostasis*) of Christ (the latter debates being in contrast essentially metaphysical rather than historiographical). In fact, let me again suggest that there seem to be three such temptations of confusion in this area, equally seductive and equally misleading christologically. Each has relevance for the contested question of Jesus's 'identity', which we seek to clarify.

The first temptation causes one to slide straight back to the epistemological pole. It assumes, in neoRitschlian mode, that talk about 'Jesus' is a matter of establishing 'fact', whilst response to 'Christ' is a question of 'value'. The crudest form of this misapprehension is the naïve empiricist attempt to 'justify' an ascription of divine 'identity' to Jesus by reference to historical 'evidences', a ploy which has in the past much exercised evangelical and British empiricist approaches to Christology, but which I myself take to be a category mistake: evidences may at best *suggest* the presence of divinity, but cannot logically compel such a conclusion. There is however also a more subtle version of the same fact/value distinction, to which we shall have reason to return later. To cite a suggestive essay by Rowan Williams, the response of faith to Christ is *not* a matter of dispassionate factual investigation, but 'everything depends, in our reading of the gospels, on whether the story displaces or decentres us, whether we read it as an address to us, a call to *dispossession*'.[14] Williams himself, then, is careful to go on to deny that 'fact' and 'response' can be rent apart here, as might appear to be the case: 'There is no path to a secure portrait of Jesus independent of how he has been responded to; ... Part of the "reality" we seek is that the history of Jesus did indeed begin the process that led to the definition of faith in the Christian sense'.[15] In other words, not only is the quest for 'facts' about Jesus strongly already entangled with implicit issues of 'valuation', but underlyingly too there is a metaphysical *reality*, Jesus, with whom both historians and believers have to do; the temptation to slice him in half is to be sternly resisted. Yet that temptation, we may note, may also come in another two forms as well. The modernistic template may suggest, secondly, either that *clarity* may be achieved in the area of 'Jesus', whereas 'mystery' necessarily attends the figure of 'Christ', or – thirdly, and worse – that 'Jesus' is code for the *humanity* of the God/man, and 'Christ' for his divinity. But in both cases, this is to divide the 'natures'.

Only when we have shaken off these misapprehensions like dust from our feet, can we proceed to less misleading ways of framing the

---

[14] Rowan Williams, 'Looking for Jesus and Finding Christ', in eds. D. Z. Phillips and Mario von der Ruhr, *Biblical Concepts and our World* (Basingstoke: Palgrave Macmillan, 2004), 150, my emphasis.

[15] Ibid., 151.

metaphysical question about Jesus's own 'identity'. What we have suggested so far, then, is that this *one* 'person' is the subject both of 'historical' enquiry and of the arousal of faith; that he is no less personally mysterious and elusive in his 'earthly' life as in his 'risen' existence; and that (from the perspective of faith, not of 'secular' historical research) we must speak of his personal, 'hypostatic' identity in the incarnation as involving a *co-existence* of the human with the divine.

Once we are talking about personal 'hypostasis' as the locus of Jesus's identity, we have declared a sort of dogmatic *fiat* (some would say by a mere sleight of hand): we have not exactly clarified the issue intrinsically, but at least we have shed certain modernistic muddles. The word 'hypostasis' in fact merely serves here as a place-holder for a strong metaphysical claim: that Jesus was God's Son incarnate. It does not provide an answer to the notoriously complex philosophical problems of 'personal identity' in general – indeed, it complicates them not a little! Whereas debates about 'personal identity' in analytic philosophy focus on whether to appeal to mental states (memory in particular), or to physical ones (bodily features), as criteria of 'identity' through time – a debate which has given rise to a memorable range of fantastic counter-factual thought-experiments about brains-in-vats[16] – the concept 'hypostasis' does nothing to *solve* such debates in this christological context; it merely trumps them in Jesus's case by appeal to an unchanging, divine locus of 'identity' (the Logos, the second 'person' of the Trinity) that is inseparably conjoined to a human 'nature' at the incarnation.

Is then the 'risen Jesus' *also* human in his 'identity'? The question is, in a sense, a trick one, and has had no clearly unanimous answer from the Christian theological tradition.[17] However, if we take the gospel 'appearance' narratives as broadly credible, we must surely answer Yes rather than No: this 'risen Jesus' seemingly *claims* to be the 'same' Jesus who taught and healed and suffered and died (the Lockean memory

---

[16] A fine, if now somewhat dated, collection of essays on these issues, which gives the flavour of the analytic debate is ed. Amélie Oksenberg Rorty, *The Identities of Persons* (Berkeley: U. California Press, 1976).

[17] At the Reformation this question became inextricably entangled with debates in the *Abendmahlstreit* about the sort of presence Christ has at the eucharist. Those denying a 'real', that is, physical, presence would also be inclined to question the risen Jesus's present 'human', bodily availability in general.

criterion for personal identity); and he is recognizable to at least some of his followers and acquaintances, has wounds and scars consistent with an experience of crucifixion, and a voice that also evokes recognition; so secondly, too – on the physical criteria for 'personal identity' mentioned above – he is 'the same' Jesus as was known to his disciples before his arrest, trial and death. Yet it seems that his human 'identity' has also undergone a significant change: he is strangely unrecognizable at times to some who knew him before (an epistemic problem which we shall address shortly); he moves around in ways incompatible with normal human bodiliness; and he is perceived as densely 'present' in ways and places not strictly compatible with ordinary human physical existence. Perhaps we must therefore call the 'risen Jesus' 'human' in some expanded, intensified or transformed sense, no longer simply '*a* man'; he is rather – as Luther as would have put it – the 'proper man', as only one who is also 'God' can be: God 'for us'.

But this conclusion of course raises further complications for our 'identity' issue. For especially as the era of physical resurrection appearances seems to draw to a close in the biblical text, we are again pushed up against the question of how *physical* criteria of 'identity' could continue to apply in the identification of the 'risen Jesus'. What has now become of the 'individual' who is/was 'Jesus'? Simply to re-summon the patristic argument of metaphysical fiat at this point may not adequately satisfy us: it may rather at times strike us as too much lifted away from the known contours of individual bodily existence. Docetism again looms. Perhaps then we need to step back at this point and distinguish several *different* ways in which we now see that the question of the 'identity' of 'Jesus' may be tackled, and also return to the question of what part, if any, may be played in this by the modern project of 'historical reconstruction'.

At one level of discussion, as we have now shown, the question of Jesus' 'identity' is metaphysically straightforward, if deeply mysterious and unique: for those who subscribe to an 'orthodox' Christology, Jesus simply *is* God incarnate; his 'identity' *is* the divine 'hypostasis' of the Word. As such, the mystery of his 'personhood' has an 'apophatic' dimension qualitatively different even from the mystery of every human 'personhood'; for he, alone amongst humans, is also 'God'. But if it be objected that this claim merely begs the question of the relation of this metaphysical pronouncement to historical manifestation, we have to acknowledge the challenge and take some riskier and

more complicated steps. Firstly, we have to summon the bag and baggage of the philosophically contested criteria of memory and of physical 'identity' through time, and enquire how those criteria could
possibly apply to a God-man who has undergone death and resurrection. Let us suppose, for a moment, that this first task will not defeat
us, by dint of some clever analogical reasoning. After all, contemporary philosophers such as Derek Parfit have made the ingenious claim
that a personal 'identity' over time may be more akin to a lake with its
ever-changing shores than to a strictly stable entity;[18] and if ordinary
'persons' can thus maintain their malleable identity no less than muta-
ble lakes do, surely it is also logically possible that Jesus's divine/per-
sonal 'identity' can also endure – in and through certain notable bodily
transformations of the passion and resurrection – and retain the capacity to be recognized even *as* a resurrection body?

But things get yet tougher to handle hereafter; for it seems that
the gospels and epistles also press on us the thought that the risen
Jesus's 'identity' is to be found (if not always easily recognized) even
when *individual* resurrection 'appearances' by him are not in play.
Specifically, he is to be found in 'the breaking of bread' (Luke 24.
35), and in the faces of the poor, the imprisoned, the bereaved and
the destitute (Matt. 25. 31–46). And further, if Paul's theology of the
church as the 'body of Christ' (Rom. 12, 1 Cor. 12) is to be taken as
more than a mere metaphorical frill, he is also to be 'identified',
more generically, in the very mystery of the life of the church, his
ecclesial 'body'. Analytic identity theorists may at this point throw
up their hands in horror: where is the 'identity of Jesus' then *not* to
be found ('Split the wood and I am there'?) – and this query certainly has point. But perhaps it is just at this juncture that we can
rescue our 'historian's Jesus' and at last give him/it something to do
theologically. Simultaneously, however, we can also introduce our
own distinctive proposal about the relation of continuing Christian
practices to the capacity for graced recognition of the identity of the
'risen Jesus'. To fill out these latter points, I turn now to my third
and last section of this chapter. Here, at last, historiographical and
dogmatic criteria of Jesus' 'identity' finally come together, undergirded epistemically, however – or so I shall argue – by the necessary

---

[18] See Derek Parfit, *Reasons and Persons* (Oxford: Clarendon Press, 1984).

sustaining matrix of the Christian practices of meditation, prayer, sacrament and – as we shall now proceed to explore – acts of mercy to the poor.

Recognizing the 'Anonymous' (Risen) Jesus

In a famous essay on 'meaning', J. L. Austin once averred that the word 'same' (like other difficult-to-define words such as 'real', or 'exists') is one of a group in which 'the negative use wears the trousers'.[19] Whatever we think of the gender-ascription here (a point to which we shall return), we immediately see what he means: we tend to know when something, or someone, is *not* the 'same' as another; but it is much harder to say (definitively) when it/she *is* the 'same'. And thus perhaps oftentimes – or so Austin indicates – it is better not to try too hard. So it may be, I suggest, that such a semantic intuition helps us now to discern the proper *christological* use of the 'historian's Jesus' for the broader issue of Jesus's identity. To attempt to found, or more precisely *justify*, faith in historical research is, or so I have argued (and Bultmann too insisted), a category mistake of some spiritual magnitude; but that is not to say that historical research cannot play some significant, if secondary, role as 'negative' testing for claims to the 'identity' of Jesus.[20] It can 'wear the trousers', to use Austin's phrase.

---

[19] J. L. Austin, 'Truth', in *Philosophical Papers* (Oxford: Clarendon Press, 1961), 88.

[20] I want to be clear what I mean by 'negative' in this context. First, I do not mean 'negative' in the sense of either 'hostile' or 'destructive'; I mean it rather in the sense of 'chastening' or 'constraining'. Nor do I mean, on the other hand, that 'positive' (in the sense of 'sustaining', or 'fulfilling', or 'contentful') reflection on Jesus cannot be supplied both by meditative and prayerful study of the canonical biblical literature (a requirement for any Christian spiritual life), and indeed by historical/critical study of Jesus (which, for those with access to the latter, can often be in fruitful interplay with biblical meditation). However, my point is that we must most carefully avoid, first, the supposition that we can ever 'catch' and 'hold' Jesus, let alone 'justify' our belief in him, by way of historical evidences; and thus, secondly, that the continuous need to 'chasten' and 'correct' our own incipient blasphemy or idolatry in this area can in one degree be importantly catered for by the use of historical evidences for that ('negative') purpose. (Indeed 'historical Jesus' research can be used no less significantly against a false 'captivity' of Jesus by the church, and by a smug presumption

The kinds of conclusions that secular historians may gather about a past person's 'identity' (in the loose sense, discussed above, of character qualities or distinctive personal beliefs and actions) can at least indicate when a claim about that person is palpably errant. Thus, for instance, if a self-proclaimed Christian believer avers that 'Jesus' was not a Jew (a denial on which so much hung in the twentieth century), or if she insists that 'Jesus' tells her that being obedient to him should rightly result in worldly influence and financial success (a supposition not absent from certain Evangelical forms of twenty-first-century spirituality), we may appropriately object, not only on intra-Christian biblical grounds, but also on *historical* grounds – open too to 'secular' investigation – that this cannot be the 'same' Jesus whom Christians worship and claim to encounter today, but who lived and taught and walked about and was crucified in Palestine at a known period in the first century C.E.

And so here, finally, we reach the nub to which the foregoing argument has eventually led. If historical evidences can properly supply only *negative* tests on Jesus's earthly personal 'identity', what are to be the appropriate *positive* 'tests' in the case of Jesus' risen 'identity'? To extend our gender metaphor, a little provocatively: if historical evidences 'wear the trousers', albeit only negatively, in the matter of the identity of Jesus, where are we to find the more alluring and enveloping *skirts* of this issue?[21]

---

that he is available only to the credally 'orthodox', as it can against more individual manifestations of fantasy or self-righteousness). I shall argue shortly below, however, that this continuous task of a 'negative' use of *historical* evidences must always be balanced, indeed undergirded, by a *spiritual* erasure of self-certainty, in and through the Holy Spirit, who alone discloses the identity of the risen Jesus to us. I trust it will thus also be clear that I am using the word 'negative' here in a distinctly nuanced way, as explained, to be contrasted with Albert Schweitzer's famous utilization of the same word at the end of his *The Quest of the Historical Jesus* (London: Adam and Charles Black, 1952), when he writes (p. 396), under the heading *Results*: 'Those who are fond of talking about negative theology can find their account here. There is nothing more negative than the result of the critical study of the Life of Jesus'.

[21] One cannot help recalling here the famous – albeit unnecessarily sceptical – remark of R.H. Lightfoot (*History and Interpretation in the Gospels* (London: Hodder and Stoughton, 1935), 255, my emphasis, that 'we trace [in the gospels] but the *outskirts* of his ways'. I do intend a playful gender allusion here (in the spirit of the

The investigation of the identity of the 'risen Jesus', surely, shares something special with the investigation of the 'identity' of any other *living* human 'person', but also has something entirely unique to it. What it shares with the investigation of living 'personhood', it seems to me, is the possibility of relationship: I do not only 'grasp', but am also 'grasped', by the living mystery of the 'other' (something not possible in the same way, note, in a detective's investigation of the technical 'identity' of a dead body, nor in the secular historian's reconstruction of a deceased personality). But what I now suggest is unique to the risen Jesus, if his hypostatic identity *qua* second divine 'person' is to be properly intuited and responded to, is the necessity of my first being grasped – not just directly by the mystery of the 'person' of Jesus himself – but by that in God (what Christians call the Spirit) which so *dispossesses* me that I can truly 'see' 'Jesus', and not merely my own face at the bottom of a well. Note here that I am picking up a theme – dispossession – that we earlier saw adumbrated briefly by Rowan Williams; but I am giving it now a particular, and we might say *semiotic*, significance, in terms of the transformative, even de-stabilizing conditions of entry into inner-trinitarian participation. In other words, what is needed here – in the richest theological sense of 'identifying' the risen Jesus – is some prior, interruptive, undoing of epistemic blockage, some mending of the blindness of the ravages of sin, in order that the 'person' of Jesus truly be 'identified'. Paul memorably puts it thus, heading off a proto-gnostic threat before he discloses his teaching on the 'body' of Christ: 'No one can say Jesus is Lord *except by the Holy Spirit*' (1 Cor. 12. 3); and in the contemporary period, Hans Urs von Balthasar has expressed a similar sentiment, precisely in relation to the problem of our contemporary obsession with the historical reconstruction of 'Jesus': we need, he says, to avoid 'fixing [our] eyes so narrowly on the historical aspect of Christ's revelation, as the thing of ultimate significance, that [we] neglect the Holy Spirit'.[22] In other words, to 'see' God (the Son) – to identify the risen Jesus – involves a profound epistemic transformation, one that may first

---

Lacanian category of the 'semiotic'), for as we shall see, a very particular, and normally undiscussed, form of epistemic receptivity is here required of us, which is spiritually transformative rather than gender-stereotypical or essentialist.

[22] H. U. von Balthasar, *Love Alone is Credible* (San Francisco: Ignatius Press, 2004), 149–150.

throw me out of kilter but ultimately knit me participatively into the life of the Trinity. And *this* is why acknowledging the 'identity' of Jesus is different from any other such 'identifying' of 'persons'.

Let me now try, in what remains of this opening chapter, to spell this suggestion out a little further in order to bring this argument to its climax and conclusion.

I have attempted in an earlier publication[23] to explicate the possible conditions for contemporary 'seeing' of the resurrected Jesus by reference to the patristic 'spiritual senses' tradition, so-called. This tradition charts in some detail the proposed capacity of our gross physical senses to undergo profound transformative change, or sharpening, in the Spirit in order to come, ultimately, into desired recognition of, and union with, the risen Jesus. The tradition is founded originally in the work of Origen, in his *de Principiis,* his *Contra Celsum,* and perhaps most richly in his *Commentary on the Song of Songs;*[24] but there is some continuing debate as to whether Origen's own rendition of this type of epistemology is at times rendered problematic by a sharp disjunction between 'inner' (spiritual) and 'outer' (physical) senses: does this suggest a certain squeamishness about the ultimate redeemability of the 'flesh' on his view?[25] The subtle extension and adjustments made to Origen's approach by the fourth-century Gregory of Nyssa, I have argued, present a telling and creative alternative, in which 'spiritual senses' are developed by the grace of the Holy Spirit and through patient Christian practice over a life-time of purgation and transformation *starting with the raw material of the 'fleshly minded'* (as Gregory

---

[23] Sarah Coakley, *Powers and Submissions* (Oxford: Blackwell, 2002), ch. 8.

[24] For a recent, and discerning, account of Origen's understanding of 'spiritual sensation' and its modern reception, see Mark J. McInroy, 'Origen of Alexandria', in eds. Paul L. Gavrilyuk and Sarah Coakley, *The Spiritual Senses: Perceiving God in Western Christianity* (Cambridge: C.U.P., 2012), ch. 1.

[25] This is the view I adumbrated in *Powers and Submissions*, 136–141; but more recently I have somewhat revised my thoughts on the relationship of Origen and Nyssen on this theme: see Sarah Coakley, *Sensing God? Reconsidering the Patristic Doctrine of "Spiritual Sensation" for Contemporary Theology and Ethics* (Milwaukee: Marquette University Press, the Père Marquette Lecture, 2022), for a more nuanced discussion. I now see that Origen's views on 'spiritual sensation', especially when viewed as anticipatory of the resurrection body, do not always rehearse a disjunctive view of the relation of body and soul.

himself puts it in the introduction to his *Commentary on the Song*).[26] In other words, for Gregory, it is precisely the stuff of my flesh that is worked on, rather than disdained, in this process towards Christic recognition and union. Yet what is also distinctive to Gregory's account is an insistence that a de-throning darkness – a 'blinding' of normal sight and intellectual power – will necessarily attend any *close* approach to intimacy with the bridegroom, Christ; the soul must adopt the ostensibly 'feminine' posture of virgin/lover, must embrace what we might now call the destabilizing realm of the 'semiotic', in order to reach the goal of closeness and embrace of the Logos.[27] 'She' (for it is 'she' in a novel and *sui generis* sense) must exercise her epistemic responses in new, and subtle, ways – by dark touch and taste and smell (the supposedly 'lower' senses of classical philosophy, now elevated to superior significance) – if Christ is to be truly encountered. Only through this lengthy process is the soul sufficiently cleansed to be able see, because also *reflect*, the beauty of the risen Jesus: 'So too', says Gregory, 'the soul reflects the pure image of that unsullied Beauty, when she has prepared herself properly and cast off every material stain. Then may the soul say – for she is a kind of living mirror possessing free will: When I face my Beloved with my entire surface, all the beauty of His form is reflected within me.'[28]

---

[26] See again *Powers and Submissions*, 138: the idea that the 'fleshly-minded' could be drawn into the higher realms of contemplation required to comprehend *The Song* is unique to Gregory, and marks a real difference of emphasis between his and Origen's Prologues to their *Song* commentaries. See tr. Richard A. Norris, Jr., *Gregory of Nyssa: Homilies on the Song of Songs* (Atlanta: Society of Biblical Literature, 2012), 2–13, at p. 3 for 'fleshly folk'.

[27] I discuss in detail the issue of how gender is not merely 'destabilized', but substantively re-made as relationship to Christ, according to Gregory of Nyssa, in *Powers and Submissions*, ch. 9. To read him as re-establishing a 'worldly', subordinated, view of 'femininity' would be entirely to miss his subtlety here. For the most recent, and detailed, account of Nyssen on the body and gender (including some astute criticism of my own earlier views), see Raphael A. Cadenhead, *The Body and Desire: Gregory of Nyssa's Ascetical Theology* (Oakland, CA: University of California Press, 2018), esp. Part III.

[28] 'Commentary on the Song of Song, 15', tr. in ed. H. Musurillo, *From Glory to Glory* (New York: Charles Scribner's Sons, 1995), 282.

Why, then, do I argue that the 'spiritual senses' give us the final and necessary epistemic key to the problem of the 'identity' of the risen Jesus? It is partly because I see this tradition as able to explain, retro-actively, certain characteristic features of the New Testament stories of the resurrection which otherwise remain obscure or quirky: the pos-sibility of being with the risen Jesus and *not* recognizing him, for instance; of having to go through a personal process of change or of particular ritual acts in order to 'see' him; of the context of uncer-tainty and disturbance and 'fear' in which the resurrection is distinc-tively encountered; or of the significance of women's testimony to the resurrection that was so quickly sidelined or superseded. But I am also, and more systematically, wishing to highlight the significance of the spiritual senses because I take it they indicate a particular sort of knowing that is alone *appropriate* to the solution of the problem of the mystery of the 'identity' of Jesus: a knowing by destabilized unknow-ing, a knowing by so-called 'feminine' desire, a knowing by a gradual spiritual transformation and merging into the object of longing.

Predictably, perhaps, my initial essay on this theme produced some vehemently negative response: it is surprising, but noteworthy, how committed most contemporary theologians seemingly are to the *impossibility* of any present 'physical' re-identification of 'the risen Jesus' at all, of whatever sort. Ingolf Dalferth put it thus, and uncom-promisingly, scolding me for what he saw as a major category error: ' ... "*seeing*" *the risen Christ* [he said] is not a case of seeing at all, but a metaphorical way of expressing the fundamental change of life brought about [in the believer in relation to the resurrection]'.[29] However, I beg to differ: if we cannot, by definition, respond to Jesus's identity through our bodies – our eyes, our hands, our lips, our ears – what is the cost to our Christian principle of 'incarnation'? Who is 'wearing the trousers' here? And that is why, in the closing portion of this chapter, I wish – doggedly – to repeat, and extend, this earlier line of argument on the 'spiritual senses' with a further responsive sugges-tion. I want to say that that supposed '*impossibility*' (as Dalferth puts it) of relating physically to the risen Jesus is really, and more truly, a profound *possibility* of a paradoxical and 'apophatic' sort – one that intrinsically undercuts my natural longings to control and predict the

---

[29] Ingolf U. Dalferth, 'The Resurrection: The Grammar of "Raised"', in Philips and von der Ruhr, *Biblical Concepts and our World*, 202, my emphasis.

epistemic outcome. And it seems to me that even the New Testament authors already show us – and the patristic authors on the 'spiritual senses' ramify this approach – that the 'spiritual' or epistemic conditions for the recognition of the 'risen Jesus' (involving crucially, as I have hinted, a radical dispossession to the Spirit) demand a cumulative tangle of *practices* – meditative, sacramental, but also moral, in order to sustain this paradoxical form of unknowing/knowing.[30]

The repetitive 'emptying' of self, in the Spirit, towards the possibility of seeing and finding 'Jesus', has to be formed and shaped by deep positive meditative immersion in the narrative of the gospels, firstly, to be sure, but no less also by the sort of *rupture* of expectation that the sacramental 'breaking' of bread implies.[31] He is made known in 'the *breaking* of bread' (Luke 24. 35), but only because his '*death*' is proclaimed 'until he comes' (1 Cor. 11. 26).[32] It is through this paradox of making and breaking of my sense of 'Jesus' that my true sense of Jesus, by grace, emerges. It involves a sort of 'turning', and 'turning' again – as the Magdalene did before she recognized the gardener for 'Rabboni' (John 20. 14, 16) – that I am ever engaged in as I seek the identity of the 'risen Jesus'. By the same token, in my moral life, in my intended acts of mercy, though it is 'Jesus' I seek to obey and emulate, it is always in the *erasure* of expectation that Jesus truly presents himself to me – in the entirely unromantic 'other', in the exhausting and defeating poverty of my 'neighbour', in the nuisance of the beggar at my gate. And that 'apophatic' lesson surely sustains the insights of the parable

---

[30] Marianne Sawicki creatively develops a somewhat similar line of approach to 'practice' and resurrection in *Seeing the Lord: Resurrection and Early Christian Practices* (Minneapolis, MN: Fortress Press, 1994), and does so in a way that gives close attention to particular New Testament evidences. However she does not systematically develop the 'apophatic' dimension of the argument in the way I am suggesting here.

[31] It strikes me that the 'doing in memory' of the eucharist might itself be seen as a sort of extension of the 'identity' criterion of 'memory' for the existence of 'persons' through time (the Lockean tradition on personal identity), but here extended by means of Jesus's followers *identifying* themselves with the body of Jesus who has to suffer Passion and death.

[32] I discuss in more detail this reading of the eucharistic 'breaking' as a questioning and chastening of desire in the chapters in the final section of this book. A discerning reading of the Emmaus story as both 'demanding and surprising', especially in a Jewish/Christian context, may be found in R. W. L. Moberly, *The Bible, Theology and Faith: A Study of Abraham and Jesus* (Cambridge: C.U.P., 2000), ch. 2.

of the sheep and the goats in Matt 25. 31–46, if anything does. Whatever the original provenance and intention of this 'parable', its paradoxes in the Matthaean redaction are striking and powerful: the true 'recognizers' of Jesus are precisely the ones who are unaware of it (Matt 25. 37–39); yet presumably their moral antennae have in some sense been trained, spiritually if unconsciously, and by repetitive breakage, to respond to the 'identity of Jesus' in those whom they serve. 'Jesus' is found precisely in the incarnational *physicality* of these poor and destitute to whom they have given their acknowledgement and aid; 'Jesus' is ignored, unrecognized, despised, by those who fail so to act and will. Such is not merely a question of ethical rectitude, let alone a worthy project of human self-improvement; it is a subtle matter of 'seeing' – of identification and response. And perhaps more: for according to at least one strand in patristic exegesis of Matt 25, what is given back to us by the poor whom we serve (Jesus himself) is far greater a gift than anything we could ever give to them.

It is, indeed, Gregory of Nyssa's elder brother, Basil, who expresses this point with the greatest spiritual acuity and daring. Although all the Cappadocian Fathers insist on the revolutionary social signifi-cance of donation to the poor,[33] the possibility thereby of up-ending the network of class and privilege that sustains the order of the 'world',

---

[33] This is a striking theme throughout the writings of the Cappadocian fathers: see, e.g., Gregory of Nyssa, GNO 9 (Leiden: Brill, 1967), 93–127; and, for Gregory of Nazianzus and Basil on the same issue, see tr. M. F. Toal, *Sunday Sermons of the Great Fathers* 3 (Chicago: Regnery, 1959), 43–64, and 325–332. Two of the most important homiles by Gregory of Nyssa on *philanthrōpia* to the poor are edited, with commen-tary, by Adrianus van Heck, *Gregorii Nysseni de Pauperibus Orationes Duo* (Leiden: Brill, 1964). A compendium of patristic and later interpretations of Matt 25 can be conveniently found in Sherman W. Gray, *The Least of My Brothers: Matthew 25: 31–46 – A History of Interpretation* (Atlanta, GA: Scholars Press, 1989). However, Gray is mostly interested in whether the text is interpreted in a universalistic or intra-Christian way, and this leads to neglect of other themes that the patristic authors (such as the Cappadocians) also cover. I am much indebted, in this final section of this chapter, to Brian E. Daley's lecture, 'Building a New City: The Cappadocian Fathers and the Rhetoric of Philanthropy', *Journal of Early Christian Studies* 7 (1999), 431–461, and also to the continuing work of Susan R. Holman on the theme of poverty in the patristic era: see her *The Hungry Are Dying: Beggars and Bishops in Roman Cappadocia* (New York: O.U.P., 2001).

it is Basil who first presses home the radical point that gifts to the poor are not really 'free' donations at all, but rather the paying back of an initial debt that God lays on us even as we are created. Since life itself is a gift, all of life is also a repayment. But if we are all debtors to start with, then our response to the poor is not some good civic duty of supererogation, but a *necessity* – which, however, to our great surprise, issues in yet further divine gift, the gift of being given Jesus back by the poor. As Basil puts it, 'And you, whatever fruits of beneficence you do yield, you gather up for yourself; for the grace of good works and their reward is returned to the giver. Have you given something to a person in need; what you have given becomes yours, and is returned to you with an increase'.[34] Gregory of Nazianzus, Basil's great friend and collaborator, finishes his great sermon 'On the Love of the Poor and Those Afflicted with Leprosy', with a similar sentiment, expressly summoning the paradoxes of Matt 25: 'If, therefore, I have convinced you of anything, O Servants of Christ, who are my brothers and my fellow-heirs, let us, while there is yet time, visit Christ in his sickness, let us have care for Christ …, let us give to Christ to eat, let us clothe Christ in his nakedness, let us do honour to Christ … not only with precious ointments, as Mary did, not only in his tomb, as Joseph of Arimathea did, ….; but let us honour Him because the Lord of all will have mercy … Let us give Him this honour in His poor, in those who lie on the ground here before us this day, so that when we leave this world they may receive us into eternal tabernacles, in Jesus Christ our Lord…'.[35] The Cappadocian view of acts of mercy, then, must finally be seen as intrinsically connected to the question of the identification of 'Jesus'; to know Christ *is* to have served the poor, to have felt the indebtedness of the very gift of life that animates such service, yet also to have received the 'identity of Jesus' back afresh in the process.[36]

---

[34] Basil in Toal, *Sunday Sermons* 3, 327.

[35] Gregory of Nazianzus in Toal, *Sunday Sermons* 3, 63–64.

[36] Perhaps this is most beautifully expressed in Gregory of Nyssa's explicitly christo-logical remarks: 'Do not look down on those who lie at your feet, as if you judged them worthless. Consider who they are, and you will discover their dignity: they have put on the figure (*prosōpon*) of our Saviour …' Van Heck, *de Pauperibus*, 8. 23–9.4, cited in Daley, 'Building a New City', 451.

Conclusions

Let me now sum up the results of the somewhat complex argument in this first chapter of this volume. We started with the question: *'Who, or why, or which, or what, is the risen Jesus?'* As we have seen, when we ask what are the conditions for the recognition of the 'identity' of Jesus, we are asking a deep and complicated question, one in which epistemic, sacramental and moral factors are profoundly entangled, as well as necessary speculations about the historical investigation of Jesus's life and about the metaphysics of divinity. We have come a long way from the original quest for the 'historical Jesus', with its optimistic positivism about 'the facts'. Yet along the path, we have suggested a 'trouser'-like part – significant but circumscribed – that historical work can and indeed should play in responding to the 'identity of Jesus'; but we have been far more interested in developing less well-worn lines of approach. Thus we have identified some of the confusions caused by the superimposition of modern disjunctions between 'Jesus' and the 'Christ' on traditional christological metaphysics, and have attempted to give new coinage to that metaphysics with the help of analytic reflection on philosophical criteria for 'personal identity'. Finally, we have suggested that the full recognition of the 'identity of Jesus' may be a unique and life-long task, one that necessarily 'skirts' – as I have put it – the borderlands of desire and nescience; it is the product of an only gradually emerging spiritual and erotic maturity, and rooted transformatively in sacramental practice, prayer and service to the poor. But only in the light of the union with Christ to which the Spirit draws us, it has been suggested, will our epistemic responses be fully cleansed and engaged to receive him; only then shall we realize that we have seen Christ most fully in the 'least of our sisters and brothers'; only then, indeed, shall we *know*, with the appropriateness of a continuing and paradoxical 'unknowing' brokered by the Spirit, the full mystery of the 'identity of the risen Jesus'.

★

In this first chapter of this volume, then, I have begun to delineate – but deliberately not to confine – the complexity of the various pieces that should make up a fully formed Christology for today; and I have pointed especially to that strange, primary epistemic 'displacement' in the Spirit that I have argued any authentic response to the risen Christ demands. Armed with these insights, we go on now, in chs. 2 and 3, to reconsider certain christological modes and *strategies* of discourse (ones that were, again, uniquely attuned to the 'apophatic' transcendence of the divine), and which arose in the contested period of christological discussion leading up to the political *dénouement* that precipitated the Council of Chalcedon (451 CE). Just as we have noted in this chapter that Gregory of Nyssa's spiritual insights led to an insistence that a special recognition of the risen Christ could be found in the 'faces' of the poor, we shall now trace two other – underrated, or misunderstood – elements in his pre-Chaldeconian 'apophatic' christological armoury. In the first (ch. 2) we consider the various renditions of divine 'self-emptying' (*kenōsis*) of Philippians 2 in the fourth to fifth century patristic discussion, and bring to the forefront a neglected and original exegesis of this key passage by Nyssen himself, in which he traces the unspeakably transcendent outpouring (*kenōsis*) of divine grace into the fragile, but malleable, container of Jesus's human nature, with all its passionate elements opened transformatively to this divine infusion. In the second example (ch. 3), we expound Nyssen's equally misunderstood account of how the divine and the human thus 'mingled' in the incarnation, again in such a way that the divine fully *suffused* the human for our healing and salvation, but without in any way overwhelming or obliterating it.

From the later perspective of Chalcedon, both these exegetical endeavours would come to seem obtuse, if not wayward. But once we free ourselves from the modernistic presumption that all pre-Chaldeconian Christologies were either false starts or merely clumsy approximations of the supposedly 'final' clarification that Chalcedon would deliver, then we are also released to attend afresh to the subtle alternatives that Nyssen proposed. And in particular, we are able to see how certain discrete 'apophatic' strategies were here applied by him, and with considerable sophistication and depth. Once we get to ch. 4, then, we shall be able to re-assess Chalcedon itself through this 'apophatic' lens.

But that is to anticipate. For now, we turn first (ch. 2) to the great debate on the meaning of christological 'self-emptying' in the classic patristic period.

2

Does *Kenōsis* Rest on a Mistake? Three *Kenotic* Models in Patristic Exegesis

Introduction: Is *Kenōsis* Necessary?

It is a feature of contemporary philosophical analysis of 'kenotic' Christology to emphasize the particular problems of *coherence* caused by the notion of divine 'self-emptying'.[1] 'Orthodox' or 'Chalcedonian' incarnationalism is taken (not unreasonably, given the normative

---

[1] As witnessed, for instance, by the analytic philosophical discussion of this issue in ed. C. Stephen Evans, *Exploring Kenotic Christology: The Self-Emptying of God* (Oxford: O.U.P., 2006), esp. chs. 1 and 8 (C. Stephen Evans), and ch. 5 (Stephen T. Davis). The characteristic approach here is to provide lists of divine and human characteristics which are then lined up side by side and found to be logically incompatible with one another, leading to one potential solution in a 'kenotic' *loss* of divine characteristics in the incarnation. For a more recent, and very rich, account of the history and contemporary philosophical reception of the topic of christological *kenōsis*, see David Brown, *Divine Humanity: Kenosis and the Construction of a Christian Theology* (London: S.C.M. Press, 2011).

The Broken Body: Israel, Christ and Fragmentation, First Edition. Sarah Coakley.
© 2024 John Wiley & Sons Ltd. Published 2024 by John Wiley & Sons Ltd.

interpretation of Chalcedon from the time of Constantinople II[2]) to imply an assumption that the subject of such 'incarnation' simply *is* the divine, pre-existent Logos, who had an existence in some sense 'prior' to the taking of humanity,[3] but who, in becoming human must – according to this reading of *kenōsis* – have undergone some modification, or 'retraction', of divine characteristics such as impassibility, omniscience and omnipotence. The question of whether, and how, such a modification can be seen as philosophically and religiously coherent then moves from this base of assumptions. And much then hangs, of course, on whether philosophically grounded notions of the divine perfections are allowed to triumph over the biblical witness to the characteristics of Jesus's life, or vice versa.

When we turn to the patristic witness to the possible meanings of Phil 2. 5–11, however, we must immediately be struck by a different set of assumptions. For a start, as is often pointed out (sometimes as a slightly supercilious dig), our patristic authors – for all their bewildering creative difference in the exegesis of this passage – rarely even *consider* the possibility of the questioning of divine impassibility or other cognate characteristics in the light of the incarnation. The fact is that they have other, and complex, strategies for dealing philosophically and doctrinally with the issue of divine 'self-emptying' in Phil 2, and it will be the purpose of this chapter to compare and contrast three such (well-developed) strategies from the fourth and fifth centuries. In so doing, I aim to play devil's advocate (or is it Socratic gadfly?), and urge that the sophisticated – and different – readings of

---

[2] In the Chalcedonian Definition itself it is not clear that the *hypostasis* is to be straightforwardly identified with the pre-existent Logos, since it (the *hypostasis*) is mentioned only in the context of its being the point of 'concurrence' of the humanity and the divinity. (It might be said that the identification is *implied* by the placement of the 'Definition' in the context, in the *Acta*, of a recapitulation of the earlier conciliar creeds, but the strands are not actually drawn together here in 451 CE.) The *explicit* identification of the *hypostasis* with the Logos, then, is made only later, at the second Council of Constantinople (553). For further reflection on this point, see ch. 4, *intra*.

[3] This metaphoric use of 'prior' is of course complicated by the fact that, strictly speaking, an 'eternal' Son does *not* 'precede' the incarnation in any ordinary chronological sense.

the *communicatio idiomatum*[4] that we find sketched in these three authors are highly instructive for our contemporary philosophical debates about Christology. For what we see first, in the light of them, is that the contemporary philosophical analysis has largely ignored the technical issue of the relation of the two natures (and possible variations thereon) in its setting up of the *kenotic* problem. Yet a failure to consider the complexifications afforded by these readings of the *communicatio* causes the contestants in the debate to overlook potentially sophisticated ways of avoiding a modification of the divine nature as a result of the incarnation. In short, this contemporary philosophical discussion has in large part tended to overlook the importance of the doctrine of the 'communication of idioms' altogether.

   More particularly, and secondly, one of our chosen authors, Gregory of Nyssa (whose Christology has been unduly neglected until quite

---

[4] The doctrine of the 'communication of idioms' (i.e., the account of the precise relationship of the 'distinctive characteristics' of the human and the divine in Christ) has a complex history on which – unfortunately – even now there is no one definitive scholarly monograph. In the Anglophone literature Richard Cross has recently begun to attempt this task of analysis: see, for example, his 'Perichoresis, Deification, and Christological Predication in John of Damascus', *Medieval Studies* 62, 2000, 69–124, and his retroactive treatment of the patristic account of the *communicatio* in his *Communicatio Idiomatum: Reformation Christological Debates* (Oxford: O.U.P., 2019), 1–38. For an important and suggestive monograph on the topic of the *communicatio* in Italian, see Grzegorz Strzelczyk, *Communicatio Idiomatum: Lo scambio delle proprietà: Storia, status questionis e prospettive* (Rome: Pontificia Università Gregoriana, 2004). One should note that pre-Chalcedonian authors whom we treat in this chapter will often talk – somewhat loosely – of *linguistic* 'attribution', or 'appropriation', of the characteristics of one nature to the other, without clarifying precisely the implied *ontological* relation of the two. And Chalcedon itself does not pronounce, normatively, on the way this matter should be construed. There is a certain anachronism, then, in speaking in this chapter in a way that suggests that the *communicatio idiomatum* already had, in the period we are considering, a clearly defined status as a point of theological decision (with various analytically distinguished options to be weighed and considered). Part of what is offered here, then, is a 'back-formation' attempt at such clarification *re* the relevant patristic material; the much later intra-Reformation debates on the same topic produced, at last, a set of clearly distinguished options: see, for a brief introductory account, Wolfhart Pannenberg, *Jesus – God and Man* (London: S.C.M. Press, 1968), 296–307, and, in more detail, and with some corrections and complexifications, Cross, *Communicatio Idiomatum*.

recently on account of its apparent failure to conform to later, Chalcedonian standards), presents us – I believe – with a peculiarly cogent understanding of Phil 2 which seems anticipatorily to satisfy all the requirements of 'modern' historical consciousness whilst also avoiding divine modification. This is what causes me to title this chapter as I have: could it be that the philosophical contortions required to make the notion of divine 'retraction' plausible are unnecessary, and thus 'rest on a mistake'?[5] Finally, we shall also remark briefly in closing on how even the philosophical interpretation of these arcane patristic issues may be subliminally affected by gender associations, given an assumption made by most contemporary philosophical interlocutors about the normative nature of freedom (both human and divine) and thus about their proposed form of intersection. This will be held up for new critical reflection in the light of the patristic material that we reflect upon.

Such is enough by way of introduction.

Philippians 2 in Patristic Exegesis

A quick perusal of the relevant sections in the first seven volumes of the *Biblia Patristica*[6] should be enough to convince the patristic neophyte of the immense significance for patristic exegesis of Phil 2. The material is of overwhelming complexity and density; in Origen alone, for instance (to whom a whole volume of *Biblia Patristica* is devoted), there are 219 discussions of the 'hymn' (Phil 2. 5–11), or verses within it. Any pert generalizations about patristic interpretation of this matter would therefore be foolhardy, although more confident scholars of an earlier generation did attempt them. In a now-classic

---

[5] I do intend a (slightly ironic) allusion to M. F. Wiles's now-classic paper, 'Does Christology Rest on A Mistake?' in eds. Sykes and Clayton, *Christ, Faith and History* (Cambridge: C.U.P., 1973), 3–12. In my case the 'mistake' I am attempting to expose is the presumption made by modern philosophical analyses of *kenōsis* that there is a necessity to bring 'divine' and 'human' characteristics into the *same plane* and make them into a 'coherent' package. I draw these critical conclusions at the end of this chapter.

[6] *Biblia Patristica: index des citations et allusions bibliques dans la littérature patristique* (Paris: Editions du Centre national de la recherche scientifique, 1975).

article for the first edition of *The Encyclopedia of Religion and Ethics*,[7] for instance, Friedrich Loofs suggested that patristic exegesis of 'kenosis' could conveniently be tidied into three categories: (a) that which straightforwardly identified the subject of the 'emptying' as the *logos asarkos*; (b) that which adopted a 'Pelagian' reading (pre-eminently, of course, Pelagius himself), and saw the 'historical Jesus' as *earning* his 'name above every other name' by a human act of obedience; and (c) a third, median category (which Loofs slightly confusingly terms 'Antiochene/Occidental'), which brought together elements of the first two categories by seeing the 'decisive' act of 'emptying' as the Logos's incarnation, the implications then being wrought out in the 'historical Jesus Christ', such that there was a '*co-existence*' of the 'forma Dei' and the 'forma servi'.

Now this three-fold typology obviously has its pedagogical uses: Pelagius has a nicely unambiguous position in it as official 'heretic' (b); and Cyril and Nestorius, the great fifth-century Christologians vying for hegemony in the preamble to Chalcedon, can be conveniently ascribed, dialectically, to (a) and (c). But whether it is clear that the distinction between (a) and (c) can always be unambiguously maintained (granted that Tertullian is positioned by Loofs, with Origen, in (a), and Hilary and Augustine, with Ambrosiaster, in (c)) seems to me a moot point. Moreover, we note that Gregory of Nyssa (and indeed the other 'Cappadocian' fathers of the late fourth century) get virtually no mention at all in Loofs' account; and this is an extraordinary omission that can only be explained as part of the selective principle of an earlier *Dogmengeschichte* bent primarily on clarifying 'false-starts and approximations' *en route* to normative 'Chalcedonianism'. Yet – as I shall shortly argue – Gregory of Nyssa seems to me to represent a distinct (other) type of exegesis of Phil 2, which cuts through many of the difficulties left by Loofs' categories (a) and (c), especially for those of 'modern' and 'post-modern' historical consciousness. Accordingly I shall, in what follows, adopt the slightly anachronistic procedure of discussing Cyril and Nestorius's exegesis of Phil 2 first; then I shall cut

---

[7] Friedrich Loofs, art. 'Kenosis', in ed. James Hastings, *Encyclopedia of Religion and Ethics* (Edinburgh: T & T Clark, 1914), VII, 680b–687b. Also worth comparing is P. Henry, 'Kénose', in the *Dictionnaire de la Bible Supplément* (Paris: Librairie Letouzey et Ané, 1957), V, 7–162.

back a generation to the neglected Gregory of Nyssa, in order to highlight his distinctiveness and originality. Note, however (as Loofs does also after his long and learned exposition of his three 'types'), that in *all* this patristic material, and for all its extraordinary variety and ingenuity, there is rarely a whiff of any actual modification of divine characteristics in the incarnation: 'The truth is', remarks Loofs, 'that no theologian of any standing in the early Church ever adopted such a theory of *kenōsis* of the Logos as would involve an actual supersession of His divine form of existence by the human – a real "*becoming*-man", i.e., a transformation on the part of the Logos'.[8]

Was this a prejudicial weakness, a failure of philosophical nerve, an unwillingness to take as fully authoritative the givenness of Scripture? Or was it an insight of greater wisdom than that evidenced by what Loofs calls 'popular' exegesis and the tug of Arianism? This matter we shall now consider through the comparison, firstly, of the accounts of Phil 2 in Cyril and Nestorius. These figures will well exemplify the two dominant types of patristic *kenotic* theory ((a) and (c)) adumbrated by Loofs.

(a) Cyril of Alexandria (c. 376–444)

It has been well said that Cyril's entire christological undertaking could be ranged under the heading of an extended exegesis of Phil 2.[9] The force of his Logos Christology lies largely in its intense stress on the integrity and mysterious unity of the Logos's act of soteriological condescension in taking on human nature: the personal identity of Christ lies squarely in the pre-existent Logos, and what is 'assumed' (all the characteristics of human nature, including – *contra* Apollinarius – a human mind) involves no change to that identity, but merely an *extension* of its range for the sake of the salvific process. There is an ostensible loss of stature in this act of condescension, to be sure, but no actual ontological transformation of the Logos itself.

---

[8] Loofs, art. 'Kenosis', 683a.

[9] See esp. Frances Young, *From Nicaea to Chalcedon* (London: S.C.M., 1983), 260–263, drawing also on R. A. Norris, 'Christological Models in Cyril of Alexandria', *Studia Patristica* 13, 1975, 255–268.

Kenōsis here, then, is really *assumption* (the word 'addition' would, in contrast, suggest a false duality for Cyril); for there is no question here of any actual, ontological 'emptying' of divine characteristics, but rather the Logos's act of complete soteriological integrity in his *taking on* of the human condition. The exegesis of Phil 2 thus proceeds accordingly:

> What sort of *emptying* is this? To assume the flesh, even in the form of a slave, a likeness to ourselves while not being like us in his own nature but superior to the whole creation. Thus he humbled himself, descending by his economy into mortal bounds.[10]

Or again:

> Since … the divine Logos who came down from above and from heaven 'emptied himself and took the form of a slave' [Phil 2. 7] and was also called 'Son of Man' while remaining what he was (that is, God; for he is unchangeable and unalterable by nature), he is said to have come down because he is now conceived to be one with his own flesh, and so he is called 'the human being from heaven', the same one being complete in his deity and complete in his humanity and understood to exist in one person. There is one Lord Jesus Christ, even though we do not ignore the difference of the natures out of which we say the inexpressible union has been made.[11]

This being so, how then is the so-called *communicatio idiomatum* being construed in Cyril? The matter is a little complex. On the one hand, as is well explicated by Grillmeier,[12] there is no real doubt

---

[10] 'On the Unity of Christ', cited and translated in ed. Mark J. Edwards, *Ancient Christian Commentary on Scripture*, VIII, *Galatians, Ephesians, Philippians* (Downers Grove, Illinois: InterVarsity Press, 1999), 243; Greek text in Migne PG 75: 1301B [742].

[11] Letter to John of Antioch', in R. A. Norris, *The Christological Controversy* (Philadelphia, Fortress Press, 1980), 143; Greek text in eds. Josepho Alberigo et al., *Conciliorum Oecumenicorum Decreta* (Bologna: Istituto Per Le Scienze Religiose, 1972), 72, lines 11–28.

[12] Aloys Grillmeier, *Christ in Christian Tradition*, I (Atlanta: John Knox Press, ²1975), 476.

that – in the Alexandrian tradition of Athanasius – Cyril is assuming a (one-way) *ontological* communication of divine *energeia* from the divine nature to the human; were this not so, the human nature assumed in the incarnation would not be *changed*, and the salvific point of the whole exercise undermined. But on the other hand, Cyril is extraordinarily anxious that this exchange not be seen as a 'mixture' or 'blending' (a technical and semantic point that will prove an instructive axis of comparison with Gregory of Nyssa[13]); for this could lead, according to Cyril, to the false conclusion that the divine nature has somehow been contaminated by the human. Where 'appropriation' of the human characteristics to the divine is concerned, then (and this is Cyril's way of talking about the *communicatio*), this is emphatically *not* a matter of ontological leakage, but a mysterious 'attribution' for the sake of salvation:

> … we all confess that the divine Logos is impassible, even though, since he himself carries out the mystery [of salvation], he is seen to attribute to himself the passions that occur in his own flesh…. In order that he may be believed to be Savior of the universe, Christ refers the passions of his own flesh – as I have said – to himself by means of an appropriation which occurs for the sake of our salvation.[14]

Now so far the picture looks consistent, if a little *mysterious*. *Kenōsis* involves no change in the divine nature, but a means of transference of divine 'energy' into the human nature. However, the 'mysterious' dimension *re* the 'attribution' of human characteristics to the divine Logos (never fully explained) becomes conceptually strained when Cyril is forced to confront some of the issues of Christ's suffering in the passion narratives, and it is here (I am going to argue) that his predecessor Gregory had a more convincing and effective approach that Cyril does not consider. For Cyril there seem to be two basic ploys for 'explaining' the displays of human suffering, nescience and even despair that we find in the story of Christ's death. One is to play

---

[13] By the time of Cyril the language of 'mingling' has become suspect of the overtones of 'confusion': see further, below.

[14] 'Letter to John of Antioch', in Norris, *The Christological Controversy*, 144; Greek text in eds. Alberigo et al., 72, lines 42–44, and 73, lines 1–11.

the paradox card hard: to underscore the utter 'ineffability' of the *hypostatic* union, and thus to declare that 'he suffered unsufferingly'. This has the force of rhetorical *fiat*, and doggedly defends the personal unity, but it can scarcely count as an *explanation*. The other ploy is actually to admit the separation-out of suffering into the human side (an admission in some tension with the maintenance of *absolute* personal unity):

> We assert that this is the way in which he suffered and rose from the dead. It is not that the Logos of God suffered in his own nature, being overcome by stripes or nail-piercing or any of the other injuries; for the divine, since it is incorporeal, is impassible. Since, however, the body that had become his own underwent suffering, he is – once again – said to have suffered these things for our sakes, for the impassible One was within the suffering body.[15]

We must conclude, then, from this brief account of *kenotic* themes in Cyril, that the magisterial avoidance of divine passibility is not effected without some remaining element of strain attending the discussion of Christ's human weakness. For here are precisely those elements of the biblical narrative that modern kenoticists have fastened onto as in need of clearer and more unembarrassed metaphysical explanation. In Cyril, the divine *unity* of Christ's person is the supposedly greatest strength: it guarantees the salvific efficacy of the incarnation *tout court*; it rejects the possibility of disjunct duality in the person. But can it do so without ultimately 'supervening' over those elements of humanity most in need of salvation? The weakness seems to lie finally in the working out of the details of the *communicatio*.

These potential weaknesses were however also of course in the mind of Nestorius, Cyril's notorious christological rival and one of the more maligned thinkers of the patristic era. Let us see whether, and how, he might be said to improve on the matter.

---

[15] 'Second Letter to Nestorius', in Norris, *The Christological Controversy*, 133; Greek text in eds. Alberigo et al., 42, lines 20–29.

(b) Nestorius (386–c. 451)

Since Nestorius's christological starting point is notably different from Cyril's, we should not be surprised to find a different reading of the significance of Phil 2. In Nestorius we have what has been called an 'additive'[16] view of Christ's person: rather than starting from a (Cyrilline) straightforward *identification* of the person of Christ with the pre-existent Logos, it is in the 'conjunction' or 'union' of the Logos with *a* 'human being' that we locate the person of 'Christ'. 'Christ' therefore 'signifies the two natures', at once God *and* man. Yet Nestorius is no less passionately committed than Cyril to the maintenance of divine impassibility (indeed, he fears Cyril's 'solution' to the christological paradox precisely endangers it); hence, in his exegesis of Phil 2, he is exceedingly careful to underscore how the 'natures' remain distinct. A lengthy quotation from him is here in order:

A creature [*sc.*, the Virgin] did not produce the Creator, rather she gave birth to the human being, the instrument of the Godhead. The Holy Spirit did not create God the Logos … Rather, he formed out of the Virgin a temple for God the Logos, a temple in which he dwelt. … Paul … recounts all at once everything which happened, that the [divine] being has become incarnate and that the immutability of the incarnate deity is always maintained after the union. That is why … he writes … 'Let this mind be in you which was also in Christ Jesus, who being in the form of God … emptied himself, taking the form of a slave' [Phil 2. 5–7]. He did not say, 'Let this mind be in you which was in God the Logos, who being in the form of God, took the form of a slave'. Rather, he takes the term *Christ* to be an expression which signifies the two natures, and without risk he applies to him both the style 'form of a slave', which he took, and that of God. The descriptions are different from each other by reason of the mysterious fact that the natures are two in number.

Furthermore, it is not only this – that Christ as God is unaffected by change – which must be proclaimed to Christians but also that he is benevolent, that he takes the 'form of a slave' while existing as he was,

---

[16] This is Grillmeier's appellation: see *Christ in Christian Tradition*, I, 453.

in order that you may know not only that he was not altered after the union but that he has been revealed as both benevolent and just.[17]

Nestorius goes on from here to recount how, in his earthly life, Christ systematically undoes all the wrongs of Adam; throughout, it is his *historical* 'obedience' in *forma servi* (conjoined with his equal status in *forma dei*) that effects salvation: 'Because of his disobedience in the case of a tree, Adam was under sentence of punishment; Christ made up for this debt, too, 'having become obedient' [Phil 2. 8] on a tree.'[18]

From this, we can judge how apt is Loofs's explication of Nestorius's reading of Phil 2 as a 'mixed type' between the 'Alexandrian' and the 'Pelagian'.[19] The 'emptying' is *both* the metaphysical act of incarnation, construed now as a *conjunction* of natures (rather than Cyril's *assumption* by the divine Logos), and *also* Christ's human/historical undoing of the effects of Adam's sin, his radical outworking of 'obedience'. The possibility of the double-reading is of course precisely the outcome of Nestorius's distinctive construal of the 'two natures' doctrine.

But what, then, of Nestorius's understanding of the *communicatio*? Here, again, unfortunately, things get a little murky. Much depends on how much evidence for Nestorius's position we may deduce from the enigmatic *Bazaar of Hericleides* (only preserved in Syriac, and exceedingly hard to evaluate); but if we take this following passage to be authentic to Nestorius, we arrive at a distinctive understanding of the *communicatio* that was later – in an admittedly clearer form – to have a long and honourable history:

> There must be two natures, that of the divinity and that of the humanity. The divinity has emptied itself into the likeness of a servant. The humanity, in the likeness of a servant, has been raised into *the name which is above all names* ... This is in fact what summarizes the chief greatness of the nature of humanity. It is he who accepts *a name that is more excellent than all names*. He does this neither in

---

[17] 'First Sermon Against the *Theotokos*', in Norris, *The Christological Controversy*, 124–126; Greek text in ed. Friedrich Loofs, *Nestoriana: die Fragmente des Nestorius* (Halle: Niemayer, 1905), 252, lines 10–15.

[18] Ibid., in Norris, *The Christological Controversy*, 127; Greek text in ed. Loofs, *Nestoriana*, 256, lines 13–14.

[19] 'Pelagian' is actually misleading, if it assumes a need to 'earn' divine status.

consequence of moral progress nor in consequence of knowledge and faith. Rather he accepts that it has come about that humanity should be transformed in his image and person. In this way humanity becomes by exaltation what God is, the name which is above all names.[20]

If this is rightly understood, then Nestorius is insisting that each nature, maintaining its distinctiveness, is nonetheless referred to the person of Christ, such that *in him* there may be a transformative and salvific exchange without detrimental effects for the integrity of either: neither the divinity is besmirched, nor the humanity magicked into a form that denies or represses its natural and embodied frailty. But it might be objected that this (a) reads Nestorius over-charitably (a moot point) and/or (b) glosses the difficulties of this apparent metaphysical *fiat*. For if Cyril was problematic over the final integrity and significance of Christ's human sufferings, Nestorius remains equally elusive about the precise ontological significance of the *communicatio*. At times, he can suggest that the attribution of divine and human characteristics to the 'person' is merely *linguistic*;[21] yet if that were so what would be changed, ontologically, by the event of incarnation, a change that he clearly wishes to endorse *vis-à-vis* the humanity? At other times, he tries to effect a compromise by suggesting a real exchange at the level of the *prosōpon* (a sort of outer, 'crust' interaction), which somehow does not finally affect the integrity of the separable natures at a deeper level.[22] The matter is made the more obscure by trying to interpret Nestorius through the veil of Syriac terms, but the result is neither clear nor obviously coherent. So again, as with Cyril, we confront a paradox: there is seemingly the *potential* for a philosophically coherent position here, and one as animated as is Cyril's (if not more so) by the desire to protect the divine characteristics from change; yet the outcome *vis-à-vis* the technical outworkings of the *communicatio* is far from fully satisfactory or consistent.

---

[20] *The Bazaar of Heracleides, 58,* 61, in Edwards, *Ancient Christian Commentary on Scripture,* VIII, 253, using the translation from the Syriac of G.R. Driver and L. Hodgson, *The Bazaar of Heracleides* (Oxford: Clarendon, 1925).

[21] See Norris, *The Christological Controversy,* 130, 139, for passages that suggest this approach.

[22] Grillmeier discusses this theme in the *Bazaar* at length, and highly critically: see *Christ in Christian Tradition,* I, 510–519.

With these remaining problems in mind, let us now turn back a generation to Gregory of Nyssa. Can we find in him a more satisfactory or coherent position?

(c) Gregory of Nyssa (c. 335–c. 395)

We have dubbed Cyril's reading of Phil 2 under the metaphor of *assumption*, and Nestorius's under that of *conjunction* (or *addition*); it might be apt in contrast to term Gregory's exegesis as that of a *progressive divine transfusion*. Let me explain.

From the perspective of later Chalcedonianism, Gregory's position (and his concomitant exegesis of Phil 2) hovers somewhat ambiguously, it might seem, between the poles of so-called 'Alexandrian' and 'Antiochene' readings. This may be one of the reasons he has been found hard to categorize by the old-style proponents of nineteenth-century *Dogmengeschichte*; some see him as covertly Apollinarian (though Gregory is actually *countering* Apollinarius), and others as nascently 'Nestorian': Tixeront, in his *Histoire des dogmes* (1912) points out that both patterns are present.[23] The reason for this assessment, as we shall see, is that Gregory simultaneously accepts the 'Alexandrian' tradition of the incarnation involving an actual, ontological transformation of the human in virtue of the Logos's *kenōsis*, but also insists on the integrity of *a* (particular) human being, Jesus Christ, as being the 'tabernacle' where this transformation occurs.[24] The crucial difference from both the (later) models of Cyril and Nestorius, however (and this also constitutes the *novum* that may be attractive from a modern, 'historical-critical' perspective), is that in Gregory's

---

[23] See Joseph Tixeront, *Histoire des dogmes dans l'antiquité chrétienne*, II (Paris: J. Gabalda, 1912), 128; cited and discussed by Brian E. Daley, S.J. in 'Divine Transcendence and Human Transformation: Gregory of Nyssa's Anti-Apollinarian Christology', *Studia Patristica* 32, 1997, 87–95; at 87. (This article by Daley is reprinted in ed. Sarah Coakley, *Re-thinking Gregory of Nyssa* (Oxford: Blackwell, 2003), 67–76, but page references are given here from the original *Studia Patristica* version of the essay.)

[24] See, for instance, GNO II/2: 126; quoted by Daley, 'Divine Transcendence', 87. Gregory of Nyssa's works are cited by reference to the critical edition, *Gregorii Nysseni Opera* (GNO) (Leiden: Brill, 1958).

understanding of the transformation of the human in Jesus, the process is not *immediate*, not effected instantaneously at the moment of conception. Rather, it is throughout the lifetime of Jesus's ministry, life and death – and supremely and decisively in the resurrection – that this purification and transformation occurs; not that there is sin to be removed in Jesus himself, but merely a plumbing of every vulnerable weakness and *pathos* that is characteristic of the genuinely human: the move from immaturity to maturity, from uncertainty to triumph, from fear to certitude, from grief to confidence is effected in this purification of the human. The 'personhood' of Christ is thus not, as in Cyril, already pre-identified (*qua* Logos), such that the danger of the reading of the *kenōsis* is that the 'assumption' of human character-istics looks like a mere take-over bid that instantly trumps weakness – or else rhetorically declares the Logos the subject of it without further explanation. But nor is the dualism in Christ so uncomfortable as we tend to find Nestorius's 'solution', with its understandable attempts to 'stop' the characteristics of humanity and divinity from direct mutual exchange in the 'person', yet with its own apparent uncertainties about whether this is finally soteriologically convincing. Rather, what Gregory proposes is a *real*, but gradual, transfusion of divinity into the human, until, as he memorably puts it, the humanity is 'absorbed by the omnipotent divinity like a drop of vinegar mingled in the bound-less sea'.[25] Thus, the seemingly unguarded language of 'mingling' or 'mixture' (later to become a negative *shibboleth* to Cyril, and indeed explicitly deflected by the Chalcedonian Definition[26]) is here fully advised: the divine characteristics are progressively absorbed by the human, but not without every dimension of authentic humanity

---

[25] GNO III/1: 126–7; Gregory uses this metaphor in various places: see also GNO II/2: 132–133, and GNO III/1: 201. For an earlier account of the interpretative problems and interest of Gregory's metaphor of 'mingling', see J.-R. Bouchet, 'Le vocabulaire de l'union et du rapport des natures chez saint Grégoire de Nysse', *Revue Thomiste* 68, 1968, 533–582; and in more detail, see ch. 3, *intra*, for my own further analysis and defence of this theme in Nyssen.

[26] Only consider the requirements of the Chalcedonian Definition: 'without confu-sion, without change …' However, if the crucial point of identity in Christ is the divine Logos, then a transformation of the *human* in Christ need not necessarily abrogate this principle: see again ch. 3, *intra*.

being held up and retained in this transformative interaction, until, in the resurrection, the process is found complete.

What reading of Phil 2 attends and supports this view? Whilst Gregory's Christology is scattered throughout many of his writings, three passages from the *Antirrheticus Against Apollinarius* are especially revealing here:

> He *emptied himself*, as the Scripture says, so that as much as nature could hold it might receive . . ..[27]

And again:

> And even the word *emptied* clearly affirms that he was not always as he appeared to us in history ... He *emptied himself*, as the apostle says, by contracting the ineffable glory of his Godhead within our small compass. In this way *what he was* remained great and perfect and incomprehensible, but *what he assumed* was commensurate with the measure of our own nature.[28]

This is further explained:

> Since the human is changeable, while the divine is unchangeable, the divinity is unmovable with respect to change, neither varying for the better nor for the worse (for it cannot take into itself what is worse, and there is nothing better); but human nature, in Christ, undergoes change towards the better, being altered from corruption to incorruption, from the perishable to the imperishable, from the short-lived to the eternal, from the bodily and the formed to what is without either body or form.[29]

Now we note from this particular exegesis that the 'mingling' of which Gregory regularly speaks obviously does not mean a *two-way* ontological exchange (Cyril's major worry). It is more like a glass

---

[27] GNO III/1, 123; in Edwards, *Ancient Christian Commentary on Scripture*, VIII, 244.

[28] GNO III/1, 159; in Edwards, *Ancient Christian Commentary on Scripture*, VIII, 242.

[29] GNO III/1, 223; this translation from Brian E. Daley, S.J., '"Heavenly Man" and "Eternal Christ": Apollinarius and Gregory of Nyssa on the Personal Identity of the Savior', *Journal of Early Christian Studies* 10, 2002, 469–488, at 480–481.

being filled from an (incomprehensibly larger, indeed qualitatively and 'incomprehensibly' different) container, till everything divine has been taken in *that can be*. Not – says Gregory – that the characteristics of divinity and humanity are *compatible*, but nor are they meant to be: one (the divine) is infusing the other (the human) until it is fully restored to its proper perfection in the resurrection.[30] This, then, is Gregory's distinctive, and original, contribution to the exegesis of Phil 2, and thus also to the store of possible renditions of the *communicatio*. We turn now to essay a brief contemporary assessment of these various alternative readings.

Contemporary Philosophical Implications

When moving forward from the patristic thought-world to that of contemporary analytic philosophy of religion, we may be struck, firstly, by two (I believe debatable) assumptions made by those current 'kenoticists' who feel compelled to propound a 'substantive change' in the divine characteristics as a result of the incarnation. These assumptions seem to be suggested by such philosophers as C. Stephen Evans and Stephen T. Davis, for instance, when they write as follows:

> It seems safe to say that a conception of God as timeless and immutable would not be the most natural view of God if one took seriously the idea that the incarnation itself is our primary window into God's being. For the incarnation seems to shout to us that God is intimately involved in the temporal world and capable of change that is radical and even shocking in character. What is missing, in my view, if we think of the incarnation merely as the temporal outcome of a timeless divine intention, is any sense that God himself enters the human condition, takes on human flesh, and experiences reality as a human does.

---

[30] See esp. GNO III/1, 156–57, 158–9; in the excerpted translation from the *Antirrheticus* in Anthony Meredith, *Gregory of Nyssa* (London: Routledge, 1999), the relevant passages are at 54, 56–57. A more detailed account of Gregory's Christology that fills out these themes with exactitude is to be found in John Behr, *The Nicene Faith: The Formation of Christian Theology* II/2 (New York: St. Vladimir's Seminary Press, 2004), 435–458.

A real incarnation must not merely be an addition to God; it must make some difference to God as God.[31]

And:

The basic idea [of a kenotic theory] is that Christ was indeed simultaneously truly divine and truly human, possessing as he did all properties essential to divinity and humanity, and this was made possible by the Logos emptying itself, during the period of Jesus's earthly life, of those properties that normally characterize divinity but are inconsistent with humanity. ... [For] *it is logically impossible for any being simultaneously to have all the members of both properties* [sc. human and divine].[32]

It is precisely in these kinds of statements, I suggest, that we see the effects of not considering the implications of some form of the doctrine of *communicatio idiomatum* seriously at the outset. For on the one hand (see Evans's remarks, first) we have the suggestion that 'God' (*tout court?*) becomes human in the incarnation, and thus that this must thereby imply 'change' to Godself. But this proposal stops neither to consider the trinitarian base of incarnation theory (i.e., to locate the incarnation as a specific undertaking of the *second person*), nor does it distinguish between 'incarnation' and *metamorphosis or transmogrification*. Yet the doctrine of the *communicatio* is, as I hope to have illustrated already, precisely intended to guard this crucial distinction. What happens in the incarnation is *not* a simple turning of God *into* a human (this spectre was already headed off in the Sabellian controversy), but rather the coming into 'union' (however construed) of the divine Logos and humanity. The issue is thus not how divine characteristics can *be* or *become* human characteristics, but rather how one will affect and change the other (if at all) by their 'concurrence' (to use the later language of Chalcedon). And this is what the discussion of the *communicatio* specifically addresses, in all its various possible forms. So the first misunderstanding that needs to be allayed is the suggestion that incarnation involves 'God' *turning into* 'man'.

---

[31] C. Stephen Evans, 'Kenotic Christology and the Nature of God', in ed. C. Stephen Evans, *Exploring Kenotic Christology*, ch. 8, at 197.

[32] Stephen T. Davis, 'Is Kenosis Orthodox?' in ed. C. Stephen Evans, *Exploring Kenotic Christology*, 115, my emphasis.

Davis's remarks here are initially much more explicit about the necessary duality of the incarnation than are Evans's; but he too, it seems to me, makes a further (and second) questionable assumption that the categories of 'divinity' and 'humanity' must somehow be *merged* so as to effect 'coherence' (just as, in an earlier piece of writing on the subject, he gave the analogy for the incarnation of a tennis player [God] operating with one hand tied behind his back [the *kenotic* effects of *becoming* man][33]). What is lost here is precisely, again, what the *communicatio* is striving to convey – that 'divinity' and 'humanity' *are* indeed radically distinct and qualitatively different categories, which cannot thus be collapsed into one, flat package without seriously deleterious effects for the whole understanding of the salvific process.

In her excellent little book, *Jesus, Humanity and the Trinity*, Kathryn Tanner has exposed precisely these sorts of 'modern' assumptions to critical gaze. Her central point – in which she evidences influence from Karl Rahner[34] – is that any Christology that intends to be 'orthodox' radically loses its way if it starts from the assumption that the humanity and divinity of Christ are like two vying (but potentially well-matched?) contestants striving to inhabit the same space. As she well puts it, '[human] relations with God are utterly non-competitive because God, from beyond this created plane of reality, brings about the *whole* plane of creaturely being and activity in its goodness'.[35] And the same principle applies, mutatis mutandis, to human/divine relations in Christ; thus, as Richard Norris has also argued (with the use of a similarly memorable metaphor), we must give up the 'two baskets' image of humanity and divinity if we wish to be true to the intentions of classical (and especially Chalcedonian) Christology.[36] We are not trying to squeeze together, or coalesce, two sets of features which (disturbingly or annoyingly?) present us with logical

---

[33] S. T. Davis, *Logic and the Nature of God* (Grand Rapids, MI: Eerdmans,1983), 125; discussed in my *Powers and Submissions: Spirituality, Philosophy and Gender* (Oxford: Blackwell, 2002), 23–25.

[34] See, e.g., Karl Rahner, *Theological Investigations*, I (Baltimore: Helikon Press, 1961).

[35] Kathryn Tanner, *Jesus, Humanity and the Trinity* (Minneapolis: Fortress Press, 2001), 4.

[36] See R. A. Norris, 'Chalcedon Revisited: A Historical and Theological Reflection', in ed. B. Nassif, *New Perspectives on Historical Theology* (Grand Rapids, MI: Eerdmans,1996), 140–158.

opposites; rather, we are attempting to conceive of a unique inter-section precisely *of* opposites, in which the divine – that which is *in se* unimaginably greater and indeed creator and sustainer of the human – is 'united', *hypostatically*, with that 'human', forming one concrete subject.

If this is so (and of course, it may be debated or disbelieved), then where does it leave us in regard to the coherence of 'kenotic' Christologies? Let me end this chapter with some enumerated lessons and questions that may accrue from our visit to the exotic world of fourth- and fifth-century exegesis of Phil 2. I do not pretend to pro-vide definitive answers to all the issues I raise here in closing; my main goal in this chapter has simply been to attempt to shift the focus of the philosophical discussion of *kenōsis* in some potentially creative new directions.

Conclusions

1. The lessons of our constellating 'heroes' from the patristic thought-world may be seen to be mixed. I have tried to suggest that both Cyril's and Nestorius's alternative readings of the *communicatio* are worthy of consideration, and – whilst enshrining remaining internal difficulties of their own, which I have highlighted – both are capa-ble, in principle, of being refined and improved in ways compatible with later 'Chalcedonianism', broadly understood.[37] However, both also, for reasons we have explored above, present us with difficulties relating to the areas of Jesus's humanity that have evinced most interest in 'modern' 'historical-critical' readings of the Gospels (and indeed therefore amongst modern 'kenoticists'): his apparent occasional nescience, his need for growth and psychological devel-opment, his frailty and fear in the face of suffering and death. Whilst these difficulties may not be entirely insuperable, they tend

---

[37] I think of Thomas Weinandy's defence of Cyriline/Chalcedonian impassibility on the one hand (see Thomas G. Weinandy, *Does God Suffer?* (Edinburgh: T & T Clark, 2000), esp. 172–213), or of Herbert McCabe's defence of an Antiochene/Chalcedonian version of the *communicatio* on the other (see Herbert McCabe, *God Matters* (London: G. Chapman, 1987), esp. 39–51).

to involve what I have termed a heavy playing of the 'paradox card', and it is always an interesting question when, and to what degree, a theologian/philosopher is willing so to play.

2. Thus, it has been my particular interest in this chapter to place in the forefront an alternative (but only *questionably* 'proto-Chalcedonian'[38]) christological alternative, that represented by Gregory of Nyssa; for it seems to me that his distinctive reading of Phil 2 avoids many of the difficulties of the other two renditions of the *communicatio* considered, whilst also providing a plausible and cogent account of the features of Jesus's humanity (just mentioned) that have so exercised modern 'kenoticists'. If, as I have suggested, his alternative could indeed be found to be finally coherent,[39] we might indeed be able to declare that *modern* kenoticism 'rests on a mistake'.

3. The final concluding point is one I have raised in earlier essays on *kenōsis*. It is that (in my view) the 'competitive' reading of the human/divine relations in Christ has gender overtones that need to be faced, and – if necessary – exorcised in any contemporary philosophical attempt to give credibility to 'Chalcedonian orthodoxy', whether *kenotically* conceived or otherwise. Here I can only repeat what I have suggested elsewhere at greater length,[40] viz., that the strong commitment to an 'incompatibilist' view of freedom in much analytic philosophy of religion today, combined with the 'competitive' view of divine/human relations just described,

---

[38] I say this because of the remaining difficulties of reconciling Gregory's reading of Phil 2 with the Chalcedonian requirement 'without change' (see above). Yet Cyril's understanding is also problematic on that score.

[39] In this chapter I have concentrated on the way in which Gregory's rendition of the human nature in Christ allows for genuine change and transformation in ways coincident with the gospel texts and 'modern' historical approaches to them. It would be a larger task to attempt a full defence of the coherence of Gregory's Christology, and certain prima facie problems do remain, for example, how to understand the relation of his language of the 'Logos' and of the 'man Jesus' within his christological texts without fear of suggesting 'two Christs'.

[40] In *Powers and Submissions*, esp. 3–39 and 98–105; and in 'Kenosis: Theological Meanings and Gender Connotations', in ed. John Polkinghorne, *The Work of Love: Creation as Kenosis* (Grand Rapids, MI: Eerdmams, 2001), 192–210.

has unacknowledged overtones of a valorized 'masculinism'[41] (freedom from constraint, relationship, dependence) which leads to a *false choice* christologically: *either* a ceding of certain divine characteristics in a *kenotic* understanding of the incarnation based subliminally on competition (so Stephen T. Davis, C. Stephen Evans); *or* a 'two minds' dualism infected by thought-experiments which vividly reconfirm the dominance of the dependence/ control anxiety (variously, Thomas V. Morris, Richard Swinburne, David Brown[42]). This chapter has been devoted to arguing that we need to get beyond these alternatives, and to re-embrace alternative readings of *kenōsis* that take the *communicatio* tradition seriously, along with its understanding of the radical difference of status of the 'divine' and the 'human'. Such a view need not think of human 'freedom' as involving divine 'self-restraint' at all, I suggest, but rather as being enabled precisely *by* the sustaining and continuing matrix of divine creative power. It is not for nothing that it is Gregory of Nyssa who memorably insists that the *kenōsis* of the incarnation is the sign *of* supreme divine power, not of the loss of it.[43]

---

[41] I do not intend by the use of this term any suggestion of physiological or psychological gender essentialism.

[42] These authors and their christological views are discussed critically in some detail in my *Powers and Submissions*, 25–30. The relevant monographs are Thomas V. Morris, *The Logic of God Incarnate* (Ithaca, NY: Cornell University Press, 1986), Richard Swinburne, *The Christian God* (Oxford: Clarendon Press, 1994), and David Brown, *The Divine Trinity* (London: Duckworth, 1985).

[43] See GNO III/4, 60–62; the English can be found in 'Address on Religious Instruction', ed. E. R. Hardy (Philadelphia: Westminster Press, 1954), 300–301.

3

'Mingling' in Gregory of Nyssa's Christology: A Reconsideration

Introduction: Re-Thinking Gregory of Nyssa's Christology of Union

The purpose of this chapter is to essay a reconsideration and analysis of a controversial element in the Christology of Gregory of Nyssa (c 330–c 395). What is offered here is a reflection on Gregory's distinctive and radical reading of christological 'union', a reading indeed so radical as to suffer later misapprehension by those retrospectively fearful of the dangers of 'unorthodoxy'. My claim is that this strand of tradition is now worthy of positive review and reinterpretation. To attempt this reinterpretation, however, we have to attend especially closely to the relation of biblical exegesis and philosophical allusion in Gregory's argument. We also have to take account of the distinctive and subtle entanglement of doctrinal exposition, narrative substructure and implied ascetical demand in his christological approach.[1]

---

[1] Few secondary authors have achieved a balanced assessment of these different dimensions of Nyssen's Christology. The best overall existing study, in my view, is that supplied by John Behr, *The Nicene Faith: The Formation of Christian Theology* II/2 (Crestwood, NY: St. Vladimir's Seminary Press, 2004), ch. 8, in a volume which

The Broken Body: Israel, Christ and Fragmentation, First Edition. Sarah Coakley.
© 2024 John Wiley & Sons Ltd. Published 2024 by John Wiley & Sons Ltd.

As we shall see, this is a rich nexus which has some surprising implications. It even brings technical christological debate into relation with what we would now call issues of 'sex' and 'gender', suggesting an intrinsic connection between various levels and types of intimate relationship – between the divine/human in Christ himself, the divine/human in contemplation and the human/human in sexual union.[2]

---

appeared a year after I had originally presented this chapter at the Oxford Patristics Conference, 2003. I am very grateful to John Behr for subsequent conversations which have helped me to refine my argument. In broad terms we agree that Nyssen should *not* be read as endangering the obliteration of the human in Christ; and that most twentieth century commentators have failed to appreciate the distinctively narrative propulsion of his christological approach. (On this latter point, however, we are both indebted to Brian E. Daley, S.J., 'Divine Transcendence and Human Transformation: Gregory of Nyssa's Anti-Apollinarian Christology', in ed. Sarah Coakley, *Re-Thinking Gregory of Nyssa* (Oxford: Blackwell, 2003), 67–76). This chapter may be read as complementing Behr's analysis (a) by providing a detailed account, and new interpretation, of Gregory's use of the various meanings of 'mingling' in Greek philosophical discussion, and (b) by drawing attention to the material in Gregory's *Commentary on the Song* which links 'mingling' to 'erotic' themes. Earlier work on Gregory's Christology which I have consulted should also be mentioned here. The invaluable word studies by Jean-René Bouchet, O.P. ('À propos d'une image christologique de Grégoire de Nysse', *Revue Thomiste* 67 (1967), 584–588, and idem, 'Le vocabulaire de l'union et du rapport des natures chez sainte Grégoire de Nysse', *Revue Thomiste* 68 (1968), 533–582), are necessary starting points in any assessment of Gregory's complex Christology, and esp. of the theme of 'mingling'. One should also note: Elias D. Moutsoulas, *The Incarnation of the Word and the Theosis of Man According to the Teaching of Gregory of Nyssa* (Athens: Eptalophos, 2000); George D. Dragas, 'The anti-Apollinarist Christology of St. Gregory of Nyssa: a first analysis', *The Greek Orthodox Theological Review* 42 (1997), 299–314; Bernard Pottier, *Dieu et le Christ selon Grégoire de Nysse* (Namur: Culture et Vérité, 1994); Reinhard M. Hübner, *Die Einheit des Leibes Christi bei Gregor von Nyssa: Untersuchungen zum Ursprung der 'physischen' Erlösungslehre* (Leiden: Brill, 1974); and the still-valuable Karl Holl, *Amphilochius von Ikoniumin seinem Verhältnis zu dem grossen Kappadoziern* ([1]1904, repr. Darmstadt: Wissenschaftliche Buchgesellschaft, 1969), 220–235.

[2] In my 'Introduction: Gender, Trinitarian Analogies, and the Pedagogy of *The Song*', in *Re-Thinking Gregory of Nyssa*, 1–13, I argue that Gregory is ill-served by interpretations which force a disjunction between his writings on doctrine and 'spirituality', respectively. The latter category is an (early-) modern one, and its retrospective imposition on Gregory's *oeuvre* is misleading.

Outline of the Thesis: The Misunderstanding of Gregory of Nyssa's Christological Use of 'Mixture' Terms

The precise christological question at stake in this discussion concerns the evocations of the language of 'mixture' or 'mingling' (μίξις, κρᾶσις) and related cognate terms) in Nyssen's understanding of the divine and human in Christ. The 'mingling' language of Cappadocian Christology later came, of course, to be besmirched by association with the very Apollinarianism that Gregory was countering at the time,[3] since after the Apollinarian crisis Chalcedon was to shun the language of 'mingling' for fear of docetic or 'monophysite' overtones. Gregory's persistent use of such language has thus been a crucial factor in the side-lining of his Christology by a tradition of modern Western *Dogmengeschichte* bent primarily on recounting foreshadowings of later Chalcedonian 'orthodoxy'. (One thinks here not only of earlier twentieth-century commentators such as Tixeront, but of more recent, and equally damning, assessments in the work of Grillmeier and Pannennberg.[4]) Much hangs, then – at least for the dogmatician – on the precise *meaning* of 'mingling' for Gregory, and whether its overtones would fall foul of the 'without confusion' and 'without change' of the later Chalcedonian Definition. But even if we avoid such anachronistic judgements, Gregory's own notable unwillingness to use the new normative trinitarian language of ὑπόστασις ('person') in the context of his Christology[5] makes the precise exploration of his favoured 'mingling' metaphor the more pressing. What exactly does Gregory mean by the 'mingling' of the human and divine in Christ? Does the humanity dissolve into the divinity here, as many have charged?

---

[3] This problem has been discussed and illuminated by Brian E. Daley, S.J, in his ' "Heavenly Man" and "Eternal Christ": Apollinarius and Gregory of Nyssa on the Personal Identity of the Savior', *Journal of Early Christian Studies* 10 (2002), 469–488.

[4] See Joseph Tixeront, *Histoire des dogmes dans l'Antiquité chrétienne*, II (Paris: J. Gabalda, 1912), 128–130; A. Grillmeier, *Christ in Christian Tradition*, I (London: Mowbray, ²1975), 370–372; Pannenberg, *Jesus – God and Man*, 297.

[5] This feature is remarked upon in Daley, 'Divine Transcendence and Human Transformation', 72.

Almost all the previous modern discussions of this problem, we should note at the outset, have proceeded as if the only issue to consider is one of *philosophical* allusion – to the various technical discussions of different sorts of 'mixture' in Aristotle and the Stoic writers with which Gregory was certainly familiar. But it is precisely this initial presumption that I wish to contest. More is at stake, I believe, than an artful set of allusions to philosophical debates about 'mixture' (although they are certainly there); a primary sense of biblical authority is more fundamentally in play, as too are certain underlying presumptions about divine power and intimacy, and human analogues thereto, which come into question for Gregory when 'union' or 'mingling' in Christ are discussed. My own exegetical argument on this issue of 'mingling' has in fact two prongs, which may be described succinctly at the outset. I shall then go on to spell out the two sides of the argument in some greater detail, and bring their combined force to some systematic conclusions in closing.

Firstly, in relation to the different philosophical meanings of 'mingling' discussed in Greek pagan philosophy (to which Nyssen is clearly alluding), I want to argue that it is extremely misleading to say that the Aristotelian category of the 'mingling of predominance' fits Nyssen's christological use with exactitude. This latter position, however, is precisely the view of H. A. Wolfson, in an analysis whose influence has proved wide-ranging.[6] Such an interpretation, as we shall see, would have Christ's divine power effectively obliterate his human nature. But this I cannot find to be Gregory's intention: he is certainly not so foolish as to fall foul of the dangers of the very Apollinarianism which he is combatting. On the contrary, it seems that Nyssen is doing something much more subtle. For a start, he is primarily engaged here in a complex negotiation of relevant biblical texts (in particular, as we shall see, of 1 Corinthians 15), which factor modern writers of *Dogmengeschichte* have curiously ignored, but which gives the lie – as we shall show – to Wofson's and others' conclusion that Gregory simply succumbs to an unconscious Apollinarianism.

---

[6] H. A. Wolfson, *The Philosophy of the Church Fathers*, I: *Faith, Trinity, Incarnation* (Cambridge, MA: Harvard University Press, 1970), 372–386 (for 'Five Types of Physical Union' in pagan philosophy); and 396–399 (for the analysis of Gregory of Nyssa on the 'union of predominance').

But in addition, it seems he is also summoning out of his notable philosophical armoury suggestions of Stoic, as well as Aristotelian, categorizations of 'mixture',[7] and deliberately setting them into a mutually de-stabilizing conjunction, whilst simultaneously overlaying them both with an allusion to a medical 'mixture' appropriate to Christ's healing powers.[8] If I am right, this playful strategy of utilizing overlapping (but mutually corrective) philosophical evocations, whilst also implicitly trumping them by appeal to a relevant scriptural text, is entirely deliberate on Gregory's part. It may cause us to question Wolfson's verdict in a way that has important implications for resisting the charges of covert Apollinarianism or proto-'monophysitism' in Gregory, but also for better comprehending his christological intentions, *tout court*. As elsewhere in his theology (his theory of universals and his doctrine of the soul immediately come to mind), Gregory deliberately sets off allusions to various competing possibilities from ancient philosophy, and then resolutely refuses to be boxed into any of them.[9] Scriptural authority, we might say, finally triumphs, rendering even paradoxically related philosophical tags sublated and overcome.

But this is not even yet the whole picture; for – secondly – we must also take account, in our full assessment of Gregory's christological repertoire, of his use of the same language of 'mingling' with the completely different evocations of sexual union. As far as I know, no one has previously charted the christological significance in Gregory of such an erotic allusion, perhaps because his biblical commentaries have been under-used sources for textbook accounts of his doctrinal contribution. But in a highly revealing passage in his fourth homily on *The Song of Songs*,[10] utilizing again the language of 'mingling' (but

---

[7] Wolfson (ibid., 379–387, esp. 385 for his typology) does discuss Stoic views; but – as we shall see – he slightly distorts his account of one of them (that expressed by Stobaeus and other Stoics) which is peculiarly applicable to Gregory's case.

[8] This last point was already noted by Bouchet, in 'À propos d'une image', 587–588.

[9] On this point, see again my 'Introduction' in ed. Coakley, *Re-Thinking*, 7–8.

[10] *In Cant*. IV (*GNO* VI: 108–109), discussed in detail below. In this volume I follow the usual convention of citing Gregory of Nyssa's works by reference, where applicable, to the critical edition: *Gregorii Nysseni Opera* (*GNO*) (Leiden: Brill, 1958).

this time with its sexual meaning), Gregory ranges side by side, in analogical relation, three levels of such intimacy: firstly, the divinity and humanity in Christ; secondly, the nuptial love of Christ for the individual soul; and thirdly, the sexual love of husband and wife. Commenting here on *The Song of Songs* 1.16 (where, in the LXX version, the male lover 'overshadow[s] [the] bed'),[11] Gregory presents us, as we shall see, with another bundle of superimposed and mutually bombarding allusions, both biblical and philosophical, on the crucial issue of 'mingling'. He cites, or makes allusion, to Philippians 2. 5–11, for the *kenotic* act of incarnation; to Ephesians 5. 22–33, for the analogy between married love and Christ's love for the church; and then finally – by way of philosophical polemic – to the Plotinian view of the soul as besmirched by contamination with the body, a view which, for Gregory, Christ's incarnation decisively refutes. But we shall see here once more that it is not only philosophical debates about 'mixture' that Greogry is alluding to in his chosen christological form of speech; overarching questions of scriptural exegesis, and – with that – issues of power, intimacy and gender, are also in play in intriguing ways.

Let me now turn to a slightly more detailed textual exposition of each of the two prongs of this argument in turn, before drawing some final systematic conclusions about the wider implications of this analysis for contemporary Christology.

'Mixture' Revisited: Nyssen's Strategies for Describing the Indescribable in Christ

For the first prong of my argument, I shall take as representative one of the important passages (in the letter to Theophilus – there are two other parallel ones, in the *Contra Eunomium* and *Antirrhetikos*, respectively[12]), where Gregory famously specifies the type of 'mingling' of

---

[11] This reading of *Song* 1.16b in the LXX is seemingly the result of an interpretative rendition or misunderstanding of the Hebrew word for 'green' or 'luxuriant', which applies in the Hebrew to the bed; in the LXX it is taken to apply to the lover who 'shades' or 'overshadows' the bed.

[12] *Ad Theophilum* (*GNO* III.1: 126), discussed in detail here; cf. *C. Eun.* 3, 3. 68–69 (*GNO* II.2: 132–133); *Antirrh.* (*GNO* III.1: 201).

the human and the divine involved in Christ's incarnate life to be akin to a drop of vinegar dissolved in the ocean. Since it is here – and in the parallel passages – that nervous commentators fear an actual loss of the human nature of Christ, the text presents an especially important test case; and we must first attend to its details, in both Greek and English, before assessing its full significance. The language is indeed startling:

Text 1: **Ad Theophilum** (GNO III.1: 126–127):

ἀλλὰ τὸ μὲν θνητὸν ὑπὸ τῆς ζωῆς κατεπόθη, ὁ δὲ σταυρωθεὶς ἐξ ἀσθενείας ἔζησεν ἐκ δυνάμεως ἥ τε κατάρα εἰς εὐλογίαν μετεποιήθη καὶ πᾶν, ὅσον ἀσθενὲς τῆς φύσεως ἡμῶν καὶ ἐπίκηρον ἄνακραθὲν τῇ θεότητι ἐκεῖνο ἐγένετο, ὅπερ ἡ θεότης ἐστίν. πόθεν οὖν ἄν τις τὴν δυάδα τῶν υἱῶν ἐννοήσειεν ὡς ἀνάγκῃ τινὶ διὰ τῆς κατὰ σάρκα οἰκονομίας πρὸς τήν τοιαύτην ὑπόληψιν ἐναγόμενος;
Ὁ γὰρ ἀεὶ ἐν τῷ πατρὶ ὢν καὶ ἀεὶ ἔχων ἐν ἑαυτῷ τὸν πατέρα καὶ ἡνωμένος αὐτῷ, ὡς ἦν καὶ πρώην, οὕτω καὶ ἔστι καὶ ἔσται καὶ ἄλλος παρ' ἐκεῖνον υἱὸς οὔτε ἦν οὔτε ἐγένετο οὔτε ἔσται· ἡ δὲ προσληφθεῖσα τῆς ἀνθρωπίνης φύσεως ἀπαρχή, ὑπὸ τῆς παντοδυνάμου θεότητος (ὡς ἂν εἴποι τις εἰκόνι χρώμενος) οἷόν τις σταγὼν ὄξους ἀπείρῳ πελάγει κατακραθεῖσα, ἔστι μὲν ἐν τῇ θεότητι, οὐ μὴν ἐν τοῖς ἰδίοις αὐτῆς ἰδιώμασιν. οὕτω γὰρ ἂν ἡ τῶν υἱῶν δυάς ἀκολούθως ὑπενοεῖτο, εἰ ἐν τῇ ἀφράστῳ τοῦ υἱοῦ θεότητι ἑτερογενής τις φύσις [ἐν] ἰδιάζουσι σημείοις ἐπεγινώσκετο, ὡς εἶναι τὸ μὲν ἀσθενὲς ἢ μικρὸν ἢ φθαρτὸν ἢ πρόσκαιρον, τὸ δὲ δυνατὸν καὶ μέγα καὶ ἄφθαρτον καὶ ἀίδιον· ἐπειδὴ δὲ πάντων τῶν τῷ θνητῷ συνεπιθεωρουμένων ἐν τοῖς τῆς θεότητος ἰδιώμασι μεταποιηθέντων, ἐν οὐδενὶ καταλαμβάνεται ἡ διαφορά (ὅπερ γὰρ ἂν τις ἴδῃ τοῦ υἱοῦ, θεότης ἐστί, σοφία, δύναμις, ἁγιασμός, ἀπάθεια), πῶς ἂν διαιροῖτο τὸ ἓν εἰς δυϊκὴν σημασίαν, μηδεμιᾶς διαφορᾶς τὸν ἀριθμὸν μεριζούσης;

But death has been swallowed up by life [1 Cor 15. 54, 2 Cor 5. 4], the Crucified has been restored to life by power from weakness, and the curse has been turned into blessing. And everything that was weak and perishable in our nature, mingled with the Godhead, has become that which the Godhead is. How then would anyone suppose there to be a duality of Sons, when of necessity one is led to such a rejoinder as this by the [Son's] 'economy' in the flesh? For he is always in the Father, and always has the Father in him, and is one with him, as it was in the beginning and is now and always will be; and there never was any other Son beside him, nor is there, nor will there be. The first-fruits [1 Cor 15. 20] of the human nature which he has taken up – absorbed, one might say figuratively – by the omnipotent divinity like a drop of vinegar mingled in the boundless sea, exist in the Godhead, but not in their own [sc. human] distinctive characteristics. For a duality of Sons might consistently be presumed, if a nature of a different kind could be recognized by its own proper signs within the ineffable Godhead of the Son – as being weak or small or perishable or temporary, as opposed to powerful and great and imperishable and eternal. But since all the traits we recognize in the mortal [person] we see transformed by the characteristics of the Godhead, and since no difference of any kind can be perceived – for whatever one sees in the Son *is* Godhead: wisdom, power, holiness, *apatheia* – how could one divide what is one into double significance, since no difference divides him numerically?[13]

Read on its own, and in isolation from a proper understanding of the distinctively progressivist logic of Gregory's Christology,[14] this passage might indeed seem to imply that the humanity of Christ is completely subsumed into his divinity. There is none of the cautious emphasis on a consistent and continuing duality that we would expect from an earlier Latin writer such as Tertullian, for instance, or from the later Tome of Leo: that must be readily acknowledged at the outset. Gregory's entire christological project assumes that the task of the incarnation is the *gradual* purgation and transformation of the nature of the human in Christ, and its final restoration to an unsullied condition, as before the Fall, in the resurrection. Here he is describing that achieved transformation of the human in Christ's resurrected body, in

---

[13] The translation of this passage is by Brian Daley, S.J. ('"Heavenly Man" and "Eternal Christ"', 483), slightly adjusted and expanded.

[14] As Behr's analysis (*The Nicene Faith*, II/2, 435–451) well emphasizes, it is vital to understand that Gregory's talk of the human nature of Christ being 'swallowed up' refers to a *process* only completed in the resurrection and exaltation. For Gregory, it is in the earthly sojourn of the Son, and especially through the events of the Passion, that the purgation and transformation of the human is effected.

which the human nature, whilst assuredly continuing in existence, operates now in its fully perfected mode, 'in the Godhead'. And the language of 'mingling' here is made to do some very interesting work, which we must now explore in detail.

What Gregory is doing, it seems, is superimposing on the metaphor of 'mingling' as utilized in pagan philosophy another, biblical, metaphor ('first-fruits'), which helps him explicate with exactitude the precise sort of 'mingling' he has in mind. By doing things this way he is indicating how the unique christological 'mingling' of human and divine falls out, or rather *fails to fall out with exactitude*, in the range of available philosophical meanings of 'mingling' with which his educated readers would be familiar. Two such philosophical views of 'mingling' might immediately come into mind, out of about five different possibilities explicated in Aristotelian and Stoic thought.[15] According to the different categories of 'mixture' or physical union discussed in Aristotle's *de generatione et corruptione* Bk I, firstly, it is surely right to say, with Wolfson, that Aristotle's so-called 'union of predominance', is quite deliberately being alluded to by Gregory here.[16] If that

---

[15] The two relevant ones are the Aristotelian 'union of predominance' (in which one component virtually disappears, as, for example, a drop of wine in gallons of water), and a Stoic understanding of 'mingling' in which the substances and qualities of the two elements remain, even as the two interpenetrate each other. See Wolfson, *The Philosophy of the Church Fathers*, I, 385, for his list of the full five such types of 'union' or 'mingling'; but note that his account has been challenged on his representation of the crucial third (Stoic) one: see Richard Sorabji, *Matter, Space and Time: Theories in Antiquity and Their Sequel* (Ithaca, NY, Cornell University Press, 1988), chs. 5–6; and more recently, Richard Cross, 'Perichoresis, Deification, and Christological Predication in John of Damascus', *Mediaeval Studies* 62 (2000), 69–124, esp. 72, 86–97. I follow Sorabji and Cross here in their modification and correction of Wolfson's understanding of the Stoic view. My own account differs from Cross's in that, unlike him (see ibid., 86), I precisely disagree that 'the Cappadocians' used the language of 'mixture' in 'a way that suggested a complete obliteration of the human nature' (a conclusion that Cross simply takes on from Wolfson, both of them presuming that only the Aristotelian 'union of predominance' is in play in Gregory of Nyssa's discussion of 'mingling'). On the contrary, I am arguing here that the complex Stoic background that Cross rightly highlights for John of Damascus's use was *already* in play in Gregory of Nyssa's christological use.

[16] See Aristotle, *de gen. et. corr. 1. 10* (328a, 27–29). Arguably this allusion is even more strongly enunciated in the other two passages in which Gregory uses this analogy: *C. Eun. 3, 3. 68–69 (GNO II.2: 132–133)*; *Antirrh. (GNO III.1: 201)*.

were the full picture, in fact, then Wolfson would be right to conclude that 'the weaker has changed into the stronger',[17] and the charge of proto-'monophysitism' would stand.

But artfully and deliberately, it seems, Gregory has changed the classic Aristotelian example of wine and water to *vinegar* and water. He must surely have done this for a reason – or perhaps, I would suggest, for two reasons. Not only does this change set off another sort of philosophical allusion, this time to one of the Stoic types of 'mixture' discussed by Stobaeus, in which vinegar significantly features (with notably different allusions of mutual interaction rather than near obliteration)[18], but it also introduces a well-known medical allusion, since a 'mixture' of sea-water and vinegar is discussed more than once by Hippocrates as alleviating all kinds of chronic aches and pains.[19] Since Gregory is regularly wont to describe Christ as the ultimate 'physician', and often uses the metaphor of different sorts of divine 'prescriptions' required for different souls,[20] this final evocation makes clear the *soteriological* impact of this unique christological 'mixture'. Once we see this, we can better understand the decisive, and undergirding, layer of biblical meaning created by the appeal in this same passage to the 'first-fruits' of 1 Corinthians 15. 20. This particular 'mingling' of divine and human in Christ that is being discussed is one in which we are also destined to participate: it is the 'first-fruits' of 'them that slept', and hence the union (or 'mingling') of human and divine that occurs in Christ is what enables *our* final union with Christ – a mysterious eschatological change to the body/soul 'in the twinkling of

---

[17] Wolfson, *The Philosophy of the Church Fathers*, I, 397.

[18] As we have noted, Wolfson misrepresents this type (see again Cross, 'Perichoresis', 89, 93). He mentions Stobaeus (*Eclogae* I, 17; *The Philosophy of the Church Fathers, I,* 379), but fails to point out that an allusion to this particular Stoic type would involve contesting his reading of 'the mixture of predominance' as alone applicable to Gregory of Nyssa's Christology.

[19] See Émile Littré (ed.), *Oeuvres Complètes d'Hippocrate, V* (Paris, J. B. Ballière, 1846), 240–241, 434–435.

[20] He does so, in fact, in the *Ad Theophilum* (*GNO* III/1: 124) just before the passage here under discussion, making the point that the incarnation allowed the cure for those of a more fleshly minded disposition. For a more complete account of Nyssen's fondness for medical metaphors, see Mary E. Keenan, 'St. Gregory of Nyssa and the Medical Profession', *Bulletin of the History of Medicine* 15 (1944), 150–161.

an eye'. It cannot therefore be an *obliteration* of the human which is implied by this 'mingling' (which would make nonsense of Paul's entire argument in 1 Corinthians 15). Rather, it is its unique *transformation*.

All in all, an artful reading of this dense and crucial passage shows us that Gregory refuses to allow just one metaphor, or philosophical category, to dominate his argument. The clear and primary allusion to the Aristotelian 'mixture of predominance' illustrates his insistence on the indescribably greater power of divinity over humanity, its capacity to transform it, and the unity of what is achieved. But the simultaneous hint of the Stoic example of vinegar and water refuses the possibility of the total loss of existence or identity by the lesser element: there is neither a *tertium quid* created here, nor a simple obliteration of the weaker element by the stronger. A 'suffusion' is perhaps the happiest English translation of this kind of 'mixture' of the divine with the human in Christ,[21] and accords best with the meaning implied by the appeal to 1 Corinthians 15.

Let us now compare the lessons from this first passage with those of the apparently quite different, *erotic* overtones of 'mingling' in the fourth *Homily on the Song*. We may be surprised by how consistent with our first example is the overall impact:

Text 2: ***In Cant. IV*** (GNO VI: 108–109):

εἰ γὰρ μὴ συνεσκίασας αὐτὸς σεαυτὸν τὴν ἄκρατον τῆς θεότητος ἀκτῖνα συγκαλύψας τῇ τοῦ δούλου μορφῇ, τίς ἂν ὑπέστη σου τὴν ἐμφάνειαν; οὐδεὶς γὰρ ὄψεται πρόσωπον κυρίου καὶ ζήσεται. ἦλθες τοίνυν ὁ ὡραῖος, ἀλλ' ὡς χωροῦμεν δέξασθαι τοιοῦτος γενόμενος· ἦλθες τάς τῆς θεότητος ἀκτῖνας τῇ περιβολῇ συσκιάσας τοῦ σώματος. πῶς γὰρ ἂν ἐχώρησε θνητὴ καὶ ἐπίκηρος φύσις τῇ ἀκηράτῳ καὶ ἀπροσίτῳ συζυγίᾳ συναρμοσθῆναι, εἰ μὴ τοῖς ἐν σκότῳ ζῶσιν ἡμῖν ἡ σκιά τοῦ σώματος πρὸς τὸ φῶς

---

[21] Daley fleetingly uses this term in 'Divine Transcendence and Human Transformation', 71. I make greater use of it in my own analysis of Gregory's unique reading of Philippians 2, in which Christ's 'emptying' is seen neither as a loss of divinity, nor as a mere 'assumption' of humanity, but as a 'suffusing' outpouring of divinity into the human: see ch. 2.

ἐμεσίτευσεν; κλίνην δὲ ὀνομάζει ἡ νύμφη τῇ τροπικῇ σημασίᾳ τὴν
πρὸς τὸ θεῖον ἄνκρασιν τῆς ἀνθρωπίνης φύσεως ἑρμηνεύουσα, ὡς
καὶ ὁ μέγας ἀτόστολος ἁρμόζεται τῷ Χριστῷ τὴν παρθένον, ἡμᾶς,
καὶ νυμφοστολεῖ [τὴν ψυχὴν] καὶ τὴν προσκόλλησιν τῶν δύο εἰς
ἑνὸς σώματος κοινωνίαν τὸ μέγα μυστήριον εἶναι λέγει τῆς τοῦ
Χριστοῦ πρὸς τὴν ἐκκλησίαν ἑνώσεως· εἰπὼν γὰρ ὅτι Ἔσονται οἱ
δύο εἰς σάρκα μίαν ἐπήγαγεν ὅτι Τὸ μυστήριον τοῦτο μέγα ἐστίν,
ἐγὼ δὲ λέγω εἰς Χριστὸν καὶ εἰς τὴν ἐκκλησίαν. διά τοῦτο τοίνυν
τὸ μυστήριον κλίνην ἡ παρθένος ψυχὴ τὴν πρὸς τὸ θεῖον κοινωνίαν
ὠνόμασεν. ταύτην δὲ οὐκ ἄλλως ἦν δυνατὸν γενέσθαι εἰ μὴ διὰ
τοῦ σύσκιον ἡμῖν διὰ τοῦ σώματος ἐπιφανῆναι τὸν κύριον,

For unless you 'shaded yourself over with the form of a servant' [Phil
2. 7] while unveiling the pure rays of your divinity, who could stand
your appearance [Mal 3. 2]? 'For no one can see God's face and live'
[Ex 33. 20]. You have now come as one who is timely, but as one we
are we are capable of receiving. You came with the covering of your
body which is shadowed over by the rays of your divinity [Luke 1. 35].
How could a mortal, perishable nature be capable of union with an
imperishable, inaccessible nature unless the shadow of the body acted
as a mediator of the light for us who live in darkness? The bride uses
the term 'bed' to interpret in a figurative sense the mingling of human
nature with the divine. In the same way, the great Apostle Paul joins
us as virgins to Christ and acts as an escort for the bride. He says that
the affixing together of two persons in the union of one body is a
great mystery of Christ's union with the church. For he said, 'The two
shall be one flesh', and then added, 'This is a great mystery with reference to Christ and his church' [Eph 5. 31–2]. Because of this mystery,
the virgin soul names the union with the divine a 'bed'. This could
not have happened at all unless the Lord had appeared 'overshadowed'
to us in a human body'.[22]

---

[22] This translation is a modified version of that by Casimir McCambley, OCSO, *Gregory
of Nyssa, Commentary on the Song of Songs* (Brookline, MA: Hellenic College Press,
1987), 94. (The more recent, and superior, translation by Richard A. Norris, Jr., *Gregory
of Nyssa: Homilies on the Song of Songs* (Atlanta: Society of Biblical Literature, 2012), had
not appeared at the time that the first version of this chapter was written; the relevant
passage here, however, in both Greek and English, can be found at ibid., 118–121.)

This passage in Gregory's fourth *Homily* is discussing *The Song* 1.16, read, as in the LXX, as the male lover 'overshadowing [the] bed'. The first reading Gregory makes of this is to see it as a 'figurative' way of talking of the 'mingling' of the human nature with the divine in the incarnation. The reference to Philippians 2.7 (with the phrase 'the form of a servant') summons up all the overtones of the highly distinctive way that Gregory interprets *kenōsis* elsewhere in his work – not as a mere 'assumption' of humanity, but as a veritable pouring out of divinity into it, here effected by the bridegroom. It is this outpouring that causes the need for 'overshadowing', as is well brought out in a discussion of this passage in Gregory's *Commentary* by Alessandro Cortesi.[23] 'Shadow' does not have here for Gregory the connection to sin that darkness can often symbolize in the *The Song*, but rather indicates the apophatic mysteriousness that necessarily attends the effusive revelation of the divine when it comes into the human incarnationally (as in the annunciation in Luke 1. 35). Yet even as Gregory alludes to the biblical text in Luke, there is almost certainly also a polemic implied here against Plotinus's well-known discussion in *Enneads* Bk 1 of the 'mingling' (μίξις and κρᾶσις) of soul with body which inevitably involves a beschmirchment of the soul and a darkening of its light.[24] But for Gregory, in contrast to Plotinus, the divine Logos's effusion into a human body/soul is 'shadowed' only because of its ineffable greatness.

Now as Christ's fructifying divinity is represented as the bridegroom here, so it follows that the human nature of Christ is figured as 'feminine', as the bride. But it is by no means clear from this that 'she' (the humanity in Christ) is simply passive: as Bernadette Brooten has noted, the verb μείγνυμι, used for sexual intercourse, is one of the few

---

[23] Alessandro Cortesi, *Le Omelie sul Cantico dei Cantici di Gregario di Nissa: proposta di un itinerario di vita battesimale* (Rome: Augustinianum, 2000), esp. 81–87. Cortesi provides an elegant analysis of this section of Gregory's *Song* commentary, noting some of Gregory's allusions to pagan philosophy as well as comparing Gregory's exegesis to that of Origen.

[24] *Enneads* I, 6, 5: 'the soul becomes ugly by mixture and dilution and inclination towards the body and matter', ed. and tr. A. H. A. Armstrong, *Plotinus, I* (Cambridge, MA: Harvard University Press), 248–249.

in Greek that allows a sense of genuine mutuality;[25] and, as we have
seen above, ἀνάκρασις and μίξις are inexorably linked for Gregory in
the christological sphere. Finally, not the least significant aspect of this
passage is the way that the ἀνάκρασις, ἕνωσις and συζυγία of the
incarnation are then seen as the primary exemplifications and enable-
ment of the other two levels of interaction. There is then what we
might call an 'erotic sliding-scale' here, which moves downwards:
firstly, the primary 'mingling' between the divine and the human in
Christ, then the union between Christ and each human soul in the
church, then sexual union between husband and wife. It is an interesting hermeneutical expansion on the way that merely the latter two
levels are linked in Ephesians 5. 21–33; and the whole passage differs
markedly from Origen's reading of the same passage in his second
Homily on the Song, in which the 'overshadowed' body is not about
what we might call the 'proto-erotic' incarnate body of Christ, but
about the sinful and unhealed state of the human body in general,
represented here for Origen by the paralytic of Mark 2. 1–12 and
parallels.[26] For Gregory, in contrast, human sexual union in the
Christian context is precisely one of the outworkings of the primary
'mingling' of the divine and human in Christ, and thus – when rightly
understood – it can be seen as a proper, albeit finally mysterious,
metaphor for the workings of the incarnate life.

---

[25] See Bernadette J. Brooten, *Love Between Women: Early Christian Responses to Female
Homoeroticism* (Chicago: University of Chicago Press, 1996), 246: 'The specific verbs
for sexual intercourse are usually active when they refer to men and passive when
they refer to women. … Some verbs, such as "to mingle" … do occur in the active
for both women and men, but the more common pattern is to use an active verb for
the male and a passive one for the female'.

[26] Origen in fact exegetes *Song* 1.16 twice, in illuminatingly different ways. In his
second *Homily on the Song*, the 'bed' is first understood as the 'human body' in its
unhealed state, as 'the feeble body of [the paralytic's] limbs', awaiting Christ's healing
(see tr. R. P. Lawson, *Origen: The Song of Songs – Commentary and Homilies* (New York:
Newman Press, 1956), 291. But in his *Commentary*, which (see Lawson's introduction, ibid., 16–19) is written for those of greater spiritual maturity, the interpretation
is closer to that of Gregory's (and indeed probably influenced Gregory). Here the
bed/body has become fit for Christ as bridegroom, suitably spiritualized: 'Such a
soul as this rightly shares her bed – that is, her body, with the Word' (ibid, 174); and
the 'shady' bed is read as 'a thicket of good works' (ibid, 172).

Conclusions: Christology, Soteriology and the Ascetic Task in Gregory of Nyssa

What then are we to conclude from this exploration about the many different overtones of μίξις, κρᾶσις and other cognate nouns in Gregory's Christology? A full search of this cluster of terms in Nyssen − following Bouchet's excellent lead[27] − produces an enormous, even chaotic, range of other and different contexts in which these terms are applied, and we have only been able to explore some of these. But in the specifically christological application, I think that through the two rich and revealing examples discussed here, I have indicated the main points of allusion, showing that in Gregory's ingenious and consciously anti-Apollinarian uses of the terms, we must attend at all times to the cat's cradle of biblical symbolism that he weaves around his theme of 'mingling', and hence as much to evocations of divine power, resurrection and the ascetical training of desire, as to philosophical and medical niceties and distinctions.

It has been said of late (by Brian Daley, S.J.) that Gregory is more interested in 'narrative' soteriology than metaphysical Christology; and maybe − Daley avers − this explains why his language of 'mingling' is less precise or clear than we might like it to be.[28] But this little investigation has led me to a slightly differently nuanced conclusion. Whilst it is certainly true, as we have indicated, that the soteriological theory of suffusing 'deification' sustains Gregory's whole christological undertaking, and gives it its narrative substructure, I would prefer to say that Gregory has deployed a particular, and very subtle, form of 'apophatic speech' in expressing his Christology, than that he is metaphysically imprecise, defective or sloppy. By adopting a policy of mutually bombarding (and thus mutually correcting) metaphorical allusions in his key christological passages, Gregory has utilized the key metaphor of 'mingling' in ways that never claim finally to *explain* the mystery of the incarnation (which must always remain 'shadowed'

---

[27] See again Bouchet, 'Le vocabulaire de l'union', *passim*, who covers most, if not all, of the necessary christological ground. A wider search in the *TLG* for 'mixture' terms in Gregory provides a veritable maze of interconnected associations and patterns, too complicated to chart here.

[28] Daley, 'Divine Transcendence and Human Transformation', 72–73.

to the sinful human eye), but which indicate with unusual precision what he does and does not want to say.[29] There are striking anticipations in this regard of the linguistic strategies of the later negative theology of the pseudo-Dionysius, here applied explicitly to the christological sphere. Once we read Nyssen in this way, I see no reason to dub his Christology as either covertly Apollinarian or, for that matter, naively proto-'Nestorian' (as Tixeront charged). Whilst the jury may be still out on the final coherence or consistency of Gregory's Christology, *tout court*,[30] his theory of 'mingling' seems to me remarkably rich and strange, not happily acceptable to those bred on the clarificatory dualisms of Leo's Tome, to be sure, but continuing a tradition of participatory 'deification' which goes back to Athanasius and then stretches forward (with huge and conscious debts to Nyssen) to Leontius, Maximus and John Damascene.[31] From here, it was ultimately to leave its contentious mark on Luther's eucharistic theology, a tradition which the Calvinist position then, in turn, strongly opposed.[32] But in Nyssen's own treatment, as we have seen, there was

---

[29] We should not forget that Gregory is ever wont to stress the final *incomprehensibility* of the 'mingling' of the incarnation. See his *Oratio Catechetica* 11 (*GNO* III/4, 39), tr. Cyril G. Richardson, in ed. E. R. Hardy, *The Christology of the Later Fathers* (London: S.C.M, 1954), 288: 'we are unable to detect how the divine is mingled with the human. Yet we have no doubt, from the recorded miracles, that God underwent birth in human nature. But *how* this happened we decline to investigate as a matter beyond the scope of reason'.

[30] There are certainly remaining difficulties, which cannot be addressed in this context; but they indicate where my assessment of Gregory's Christology might still differ somewhat from that of John Behr (see n. 1, above). Thus, the problem of how, *exactly*, the 'human Jesus' relates to the Word in the incarnation, and what happens to 'the human' in Christ after the resurrection/exaltation, are both issues in need of further probing and critical explication.

[31] Gregory's interest in the transforming humanity of Christ, including his human soul, arguably owes more to Origen than to Athanasius (a topic worthy of further research); but otherwise his presumptions about the pattern of participatory deification in Christ is strongly indebted to Athanasius: on this Eastern tradition of 'deification', and its subvariants, see Norman Russell, *The Doctrine of Deification in the Greek Patristic Tradition* (Oxford: O.U.P., 2004).

[32] Cross, 'Perichoresis', 70, 123, briefly clarifies the extent and nature of John of Damascus's influence on Luther's eucharistic theology and on the later Lutheran christological category, the *genus maiestaticum*. It has been the burden of this chapter

a remarkable integration of biblical witness, philosophical insight and implied ascetic demand, albeit always without abrogating an essential aspect of apophatic mystery. A rich heritage of ingenious biblical exegesis could itself be 'mingled' with, but ultimately trump, sophisticated philosophical analysis and allusion. The 'mingling' found in Christ's person could thus become, through prayerful living of the Christian life, a derivative 'mingling' equally available now to the blessed: Christology could 'erotically' guide spirituality, and even – by implication – cause a certain rethinking of faithful sexual practice. Such an integrative approach to Christology, asceticism, and 'sexuality' seems, at the very least, worthy of reconsideration in our current era of the renegotiation of the 'systematic' theological task.

---

to suggest that some of the subtle moves made by John of Damascus on the *communicatio idiomatum* are already intimated by Gregory of Nyssa. If this hypothesis is correct, then it would be interesting to explore further how the Calvinist tradition, in contrast to the Lutheran, assimilated the Greek patristic theme of 'participation' (both christologically and trinitarianly), even as it took a polemically different approach to eucharistic theology. For an important assessment of the theme of 'participation' in the theology of Calvin, and esp. of Calvin's debt to the Greek patristic tradition (as well as to Augustine), see Todd Billings, *Calvin, Participation and the Gift: The Activity of Believers in Union with Christ* (Oxford: O.U.P., 2007).

4

What Does Chalcedon Solve and What Does It Not? Some Reflections on the Status and Meaning of the Chalcedonian 'Definition'

Following, then, the holy Fathers, we all with one voice teach that it should be confessed that our Lord Jesus Christ is one and same Son, the Same perfect in Godhead, the Same perfect in manhood, truly God and truly man, the Same [consisting] of a rational soul and a body; *homoousios* with the Father as to his Godhead, and the Same *homoousios* with us as to his manhood; in all things like unto us, sin only excepted; begotten of the Father before ages as to his Godhead, and in the last days, the Same, for us and for our salvation, of Mary the Virgin Theotokos as to his manhood; One and the same Christ, Son, Lord, Only begotten, made known in two natures [which exist] without confusion, without change, without division, without separation; the difference of the natures having been in no wise taken away by reason of the union, but rather the properties of each being preserved, and [both] concurring into one Person (*prosōpon*) and one *hypostasis* – not parted or divided into two persons (*prosōpa*), but one and the same Son and Only-begotten, the divine Logos, the Lord Jesus Christ; even as the prophets from of old [have spoken] concerning him, as the Lord Jesus Christ has taught us, and as the Symbol of the Fathers has delivered to us.

The Broken Body: Israel, Christ and Fragmentation, First Edition. Sarah Coakley.
© 2024 John Wiley & Sons Ltd. Published 2024 by John Wiley & Sons Ltd.

Introduction: What Can Chalcedon Solve?

The purpose of this chapter is to examine a question of some subtlety and importance, which is nonetheless often overlooked in the contemporary Anglo-American philosophical debates about the Chalcedonian 'Definition' of 451. I shall be asking, in the main body of the chapter, what *sort* of statement this particular statement about Christ is; and this apparently innocent and simple question will be discovered to be capable of a wide range of possible answers. In particular, I shall focus on three answers to this question that are all current and influential, but which strike me as rather far from the properly understood intentions of the original authors of the document. These are the views: (1) that the 'Definition' is *linguistically regulatory* rather than ontological in intent; (2) that its language is rightly understood today as *metaphorical;* and (3) that its purpose is to 'define' the personal identity of Christ (as God-man) in a '*literal*' manner leaving as little room as possible for further ambiguity. It will be immediately obvious that these three approaches arise from very different schools of theological and philosophical understanding, all of which are worthy of close and sympathetic reflection, but none of which, in my view, probes to the heart of the document's simultaneous richness and elusiveness.

My *second* undertaking, thereafter, will be to indicate a properly *apophatic* reading of the Definition (in a sense of 'apophatic' to be carefully defined). It will be underscored that this approach in no way excuses laxity of thinking, nor does it invite a glorying in the irrational or incoherent, but rather involves a form of precision exactly at the 'horizon' (*horos*) of defining what can, and cannot, be said. It will be underscored that this view is not novel; indeed, there is some reason to think that it was what was in (at least some of) the minds of those shaping the document, and certainly in the minds of important later Eastern defenders of it. The closeness to (and slight difference from) a famous reading of Chalcedon by Karl Rahner will also be noted. I shall end by enumerating a list of pressing christological questions that were *not* 'solved' by Chalcedon, and indeed *could* not be, given the sort of document I have shown that it was (and is). The effect of this explication will, I trust, be to preempt a significant range of responses to Chalcedon that simply miss the mark by misreading its intent.

Let us now turn, firstly, to the task of explicating the recent views that I find in different ways defective. It is perhaps a nice mimetic

touch that by proceeding in this way (that is, by ruling out erroneous
interpretations in order to leave room for a more creative and expan-
sive alternative), we shall be following precisely the means of argument that Chalcedon itself also employs.

Chalcedon as 'Linguistic Regulation'

The circumstances of the summoning of the Council of Chalcedon
(451 CE) are well-known and do not here need another rehearsal.[1]
The immediate crisis was an attempt to find a way through the tortured debate between the rival Alexandrian and Antiochene schools
of Christology. Whether we should see the resultant 'Definition' as an
effective 'compromise' between the two is a moot point: the hostile, and
secessionist, response of the 'Monophysite' churches of the East thereafter painfully demonstrated the lack of balance that some felt was
manifest in it. Nonetheless, its aim to reconcile warring parties (whilst
ruling out decisively three unacceptable understandings of Christ's
person in the form of Apollinarianism, Eutychianism and extreme
Nestorianism) was clear. What is less commonly remembered in contemporary textbooks and commentaries (given the regrettable tendency to reprint the 'Definition' in isolation from the surrounding
text), is that the assembled Bishops were deeply reluctant to come up
with any new formulas at all, their preference being to reaffirm – as
they now did – the faith of Nicaea, itself grounded and founded in the
biblical narratives of salvation.[2] Close attention to the *Acta*, therefore,
gives the lie to the suggestion (associated with a critique of Henry

---

[1] See, *inter alios*, A Grillmeier, *Christ in Christian Tradition*, i (London: Mowbrays,
1975), esp. 443–557; eds. A. Grillmeier and H. Bacht, *Das Konzil von Chalkedon*,
3 vols. (Würzbur: Echter-Verlag, 1951–1954); A. de Halleux, 'La définition
christologique à Chalcédoine', *Revue théologique de Louvain* 7 (1976), 3–23, 155–170;
R.V. Sellars, *The Council of Chalcedon* (London: SPCK, 1961); M. Slusser, 'The Issues
in the Definition of the Council of Chalcedon', *Toronto Journal of Theology* 6 (1990),
63–69; L. R. Wickham, 'Chalkedon', *Theologische Realenzyklopädie*, vii, 668–675.
[2] Ed. E. Schwartz, *Acta Conciliorum Oecumenicorum*, 4 vols. (Berlin: de Gruyter, 1914–1984);
T. II, *Concilium Universale Chalcedonense* (1932–1938) is devoted to the Council of
Chalcedon. I am aware of the irony of having myself quoted the 'Definition' in isolation
at the opening of this chapter: such can only be a point of departure.

Chadwick[3]) that the 'Definition' lifts away abstractly from the events of salvation and the biblical economy. On the contrary, the 'Definition', set in context, can be seen precisely to presume and reaffirm those events and then to provide a regulatory *grid* through which to pass them interpretatively. The special committee group which, under pressure, honed the linguistic terms for this grid was mainly concerned with finding an acceptable solution to the Alexandrian/Antiochene problem: cherished terminology from both sides of the debate was craftily pasted into the collage, along with inputs from Leo's *Tome*, but this is not to say that the result was a bodged or incoherent compromise.[4]

But was then the goal and achievement of Chalcedon *only* linguistic and regulatory? Such, at any rate, is the sophisticated thesis of Richard A. Norris in an important article for John Meyendorff's memorial volume, entitled 'Chalcedon Revisited: A Historical and Theological Reflection.'[5] Norris's thesis is complex and subtle, and deserves a full rehearsal.

Firstly, he points out that the bishops assembled at Chalcedon were not 'professional philosophers' or even 'professional theologians'. They were not pronouncing a 'theoretically devised "christology"' (a modernist term with which they were in any case not familiar). Rather, they were weaving together a 'pastiche of allusions and quotations' – tidbits from Leo's *Tome* and from Cyril's letters, fragments or terms from the *Formulary of Reunion*, from Flavian, and from Proclus.[6] Their central question was how Christ (the 'one and the same', a phrase repeated five times) could be simultaneously God and human, an issue 'solved' by the crucial distinction between *phusis* and *hypostasis*. Yet the 'solution' here, as Norris emphasizes, was actually a form of evasion: the terms were *linguistically distinguished* but never given substantial content. Hence, 'The Chalcedonian *Definition* … offers little more

---

[3] In tr. André-Jean Festugière, Henry Chadwick (preface), *Actes du Concile de Chalcédoine* (Genève: Patrick Cramer, 1983), 7–16, at 15–16.

[4] See Slusser, 'Issues in the Definition', 67.

[5] Ed. B. Nassif, *New Perspectives on Historical Theology* (Grand Rapids, MI: Eerdmans, 1996), 140–158. A related argument is mounted by Norris in an earlier volume: ed R. A. Norris, *Lux in Lumine* (New York: Seabury Press, 1966); here I concentrate on the later essay.

[6] Ibid., 141–142.

than a paradigm. It does not explicitly explain or define what "nature" and "hypostasis" mean, save by tacit reference to the way in which the Nicene symbol *speaks* of Christ; ... what it provides is essentially a transcription and an account of a pattern of predication.'[7]

Norris then argues that this merely 'paradigmatic' gesturing of the Definition has to be sharply distinguished from the approach of 'contributors to the debate that *surrounded* Chalcedon', who in contrast saw the two sets of predicates as referring to things or substances of the ordinary sort; and hence the 'natures' become, as he puts it, 'reified'. (Norris cites, as instances of this 'reification', Severus of Antioch's comparison of the union of natures to the wedding of soul and body in the human individual, or John of Damascus' later identification of the human intellect as the 'medium' through which the Word united with flesh.[8]) Driving a wedge between Chalcedon's supposedly merely regulatory agenda and this 'reification' via 'analogies' and 'metaphors' which others applied to it, Norris concludes that the latter 'appears to insist upon a synthesis or union of *incompatibles* – precisely because it takes its physical models too seriously.'[9] In other words, the concretization of thought about the 'natures' leads, he avers, to the supposition of their 'incompatibility'. And whereas in the patristic debate, this false disjunction resulted in an overemphasis (claims Norris) on Christ's divinity, the modern form of this aberrant perception of Chalcedon's intent has been the opposite: 'a new type of Monophysitism – a tendency, in the face of its own strong sense of the incompatibility of divine and human agencies, to reduce the Christ not to a God fitted out with the vestiges of humanity but to a human being adorned with the vestiges of divinity.'[10]

Both these alternatives, however, suffer from a misconception of the 'natures' as 'interchangeable contraries' – as 'differing items of the *same* order',[11] competing against one another for the same space. If we could counter this misconception, says Norris, we would see that Chalcedon merely presents us with a 'rule of predication'; it is non-committal on the 'logical relations' between the divine and human natures, and it makes no attempt to give an account of what those two natures consist in.

---

[7] Ibid., 151.

[8] Ibid., 149–151.

[9] Ibid., 154.

[10] Ibid., 155.

[11] Ibid., 155, 158, my emphasis.

Thus, finally, we need a 'negative theology' here in a particular sense, one that *denies* that the difference between God and humanity is a matter either of 'contrariety' or of 'contradiction'. It is not an issue of 'how to fit two logical contraries together into one, as its ancient and modern interpreters have all but uniformly supposed, but how to dispense with a binary logic in figuring the relation between God and creatures'.[12]

Norris' exposition is refreshingly direct and suitably challenging to much current writing on Chalcedon, even now. It appears to this writer to be correct about several matters. Firstly, his underscoring of the relatively *undefined* state of the key terms 'nature' (*phusis*) and 'person' (*hypostasis*) in the so-called Definition rightly draws attention to the open-endedness of the document, its unclarity about the precise meaning of key terms. If anything is 'defined' in the 'Definition' it is not these crucial concepts. To be sure, these terms had a pre-history, but it was an ambiguous one, and the 'Definition' does not clear up the ambiguity. This is a point to which we shall return in due course; for we are left wondering whether this feature 'looks like carelessness' (to reapply a phrase of Oscar Wilde), or whether it is a subtle and intentional ploy. Norris implies, though does not fully document, the latter alternative. He also correctly notes that not only the *content* of these key terms ('person' and 'nature'), but also their 'logical relation' to one another, is left undefined.

Secondly, we may agree with Norris that to gloss the human and divine 'natures' as inherently two of the same kind, and/or in 'contradiction' with one another, is not implied by the text of the 'Definition', *per se*. However, it has to be said that the text does not rule out that interpretation either; we have to probe into the debates that preceded and succeeded Chalcedon, especially over the human sufferings of Christ, to discover how 'divinity' and 'humanity' were deemed to constitute different, and mutually exclusive, ranges of characteristics.[13]

---

[12] Ibid., 158.

[13] See e.g. Grillmeier, 'Die theologische und sprachliche Vorbereitung der christologischen Formel von Chalkedon', *Das Konzil von Chalkedon*, 5–202; and for a particularly sympathetic reading of Cyril, J. A. McGuckin, *St Cyril of Alexandria: The Christological Controversy* (Leiden: Brill, 1994), especially on the vexed question of Christ's human sufferings. Norris's own important contribution to an understanding of Cyril's Christology as essentially founded in a *narrative* of *kenōsis* can be found in R. A. Norris, 'Christological Models in Cyril of Alexandria', *Studia Patristica* XIII 2, in *Texte und Untersuchungen* 116 (1971), 255–268.

There is a certain *fiat* on Norris' part, it seems, in attempting to rule out *any* logical incompatibility between the 'natures': this too goes beyond the (skimpy) evidence before us in the 'Definition' and depends on him successfully driving his wedge between 'regulatory' and 'reified' readings of the document.

Thirdly, however, Norris is certainly right to claim that the major achievement of Chalcedon is its 'regulatory' vocabulary, on which semantic grid the events of salvation are now plotted. As with Nicaea, so here, unbiblical 'substance' language of ill-defined reference is wielded in order to 'settle' a set of problems that have their roots in the less consistent witness of the scriptural narratives. The 'rules' of predication are now that duality resides in the *phuseis* and unity in the *hypostasis*. Yet what does this imply ontologically? And why is Norris so evidently coy about the metaphysics of incarnation?

It is here that we must turn the tables on Norris and enquire whether his own agenda, illuminating as it is, is not also driven by contemporary (but less than explicit) theological assumptions. Firstly, and perhaps most obviously, Norris' insistence that Chalcedon is attempting not an ontological *proposition* but a more modest set of linguistic 'rules of predication' smacks immediately of a Lindbeckian 'post-liberal' programme. We recall the main themes of Lindbeck's *The Nature of Doctrine* (1984),[14] which fit exactly with Norris' strong disjunction between 'regulatory' and ontological ascriptions; for Lindbeck in that book identifies three basic models for theological work, the 'cognitivist', the 'experiential-expressive' and the 'cultural-linguistic', and opts strongly for the last whilst eschewing the other two.[15] 'Cognitivist' theories according to Lindbeck understand doctrines as veridical truths, informative 'propositions' about objective realities; 'experiential-expressive' theories see religion as linking with 'pre-reflective experiential depths of the self';[16] whereas 'cultural-linguistic' theories, clearly favoured by Lindbeck, are set carefully apart from the other two, since here doctrines provide merely the 'grammar' for comprehensive interpretative schemes. On this view, doctrines do not even *attempt* to convey first-order beliefs, since 'their

---

[14] George A. Lindbeck, *The Nature of Doctrine: Religion and Theology in a Postliberal Age* (Philadelphia: Westminster Press, 1984), 16–19.

[15] Ibid., 30–45.

[16] Ibid., 21.

communally authoritative use hinders or prevents them from specifying positively what is to be affirmed.'[17]

Lindbeck's highly influential work owes much to a non-realist reading of the late Wittgenstein which now, incidentally, seems questionable to an increasing body of philosophers.[18] But only thus can it drive so significant a wedge between 'ontological' and 'linguistic' claims, the (dubious?) apologetic advantage being a bashful 'recession from reality'[19] and into the buffering and protective 'hermeneutical circle' of the church community. Thus Lindbeck, like Norris after him, can dub the efforts of Nicaea and Chalcedon mere 'second-order guidelines', not 'first-order affirmations about the inner being of God or of Jesus Christ'.[20] The trouble with this assertion, of course (even if it proves suitable as a somewhat defensive post-modern apologetic ploy, which this writer would question), is whether it bears any relation to what the writers of the Chalcedonian 'Definition' and their sources thought they were up to themselves. And in this area, there appears to be no confirming evidence whatsoever. Indeed the very disjunction between 'ontological', 'experiential' and 'linguistic' appears anachronistic in the fifth-century *milieu*. Whereas writers like Augustine certainly discourse lengthily on language's relation to reality,[21] they do not make this fine-tuned Lindbeckian distinction between 'doctrinal' assertions as merely regulatory and other (separable) *propositional* claims. And later, when (for instance, in the sixth-century Eastern discussions of the Chalcedonian tradition), fine-tuning about very particular linguistic uses applied to Christ became a focus of intense debate, this was done 'precisely with the understanding that these [uses] refer to realities, and that the realities rather than our

---

[17] Ibid., 19. It is, however, debatable whether Lindbeck can keep up this line consistently: see, for example, ibid., 68–69.

[18] See esp. Hilary Putnam, *Renewing Philosophy* (Cambridge, MA: Harvard University Press, 1992), chs. 7 and 8.

[19] The phrase is used by Alvin Plantinga in his critique of the work of Gordon D. Kaufman, in A. Plantinga, *Warranted Christian Belief* (New York: O.U.P., 2000), ch. 2, esp. 31–42.

[20] Lindbeck, *The Nature of Doctrine*, 94.

[21] Augustine, *De doctrina christiana*, bks II and III.

language about them are what is important.'[22] In short, I can find no
evidence from either Aristotelian or Platonist-inspired circles of the
patristic period that linguistic terms for 'Christ' could be divorced
from ontological commitment, or indeed from 'experience' (despite
the notable dearth of discussion of that latter category); for why else
would this matter have evinced such intense and passionate controversy, if it were not about the very *reality* of experienced Christian
salvation?

If I am right, then, Norris's thesis is propelled by an anachronistic
Lindbeckian engine. Oddly, too (again, if I am right), it contains two
other covert strands of contemporary theological commitment, in
somewhat paradoxical relation to this first one. The second, which
emerges in Norris's allusions to the need for a form of 'negative theology' in relation to an appropriate reading of Chalcedon, suggests a
slippage – even on his own terms – into a more 'cognitive' claim than
his own 'regulatory' approach would allow; for here he insists that
God is no part of the natural order and that therefore *all* language
used to speak of God is radically improper.[23] The claim sits oddly, we
note, alongside his non-propositional interpretation of the 'Definition';
but it helps to explain the puzzling features of his theory, already
mentioned, that 'metaphorical' and 'analogical' explications of
Chalcedon's abstract terms *all* fall equally short of the mark and result
in inappropriate 'reification'. What I suspect at this point is obtruding
into Norris's text is a post-Kantian understanding of God's 'ineffability' (associated in the North American theological scene with the
work of Gordon D. Kaufman and Sallie McFague),[24] where an insistence on God's *noumenal* unavailability is conjoined with a non-
cognitive understanding of 'metaphor' and a tendency to smudge
altogether the distinction between 'metaphorical' and 'analogical'

---

[22] Brian Daley, S.J., in private correspondence. Also see idem, 'Nature and the "Mode
of Union": Late Patristic Models for the Personal Unity of Christ', in eds. Stephen
T. Davis, Daniel Kendall, S.J., and Gerald O'Collins, S.J, *The Incarnation: An
Interdisciplinary Symposium on the Incarnation of the Son of God* (Oxford: O.U.P., 2002),
164–196.

[23] Norris, 'Chalcedon Revisited', 153.

[24] See, e.g., Gordon D. Kaufman, *In Face of Mystery* (Cambridge, MA: Harvard
University Press, 1993); S. McFague, *Metaphorical Theology* (Philadelphia: Fortress
Press, 1982).

speech for God. Since God *in se* is assumed to be completely off limits epistemologically, then figurative speech about him/her is all at the same level of 'reified' inappropriateness: it is (paradoxically) *both* harmlessly ornamental *and* simultaneously 'radically improper'. Consequently, it is not clear, on Norris's view, how anyone *could* apply the 'rules' of Chalcedon appropriately except by repeating its empty-sounding phrases. This form of 'apophaticism' is a far cry, we note, from the 'negative theology' of the pseudo-Dionysius, for whom even negations about God's nature must be negated linguistically, yet where a vision of ecstatic *encounter* with the 'dazzling darkness' of the divine is promised *hyper noun* ('beyond the mind');[25] and it is perhaps yet further still from Thomas's sophisticated appropriation of Dionysius, which results in a theory of 'analogical' speech for God intentionally distinguished (by its 'appropriateness') from 'metaphor', and sustained by an ontology of participation.[26] Norris, however, does not even explore these more ancient theories of 'negative' religious language; instead, it seems that the shadow of Kant falls upon his path.

Finally, we once again suspect a modern dogmatic commitment when Norris insists (again, more fervently than his 'regulatory' approach would seem to vindicate) that the divine and human 'natures' must be read without any possibility of 'contrariety' between them. How, we may ask, does Norris know this, when he has rightly pointed out that the term *phusis* in itself imparts no clear description of the attributes of each – the human and the divine? In principle, on this (supposedly) 'contentless' reading of the linguistic 'rules', contrariety or non-contrariety between the natures could surely equally well apply. In a lightly footnoted article such as Norris's, we are again left guessing at influence for his own *penchant* here; but it seems likely this time that Karl Rahner is in the background here, Rahner who in a justly famous article in *Theological Investigations* (to which we shall return later) urges that God should be thought of as capable of creating

---

[25] Pseudo-Dionysius, 'Mystical Theology', in *Pseudo-Dionysius: The Complete Works* (New York: Paulist Press, 1987), 133–141.

[26] See David Burrell's important reconsideration of the topic of 'analogy' in Aquinas, 'From Analogy of "Being" to the Analogy of Being', in eds. T. Hibbs and John O'Callaghan, *Recovering Nature: Essays in Natural Philosophy, Ethics, and Metaphysics in Honor of Ralph McInerny* (Notre Dame, IN: University of Notre Dame Press, 1999), 253–266.

in distinction from God-self a humanity 'absolutely open upwards',[27] not by definition therefore set in 'contrariety' to the divine nature, nor competing for space over against it. That this reading might indeed commend itself to us (as an adjunct to Rahner's developed 'transcendental anthropology', and as a particular exposition of Chalcedon) is a matter here to be left open for the meantime. All that we have established, however, is that Norris's thesis at this point technically extends beyond the 'regulatory' reading of Chalcedon that he himself has set up.

To sum up, then, on Norris' important and challenging article: we have shown that he rightly identifies the regulatory force of the 'Definition' as technical–cum–linguistic, but he also shows that the very terms that are proposed as solutions to the christological dispute are left deliberately undefined (an ostensibly surprising state of affairs for a 'Definition'). Where he errs is in suggesting that the 'Definition' required no concomitant ontological commitment, and in implying a theory of 'negative theology' that looks suspiciously, and anachronistically, modern.

Let us now take these points forward in examination of the theory that 'incarnation' language *tout court* should be read as 'metaphorical'. Since we have already cleared some of the philosophical ground here, this theory can be considered rather more summarily.

Incarnation Language as 'Metaphorical'

John Hick's famous (or notorious) assertion in *The Myth of God Incarnate* (1977) that the idea of a God/man is 'as devoid of meaning as to say that this circle drawn with a pencil on paper is also a square'[28] drew an immediate storm of defensive protest.[29] The most obvious riposte was that we cannot *know* that the notion of a God/ Man is incoherent unless we antecedently and exhaustively know

---

[27] K. Rahner, 'Current Problems in Theology', tr. and introd. Cornelius Ernst, *Theological Investigations* i (Baltimore: Helicon Press, 1961), 183.

[28] 'Jesus and the World Religions', in ed. J. Hick, *The Myth of God Incarnate* (London: SCM Press, 1977), 167–185, at 178.

[29] Most immediately in ed. M. Green, *The Truth of God Incarnate* (Grand Rapids, MI: Eerdmans, 1997).

what divinity and humanity consist in (which evidently we do not). However, it is ironic that Hick points precisely to those elements of indeterminacy in the Chalcedonian Definition which Norris also highlights, but uses them to insist that the God/Man formula makes no sense: 'orthodoxy insisted upon the two natures, human and divine, coinhering in the one historical Jesus Christ. But orthodoxy has never been able to give this idea any content. ... The Chalcedonian formula, in which the attempt rested, merely reiterated that Jesus was both God and man, but made no attempt to interpret the formula.'[30]

Rather oddly, the effect on Hick of his views about Chalcedon's supposed incoherence is to object (in his later book, *The Metaphor of God Incarnate*) that 'incarnation' language must therefore be seen as 'metaphorical' in nature rather than 'literal'. More usually, he agrees, such a linguistic process moves in the opposite direction: speech originally coined as metaphor settles into literalness over time. But here, with the claim of 'incarnation', what was once thought to be 'literal' (God becoming human in Christ) must now be seen to have failed as literal speech: 'in the case of divine incarnation the initial idea has proved to be devoid of literal meaning and *accordingly* identified as metaphor... .'[31] The effect of this attribution of 'metaphorical' status thus seems to imply a 'recession from reality' of the sort that Norris also entertained: unable to perceive 'metaphor' as cognitive, as precisely giving us a new purchase on reality, Hick instead assumes that to use 'metaphorical' speech is to say something with *less* firm ontological commitment than if one spoke literally. But it should immediately be responded that this conclusion by no means follows: it is often by the means of a freshly minted metaphor that one can make the most intense claims on the real. As Soskice well illustrates, the coinage of new and striking metaphor ('speaking of one thing in terms suggestive of another'[32]) has more often sprung in Christian tradition from a realist commitment, especially amongst mystical theologians,[33] than from a coyness such as Hick's about realist claims. Again, as we suggested with Norris, but here more explicitly, it is

---

[30] Hick, *Myth*, 178.

[31] *The Metaphor of God Incarnate* (London: SCM Press, 1993), 104, my emphasis.

[32] Janet Martin Soskice, *Metaphor and Religious Language* (Oxford: O.U.P., 1985), 54.

[33] Ibid., 152.

Hick's post-Kantian appeal to the *noumenal* that dictates his understanding of how 'metaphor' should remove us from reality rather than engaging it.[34]

So it seems that Hick has created a confusion here. He is right to imply that 'metaphorical' speech has an *oddness* characterized by a novel conjunction of ideas. But the oddness of the idea of 'incarnation' (or for that matter of the 'Definition' of Chalcedon) cannot be assumed to be the same oddness as that of the metaphorical *trope*; nor can its oddness be alleviated simply by asserting that 'God/Man' talk is *outré* and empty, or that it is time we acknowledged religious claims other than the Christian one.[35] Indeed, the whole attempt to dub 'incarnation' 'metaphorical' *tout court* at this second-order level looks misguided when compared with a close attempt to discern, in the terms of the 'Definition' of Chalcedon, how particular terms and words are being used. There, in comparison, it is surprisingly hard to clarify whether the key terms *phusis* and *hypostasis* are being applied 'literally', 'metaphorically', or 'analogically', since these are 'substance' words with a bewildering range of uses elsewhere and, as we have already underlined, a non-specified use in this case.[36]

If the oddness of the claims of the 'Definition' is not the oddness of metaphor, then is it perhaps more truly the oddness of 'paradox' or 'riddle'? It is worth considering these two alternatives before passing on to our final (and very different) contemporary assessment of how to read Chalcedon.

In a broadly accepted sense, the Chalcedonian 'Definition' does indeed involve a 'paradoxical' claim – the claim that 'God' and 'Man', normally perceived as strikingly different in defining characteristics, find in Christ a unique intersection. Here 'paradox' simply means 'contrary to expectation', and the mind is led on from there to eke out an explanation that can satisfy both logic and tradition. However, we should be careful to distinguish this meaning of 'paradox' from a tighter one in which not merely something 'contrary to expectation'

---

[34] See esp. J. Hick, *The Interpretation of Religion* (New Haven: Yale University Press, 1989).

[35] Hick, *Myth*, 177–184.

[36] See G. C. Stead, *Divine Substance* (Oxford: Clarendon Press, 1977), which painstakingly charts the different evocation of 'substance' terms in the formative patristic period.

is suggested, but something actually 'self-contradictory' or logically incoherent. In this latter sense, of course, Hick could most happily apply the term 'paradoxical' to the incarnation (and indeed less confusingly in my view than his chosen epithet 'metaphorical'); but it has to be said that, again, the 'Definition' of Chalcedon does not tell us, in and of itself, how to read its 'paradoxical' claim. The overwhelming impression from following the debate leading up to Chalcedon, however, as well as that which succeeds it, is that the 'paradoxical' nature of the incarnation in the *first* sense is embraced (with greater or lesser degrees of enthusiasm), but that 'paradox' in the latter sense is vigorously warded off.[37] The 'Definition' is propelled by an assumption of coherence, not by a glorying in incoherence.

The question of whether Chalcedon may be read as a 'riddle' is perhaps even more subtle a question. A playful case could be made, I think, for reading the famous negative epithets ('without confusion', 'without change', 'without division', 'without separation') in the form of a riddle. (*Q*: What is 'without confusion', 'without change', 'without division', 'without separation'? *A*: Two natures in one person, Christ.) But this is not just any riddle, for riddles can take various forms. Some, notoriously the Mad Hatter's ('Why is a raven like a writing desk?') have *no* answer, whereas others play on words to indicate a disjunction. (*Q*: What is the difference between God and Ninian Smart? *A*: God is everywhere, but Ninian is everywhere but *here*.) The sort encoded in the 'Definition', by contrast, is more truly the kind analysed by Wittgenstein in relation to a mathematical problem whose solution one cannot yet guess, but where one drives between the horns of a dilemma:

[it is] like the problem set by the king in the fairy tale who told the princess to come neither naked nor dressed, and she came wearing fishnet. That might have been called not naked and not dressed either. He didn't really know what he wanted her to do, but when she came thus he was forced to accept it. It was of the form 'Do something which I shall be inclined to call neither naked or dressed'. It's the same with the mathematical problem. 'Do something which

---

[37] See Grillmeier, 'Vorbereitung', 199–202.

I shall be inclined to accept as a solution, though I don't know now
what it will be like.'[38]

In a justly famous article by Cora Diamond applying this understanding of 'riddle' to Anselm's ontological argument, Diamond
clarifies this particular use of riddle thus: 'that reality may surprise
us, not only by showing us what *is* the case, when we had not sus-
pected it was, but also by showing us something beyond what we
had ever taken to be possible, beyond anything we had thought of at
all'.[39] By pointing disjunctively to what is *not* the case, one moves
through to a novel level of perception: 'We express and do not
express a thing, see and do not see a thing, when we express it in
riddles ...'[40] Now this seems to me a particularly apt way of describing what is going on in the Chalcedonian 'Definition' in the ruling
out of disjunctive possibilities: a new, and surprising, reality which
we could not previously have thought possible is being gestured
towards, in this case the reality of Christ's *hypostasis*. And this seems
to me infinitely more illuminating of the Definition's intent than a
focus on metaphor. To this point we shall return in our last section,
when we consider the status of the 'Definition' as an 'apophatic'
document. Let us now look at the other end of the spectrum of
contemporary debate and briefly chart the responses to Hick
amongst the 'literalists'.

Incarnation Language as 'Literal'

The tactics of both Norris and Hick, as we have seen, involve a loos-
ening of the relation between language and reality in the case of the
Chalcedonian 'Definition': their distrust of 'literalism' (Hick) or

---

[38] Margaret MacDonald's notes to Wittgenstein's lectures in 1935, cited in C.
Diamond, 'Riddles and Anselm's Riddle', *The Realistic Spirit* (Cambridge, MA: MIT
Press, 1991), 267.

[39] Ibid., 279–280.

[40] Ibid., 288. I do not see this reading of the negative epithets as necessarily in com-
petition with the careful study of the terms in L. Abramowski, 'ΣΥΝΑΦΕΙΑ und
ΑΣΥΓΧΥΤΟΣ ΕΝΩΣΙΣ als Bezeichnung für trinitarische und christologische
Einheit', in *Drei christologische Untersuchungen* (Berlin: de Gruyter, 1981), 63–109.

'reification' (Norris) has roots in a post-Kantian withdrawal from 'things-in-themselves'. In stark contrast, the analytic philosophers of religion who of late have leapt to the defence of incarnationalism in general, and Chalcedonianism in particular, affirm both the possibility, and indeed the necessity, of asserting the 'literal' truth of the incarnation. It is worth now enquiring a little more closely what they mean by this.

Let us take here two celebrated instances of this embracing of the claim of 'literalism' and then probe a little further into what it implies for the philosophers concerned. Thomas V. Morris, first, opens his book on *The Logic of God Incarnate* thus: 'The core claim of the traditional Christian doctrine of the Incarnation, the fundamental and most distinctive tenet of the Christian faith as defined at the Council of Chalcedon (451 CE), is the claim that the person who was and is Jesus of Nazareth is one and the same individual as God the Son, the Second Person of the divine Trinity – a *literal* statement of absolute, numerical identity'.[41] Or again, David Brown, in his *The Divine Trinity*, stresses that Jesus was 'in some *literal* sense God', and according to the 'Chalcedonian model' of that view, 'simultaneously God and man'.[42] But what exactly is meant in each of these cases by 'literal'? Both authors are explicitly writing to rebuff the views of the contributors to *The Myth of God Incarnate*, and in particular replying to Hick's charge of the incoherence of the doctrine of the incarnation in that volume: they obviously, and minimally, aspire to demonstrate the doctrine's logical *coherence*. But this is probably not the only, or even the prime evocation of 'literal' for them. It is worth clarifying further, with the aid of some thoughts from an essay of William Alston,[43] what *range* of meanings can be applied to the term 'literal', because this makes a great difference to how we assess the supposedly 'literal' status of the language of the Chalcedonian 'Definition'.

In the course of an illuminating discussion on the nature of metaphor in *Divine Nature and Human Language* (1989), Alston insists that

---

[41] Thomas V. Morris, *The Logic of God Incarnate* (Ithaca, NY: Cornell University Press, 1986), 17–18, my emphasis.

[42] David Brown, *The Divine Trinity* (London: Duckworth, 1985), 102–103, my emphasis.

[43] William P. Alston, *Divine Nature and Human Language* (Ithaca, NY: Cornell University Press, 1989), 17–38.

the primary and obvious meaning of the term 'literal' is that when I speak thus I mean what I say to be *true*.[44] The trouble, however, is that the word 'literal' has become, as Alston puts it, 'adventitiously' associated with other synonyms, and herein lies the trouble and confusion for theology when wondering what it means by 'literal' statements about God (or Christ). These 'adventitious associations' with the word 'literal' include: 'precise', 'univocal', 'specific', 'factual', 'empirical' and 'ordinary'.[45]

Now this list of Alston's is extraordinarily illuminating for pinpointing potential areas of conflict and misunderstanding between parties in the debate about Chalcedon. For instance, Morris and Brown (unlike Norris, it seems, and certainly unlike Hick) want to insist that Chalcedon 'literally' makes a true, ontological statement about Christ's person. This I take to be their prime meaning of 'literal' in the statements by them I have quoted. Therein lies their main bulwark against the 'recession from reality' school, and therein too lies, as we have already argued, their clear continuity with the intentions of the fathers of Chalcedon. But when it comes to the other 'associations' with literalness which they may be harbouring, our analytic defenders of Chalcedon may prove not always to have the same set of intentions as the writers of the Chalcedonian 'Definition'. For instance, whereas Morris's and Brown's reevaluation of the Chalcedonian heritage clearly reflects their primary commitment, as those skilled in analytic philosophy, to the goals of 'precision' and 'specification', we may question whether the sort of precision they have in mind is the *same* as that of the bishops who penned the 'Definition'. In Morris's case, for instance (as in different ways in Brown and Swinburne),[46] the Chalcedonian heritage is subjected to an analytic going-over that leaves far less room for equivocation or mystery than the 'Definition' itself.[47] It is worth reminding ourselves here that the group of bishops initially charged with producing a formula at the Council was *resistant*

---

[44] Ibid., 21.

[45] Ibid., 25.

[46] For Richard Swinburne's contribution see *The Christian God* (Oxford: O.U.P., 1994), 192–238. It is worth underscoring that Swinburne avoids talking about 'literal' truth in the manner of Morris and Brown.

[47] See Brown, *Divine Trinity*, chs. 5, 6, esp. 224–228; Morris, *Logic of God*, esp. chs. 1, 3, 4, 6; Swinburne, *Christian God*, ch. 9.

to the Emperor's pressure for greater precision, a point to which we shall want to return in our concluding section.[48] However, the question of 'literalness' when glossed as 'univocity' raises another, different, set of issues which we have already touched upon earlier: the uses of *phusis* and *hypostasis* are not obviously or clearly the same as in other uses of those terms elsewhere ('univocal' with them), since that very matter remains unexplained in the 'Definition'. Although it appears that the term *phusis* is to be used univocally *within* the 'Definition' for both the human and the divine, even that is not actually prescribed. (A stronger case for the 'univocity' of the term *prosōpon* with ordinary uses as applied to humans could I think however be made.)[49] As for 'empirical' or 'factual (historical)' as other glosses of 'literal', here we have instances where the *modern* concerns of the analytic school of philosophy of religion diverge strongly from what we know of the participants in the fifth-century debate, since it was clearly not their interest, as it is the almost obsessive interest of the analytic philosophers of religion, to establish that the empirical evidence about the 'historical Jesus' could rationally be construed as either demanding, or allowing, the ascription of divinity. (Brown's and Swinburne's projects, however, are centrally concerned with this issue.[50]) Rather, the Chalcedonian 'Definition' — as Nicaea and Constantinople before it — *takes for granted* the achievement of salvation in Christ and then asks what must be the case about that Christ if such salvation is possible. In that sense, Chalcedon is much more like a 'transcendental argument' (to use an equally anachronistic Kantian term) for Christ's divinity and humanity than it is like an empiricist investigation of the evidences of Jesus's historical life.

In sum, the interest in 'literalness' in the analytic defence of incarnationalism in general (and of Chalcedon in particular) has at its core an insistence on the ontological reality of what it describes that is fully in line with Chalcedon's intentions. But in other matters which it may associate with the ascription of 'literalness', it goes beyond, or

---

[48] See Slusser, 'The Issues', 63–65.

[49] See my discussion of the use of *prosōpon* in the trinitarian context in ' "Persons" in the "Social" Doctrine of the Trinity', in eds. S. T. Davis, D. Kendall, S.J., and G. O'Collins, S.J., *The Trinity* (Oxford: O.U.P., 1999), 123–144, at 139–140.

[50] See Brown, *Divine Trinity*, 101–158; Swinburne, *Christian God*, 216–238.

goes even against, what the fifth-century debate appears to have enshrined as assumptions or goals.

Conclusions: Chalcedon as 'Horos'

Let us now in closing gather the pieces we have assembled from an engagement with these three contemporary Western approaches to Chalcedon, and see if we can find our way through to a fourth position that learns from them all but avoids the pitfalls we have highlighted along the way.

From our discussion of Norris, firstly, we gleaned the conclusion that a 'regulatory' reading of Chalcedon's terms is correct so long as we understand (a) that the terms themselves are not 'defined' in a precise way and (b) that this approach in no way implies lack of ontological commitment (as Norris appeared to endorse). From our treatment of Hick, secondly, we concluded that his attempt to dub the language of incarnation 'metaphorical' is misleading, and distinctly out of the line with the original intentions of Chalcedon; but applying the categories of 'paradox' (without the stronger evocation of logical incoherence) and 'riddle' (in a particular sense we clarified) get us nearer the heart of Chalcedon's intents. From our brief analysis of Chalcedon's treatment at the hands of analytic philosophers of religion, finally, we discerned a commendable interest in defending the propositional dimensions of Chalcedon's claims, but also a danger of smuggling in under the rubric of 'literalness' a number of issues anachronistic from the perspective of Chalcedon itself.

Taking these insights forward, let us now consider the crucial systematic issue touched on earlier, *viz.*, whether and in what sense the 'Definition' speaks 'kataphatically' or 'apophatically', and where the line is drawn between the two. Here we shall, perforce, have finally to clarify what *genre* of text this is, and what we may appropriately expect of it.

An important clue here, I suggest, is provided by the very word used in Greek for the 'Definition', that is, *horos*, or 'horizon'. The evocations are mostly not the same ones that are set off by the English term 'Definition' – that is, semantic clarity, linguistic precision, or careful circumscription (and we have already seen how Chalcedon apparently fails to deliver all of these). Rather, as a survey of the uses of *horos* in Lampe's *Patristic Lexicon* displays, meanings of *horos* in Greek range from 'boundary, 'horizon' and 'limit', to 'standard', 'pattern' and (monastic) 'rule'. The word can also be used directly of Christ with the meaning of 'expression' (Christ as the '*horos* and *logos* of God', in Gregory of Nazianzen.)[51] Thus, when it is also used of liturgical or dogmatic 'decisions' and 'decrees', it brings with it different semantic baggage from our English equivalent. In a remarkably revealing passage using a cognate term, Plotinus (*Enneads* 5. 5 [32]. 8) speaks of the Intellect's waiting on contemplation of the One as equivalent to watching the 'horizon' for the rising sun, but then finding that limit dissolved away as the One manifests itself as a light that will not be so confined.[52] In a much later passage from John Climacus (*The Ladder*, Step 28), a similar thought is entertained in the context of mental prayer: 'Enclose your mind within the words of prayer ... the mind, after all, is naturally unstable, but God can give all things firm endurance ... he who sets a *boundary* to the sea of the mind will come to you during prayer and will say, "Thus far you shall come, and no farther" (Job 38. 11). The spirit, though, cannot be bound, and where the Creator of Spirit is found, all things yield to him.'[53]

Taking this semantic background into account, and remembering again that the assembled bishops at Chalcedon resisted at one point the Emperor's demand for greater 'precision', we may perhaps begin to see the true intentions of the document. It does not, that is, intend to provide a full systematic account of Christology, and even less a complete and precise metaphysics of Christ's makeup. Rather, it sets a 'boundary' on what can, and cannot, be said, by *first* ruling out three aberrant interpretations of Christ (Apollinarianism, Eutychianism and extreme Nestorianism), *secondly* providing an abstract rule of language (*phusis* and *hypostasis*) for distinguishing duality and unity in Christ, and *thirdly* presenting a 'riddle' of negatives by means of which a greater (though undefined) reality may be intimated. At the same time, it recapitulates and assumes (a point often forgotten in considering

---

[51] *Theological Orations* 38. 13.

[52] Tr. A. H. Armstrong, Loeb, v (Cambridge, MA: Harvard University Press, 1984), 179–180.

[53] John Climacus, *The Ladder of Divine Assent*, Classics of Western Spirituality (London: SPCK, 1982), 276 (translation slightly emended).

the *horos* in abstraction from the rest of the *Acta*) the acts of salvation detailed in Nicaea and Constantinople; and then it leaves us at that 'boundary', understood as the place now to which those salvific acts must be brought to avoid doctrinal error, but without any supposition that this linguistic regulation thereby *explains* or *grasps* the reality towards which it points. In this, rather particular sense, it is an 'apophatic' document.

What category or *genre* of text, then, is the Chalcedonian 'Definition'? If my interpretation is right, it is clearly regulatory and binding as a 'pattern' endorsed by an ecumenical council: reflections on Christ's person must henceforth pass through this 'grid', as I put it at the outset. But it would be a mistake to expect it to deliver more than it can in its own terms, given its 'apophatic' dimension. As Rahner puts it famously, it is 'not end but beginning', or (more properly) 'end *and* beginning'.[54] For the East, in any case, it has always represented one – albeit crucial – moment in a process of christological clarification that continued long afterwards, through the debates of the sixth and seventh centuries and up to and including the iconographical decrees of Nicaea II. From this perspective, even Rahner is not quite modest enough in his ascription: Chalcedon is strictly speaking *neither* end *nor* beginning, but rather a transitional (though still normative) 'horizon' to which we constantly return, but with equally constant forays backwards and forwards. Whereas the West has tended to 'stop' at Chalcedon, and to expect of it something more metaphysically and substantially precise than it can yield, the East has in contrast tended to turn its phrases into liturgical prayer (especially in the *Theotokia* for Saturday Great Vespers),[55] to gesture with it in worship beyond the 'limit' that it sets. Endless ecumenical misunderstanding, of course, has resulted from this divergence.[56]

---

[54] Rahner, 'Current Problems in Theology', 149, 150.

[55] The *Theotokia* of the Saturday Great Vespers, for instance, uses language from Chalcedon to laud the Virgin.

[56] For an assessment of the significance of Chalcedon for ongoing ecumenical interchange, see D. Wendebourg, 'Chalcedon in Ecumenical Discourse', *Pro Ecclesia* 7 (1998), 307–332.

It is worth enumerating, finally and in closing, some of the vital christological issues that Chalcedon *per se* cannot and does not solve.[57] Not only is this undertaking suitably chastening, it also invites the last ecumenical reflection: is Chalcedon's 'limit' regrettable or laudable?

Thus: (1) Chalcedon does not tell us of what the divine and human 'natures' consist; (2) it does not tell us what *hypostasis* means when applied to Christ; (3) it does not tell us how the *hypostasis* and the *phuseis* are related, or how the *phuseis* relate to one another (the problem of the *communicatio idiomatum*); (4) it does not tell us how many wills Christ has; (5) it does not tell us that the *hypostasis* is identical with the preexistent Logos; (6) it does not tell us what happens to the *phuseis* at Christ's death and in his resurrection; (7) it does not tell us whether the meaning of *hypostasis* in this christological context is different, or the same, from the meaning in the trinitarian context; and (8) it does not tell us whether the risen Christ is male.

If these are some of the 'limits' of Chalcedon, does this 'look like carelessness', or is it a *felix culpa*? The answer, of course, will depend on what *genre* of text one is hoping, or expecting, it to be. All the questions I have just enumerated were bound to become pressing at some point, and to find more-or-less official responses. Such attempts at greater precision are theologically inevitable, and indeed laudable as speculative endeavours. But if my analysis in the foregoing has been at all convincing, then we shall at least have shown that expecting *Chalcedon* to answer these further questions is a mistaken hope of some seriousness: there are many issues that Chalcedon, as such, did not 'solve'. Finally, then, the intriguing question that presses ecclesiologically for today is this: should *Chalcedon* be the primary bar of ecumenical engagement and discernment in christological matters? If so, its 'apophatic' horizon (at least as I have propounded it) could shelter many more alternatives than later official clarifications,

---

[57] It is important to stress that this list of bits of 'unfinished business' that Chalcedon leaves undetermined should not be read as considerations *equivalent* to the more fundamental reflection on Chalcedon's 'apophatic' status that I have just outlined. Most of the issues here noted were returned to in later conciliar clarifications, but without – in my view – disturbing the remaining importance of the undergirding 'apophatic' dimension of the Chalcedonian tradition as a whole.

East and West, would appear to allow; and its character as *horos* could perhaps find greater understanding in circles of the West, a development that would chasten expectations in some analytic philosophical quarters, but (I suspect) release spiritual and theological creativity in others.[58]

---

[58] Even in the years since this chapter was originally published, there has been a notable new development of consciousness in Western scholarship of the importance of the post-Chalcedonian christological trajectory for understanding Chalcedon itself. Evidences of this trend, moving beyond Grillmeier's pioneering work, may be found, for example, in Brian E. Daley, S.J., *God Visible: Reconsidering Patristic Christology* (Oxford: O.U.P., 2020), and – rather differently – in Johannes Zachhuber's remarkable *The Rise of Christian Theology and the End of Ancient Metaphysics* (Oxford: O.U.P., 2020), which probes the philosophical question of how the meaning of *hypostasis* crucially shifted from its original trinitarian meaning to its implicit Chalcedonian one – and how this matter was only clarified further thereafter.

PART 2

Israel and Christ in Contestation?

PART 2

Israel and Hizbullah: Confrontations

5

'Broken' Monotheism? Intra–Divine Complexity and the Origins of the Doctrine of the Trinity

Introduction

The purpose of this chapter is to suggest the possibility of a new systematic model for thinking about the relations of Judaism and Christianity in connection with the Christian doctrine of the Trinity. As will become clear, this will also, and by implication, involve a certain re-thinking of Jewish/Christian relations *vis-à-vis* the more obviously problematic matter of Christology; but it will be a deliberate strategy on my part not to start here with the overt 'skandalon' for Jews of the fully divine status claimed for Jesus by Christians. The chapter has two parts. In the first – systematic – section, I briefly review some recent, and highly sophisticated, attempts at *rapprochement* between Christians and Jews on the matter of the Trinity, and conclude that the relative neglect of the doctrine of the Spirit (the 'third') in these contexts has led to an implicit retraction of the problems straight back to the christological base. The attempt by some 'post-liberal' systematicians to replace classic Christian supersessionism with talk of 'relations' in God (rather than speculative trinitarian

The Broken Body: Israel, Christ and Fragmentation, First Edition. Sarah Coakley.
© 2024 John Wiley & Sons Ltd. Published 2024 by John Wiley & Sons Ltd.

ontology), and by narrative 'naming' of God (rather than the Christian metaphysics of *hypostasis*), still ducks the overarching question of why there should, in the first place, be three in God rather than two. Similarly, recent textual discussions of the Jewish background to the Trinity focus on various *mediator* figures in Jewish thought of the period contemporary to Jesus (especially on the figures of Torah, or Sophia, or the Logos in Philo), and compare those with the still-subordinated divine Logos in 2nd-century Christian writers such as Justin Martyr. So once again, the emphasis is implicitly on relational twoness in God, rather than threeness. But if the Christian Trinity effectively turns out to be a binity after all, or a *residual* threeness with no very clear or distinct role given for the Spirit in contradistinction from the Son, then the central christological *skandalon* ultimately remains unmetabolized. The only possibility of alleviating it becomes either via some embarrassed liberal 'guilt' manoeuvre to try and moderate the supersessionism implied altogether, or by the already-mentioned 'post-liberal' avoidance of divine metaphysics through the collapsing of *hypostatic* distinctiveness into a narrative unfolding of the implications of the divine 'name'. As I shall indicate, neither of these alternatives seems ultimately compelling, philosophically or theologically.

In the second part of the chapter, I therefore suggest an alternative approach, based on a crucial but neglected strand of Paul's thinking on prayer and divine action in Romans 8. 14–30, which might be dubbed 'proto-trinitarian' in implication. I then prospectively compare this strand in Paul's theology with certain suggestive lines of thinking about prayer, worship and representative office in biblical, Qumran and early rabbinic sources. The hypothesis that emerges, firstly, is that these two lines of tradition on prayer share a common, and deep, Jewish root: this is not in itself of course intrinsically surprising. The more subtle and contentious proposal is that Paul's 'proto-trinitarianism', founded in prayer, *is as profoundly Jewish as it is Christian*. To see this, however, requires a certain rethinking of the origins and history of the doctrine of the Trinity. Rather than starting with the presumption that the Christian church first mused on the problem of Jesus's divine status and only thereafter turned to the problem of the Spirit (which is of course how matters appear according to the chronology of the Christian councils), we find in Romans 8 evidence for a different logic, founded from the start in the practices of prayer. This logic places the *Spirit* to the fore at the outset and perceives there to be a primary, and we might say 'reflexive' or 'dialectical', relation between the 'Father' and Spirit in their transforming and incorporative access to the creation which Jesus now infuses. On this vision, a *reflexive movement of divinity into a space of ecstatic human worship* keeps open a future for the elect in which Messianic 'Sonship' remains unfulfilled and uncompleted until the whole creation is included. It is not a coincidence, I shall urge (although this is rarely noted), that this set of reflections towards the end of Romans ch. 8 immediately precedes Paul's excursus on Jewish/Christian relations in Romans 9–11, and this contiguity may be significant for the topic in hand.

Finally, I shall attempt a slightly more extensive exploration of those select strands in Old Testament, Qumran and rabbinic thought which seem to exhibit the same pattern of 'reflexive' threeness: God (1), his incorporative, 'reflexive' (or 'dialectical') presence in the world (in the form of 'glory', Spirit or *Shekinah*) (2), and *participatory* human response to this dialectical presence in the form of prophetic prayer or Messianic election (3). In other words, something approaching the prayer-based logic of Pauline 'proto-trinitarianism' preceded it in the Jewish tradition and continued to be witnessed to sporadically thereafter. I shall close by conceding that this proposed ecumenical mode of approach to the 'Trinity' cannot, as such, soften the obvious supersessionism of classic high Christian christological claims by the time of Nicaea and the later Chalcedon; and nor can it mask, correlatively, the idolatrous offense to Jews of any claim that the human elected one *is divine* (as opposed to participatorily sharing in divinity in some way). This remaining supersessionist nettle therefore has to be grasped. What it may do, however, is open up the way that those christological claims are made in Christianity into an unfinished, and shared, future – that of the still-expected *totus Christus* that can only be manifested and effected through the unchartable power of the Spirit. Judaism and Christianity remain, according to this view, inexorably joined at the hip; the primary divine pressure of transcendent 'reflexive' presence – not here in the form of a merely underemployed 'third' – encloses Jews and Christians together even as it wrenches open a shared and mysterious eschatological future.

Systematic Background: Recent Christian Attempts to Alleviate 'Supersessionism'

My remarks about a contemporary Christian systematic framing for this discussion of Judaism and the Trinity must necessarily remain here somewhat brief and selective. I shall concentrate on the so-called 'post-liberal' approach to the Trinity (enunciated by both Christian and Jewish scholars) that has emerged in second-generation Barthianism in America, on the one hand, and, on the other, on recent attempts in textual scholarship to re-construe the relations of Judaism and Christianity at the very point of the emergence of consciously trinitarian thinking in the second century.[1]

Let me start by noting, however, that Christian systematicians' attempts to alleviate 'supersessionism' in post-War systematic theology have been marked by a certain ambiguity about what such 'supersessionism' involves. The setting aside (in virtually all post-War Christian systematics) of the view that Christianity *rejects* the so-called 'carnal' covenant with Israel and *replaces* it with a new, and spiritual, covenant (what we may call 'Supersessionism 1'), does not as such alleviate the remaining problem for Judaism of christological absoluteness ('Supersessionism 2'). Barth is a supreme case in point, as has been well shown in Katherine Sonderegger's careful study of Barth's 'Doctrine of Israel'.[2] Strong strands of classic anti-Judaism

---

[1] In what follows I shall be looking briefly below at the work of the American theologians Robert Jenson, Kendall Soulen and Peter Ochs to illustrate the first trend. For the second trend, the more recent papers in part III of the German *Festschrift* for Jürgen Moltmann, eds. Michael Welker and Miroslav Volf, *Der lebendige Gott als Trinität* (Gütersloh: Gütersloher Verlagshuas, 2006), are especially relevant and worthwhile: Christoph Markschies, 'Jüdische Mittlergestalten und die christliche Trinitätstheologie', 199–214; Christian Link, 'Trinität im israeltheologischen Horizent', 215–228; and Bertold Klappert, 'Geheiligt werde dein NAME! – Dein Torawille werde getan! Erwägungen zu einer gesamtbiblischen Trinitätslehre in isrealtheologischer Perspektive', 229–253.

[2] Katherine Sonderegger, *That Jesus Christ was Born a Jew: Karl Barth's Doctrine of Israel* (University Park, PA: Pennsylvania State University Press, 1992) carefully traces the varying written and biographical enunciations of Barth on Israel from the time of his *Epistle to the Romans* on. Her overall thesis is that 'Barth's position has demanded a sustained critique of Judaism; and that from his break with Liberalism to his mature

('Supersessionism 1') still lurk particularly in Barth's early work, as Sonderegger shows; but in the *Church Dogmatics*, 'Israel' is precisely front and centre, although in a paradoxical role: indeed, as Sonderegger puts it, Israel is 'elected – Barth does not pull back – *for rejection*'.[3] Christ becomes the representative place where Israel's 'disobedience' is both punished and resolved, through cross to resurrection ('Supersessionism 2').

Our systematic interest in this chapter resides in pressing a question here that may not immediately be obvious in its implications: to what extent is the form of Barth's immensely influential version of 'Supersessionism 2' implicitly affected by his notorious lack of a strong *pneumatology*? It is somewhat ironic that Robert Jenson, who makes one of the most important 'post-liberal' attempts to reconstrue the significance of the Trinity for Jewish/Christian relations post–Barth, should at the same time be the person who has most savagely criti- cized Barth for holding a weak doctrine of the Spirit.[4] I say 'ironic', because I am not sure that he, or others who follow his 'post-liberal' agenda for the Trinity and Judaism, have yet shown how Barth's ver- sion of 'Supersessionism 2' can be effectively moderated or transfig- ured *except* by a stronger and revisionist doctrine of the Spirit.

Let me explain. What the Lutheran Robert Jenson, the Methodist Kendall Soulen, and the pragmatist Jewish theologian Peter Ochs all share, in their laudably irenic attempts to realign Christian trinitari- anism with Jewish monotheism, is a Yale-school Barthianism that represents *philosophical speculation* as the prime enemy for Jewish/ Christian relations in classic Christian trinitarianism. Their proposal is to replace 'timeless being' with divine 'relationship', and 'hypo- static personhood' with 'narrative naming'. And so the remaining 'supersessionist' offense will be relieved, or so it is claimed. All take their cue from Barth's early remark, made already in *Church Dogmatics* 1/I, that the trinitarian God of Christianity is 'nothing other than an

---

period, Barth's anti-Judaism has reflected his unwavering commitment to the doc- trine of justification by grace through faith alone' (ibid., 167).

[3] Ibid.,173, my emphasis.

[4] R. W. Jenson, 'You Wonder Where the Spirit Went', *Pro Ecclesia* 2 (1993), 296–304. For a rather more nuanced account of Barth's pneumatology, see Eugene F. Rogers, *After the Spirit: A Constructive Pneumatology from Resources outside the Modern West* (Grand Rapids, MI: Eerdmans, 2005).

explanatory confirmation of the *name*, Yahweh/Kyrios'.[5] In Jenson's case, this project takes the form of a radically historicized Godhead, a God whose own trinitarian 'identity' actually unfolds through the narrative histories of the Old and New Testaments, and will be ratified only eschatologically.[6] It is the 'timeless substance' talk of classic Christianity that constitutes the offense of 'supersessionism', on this view, not the Trinity as such.[7]

In Kendall Soulen's work, in some contrast, a more embarrassed remnant of 'liberalism' makes its appearance amidst ploys that in other respect echo Jenson's. Soulen concludes somewhat evasively in his *The God of Israel and Christian Theology* that the 'Lord's history with Israel ... does not prepare for the gospel but surrounds the gospel as its constant horizon',[8] a concession that seemingly acknowledges more than Jenson does the remaining offense of (what I have called) 'Supersessionism 2'. Yet Soulen finally appears elusive about how that position might align with his claims elsewhere that 'YHWH's eternal life happens as a communion of 'persons' *reliably identified* as Father, Son, and Holy Spirit'.[9] For if there *is* such a communion of equal 'persons', how can 'Supersessionism 2' not remain a problem? Peter Ochs, the most prominent Jewish collaborator in this line of thinking, attempts a clearer answer of his own. He contributes an enthusiastic endorsement of the 'post-liberal' trinitarian project to repel all borders against 'philosophic intrusions': 'the creeds are misinterpreted' altogether, he announces confidently, 'if they are taken to imply supersessionism'.[10] Once we substitute 'a logic of relations' for Greek philosophical speculation, he claims, we can find a way between and beyond the false 'exclusivist' and 'assimilationist' options, and even

---

[5] Karl Barth, *Church Dogmatics* 1/I, 400.

[6] Robert W. Jenson, *Systematic Theology* vol 1: *The Triune God* (New York: O.U.P., 1997).

[7] See ibid., 90–114.

[8] R. Kendall Soulen, *The God of Israel and Christian Theology* (Minneapolis: Fortress Press, 1996), 176.

[9] Idem, 'YHWH the Triune God', *Modern Theology* 15 (1999), 25–54, at 50, my emphasis.

[10] Peter Ochs, 'Trinity and Judaism', in eds. Hermann Häring, Janet Martin Soskice and Felix Wilfred, *Learning from Other Faiths*, *Concilium* 2003/4 (London: SCM Press), 51–59, at 54, 55.

read Nicaea in a mode friendly to rabbinic Judaism.[11] The trick is to see that both Jews and Christians first need to understand something akin to the full implications of Charles Peirce's theory of 'sign relations':[12] it is modern American pragmatism, then, not classic pagan metaphysics, that should accompany a proper ecumenical understanding of trinitarian 'naming'. With an appeal to Peirce's version of 'relational' pragmatism, we can re-construe 'God creating us, redeeming us from suffering, and delivering us to community with one another and in the divine life' as a flow of *signification* shared with equal conviction by both Jews and Christians.[13]

How are we to assess these various creative attempts to moderate the divisive effect for Jewish/Christian relations of the classic Christian doctrine of the Trinity? The main trouble with this 'post-liberal' option, in its various forms – or so I see it – is that its anti-metaphysical rhetoric diverts us from two remaining systematic problems that will not go away completely: one is the problem of how 'Supersessionism 2' (the claimed absolute Messianic status of Jesus) can be magick-ed away at the same time as 'Supersessionism 1', simply by resisting Greek metaphysical 'intrusions'; the other is the evasion of the systematic significance of the status of the 'third' in the Christian trinitarian vision of divine 'relationality'. To be sure, Peter Ochs is the one member of this 'post-liberal' group who attempts to account for the necessity of relational *threeness* by appealing to the notoriously elusive notion of 'the third' in Peircean 'semiotics'. But suffice it to say that, even if the full Peircean vision can be embraced in all its subtlety and richness, it remains unclear to me that Ochs himself provides a convincing *logical* or *textual* argument against twoness being sufficient for the 'relationality' he claims to be fundamental in God. It is once more as if threeness-in-God is presumed, and then Peirce brought in, ex post facto, to explicate it philosophically.[14]

---

[11] Ibid., 56.

[12] Ibid., 57. Ochs's more extended philosophical treatment of Peirce is to be found in his *Peirce, Pragmatism and the Logic of Scripture* (Cambridge: C.U.P., 1998).

[13] Ochs, 'Trinity and Judaism', 57.

[14] Ochs does mention Kabbalist 'accounts of the various identities of God' alongside strands in both Rosenzweig's and Lévinas's thought which appear 'triadic' (Ochs, 'Trinity and Judaism', 57); but these examples appear so briefly that it is difficult to adjudicate whether their apparently triadic structure is genuinely three-fold.

It is interesting, moreover, that this same systematic problem attends some fascinating attempts by textual scholars to cast the original separation of 'Judaism' and 'Christianity' in a new light by reference to the early rabbinic attack on the idea of 'two powers in heaven'. Whereas Alan Segal famously read the eruption of this rhetoric as precisely a riposte to the emergence of Christian bintiarianism/trinitarianism,[15] Daniel Boyarin now claims that this approach gets the chronology wrong, and that even in the second century, the lines between 'Judaism' and 'Christianity' still remained blurred. Thus the causal impetus worked if anything the other way, according to Boyarin, Judaism 'creating Christianity' and only then the opposite occurring in dialectical return: 'The Rabbis', he writes, 'by defining elements within their own religious heritage as not Jewish, were, in effect, *producing* Christianity, just as Christian heresiologists were, by defining traditional elements of their own tradition as being not Christian, thereby *producing* Judaism'.[16] However we decide on the issue of the chronological separation of conscious 'Jewish' and 'Christian' identities (and this matter of course remains contentious), my point is that the systematic problem of 'threeness' cannot be settled by the '*two* powers in heaven' controversy. And Boyarin's concentration on Justin Martyr as his prototype of a Christian identity only scarcely emerging as such at this time, is also revealing: for it is precisely Justin's interest in the Logos as a subordinated, mediatorial 'second God', and his notorious neglect of the Spirit, that makes his thinking unable to help us with this question either.[17] Is there, then, anywhere else in earliest (Jewish) Christianity that the problem of threeness finds its solution? I think so, but it is easy to overlook. To provide an answer, we now move to our second section, and back to Paul.

---

[15] See Alan Segal, *Two Powers in Heaven: Early Rabbinic Reports About Christianity and Gnosticism* (Leiden: Brill, 1977).

[16] Daniel Boyarin, *Border Lines: The Partition of Judaeo-Christianity* (Philadelphia: University of Pennsylvania Press, 2004), 130, my emphasis.

[17] See ibid., 128–147. Justin Martyr refers to the Spirit at one point in his *First Apology* (6. 1–2) as subordinate even to the angels.

Why Three? The Phenomenon of Deep Prayer and Its Implications for Election

At the climax of his long argument about sin, justification, law and baptism in Romans, chs. 1–8, Paul suddenly introduces one of the most profound discussions of prayer in the Bible, indeed arguably in the whole classic Christian corpus. The point is that prayer, strictly speaking, is not done by us at all, for when pushed to the edge, we realize that we are so weak, desperate, or sin-bound that we do not even know how to begin, or what to ask for. The crucial passage, Romans 8. 26–7, has been freshly translated by Joseph Fitzmyer thus: 'Similarly, the Spirit too comes to the aid of our weakness, for we do not know for what we should pray. But the Spirit itself intercedes for us with ineffable sighs (*stenagmois alalētois*). Yet he who searches our hearts knows what the mind of the Spirit is, because it intercedes for God's dedicated people (*huper hagiōn*) in accordance with his will'.[18] This description of prayer as ecstatic – as beyond human words or comprehension – is important for our systematic purposes in this context because, as James Dunn has well put it, 'God is at both ends of the process'.[19] The Spirit, far from being 'third' in this understanding of divine relations, or a mere continuer of, or testifier to, the revelation of Son (as is the model in John's gospel: see Jn 15. 26), is the very means of God 'reflexively' talking to God *in and through the prayer*. Moreover, it is clear from the surrounding context of this chapter's argument (Ro 8. 12–39) that the effect of such reflexivity-in-God is that of binding the elect ever more deeply into the Messianic event, and opening that event to an eschatological future. The Christian pray-er is destined thus to become a true 'adopted' offspring of God, incorporated into the life of redeemed 'Sonship' (vss. 15–17), and incorporated too into the suffering implications of the Messiah for the whole physical creation, as it 'groans' towards its eschatological

---

[18] J. A. Fitzmyer, S.J., *Romans: A New Translation with Introduction and Commentary* (New York: Doubleday, 1993), 516.

[19] James D. G. Dunn, 'Spirit Speech: Reflections on Romans 8: 12–27', in eds. Sven K. Soderlund and N. T. Wright, *Romans and the People of God: Essays in Honor of Gordon D. Fee on the Occasion of His 65th Birthday* (Grand Rapids, MI: Eerdmans, 1999), 89.

end (vss. 18–23). The Christ event remains uncompleted until that participation is assured (vss. 28–30). Not for nothing, then, I now suggest again, does this eschatological vision exactly precede Paul's equally eschatological excursus on the ultimate relation of Judaism and Christianity (Ro chs. 9–11): the inexorable and inextricable connectedness of the two traditions, in ecstatic Messianic prayer as well as in final destiny, links these two visionary discussions back-to-back.

It would be deeply misleading, however, to pretend that Paul enunciates in Romans 8 a *developed* trinitarianism: such a claim would be obviously anachronistic.[20] But it would be fair, I think, to dub this a Spirit-led, incorporative, '*proto*-trinitarianism', in which the Spirit is by no means a redundant 'third', but a name for one pole in that dialectical reflexivity-in-God which precisely enables the ecstatic participation in God of the elect, and their opening up to an unknown and 'ineffable' Messianic future which includes, and indeed re-binds together, both Jewish and Christian traditions. In short, the Spirit is the wedge, the guarantor, of the 'apophatic' openness of the Christ event to a yet-unknown fulfilment.

What happened to this way of thinking about the Trinity *within* Christianity is a story that I have told elsewhere,[21] and which, perhaps not surprisingly, was to became entangled with mystical or sectarian traditions pushed largely to the edges of conciliar Christian 'orthodoxy', with its *penchant* for a more linear, even covertly hierarchical, account of the relations of 'Father', 'Son' and 'Spirit' with the church and the world.[22] But that intra-Christian story is not the narrative we are concerned with here. Rather, in this context, we want to press the particular question that I have now opened up about the origins of the doctrine of the Trinity and its Jewish backcloth in relation to the activity of

---

[20] Elements of christological subordinationism are clearly still present in Paul (e.g., 1 Cor 15. 28), as well as a confusing shift between the roles of 'Spirit' and 'Christ' in the relevant passage, Ro 8. 9–17, indicating a less-than-clear sense of the Spirit's personal identity.

[21] Originally in Sarah Coakley, 'Why Three? Some Further Reflections on the Doctrine of the Trinity', in eds. Sarah Coakley and David A. Pailin, *The Making and Remaking of Christian Doctrine: Essays in Honour of Maurice Wiles* (Oxford: O.U.P., 1993), 29–56; and more fully in *God, Sexuality and the Self: An Essay 'On the Trinity'* (Cambridge: C.U.P., 2013), 100–151.

[22] See again Coakley, *God, Sexuality and the Self*, esp. chs. 3, 6 and 7.

prayer: did this 'proto-trinitarian' vision of prayer in Paul owe anything to his own Pharisaic training? And indeed, are parallel traces of it to be found anywhere either before or after Paul in the Jewish tradition?

Are There Intimations of 'Proto-trinitarianism' in Jewish Understandings of Prayer and Election?

This is a complicated question, and any answer to it will necessarily involve some subtlety of exegesis. Many years ago now Christopher Stead wrote a two-part paper entitled 'The Origins of the Doctrine of the Trinity',[23] which has stood the test of time;[24] it provided a remarkably succinct and clear account of the exegetical problems that have to be faced in any attempt to locate emergent Christian trinitarianism in its original religio-philosophical context, whether Jewish or pagan. In regard to the Jewish backcloth Stead's view was that there was 'only one likely candidate' known to him that represented 'an actual Trinitarian pattern' (i.e., a *clear* enunciation of 'threeness' in relation to God). This was 'the image in which the Lord God sits enthroned, attended by two angels, one on the right hand and the other on the left', whether the 'two Seraphim of Isaiah's vision' or the two Cherubim 'who mount guard over the Ark'.[25] Stead went on to

---

[23] Christopher Stead, 'The Origins of the Doctrine of the Trinity', *Theology* 77 (1974), 508–517; 582–588.

[24] Only consider the outpouring of scholarly writing since then on Jewish 'hypostasizations' within the Godhead: especially interesting are Peter Schäfer, *Mirror of His Beauty: Feminine Images of God from the Bible to the Early Kabbalah* (Princeton: Princeton University Press, 2002); Gedaliahu Guy Stroumsa, 'Le Couple de L'Ange et de l'Esprit: Traditions Juives et Chrétiennes', in his *Savoir et Salut* (Paris: Les Éditions du Cerf, 1992), 23–41; and – more controversially, for its theory about the very late separation of Judaism and Christianity – Daniel Boyarin, *Border Lines* (see above, nn. 16, 17), and ibid., *The Jewish Gospels: The Story of the Jewish Christ* (New York: The New Press, 2012). It should be added that whereas discussions of incarnational/Logos/Sophia/angelic parallels are legion in this scholarly literature, few probe the more complex question of 'threeness' which is our explicit focus here.

[25] Stead, 'The Origins', 514, referring to Is 6. 2–3 and Ex 25. 18–20. Stead refers the reader here to Jean Daniélou, *The Theology of Jewish Christianity* (London: Darton, Longman & Todd, 1964),117–140 for relevant exegetical examples.

underscore, however, that in the first century CE, in particular, angel-imagery of this sort remained extraordinarily 'fluid', both in the Jewish and New Testament materials. There is, for instance, no consistent lining-up of the two-angel-idea (usually Michael and Gabriel) with other quasi-hypostatized notions of divine 'Logos' or 'Spirit', whether in Philo or other relevant texts such as *The Ascension of Isaiah*, and no 'firm distinction of roles' for Spirit, Logos, or angelic visitants in the New Testament either.[26] In fact, Stead concludes that at least *six* potentially hypostasized entities present themselves in the relevant Jewish literature of the period, in confusing interaction with one another and sometimes melding with the parallel angelic tradition: 'the list would include', he says, 'the Son of God, the Spirit of God, his Anointed, his Word, his Wisdom and his Law'.[27] It is in the nature of the discourses that contain these ideas, however, that conflations and swappings of role are endemic to the *genre*; and whilst Stead suggests a gradual 'concentration' of the six ideas into two (Messiah/Spirit and Wisdom/Torah), even this set of couplings still does not line up consistently, of course, with what was later to become normative Christian trinitarian reflection.

The image of God enthroned between the seraphim/cherubim, however, undeniably held a fundamental position in second-Temple reflection on temple worship; so the intriguing question that confronts us (and which Stead himself does not consider) is whether this model related in some way – itself perhaps also pliable in expression and thought-forms – to a triadic perception of the very nature of personal prayer or temple-worship: as animated from within by God, and as simultaneously constituting a special form of human election. Two *caveats* must however immediately be sounded, lest an overconfident quest for Jewish parallels to Paul's 'proto-trinitarianism' mislead us. Firstly, any notion of ongoing 'reflexivity-of-God' in prayer is unlikely to be identified straightforwardly as *Spirit* in this Jewish context (since, as Peter Schäfer amongst others has shown, 'Spirit' language in the Old Testament and the early rabbis is most commonly associated with being chosen for a *particular* task or

---

[26] Stead, 'The Origins', 514–515. Note that Ro 8. 26 is briefly mentioned in this regard.

[27] Ibid., 515.

office, sometimes short-term[28]). And secondly, the obvious – and unassailable – point of differentiation from the Pauline model in Jewish writings will be a resistance to the idea of an already-inaugurated Messianism, or the notion of a *fully divinized*, as opposed to an elected and participatory, human agent. Nonetheless, given the very 'fluidity' of thinking that Stead so insistently highlights, there is still room for a quest for suggestive parallels to Paul's teaching on prayer-as-triadic. Thus, in what follows I want to highlight three rather different such cases, and at the same time to draw attention to accompanying material from rabbinic teaching, which further instantiates the crucial sustaining notion of prayer as essentially God-given, 'ecstatic' or 'vatic'.[29]

It may indeed be revealing to frame and sharpen this quest for Pauline parallels, albeit from a later perspective, with a famous question about prayer that is recorded in the Babylonian Talmud (B. Berakhot 7a). Since the rabbinic sayings cited in this passage go back at least to the third century CE, and probably earlier, it might be argued that there is encoded here a key rabbinic insight about the very nature of prayer to God. At stake is the (ostensibly odd) question of whether God prays to Himself:

> R. Johanan says in the name of R. Jose: How do we know that the Holy One, blessed be He, says prayers [sc. prays]? Because it says [in Isa 56. 7]: Even them will I bring to My holy mountain and make them joyful in My house of prayer [*beit tefillati*]. It is not said "their prayer" [*tefillatam*], but "My prayer" [*tefillati*]; hence [you learn] that the Holy One, blessed be He, says prayers. What does He pray? – R. Zutra b. Tobi said in the name of Rab: "May it be My will that My mercy [*rachamay*] may suppress My anger [*ka'asi*], and that My mercy may prevail over my [other] attributes [*middotay*], so that I may deal with My children in the attribute of mercy [*middat rachamim*] and, on their behalf, stop short of the limit of strict justice [*shurat had-din*].

See Schäfer, *Mirror of His Beauty*, 92–93, on the special gifts of the Holy Spirit for prophetic purposes; and for more detail on this theme: idem, *Die Vorstellung von Heiligen Geist in der Rabbinischen Literatur* (München: Kösel-Verlag, 1972).

[29] I owe the suggestive term 'vatic' to Michael Fishbane.

The suggestion of an intra-divine prayer, here so strongly supported, might seem to be a serendipitous exegetical aside occasioned merely by an oddity in the text of Isaiah; but this interpretation should be doubted. Something deeper is at stake. The concern with the balance of 'mercy' and 'justice' in the divine attributes is of course a particular interest of the earlier tannaitic tradition;[30] and it is not hard to see how it might have been grounded in a spiritual sensibility about the very workings of prayer at its deepest: the balance of God's attributes *must* favour mercy if the creation is to be sustained in being, and this it is solely His to dispose. Thus, if prayer in 'my house (or temple)' is to be the sustaining prayer of life, it must by definition be guaranteed in some way as grounded inwardly by a prior divine propulsion ('my prayer'). The same fundamental insight, we might add, is already suggested by a discussion in the Mishnah (M. Berakhot 5.5) about the special 'fluency' of the prayer of the mystic R. Haninah ben Dosa;[31] and a similar issue is taken up in a discussion in the Babylonian Talmud of Ps 51. 15 ('O Lord, open my lips, and my mouth shall declare your praise'), a verse on which the rabbis also had reason to comment, in connection with the daily recitation of the *Amidah*, and the implied request to God to inspirit the prayer throughout.[32] Here too, *in nuce*, is the very insight basic to Paul's more floridly pneumatological rendition: human prayer and praise are always already animated by inner-divine propulsion.

---

[30] On this theme see the now-classic treatment in Ephraim E. Urbach, *The Sages: Their Concepts and Beliefs* (Cambridge, MA: Harvard University Press, 1979), esp. 452–459.

[31] This is especially the case if the textual reading is preferred (*shagrah* rather than *shegurah*) which suggests an ecstatic form of prayer: on this point see Schlomo Naeh (in Hebrew), 'Creates the Fruit of Lips: A Phenomenological Study of Prayer According to Mishnah *Berakhot* 4.3. 5.5', *Tarbiz* 63 (1994), 185–218.

[32] See B. Berakhot 4b, citing R. Yohanan: 'At the beginning of the Prayer, one says "O Lord, open my lips ..."'. For a more extended treatment of the proper mental preparation for prayer in the rabbinic tradition, see Elliot R. Wolfson, 'Iconic Visualization and the Imaginal Body of God: The Role of Intention in the Rabbinic Conception of Prayer', *Modern Theology* 12 (1996), 137–162, esp. 139–142.

Three Jewish Loci of 'Triadic' Prayer: God Praying to God in the Elect

It is in this broader context, then, that I draw attention to three other deeply suggestive *loci* in Jewish tradition for comparison with Romans 8. 26–27. They are all somewhat different in context, but a little probing of their background hermeneutics suggests confirmation of the model we seek. Recall again that the pattern we are looking for, in whatever figurative or narrative way it may be expressed, is one of divine *reflexivity* in prayer or worship, and participatory *election* (Messianic or an equivalent) in and through such prayer.

(1) *Exodus 32. 7–14 in Rabbinic Interpretation:* The first example is already to be found in Torah, in the book of Exodus; but read backwards through the Talmudic passages I have just quoted, it may perhaps strike us also as a remarkably daring instantiation of the logic sketched by Paul in Romans 8. The context here is the idolatrous disobedience of Israel in the making of the golden calf. Still on the mountain-top, where he has been communing with the Lord and receiving the tablets of stone, Moses – as prophetic representative of his people – has to confront the divine wrath:

> The Lord said to Moses, 'I have seen this people, how stiff-necked they are. Now let me alone, so that my wrath may burn hot against them and I may consume them; and of you I will make a great nation'. But Moses implored the Lord his God, and said, 'O Lord, why does your wrath burn hot against your people, whom you brought out of the land of Egypt with great power and with a mighty hand? Why should the Egyptians say, "It was with evil intent that he brought them out to kill them in the mountain, and to consume them from the face of the earth"? Turn from your fierce wrath; change your mind and do not bring disaster on your people. Remember Abraham, Isaac, and Israel, your servants, how you swore to them by your own self, saying to them: "I will multiply your descendents like the stars of heaven, and all this land that I have promised I will give to your descendents, and they shall inherit it for ever"'. And the Lord changed his mind about the disaster that he planned to bring on his people.[33]

---

[33] Exodus 32. 9–14.

Now there is, of course, an entirely straightforward and literalistic reading of this passage that takes it simply at face value: Moses confronts an anthropomorphic and angry God, and pleads with Him until he changes His mind. But even by the period of the early rabbis, it seems, that rendition was becoming less acceptable, precisely because of the more complex and emerging reflection on the tight dialectical relationship of God's mercy and His justice: by appeal to such, the suggestion of a vacillating or inconsistent divinity – famously pilloried by anti-Jewish critics of the early CE such as Marcion – could be averted. As a rich and revealing discussion by Yochanan Muffs has demonstrated,[34] a rendition of Exodus 32 arose in which Moses acted precisely as the human conduit at the base of the 'parabola' of this *intra*-divine negotiation. In the context of a desperate intercessory prayer, Moses, *qua* prophet, here stands in for the reflexive divine voice of God as the one who *pleads* His 'mercy'; he operates precisely at the painful axis of this intra-divine dialectic, and negotiates it perilously as the elected representative of Israel: 'Turn from your fierce wrath; change your mind and do not bring disaster on your people', Moses says (vs. 12) – thereby becoming the personal locus of the deflection of divine wrath into divine mercy. This interpretation, of course, is already one laden with theological meaning: that God's own *consistency* finally resides in the supervenience of His mercy over His judgment. But in this shift, Moses plays a crucial, even quasi-'incarnational',[35] role; as Muffs puts it, 'God allows the prophet to represent in his prayer His own attribute of mercy';[36] thus Moses 'stands in the breach' on behalf of his people. Muffs is able to illustrate this hermeneutic move pointedly from a medieval rabbinic midrash, although the ideas may be much older:

---

[34] Yochanan Muffs, 'Who Will Stand in the Breach? A Study of Prophetic Intercession', in *Love and Joy: Law, Language, and Religion in Ancient Israel* (New York: Jewish Theological Seminary, 1992), 9–48; Gary A. Anderson takes up Muffs's analysis from a Christian perspective in his remarkable essay, 'Moses and Jonah in Gethsemane: Representation and Impassibility in Their Old Testament Inflections', in eds. Beverly Roberts Gaventa and Richard B. Hays, *Seeking the Identity of Jesus: A Pilgrimage* (Grand Rapids, MI: Eerdmans, 2008), 215–231.

[35] This is Anderson's further gloss: 'Moses and Jonah', 231.

[36] Muffs, 'Who Will Stand in the Breach?', 33.

God said to Moses after the incident of the Golden Calf, 'Let me at
them, and my anger will rest on them and I will get rid of them'. Is
Moses holding back God's hand, so that God must say, 'Let go of me'?
What is this like? A king became angry at his son, placed him in a small
room, and was about to hit him. At the same time the king cried out
from the room for someone to stop him. The prince's teacher was
standing outside, and said to himself, 'The king and his son are in the
room. Why does the king say "stop me"? It must be that the king wants
me to go into the room and effect a reconciliation between him and
his son. That's why the king is crying, "Stop me"'. In a similar way, God
said to Moses, 'Let Me at them'. Moses said, 'Because God wants me to
defend Israel, He says, "Let Me at them'. And Moses immediately
interceded for them.[37]

In this example, then, we see the elusive 'triadology' of prayer
worked out in a dramatic form as the elected prophet bears and transforms the dialectic of divine action: at the base of the divine 'parabola'
he receives and re-instantiates his election on behalf of Israel, to open
its future even beyond apostasy and idolatry. It is in and through Moses
that that future is even assured, and the shift from divine judgment to
divine mercy is effected: 'And the Lord changed his mind about the
disaster that he planned to bring on his people' (Exodus 32. 14).

(2) *The Song of the Sabbath Sacrifice* (Qumran): The second and third
instances I have selected of a logic equivalent to the Romans 8 analysis of prayer are to be found not in reflections on the transformative
role of a prophet, but in the rather different – and perhaps more
expected – context of liturgical prayer. The first of these comes from
an earlier period: in the admittedly heterodox world of the Qumran
community, as evidenced in the Dead Sea Scrolls. Here, in the remarkable *Songs of the Sabbath Sacrifice*,[38] we read of a perception of Sabbath
liturgy as participatory and transformative in a sense that, although
ostensibly very different from that of the role of Moses in Exodus, is
evocative of the same divine dialectical engagement in prayer we have
noted, this time applied initially to the priestly ministers. The seventh

---

[37] *Exodus Rabbah* 42. 9, as cited in Muffs, 'Who Will Stand in the Breach?', 34, and
discussed by Anderson, 'Moses and Jonah', 218.
[38] See Michael Wise, Martin Abegg, Jr., and Edward Cook, *The Dead Sea Scrolls: A
New Translation* (San Francisco: Harper, 1996), 365–377.

Sabbath song enjoins on the 'priestly angels' the task of reflexively 'lift[ing] the divine exaltation on high';[39] and these exaltations are even echoed by the 'animate temple' of the community itself ('all the corners of the temple's structure'), perhaps striking a chord of recognition in Christians who are reminded of Paul's insistence that they should think of themselves as 'temples of the Holy Spirit' (1 Cor 3. 16–17). Implicitly, then, a divine reflexivity occurs here within, and participatorily transforms, the whole worshipping community, catching them up into the angelic realm and rendering them temple-like, as 'wise spirits of light', even in their constitution in the desert. Away from Jerusalem itself, and substituting a putatively corrupt earthly temple with a vision of the heavenly temple, the Sabbath community at Qumran becomes the corporate elect shot through with ecstatic divine prayer.

Thus, not only is worship itself here in the *Sabbath Songs* a participation of the *community* in divinity-answering-to-divinity, in the form of quasi-angelic worship, but – as John Collins has hinted in a fine article on this topic[40] – the *Melchizedek Scroll* from Qumran may also provide a particular, individualized, instantiation of the same logic. Equivalent to one of the principal angels in this scroll is the mysterious priest/king Melchizedek of Gen 14. 18 and Ps 110. 4, who has the elected status of *elohim*, a god or divine being: it is not clear that he was ever a mortal being according to the interpretation of the *Scroll*. But what he does stand for is an exalted priestly entity transported by

---

[39] Ibid., 371: 'Lift His exaltation on high, you godlike among the exalted divine beings – His glorious divinity above all the highest heavens. Surely He [is the utterly divine] over all the exalted princes, King of king[s] over all the eternal councils. By the wise will – through the words of his mouth – shall come into being all [the exalted godlike]; at the utterance of His lips all the eternal spirits shall exist. All the actions of His creatures are by what His wise will allows' ... 'With such songs shall all the [foundations of the hol]y of holies offer praise, and the pillars bearing the most exalted abode, even all the corners of the temple's structure. Hy[mn] the G[od a]wesome in power, [all you] wise [spirits] of light; together laud the utterly brilliant firmament that girds [His] holy temple. [Praise] Him, godli[ke] spirits ...'

[40] John J. Collins, 'Powers in Heaven: God, Gods, and Angels in the Dead Sea Scrolls', in eds. John J. Collins and Robert A. Kugler, *Religion in the Dead Sea Scrolls* (Grand Rapids, MI: Eerdmans, 2000), 9–28.

his anointing into the closest proximity with God Himself.[41] 'We are reminded', as Collins concludes this article, 'that both Jewish and Christian traditions had common roots in the rich and varied world of Second Temple Judaism'. Thus, although 'For most Jews, the scandal of Christianity was the worship of the man Jesus', ... yet 'Christianity began as a Jewish sect ... and was in some way continuous with its Jewish matrix'.[42] Secondary divine beings, elected manifestations of particular divine incorporation, are in this particular world of Jewish ideas not idolatrous exceptions to the rule, but seemingly almost everyday occurrences. We are clearly here in the realm of hypostatic 'fluidity' presciently spelled out in Stead's earlier investigation of the Jewish roots of the Christian doctrine of the Trinity. If to worship truly is to be raised to angelic status in answering God to God, then the ecstatic union of such priests and worshippers implies some sort of divine participation closely akin to the 'dialectical' model also present in Romans 8.[43]

(3) *The Shekinah and the Cherubim in Rabbinic Commentary on the Song of Songs*: Our third and last example of this intra-divine logic of prayer and election returns to Stead's key proposal about an explicit Jewish vision of liturgical 'threeness-in-God' in even more explicit mode. But in the light of the foregoing analysis, we may perhaps give it a new and clarifying gloss. We recall that Stead highlighted the importance of the biblical image of the Lord God enthroned, attended by two angels. The systematic question that remained there, however, was whether this visual 'threeness' was somehow arbitrary, rather than intrinsic to some specific divine logic of operation. In the world of rabbinic commentary on the Song of Songs, this exegetical question

---

[41] William Horbury has helpfully reminded me that it is here that there is a blending with certain heavenly perceptions of Moses in the Jewish literature of the period, thus making a further link between the different strands of tradition I am tracing in this context: see e.g., Ecclesiasticus 45. 2 (partially preserved Hebrew, restored in light of the Greek): God 'honoured him as *elohim*, and made him strong among the high ones (angels)'; or *Assumption of Moses* 11. 17 (*spiritus*).

[42] Collins, 'Powers in Heaven', 28, 9.

[43] Philip Alexander also comments illuminatingly on this ecstatic dimension of the Qumranic practice of the *Songs of the Sabbath Sacrifice* in his *The Mystical Texts: Songs of the Sabbath Sacrifice and Related Manuscripts* (London & New York: Companion to the Qumran Scrolls: Library of Second Temple Studies 61, 2006), esp. 116–117.

arguably reaches some sort of resolution.[44] What interests me especially here is that, in the comparative Christian context, it is the mystical tradition (represented originally and notably by Origen, in his *Commentary on the Song* and in his text on prayer, *De oratione*) that takes up the implications of Romans 8 most vibrantly, and realizes that prayer at its deepest demands a transformative and incorporative 'trinitarian' logic that the spiritually immature are unlikely to comprehend.[45] Nor is it safe for the immature to *try* and comprehend it, according to Origen, because the erotic metaphors in which such intimacy is necessarily couched could lead to sexual aberration on the part of those who are spiritually immature.[46] Michael Fishbane shows us that, in fascinatingly similar guise – and not coincidentally, since Origen himself was the recipient of such Jewish teaching about the Song[47] – the rabbis will speculate about what we might call a triadic 'divine ontology' above the ark in the Temple, and one with profound 'erotic' overtones of unity and ecstasy.[48] God, according to Rabbi Nathan, is as it were self-contracted as *Shekinah* between the two encircling cherubim (see again Exod 25. 19–20): as Fishbane paraphrases him, 'the special nature of the ark was that the *Shekinah* spoke from above it, between the cherubim, and "there they empower Israel"'.[49] The 'dialectical' notion is again in play. Moreover, in a

---

[44] Two texts by Michael Fishbane have especially inspired these reflections: *Biblical Myth and Rabbinic Mythmaking* (Oxford: O.U.P., 2003), 173–177; and 'Anthological midrash and cultural paideia: The case of *Songs Rabba* 1.2', in eds. Peter Ochs and Nancy Levene, *Textual Reasonings: Jewish Philosophy and Text Study at the End of the Twentieth Century* (Grand Rapids, MI: Eerdmans, 2003), 32–51. Also see the important contextualizing article by Raphael Loewe, 'Apologetic Motifs in the Targum to the Song of Songs', in ed. Alexander Altmann, *Biblical Motifs: Origins and Transformations* (Cambridge, MA: Harvard University Press, 1966), 159–196.

[45] I discuss this theme in Origen in some detail in my *God, Sexuality and the Self*, 126–132.

[46] See ibid., 129, n. 31, and Origen, *Commentarium in Canticum Canticorum*, Prologue, 2. 39–40.

[47] On this interaction see the fine article, Reuven Kimelman, 'Rabbi Yochanan and Origen on the Song of Songs: A Third-Century Jewish-Christian Disputation', *Harvard Theological Review* 73 (1980), 567–595.

[48] See Fishbane, *Biblical Myth*, 174–175.

[49] Ibid., 174.

tradition handed down by Rab Qattina, the cherubim are there said to be *erotically* entwined, but only on the presumption and demand that the worshippers at the Temple are themselves suitably prepared by participatory obedience to the Law, and so enabling of this divine erotic fulfilment. In other words, as R. Yohanan may even perhaps have instructed Origen himself, the saying 'Yes' to the Law-in-oneself was not only marked by an incorporative triadic logic, but sealed by a 'kiss … with the kisses of the mouth' of the Song 1. 2 in a way that (one might say) gave back God to God.[50] *Without* suitably obedient preparation in thus approaching God, however, the effects on the worshipper could be damaging and dangerous. In short, this rich mythological reflection on the intra-divine complexity of the presence over the ark again had its incorporative logic and flow. To be drawn into this triadic flow was to manifest true, 'erotic' obedience to be a complex, erotically entwined God; to offend against it was to be driven out by the angels facing out the other way.[51]

Conclusions

What are we to conclude from this brief survey of relevant Jewish texts? The preliminary analysis I have attempted in this chapter of the possible 'triadic' prayer-based Jewish background to Christian trinitarianism has speculatively covered a considerable amount of territory; but its aim has been to open up a fresh investigation into the indissoluble relatedness of Judaism and Christianity in this fundamental arena of

---

[50] See *Song of Songs Rabba* to Song 1. 2, II, in eds. Ochs and Levene, *Textual Reasonings*, 45: 'Another interpretation of the verse, *O let him kiss me with the kisses of the mouth.* Said R. Yohanan, "An angel would carry forth each Word [viz., Commandment of the Ten Commandments] from before the Holy One, blessed be he, and bring it about to every Israelite and say to him, 'Do you accept upon yourself this Word?' … And the Israelite would say, 'Yes'. … Immediately, [the angel] would kiss him on his mouth, as it says: *You have been shown, that you might know* (Deut. 4.25) – that is, by means of [an angelic] messenger".'

[51] See again Fishbane, *Biblical Myth*, 175, citing *BT Baba Batra* 89a on the difference between the angels on either side of the ark facing inwards or facing outwards (cp. Exod 25. 19–20 and 1 Kings 6. 23–7), as signs of divine pleasure or displeasure, respectively.

worship, and specifically in connection with those problematic realms of Christian doctrine (Trinity, Christology) which *seem* most to divide the two traditions. If I am now to attempt a succinct account of the systematic implications of this investigation in closing, I think they must be these:

1. What I earlier called 'Supersessionism 1' (the idea of an actual exclusion of the Jews from the Christian covenant with God) has been, I have noted, largely expunged in the post-Holocaust period from contemporary Christian systematic theology. But this still leaves a remaining problem with the Christian claim for a *divine* Jesus who has purportedly completed all the promises of Israel ('Supersessionism 2').

2. Christian theology cannot effectively deal with the difficulties of this 'Supersessionism 2' by evasive talk of a trinitarian 'relationality' that gives no proper account of the distinctive role of the Spirit, especially in prayer and worship.

3. A prayer-based model of reflexive divinity and incorporative election evidenced in Romans 8 does, however, provide an alternative model of considerable ecumenical potential, one in which the 'Spirit'/third is no ineffectual afterthought, but the very wedge in God that opens up the prayerful elect, both Jewish and Christian, to a shared, but ineffable, future of Messianic hope.

4. This model, in turn, provides a way, as 'Supersessionism 2' does not, of thinking of the Christ event as itself still in the *process* of cosmic completion. The christological offense for Jews of the naming of Jesus as already Messiah still has to be grasped rather than denied, to be sure; but it is pneumatologically inflected in a special way and thus opened up to a shared future which is for now as yet unknown.

5. Perhaps then in closing we may dub this proposed position for Christian theology a new 'Supersessionism 3'. It does involve a remaining and emphatic Messianic claim for Jesus by Christians, yet one which is radically demanding – *at the level of the 'economy'* – in its openness to final trinitarian fulfilment, a fulfilment that implies a compelling sharing of Jesus's sufferings on behalf of a struggling cosmos, still opened to the Messianic eschaton (see Ro 8. 15–25; 31–39). This is not, as we have seen, a spiritual option for the faint-hearted in either tradition; for as the rabbinic materials we have just surveyed make clear, the realm of prayerful intimacy-in-God

(which tends to lead back to reflection on the *Song of Songs*, one way or another, in both traditions) is a perilous realm, delightful certainly to the initiated, the pure, and the spiritually mature, but dangerous indeed to those not yet prepared to be the fragile, suffering and ecstatic receptors of God's own prayer to God. This is the shared Jewish/Christian inheritance on which we have reflected in this chapter; its ecumenical implications, I plead in closing, are still open to further exploration and fulfilment.

6

On the 'Fearfulness' of Forgiveness: Jewish and Christian Perspectives

Introduction: The 'Impossibility' of Forgiveness

One does not have to come to Israel to learn that forgiveness is impossible: the evidence is everywhere to be seen – from the botched, if seemingly trivial, failures in our own familial or collegial relations at home, through to the unspeakable recent horrors of genocide, terrorism, war, abuse and torture, worldwide. But in Israel, the pain of this 'impossibility' is supremely acute and everywhere evident; and here no theological statement can be made on forgiveness that is not simultaneously a political comment. In this chapter, then, I shall be taking the *phenomenological* facts of this 'impossibility' of forgiveness as axiomatic, a strategy that initially may seem to fly in the face both of Jewish ritual practice and of Christian dominical command. I engage this strategy, however, deeply aware of the seeming impasse that often confronts post-Holocaust Jewish/Christian discussion of 'forgiveness': Simon Wiesenthal's justly famous *Sunflower* narrative (in both its editions) has produced an array of Jewish responses that resist the human granting of forgiveness from anyone else but the victim, over against

The Broken Body: Israel, Christ and Fragmentation, First Edition. Sarah Coakley.
© 2024 John Wiley & Sons Ltd. Published 2024 by John Wiley & Sons Ltd.

Christian ones that enjoin it unconditionally.[1] The gulf seems fixed. I want to get behind this impasse – and this apparent Jewish/Christian divergence – in order to re-engage the deep theological insight that *only God forgives*; and to re-think that insight through the lens of divine 'fearfulness'.

To the modern Christian mind, the conjunction may now seem odd – forgiveness and fearfulness – but I take my cue from the remarkable psalm verse, 130.4: 'For there is forgiveness with thee; *therefore thou art to be feared*' (כִּי־עִמְּךָ הַסְּלִיחָה לְמַעַן תִּוָּרֵא [*Kî-'imměkā has-sělîḥā: lěma'an tiuwārē*]). What follows will in fact be my own selective *midrash* on this verse, a collocation of rabbinic, patristic and Reformation responses to its challenge, which give the lie to the common suggestion that 'Jewish' and 'Christian' understandings of 'forgiveness' are somehow uncomplicatedly disjunctive. In fact, both traditions contain internal tensions and also important points of contact. The systematic theological conclusion that will emerge is that there is a costly *chronology* of forgiveness (when rightly understood as divine prerogative), comprehended only in physically enacted postures of awe and 'fear'; to know *divine* forgiveness is no less to know purgative terror. In short, for the phenomenological 'impossibility' of human forgiveness to be sublated, I must pass through a transformation well beyond that of a good-hearted *fiat* of the will, let alone of 'cheap grace', to what I might call the *ecstatic* dimension of forgiveness. I must, thereby, in some anticipatory sense, glimpse – eschatologically or christologically – the divine perspective of mercy itself.

Psalm 130. 4 and Its Interpreters, I: Jewish Tradition

Let me start with a brief autobiographical aside, which may help to explain my own fascination with this topic. I well recall first learning to sing the psalms in Anglican chant when I was about 12, and feeling

---

[1] Simon Wiesenthal and symposia, *The Sunflower* (New York: Schocken Books, 1976; revised and expanded ed., 1997). The story is told here of a dying SS man who seeks forgiveness from a Jew (Wiesenthal himself) for what he has personally done to Jews in the Holocaust; the narrative, and the responses, must be read closely by anyone concerned to comment.

the eerie shock, in the psalter of *The Book of Common Prayer*, of this particular verse: 'For there is mercy with thee: *therefore* thou art to be feared'.[2] Why the 'therefore', I mused?[3] From the perspective of a regnant modern political liberalism, of course, forgiveness or mercy seemed properly associated with letting people off, even with a certain wimpishness – the very opposite, surely, of 'fearful' evocations? The puzzle stayed with me. Later, when studying the psalms in Hebrew for Cambridge Tripos examinations, I discovered that the root of the noun 'forgiveness' here (סלח [*slḥ*]) is one of the few (like ברא [*br'*], to create) reserved for God alone; it is, as Jacob Milgrom has put it (in his commentary on *Numbers*), 'exclusively a divine gift'. Milgrom goes on: 'Only God can be the subject of *salaḥ*, never man! Thus, the inherent parameters of this word set it apart from anthropopathic notions: It does not convey the pardon or forgiveness that man is capable of extending ... Thus when God extends man His boon of *salaḥ*, He thereby indicates His desire for reconciliation with man in order to ... maintain His covenant'.[4] The seemingly equivalent verb root in Akkadian (*salāhu*), interestingly, means 'asperse' or 'sprinkle', the term often used in rituals of healing. Although the connection between the two verb roots remains speculative, it is at least intriguing

---

[2] This is Coverdale's translation, using the MT.

[3] In biblical Hebrew, the particle לְמַעַן, rendered here as 'therefore' does possess multiple valences or shades of meaning, including its use as an introduction to purpose clauses – 'in order that', 'so that'. The latter is indeed a common, even predominant, rendering of לְמַעַן, and one that could resolve something of the theological difficulty raised by Coverdale's translation. But I have chosen to take advantage of the particle's subtle ambiguity in an effort to grapple with that more difficult, theologically challenging, reading. As Bruce K. Waltke and M. O'Connor observe, '[i]n Hebrew (as in many languages) expressions of purpose and consequence are not always readily distinguished; the precise sense of the relevant constructions and particles must be determined from context' (*An Introduction to Biblical Hebrew Syntax* [Winona Lake, IN, Eisenbrauns, 1990], 638). They go on to reference the study of לְמַעַן by H. A. Brongers ('Die Partikel לְמַעַן in der biblisch-hebräischen Sprache,' *Oudtestamentische Studiën* 18 [1973] 84–96), who 'suggests that *lm'n* introduces a result clause in a few cases (Lev 20. 3, 2 Kgs 22. 17, Amos 2. 7), p. 89; he also notes that sometimes the particle is elliptical in sense and a paraphrase is necessary: ' "the consequence of which will be" ' (*An Introduction to Biblical Hebrew Syntax*, 638–639, n. 25).

[4] Jacob Milgrom, *Numbers. The JPS Torah Commentary* (Philadelphia: The Jewish Publication Society, 1990), 395–396.

that the Akkadian parallel is particularly associated with purification or apotropaic protection.[5] But why then the link to 'fear', specifically?[6]

It should be noted, firstly, that the collocation of forgiveness/mercy and fear in the Hebrew Bible is by no means limited to this instance in Psalm 130. Perhaps the most striking parallel, semantically, is to be found in I Kings 8. 39–40: here, in Solomon's dedication prayer to God in the temple, the same logic of forgiveness and fear is enunciated: 'Then hear in heaven, your dwelling place, and forgive (וְסָלַחְתָּ [wĕ-sālaḥtā]) ... so that (לְמַעַן [lĕma'an]) they might fear you (יִרָאוּךָ [yirā'ûkā]) ...'. In this instance, as in the psalm verse, the fear is *consequent* on the forgiveness, note, rather than a precondition of it. But we may also find instances of the opposite logic, where human fear *precedes* divine forgiveness (e.g., Ben Sirach 2. 7–11, 15–18); and we shall shortly discuss the important way in which the penitential rituals of the New Year and Day of Atonement were to spread out this second logic along a temporal chronology of annual transformation. Yet the former motif (more puzzling, as we have noted, to the liberal Christian mind), keeps us from any easy collapse of the conundrum into the idea that fear is *supplanted* by mercy. For behind both these variations, and one might say more fundamentally,[7] lies the central insistence of Exodus 34. 6–7 on the absolute metaphysical inseparability of divine mercy and judgement: 'The Lord, the Lord, a God merciful and gracious, slow to anger, and abounding in steadfast love and faithfulness ... forgiving (נֹשֵׂא [nose']) iniquity and transgression

---

[5] *The Assyrian Dictionary of the Oriental Institute of the University of Chicago* (Chicago: Oriental Institute, 1984), *ad loc.*

[6] The root ירא (as both noun and verb), when used with God as the explicit object or in the context of an encounter with the divine, is (notoriously) multivalent in biblical Hebrew, with meanings ranging from 'awe' and 'terror' (cf. Gen 28. 17; Exod 3. 6; Ps 33. 8) to 'reverence' and even 'obedience' or 'right conduct' (cf. Gen 22. 12; Prov 8. 13; 16. 6). Robert Murray, S.J., has suggested to me that the better, simpler reading of the verse (in accord with the NRSV) would be: 'But there is forgiveness with you, so that you may be *revered*'. But taking into account the possible ambiguity of ירא, for the purposes of this chapter I would like to grapple with a more difficult, discomforting reading ('fear' or 'terror') and its theological implications.

[7] See R.W.L. Moberly, 'How May We Speak of God? A Reconsideration of the Nature of Biblical Theology,' *Tyndale Bulletin* 53.2 (2002) 177–202, for a new exegesis of the centrality of Ex. 34. 6–7 for the future of 'biblical theology'.

The Broken Body

and sin, yet by no means clearing the guilty, but visiting the iniquity of the parents upon the children and the children's children ...'

So central, in fact, is this idea of *simultaneous* divine threat and divine forgiveness, and so important for our own discussion systematically, that it is worth reflecting briefly on the rabbinic treatment of this theme before turning to the more specific history of Jewish interpretation of Psalm 130.4, to which it is intrinsically connected. Of immediate relevance is the Tannaitic saying in *Sifre* (on Deuteronomy) that '*Only in regard to God* do we find love combined with fear and fear combined with love'.[8] The exclusiveness of this statement is crucial: a lazy or careless extension of this principle to the human realm would be inherently idolatrous. In similar vein, *Midrash Rabbah* on Exodus (3. 14) famously expounds the mysterious and multi-faceted nature of the divine:

> R. Abba b. Mammel said: God said unto Moses: 'Thou wishest to know My name. Well, I am called according to My work; sometimes I am called "Almighty God", "Lord of Hosts", "God", "Lord". When I am judging created beings, I am called "God", and when I am waging war against the wicked, I am called "Lord of Hosts". When I suspend judgment for a man's sins, I am called "*El Shadday*" (Almighty God), and when I am merciful towards My world, I am called "*Adonai*", for "*Adonai*" refers to the Attributes of Mercy, as it is said: *The Lord, the Lord* (Adonai, Adonai), *God, merciful and gracious* (Exodus 34. 6). Hence *I AM THAT I AM* in virtue of my deeds'.[9]

As Urbach charts in fascinating detail in *The Sages*, this theme of God's simultaneous judgement and mercy (associated with two different names, sometimes hypostasized) was worked out in complex multiple forms in the rabbinic period, not always consistently associating the different names with the different attributes,[10] and not always maintaining the absolute indissolubility of their conjunction.[11] Thus Urbach contrasts the view of Gamaliel, who 'incorporated the

---

[8] *Sifre. A Tannaitic Commentary on the Book of Deuteronomy*, trans. Reuven Hammer (New Haven, CT: Yale University Press, 1986), 59 (Piska 32), my emphasis.

[9] *Midrash Rabbah. Exodus* (trans. Rabbi Dr. S.M. Lehrman; London: The Soncino Press, 1983), 64 (*Exodus Rabbah* III.6 *ad* Exod 3:14).

[10] Ephraim E. Urbach, *The Sages: Their Concepts and Beliefs*, trans. Israel Abrahams (Cambridge, MA: Harvard University Press, 1979), 452–453, etc.

[11] Ibid., 464 ff.

attribute of justice into that of compassion' (allowing the possibility of manipulating divine compassion by human compassionate behaviour), with the ingenious idea of the Amora R. Samuel bar Naḥman (that the divine attribute of justice could be *converted* into that of compassion); but he also compares both these opinions with the older, Tannaitic idea that the two divine attributes remain equal (and indeed are necessarily balanced in order that the creation may endure).[12] In short, it is far from the case that this fundamental theme is consistently interpreted in the rabbinic discussion; but it is indisputable that it is re-visited constantly.

It is when we examine (against this broad background) the specific liturgies of repentance associated with the High Holy Days of *Rosh Hashana* and *Yom Kippur,* and the Ten Days of Repentance between them, that the history of the interpretation of Psalm 130. 4 becomes particularly significant. The psalm is woven into the liturgies on both days.[13] And prima facie it would seem that the logic of fear *preceding* repentance is here given preeminent emphasis, and indeed is spread out chronologically through the intervening days of repentance. As we read in *Leviticus Rabbah* XXX. 7:

> ... on the eve of the New Year the leaders of the generation fast, and the Holy One, blessed be He, absolves them of a third of their iniquities. From New Year to the Day of Atonement private individuals fast, and the Holy One, blessed be He, absolves them of a third of their iniquities. On the Day of Atonement, everyone fasts, men, women, and children, and the Holy One, blessed be He, says to Israel: 'Let bygones be bygones; from now onwards we shall begin a new account'. ... R. Aḥa expounded: *For with Thee there is forgiveness* (Ps. CXXX, 4)

---

[12] Ibid., 456, 457, 459.

[13] See *The Complete ArtScroll Machzor. Rosh Hashanah. Nusach Ashkenaz* (Brooklyn, NY: Mesorah Publications, Ltd., 1985), 264–265; and *The Complete ArtScroll Machzor. Yom Kippur. Nusach Ashkenaz* (Brooklyn, NY: Mesorah Publications, Ltd., 1986), 324–325. Also see Harry P. Nasuti, 'Plumbing the Depths: Genre Ambiguity and Theological Creativity in the Interpretation of Psalm 130', *The Idea of Biblical Interpretation: Essays in Honor of James L. Kugel*, eds. Hindy Najman and Judith H. Newman (Leiden: Brill, 2004), 95–124, at 109–110.

signifies: forgiveness *waits* with thee from New Year. Why so long? *That Thou mayest be feared;* in order to impose Thy awe upon Thy creatures.[14]

It would seem, then, that the time-span of 'waiting' in 'fear' is the necessary *condition* of the coming of divine forgiveness: 'waiting' is, after all, a key theme in the same psalm (see vs. 5), and one commented upon elsewhere in the *Midrash Rabbah* in eschatological vein.[15] But in fact, on closer inspection, it is not the case that the conundrum of the 'ordering' of forgiveness and fear is hereby liturgically resolved by a transformation of fear into forgiveness; the reverse logic (from forgiveness *to* fear) is also given a new, albeit subtle, liturgical instantiation. For it is also in the liturgies of the High Holy Days that an exegetical link between Psalm 130 and the book of Jonah (read as the *haftarah* of the afternoon service on the Day of Atonement) becomes part of the exegetical nexus; so that by implication the 'depths' of Psalm 130. 1 (*de profundis*) become identified with Jonah's own perilous – but miraculously salvific – descent into the 'depths' of the sea.[16] Since judgement, mercy and repentance (and their wholly unexpected sets of conjunction in Jonah and the Ninevites) are central to the book of Jonah, the puzzle of why – as in our psalm verse – forgiveness might *result* in 'fear' also takes on new meaning. As a recent modern commentator on Jonah, Uriel Simon, puts it with grace:

> Jonah argues on behalf of strict justice against the merciful God, who repents of his sentence. ... To the advocate of strict justice it is clear that wickedness abounds not only because of the viciousness of evildoers, but also because the Judge of all the earth does not treat them with the full severity of the law. He must learn that the world can exist only through the unfathomable amalgam of justice and mercy, that fear of sin is produced not only by fear of punishment, but also by awe at the sublimity of salvation ... and by fascination with grace and absolution ('Yours is the power to forgive so that you may be held in awe' [Ps. 130. 4]). If Jonah is to be rid of the notion that divine

---

[14] *Midrash Rabbah. Leviticus*, trans. Rev. J. Israelstam (chs. I–XIX) and Judah J. Slotki (chs. XX–XXXVII) (London: The Soncino Press, 1983), 389–390 (*Leviticus Rabbah* XXX.7 *ad* Lev 23:40). This material is repeated in *Ecclesiastes Rabbah* IX.7.

[15] *Midrash Rabbah. Genesis*, vol. 2, trans. Rabbi Dr. H. Freedman (London: The Soncino Press, 1983), 964–965 (*Genesis Rabbah* XCVIII.14 *ad* Gen 49:18).

[16] See Nasuti, 'Plumbing the Depths', 110.

compassion expresses weakness of mind and softness of heart, he must experience the Lord's heavy hand directed against himself.[17]

As Simon explains, it appears to be precisely this reading of Jonah that is in play in the afternoon liturgy of the Day of Atonement; for at the end of the reading the last three verses of the book of Micah are appended (Micah 7. 18–20), 'through which Jonah, as it were, recants his condemnation of the attributes of compassion and grace (Jonah 4. 2) by reciting the praise of God'.[18] In short, Jonah *ends* with 'awe'/fear; his earlier views on justice have been dumbfounded. In similar vein, *Exodus Rabbah* 1, 6 insists that 'fear' is the outcome, not only the prerequisite, of forgiveness: 'Israel is steeped in sin through the *Evil Yezer* in their body, but they do repentance and the Lord forgives their sins every year, and *renews their heart to fear him*'.[19]

One might say, then, that the exegesis of Psalm 130.4 in early rabbinic context was vitally flavoured by its liturgical setting. It becomes woven intrinsically into the annual, embodied, practices of repentance and forgiveness, in which, as Schechter puts it, 'the prerogative of granting pardon is *entirely in the hands of God, every mediator being excluded* ...'[20] However, this development in no way resolves the conundrum of the ordering of fear and forgiveness, as we have shown; and nor does it relieve the sense of the *human* 'impossibility' of forgiveness, given the necessary divine initiative and the final mystery of the relation of the 'attributes' of God. Small wonder, then, that we find later, medieval, discussion of vs. 4 of the psalm still picking at the difficulty of its exegesis. Rashi thinks that the sole point of vs. 4 is that 'You have not given the authority to any agent/intermediary to forgive [he then quotes Exodus 23] ... and therefore no person will trust in the forgiveness of anyone else [but God]'.[21] Abraham Ibn Ezra, on the other hand, thinks that the 'fearing' means that 'when You forgive my transgressions, sinners will hear this and repent, putting aside their own sins. If You don't forgive, they will not fear You and will do

---

[17] Uriel Simon, *Jonah. The JPS Bible Commentary* (Philadelphia: The Jewish Publication Society, 1999), xii.

[18] Ibid., xiii.

[19] Cited in Solomon Schechter, *Aspects of Rabbinic Theology* (Woodstock, VT: Jewish Lights Publishing, 1993 reprint), 304, my italics.

[20] Ibid., 294, my italics. Also see Urbach, *The Sages*, 462ff.

[21] Rashi to Ps 130. 4.

their pleasure, as much as they like'.[22] Kimḥi, in turn, cites Ibn Ezra but at the same time seemingly expands on Rashi's more fundamental idea: 'God has given power to the higher intelligences to perform his *will* on earth, but *forgiveness* rests not with them but with him. Why is this so? It is in order that men may not say to themselves: if we sin, the angels will be reconciled to us and will forgive our sins. (Therefore Scripture) proceeds to make it known that forgiveness is not with them, *in order that men may fear God*, for with him there is forgiveness and with none other besides him'.[23]

Can we say, then, in concluding this section, that in the biblical and rabbinic witness forgiveness is in some sense *intrinsically* 'fearful'? On the evidence we have surveyed, that would appear now to be a non-hyperbolic conclusion, mandated by the abiding insistence that only God can forgive; yet we must not forget – before passing to a comparison with the strikingly different Christian interpretation of Ps. 130. 4 – that at key moments in the Hebrew Scriptures human *participation* in the logic of divine forgiveness also allows that same fearfulness to 'rub off' on chosen human representatives without in any way undermining the divine uniqueness. Most notable and moving here is the story of Joseph (described of late by Jon Levenson as 'the most sophisticated narrative in the Jewish or Christian Bibles'[24]); for at the end of the story, when Joseph has finally revealed himself to his brothers, and been reconciled with his father, his pronouncement to his brothers (who naturally fear a continuing resentment) coheres most strikingly with the themes of Psalm 130. 4. Both the brothers and Joseph weep as the brothers abase themselves before Joseph and ask for forgiveness (Genesis 50. 16–18); but Joseph replies: 'Do not be afraid! *Am I in the place of God?* Even though you intended to do harm to me God intended it for good …' (Genesis 50. 19–20). As Gary Anderson concludes, in a remarkable study of the Joseph narrative in Jewish and Christian exegesis, 'we are those brothers, and only the Elect One of Israel can speak the words of absolution'.[25]

---

[22] Abraham Ibn Ezra to Ps 130. 4.

[23] Eds. and trans. Joshua Baker and Ernest W. Nicholson, *The Commentary of Rabbi David Kimḥi on Psalms CXX-CL* (Cambridge: C.U.P., 1973), 37–39, my italics.

[24] Jon D. Levenson, *The Death and Resurrection of the Beloved Son: The Transformation of Child Sacrifice in Judaism and Christianity* (New Haven: Yale University Press, 1993), 142.

[25] Gary A. Anderson, 'Joseph and the Passion of Our Lord', in eds. Ellen F. Davis and Richard B. Hays, *The Art of Reading Scripture* (Grand Rapids, MI: Eerdmans, 2003), 198–215, at 215.

It is, however, with this challenging thought (to which we shall duly return at the end of this chapter) that we now pass on to examine the Christian reading of Psalm 130. 4.

And here some surprises await us.

Psalm 130. 4 (129. 4 LXX) and Its Interpreters, II: Christian Tradition

The first surprise, which mightily de-railed much of early Christian reflection on our psalm verse in Greek, was a mistranslation by the LXX of the Hebrew of Psalm 130. 4b ('therefore thou art to be feared') to read instead 'according to thy law' (and then often run on into vs. 5).[26] In short, the crucial theological 'surd' that we have been considering – the intense collocation of fear and forgiveness – was dissolved in one stroke by the Greek Bible, and so passed its adjustment into early Christian exegesis. We shall consider in a moment (and here one can only speculate) whether this change could perhaps have come about partly for *theological* reasons: did the translator baulk at the idea of the 'fearfulness of forgiveness', or was he merely misled by a variant text? Whatever lay behind the change, however, the effect on Christian exegesis was – one way or another – that of a flattening of the intensity of the paradox that had so exercised rabbinic thinking at precisely this juncture.

The second major exegetical feature we shall outline is doubtless less surprising, but nonetheless of great significance theologically for divergent Jewish/Christian reflections on the theme of forgiveness. For once the idea of 'law' is introduced into vs. 4 by the LXX, it sets off, for Christian exegesis, a stark contrast – *à la* Romans 7 – between the divine 'forgiveness' available now in *Christ*, and the era of Jewish 'law' that has been sublated. In short, the text becomes an opportunity for the enunciation of a Christian (and specifically Pauline) dispensationalism that relegates both 'law' and 'fear' to an era superseded by that of 'forgiveness': 'law' and (Christic) 'forgiveness' are set in opposition. Doubtless this change is also implicitly affected by the gospel materials on forgiveness – which we can touch on only briefly in this chapter. Interestingly, however, this move also

---

[26] *Septuaginta. X. Psalmi cum Odis*, ed. A. Rahlfs (Göttingen: Vandenhoeck & Ruprecht, 1931), Ps 129. 4–5: ὅτι παρὰ σοὶ ἱλασμός ἐστιν ἕνεκεν τοῦ νόμου σου· ὑπέμεινά σε κύριε ὑπέμεινεν ἡ ψυχή μου εἰς τὸν λόγον σου.

corresponds with a return to the Jewish liturgical association of the psalm with the book of Jonah, but along with this re-connection, especially in later (medieval) monastic interpretation, comes a Christian intensification of the idea of Psalm 130 as a 'psalm of ascent': it is 'from the depths' – like Jonah – that a pray-er of distinct maturity prays, one whose perception of 'forgiveness' has the quality both of 'profundity' and of increasing closeness to the divine.

Finally, however – and here is our third *novum* or 'surprise', though one perhaps not entirely unexpected – it is Martin Luther who restores the sense of the simultaneity of 'fear' and 'forgiveness' to the exegesis of Psalm 130. Not only does he go back, courtesy of humanistic scholarship, to the reading of the Masoretic text, and thus recoups the original reading of vs. 4b; but he interprets the psalm existentially, seeing it as a kind of witness to the maelstrom of his own experience of fear, justification and grace: it becomes an essentially 'Reformation' psalm. What is consciously discarded, however, in this Lutheran return to what we might call the 'Tannaitic' perception of simultaneous judgement and mercy in the divine, is the Christian medieval sense of spiritual 'ascent'. Bridling at 'works righteousness', Luther will no longer range the psalms of ascent upon a ladder of spiritual elevation, as had his medieval predecessors. Thus, precisely as the theme of the 'fearfulness of forgiveness' is retrieved in Lutheran thought, it is also seemingly dislocated from any mandated or manipulable *process* of 'ascent'. The simultaneity of fear and forgiveness is *fixed*, both existentially and theologically; it finds no easy resolution in a spiritual 'improvement' that might transmute or resolve that particular fear that is due only to God.

With this brief preview of the Christian exegesis of Psalm 130.4 in mind, let us now fill in some of the exegetical details of these three developments before moving to our systematic conclusions.

Firstly, the special Hebrew word for God's forgiveness (הַסְּלִיחָה [*hassĕlîḥā*]) is translated in the LXX ἱλασμός (*hilasmos*), a word with cultic overtones of expiation, and one therefore naturally referred by Christian exegesis to Christ's saving work (in the Latin it becomes *propitiatio*). The textual change in 129.5a in the LXX (130.4b MT) from 'therefore you are to be feared' to 'according to your law' (ἕνεκεν τοῦ νόμου σου [*heneken tou nomou sou*]) is a slip – if it is such – relatively easy to explain linguistically: what we have as the verb in the Masoretic text (תִּוָּרֵא [*tiwwārē'*]) has been read as תּוֹרָה (*tôrā* – 'Torah/law'), and the preceding לְמַעַן (*lĕma'an* – 'therefore' in the MT) translated in its prepositional sense as 'for the sake of'. Since all that was written in those days was the consonants, the confusion is understandable enough; on the other hand, the appearance of 'His word' (MT) or 'your word' (LXX, τὸν λόγον σου [*ton logon sou*]) in the succeeding – and perhaps parallel – vs. 5b raises the possibility that the LXX is reading a variant text rather than creatively (or defensively) exegeting the Masoretic version. As we shall see, the Greek Christian exegetes tend to flounder at this point, some of them also showing an awareness of more than one reading; and – yet more interestingly – the Syriac *Peshitta* seems altogether flummoxed, leaving out the offending two words altogether.[27] In short, this was a psalm verse that defeated a number of readers. The possibility that the change by the LXX might be a defensive reading, resisting theologically the idea of a fear *consequent* on forgiveness, is intriguing for our purposes;[28] but it cannot be said to have any obvious evidential support: there is no such parallel move by the LXX translators, for instance, to effect a similar change to the substance of I Kings 8. 39–40, where – as we have noted above – the nexus of forgiveness and fear is similarly expressed.

The result of this textual *aporia* is, for the early Christian exegesis of our verse, initially something of a disappointment, granted that the interesting collocation of fear and forgiveness has now been obliterated.[29] Unsurprisingly, Origen immediately identifies the ἱλασμός/*propitiatio* as Christ, and identifies the 'depths' of vs. 1 as a form of 'deep' prayer only achieved by the Spirit crying out in one's heart.[30] John Chrysostom, however, does not make the explicit christological identification, but simply interprets 'because with you there is propitiation', as, 'It is not in our good deeds but in your goodness that the possibility lies of escaping punishment'.[31] Interestingly, he then shows awareness of *three* possible textual variants for vs. 4b or

---

[27] With only one small textual variant showing, the *Peshitta* omits vs. 4b.

[28] See Hermann Gunkel, *Die Psalmen*, 6. Auflage (Göttingen: Vandenhoek & Ruprecht, 1986), 561, who remarks that the text may have presented an '*Anstoss*'.

[29] See Nasuti, 'Plumbing the Depths', 110ff. for a very useful treatment of the exegesis of Psalm 130 in the early Christian fathers. Nasuti is however primarily focussing on vs. 1.

[30] Origen, *Sel. Ps.* on Ps 130 (PG 12: 1647–8).

[31] *St. John Chrysostom: Commentary on the Psalms*, II, trans. Robert Charles Hill (Brookline, MA: Holy Cross Orthodox Press, 1998), 194.

5a: 'for the sake of your Law', 'for the sake of your name', and 'so that you may be fearsome'. Ostensibly floundering as a result of this variety of options, he can apparently make no sense at all of the last one: 'Fearsome to whom?' he asks rhetorically, 'To the enemy, to schemers, to my foes?'[32] We note therefore that he has instantly bracketed out the possibility that the divine might be (appropriately) 'fearsome' to *us*. Theodoret of Cyrus also shows cognizance of a variety of possible readings (including the reference to 'fear'), but again he havers, seemingly baffled; but like Origen he explicitly reads the psalm as christological: on the concluding vs. 8 he attributes the redemption of Israel to 'the Lamb of God'.[33]

The early Greek exegetes, then, make little or no sense of the theme of the collocation of fear and forgiveness, largely for reasons of textual uncertainty. When we get to the Latin tradition, however, several fascinating (and theologically important) changes occur. Although Jerome of course translated both Hebrew and Greek versions of the Psalter into Latin,[34] Augustine is commenting on the Latin that follows the LXX text of vs. 4b. However, in his case, this does not mean that he avoids the issue of the relation of judgement to mercy, because he reads the whole psalm now through the lens of the Pauline theology of justification:

> "For there is propitiation with Thee" (vs. 4). And what is this propitiation, except sacrifice? And what is sacrifice, save that which has been offered for us? The pouring forth of innocent blood blotted out all the sins of the guilty ... For if there were not mercy with Thee, if Thou chosest to be Judge only, and didst refuse to be merciful, ... Who could abide this? ... There is therefore one hope: "for the sake of Thy law have I borne Thee, O Lord". What law? That which made men guilty ... There is therefore a law of the mercy of God, a law of the propitiation of God. The one was a law of fear, the other is a law of love ...[35]

---

32 Ibid., 32.

33 *Theodoret of Cyrus: Commentary on the Psalms – Psalms 73–150*, trans. Robert C. Hill (Washington, DC: The Catholic University of America Press, 2001), 303.

34 The modern Vulgate has parallel texts of *Psalmi Iuxta Hebr.* and *Iuxta LXX*, even though the 'Gallican' version became standard under Alcuin.

35 *Augustine: Expositions on the Book of Psalms* in *Nicene and Post-Nicene Fathers* vol. 8 (reprint, Peabody, MA: Hendrickson Publishers, 1994), 613b.

Alluding then to both Galatians and Romans, Augustine re-introduces the tension of fear and mercy, despite his LXX reading of vs 4b. But the crucial Christian novelty here is that 'fear' is necessarily perceived as negative: it is the slavish 'fear' of failure in the realm of the law, and is therefore presented as that which is dispensationally *over-come* in Christic justification by faith. The possibility of a remaining 'awe/fear' that might intrinsically relate to divine 'forgiveness' is, at least in this context, rhetorically swept aside; and this is despite the fact that Augustine also recaptures the identification of the psalm with Jonah's whale. But the 'depths' are read – not as in Jewish liturgy as a place of re-learning 'fear', nor as in Origen as the deep places of the Spirit – but as the 'depths' of *sin*; for 'this mortal life is our deep', says Augustine, from which only Christ can redeem.[36]

It is in the later Western monastic interpretations of Cassiodorus and Gregory the Great, however, that we get an interesting re-reading of this Augustinian set of moves, which now stresses the importance of the psalm as one of the highest in what Jerome translated as a 'canticum graduum' (Psalms 120–134).[37] Despite the fact that in both exegetes the connection with Jonah is retained, and vs. 3 interpreted – as with Augustine – as ruling out the possibility of any human merit before God, nonetheless the 'depths' become a place from which a spiritual advance may be made. The 'depths' in Cassiodorus become the purgative place of the learning of *humility*, not – as in Augustine – the unredeemable depths of sin: 'for those who have buried themselves in the bowels of the holy humility are all the closer to the Highest'.[38] Rather differently, Gregory the Great returns to Augustine's insistence that Jonah's 'depths' *were* sinful as well as marine ones (the language of 'perversity' and 'disobedience' is used), but he continues Cassiodorus's interest in the motif of spiritual advancement and 'ascent'.[39] When Gregory comes to exegete vs. 4, however (again following the LXX reading: *propter legem tuam*), he makes the now-standard identification of the *propitiatio* with Christ; but – unlike Augustine – he does not exclusively press the psalm into the template of Paul's theory of law

---

[36] Ibid., 613a.

[37] See *Cassiodorus: Explanation of the Psalms*, vol. III, *ACW* 53, trans. P.G. Walsh (New York: Paulist Press, 1991), 311; and Gregory the Great, *Expositio in Septem Psalmos Penitentiales* (PL 49: 630–632).

[38] *Cassiodorus*, 312–313.

[39] PL 49: 632 and 630–631.

and gospel, but first stresses that 'the law of God *is* mercy', appealing to the Lukan theology of Christ's forgiveness of those crucified alongside him, and citing from Luke the dominical command to 'love your enemies'.[40] This is a significant shift, once again deflecting Western Christian exegesis of the psalm from a positive reflection on 'fear'.

With Luther, then, all is changed and made new. As Nasuti's recent article underscores, Luther saw Psalm 130 as 'the height of the Old Testament gospel', as a 'Pauline psalm', and as the basis for one of his greatest Reformation hymns: *Aus tiefer Not*.[41] The connection with Jonah is lost; but at the same time all the great Lutheran themes are constellated into his exegesis of this psalm: the unavoidability of divine judgement and human fear, the necessity of justification in Christ, the possibility of salvation (a rising 'from the deep') only through 'grace' and 'faith'. The return to the Masoretic reading of vs 4b is of course partly what enables this re-emphasis on 'fear'; but it is also Luther's particular re-reading of the Pauline gospel, and his own autobiographical experiences of *Anfechtungen*. As he opens his commentary: 'These are noble, passionate, and very profound words [*sc.*'out of the depths'] of a truly penitent heart that is most deeply moved in its distress. In fact, this cannot be understood except by those who have felt and experienced it. We are all in deep and great misery, but we do not all feel our condition'.[42] Like Augustine, then, Luther not only casts 'the depths' as a generic human condition of wretchedness, but reads 'fear' as that which characterizes the 'cross of the old man'. Nonetheless,

> ... if anyone does not fear God, he does not implore, nor is he forgiven. In order, therefore, to gain God's grace, He and He alone is to be feared, just as He alone forgives. For if anyone fears something besides God, he seeks the favor and mercy of this other thing and does not care about God. But whoever fears God desires His grace and does not care about anything that is not God; for he knows that no one can harm him if God is gracious to him.[43]

Thus this part of the commentary leads us to identify a crucial two-sidedness in Luther's treatment of 'fear': the cringing, manipulative

---

[40] Ibid., 635–636.

[41] See Nasuti, 'Plumbing the Depths', 115–117.

[42] *Luther's Works*, vol. 14, trans. Arnold Guebert (St. Louis: Concordia Publishing House, 1958), 189.

[43] Ibid., 191.

'fear' of the 'old man', and the appropriate, distinctive 'fear' of the 'new man'. For we see that Luther does not technically *resolve* (all) fear into hope; the simultaneity of the two existential responses continues in an important sense to co-exist in the justified soul, even as hope in Christ's salvation is fully acknowledged as *theologically* triumphant; that is why Luther can conclude his commentary on Psalm 130 by insisting that 'we should not be merciful to ourselves, but severe and angry, so that God may be merciful to us and not angry'.[44] The *neurotic* 'fear' of Luther's youth has gone ('those who feel that God is angry and unmerciful do not know him aright'); but the appropriate, and appropriately *unique*, sense of deference and unworthiness before God endures even as His 'kindness and mercy' is fully received. Even as 'works righteousness' is decried, then (and hence, too, all hope in purposeful 'spiritual progress' of the sort enunciated in the medieval exegesis of the 'Psalms of Ascent'), even so is right 'fearfulness' before *God* retrieved as an enduring lesson of humility and trust in 'God's grace alone'.

Systematic Conclusions: On the Fearfulness of Forgiveness

I said at the start of this chapter that Jewish and Christian exegeses of Psalm 130 are not uncomplicatedly disjunctive, that both traditions are internally complex, but that indeed they also contain important points of contact. Although this chapter has provided only a selective account of Jewish and Christian readings of Psalm 130. 4, we have proceeded far enough, I trust, to establish sufficient empirical evidence to support that initial claim. In particular, the rabbinic, and especially rabbinic/liturgical, understanding of the implications of the 'fearfulness of forgiveness' represents a startling point of convergence with Luther's thought on the matter; and that the alarmingly anti-semitic Luther should thereby present us with such a point of agreement is a spiritual irony which I can only note and leave for our reflection. If it be objected that Luther's resistance to 'spiritual progress' (in the sense of 'works righteousness') sets his position ostensibly *against* the Jewish practices of graduated repentance in the 10 days between the New Year and the Day of Atonement, it might be worth voicing a reminder that Luther nonetheless carried over from

---

[44] Ibid., 194.

Catholicism both the practices of auricular confession, and a profound commitment to the transformative liturgical experience of entering into the days of the Passion.[45]

However in closing I want to edge a little further towards my bold assertion, also made at the start of this chapter, that because – humanly speaking – forgiveness *is* 'impossible', it is a vibrant sense of the 'fearfulness of (divine) forgiveness' that needs to be recaptured if we are to move beyond the apparently disjunctive 'Jewish/Christian' alternatives that characterize the post-Holocaust period. Whilst a defence of my (implicit) claim that Jesus's own position on 'forgiveness' is entirely compatible with this stress on holy fear goes well beyond the confines of this particular chapter,[46] suffice it to say that the more one pursues the insistence on the uniquely divine characteristic of forgiveness, the higher one's Christology is pressed.[47] It is not for nothing that Teresa of Ávila's account of achieved Christic 'union' in the 7th 'Mansion' includes simultaneously a *renewed* stress on holy fear, and the passing comment that to live in such 'union' is for the first time to see what it means to love one's enemies.[48] Nor is it insignificant that Teresa's

---

[45] See Gary Anderson's treatment of the Lutheran liturgy in his 'Joseph and the Passion of Our Lord', 212–215.

[46] It would involve developing my views in the following ways: 1. that Mark 2. 1–12 (and paras.) does not mandate an easy forgiveness by 'every mother's son' (one possible rendition of the ambiguous title 'Son of Man'), but rather makes an astonishingly high christological claim for Jesus's identity; and 2. that the Matthean Sermon on the Mount makes demands about forgiveness which remain 'impossible' unless mediated *through* Jesus, the Son of God.

[47] Hence the nice irony that, in this case of 'forgiveness', an agreement between Jewish and Christian perspectives of the sort for which I have been arguing does not result in the whittling down of Christological claims, but rather the opposite.

[48] *The Interior Castle*, VII. 2, in *The Collected Works of St. Teresa of Ávila*, vol. 2, trans. Kieran Kavanaugh and Otilio Rodriguez (Washington, DC: ICS Publications, 1980), 436 (§9 '... much greater fear ...'); and VII. 3 (ibid., 439 [§5 the soul's 'love for its persecutors'], 443 [§§13–14 'living with fear']). This 'ecstatic' dimension of forgiveness as articulated by Teresa of Ávila is echoed in the twentieth century (during the time of the London *Blitz*) by Charles Williams, who, in his *The Forgiveness of Sins* (London: Geoffrey Bles, The Centenary Press, 1942, esp. chs. 6–7), argues that true forgiveness of one's enemies can occur only by means of a mystical union with Christ which enables one to pass over into one's enemies' shoes, and thus to see oneself from their perspective.

mentor and friend, John of the Cross (who shared with her a partial Jewish descent), could discourse so unforgettably on the fearful purgations of self-knowledge in the 'night of spirit' preceding 'union' as a death-like transformation equivalent to 'being in the belly of the whale'.[49] The essentially *participatory* vision that the Carmelites give us of 'mystical union' enables a glimpse at the divine perspective on forgiveness perhaps equivalent only to that which we noted in the Joseph narratives of Genesis.[50]

Let us return finally to Simon Wiesenthal and *The Sunflower*. If this reflection on the Jewish and Christian interpretation of Psalm 130. 4 has shown us anything, it has revealed a certain nexus of themes that attend the authentic perception of the 'fearfulness of forgiveness': the maintenance of awe at the *uniqueness* of the divine prerogative to forgive; the patient *waiting* on the chronology of that process; the embodied *practices* of repentance, purgation and self-knowledge; and finally the *participation* in a flow of compassion which can strictly only come from God. Seen now in this light, Wiesenthal's response to the dying SS-man, his wholly silent but compassionate reception of the German's apology, but his refusal to absolve what only God can, was as eloquent an instantiation of the principles of Psalm 130. 4 as one could hope for. Against the stark oppositions of the polarized modern 'Jewish' and 'Christian' reactions to the narrative, I therefore cast my vote with the small minority of respondents who see Wiesenthal's silent response as wholly theologically appropriate; indeed, from the perspective of the themes of this chapter, it was itself a small, but highly significant, participation in the 'fearfulness of divine forgiveness'.[51]

---

[49] *The Dark Night*, II. 6, in *The Collected Works of St. John of the Cross*, revised ed., trans. Kieran Kavanaugh and Otilio Rodriguez (Washington, DC: ICS Publications, 1991), 404.

[50] See again, Gary Anderson, 'Joseph and the Passion of Our Lord', 212–215.

[51] See for instance the contribution of Friedrich Heer to the original symposium of *The Sunflower* (1976), 125–128. Also see the important discussion of the true nature of apology and its relation to the possibility of forgiveness in Aaron Lazare, *On Apology* (Oxford: O.U.P., 2004).

7

On Clouds and Veils: Divine Presence and 'Feminine' Secrets in Revelation and Nature

Introduction and Statement of Theses

The purpose of this chapter is to unravel some of the complex associations of the metaphors of 'cloud' and 'veil' in Jewish and Christian traditions, and thereby to extend this book's detailed examination of themes that supposedly *disjoin* the two traditions through forms of Christian 'supersessionism'. Once again, I shall be aiming to highlight the richness and complexity of Jewish and Christian receptions of these core biblical topics, and how they defy any obvious binary disjunction of the sort that we might most naturally expect. The implications for contemporary Christology are themselves initially somewhat 'veiled' in this hermeneutical undertaking, but will emerge by degrees through successive textual points of comparison.

The first aim, then, is to indicate how Moses himself has figured archetypally, for both Jewish and Christian traditions, as a special locus of divine presence – and yet also, and paradoxically, of simultaneous divine occlusion or hiddenness. In Moses's story in Torah, God is both uniquely revealed and uniquely hidden: his 'glory' is shielded by cloud (see Exodus 24. 15–18), and also covered by a veil (see Exodus 34. 29–35). If we seek to explicate the subtlety of the relation of divine

The Broken Body: Israel, Christ and Fragmentation, First Edition. Sarah Coakley.
© 2024 John Wiley & Sons Ltd. Published 2024 by John Wiley & Sons Ltd.

revelation and divine hiddenness in Jewish and Christian traditions, then, we are necessarily drawn to these themes in Exodus, and to their subsequent – and varied – interpretations in both Judaism and Christianity. Here, if anywhere, are key Western *exegetical* axes for the rather different *modern* scientific interest in 'knowing the unknowable'. But it is a complex story to trace these metaphors from biblical base to modern scientific expression, and several surprising twists and turns occur along the way.

In this chapter we shall therefore attempt a selective, but illustrative, account of the exegetical history of these themes, in four moves. A brief enunciation of our main theses at the outset may aid clarity, given the complexity of the material involved.[1]

Firstly, we shall attend to the themes of cloud and veil in the text of Exodus itself, and in a selection of rabbinic commentaries upon it. Here we shall see that the question of whether direct human interaction with the deity is possible (without risk of instantaneous death) is already a point of contention even within the Hebrew sources woven into the *textus receptus* of Torah; and in early rabbinic discussion even greater squeamishness is evidenced in relation to the problem of Moses's direct access to the divine. Further, and correlatively, the exact reason for Moses's donning of a veil is also found perplexing from the start: there is surprisingly little rabbinic reflection on the veil itself, but what extended discussion there is shows a prime interest in Moses as a mediatorial figure restored in his 'image' to what God originally

[1] A much earlier version of some of the themes of this chapter was first presented at the Hartmann Institute in Jerusalem in 1995. I am very grateful to †Krister Stendahl, †David Hartmann, †Jospeh Dan, Moshe Halbertal, and Alon Goshen-Gottstein for their critical responses and suggestions at that time, which greatly helped my further development of the topic for this volume. John Bowker and Mark Nussberger provided meticulous comments on an earlier draft of this new version, and Jonathan Schofer suggested further rabbinic references. Brian Britt's *Rewriting Moses: The Narrative Eclipse of the Text* (London: Continuum, 2004) appeared some while after I presented this chapter in its new form as a paper at a conference on 'Knowing the Unknowable' in Cambridge; but ch. 4 of Britt's book covers much of the same ground as I do here, and supplies a marvellous wealth of evidence on Moses's veil and its reception history. I am most grateful to Brian Britt for generously sharing with me a version of his work on this topic before its publication in book form.

intended for human creation, and thus sharing directly, dangerously, and *uniquely*, in the divine revelatory 'glory'.

This story of the place of Moses as preeminent human locus of divine presence was therefore, and unsurprisingly, not immune from the earliest forms of Christian supersessionism. And here we come to the second set of conclusions to be drawn from this exegetical history of clouds and veils. Already in the theology of Paul (2 Cor 3. 7–18), Moses's veil was famously interpreted as that which hides a fading revelation that must necessarily give way to the superior 'glory' of Christ; and this bold subordinating move may well account for much of the silence about Moses's veil that we subsequently find in the Jewish sources. We might also expect to see Moses's complete eclipse at this point in the history of Christian reflection on divine presence, given the apparently negative Pauline reading of his veil; yet instead, in early patristic marriages between Platonism and Christianity, Moses triumphantly reappears (courtesy of the mediating inspiration of the Jewish Platonist, Philo) as the 'type' of the true *Christian* contemplative who communes with God in the divine darkness of the cloud. So here we find, in the early Christian exegesis of the figure of Moses, an interesting and revealing disjunction: the veil is read negatively, for the most part,[2] but simultaneously the cloud becomes, at least in some influential Platonizing authors, redolent with 'mystical' meaning. Soon, in fact, the cloud was to be read – in the writings of the early sixth-century 'pseudo-Dionysius' – to express an *intrinsic* mental impenetrability of divine presence, rather than of the safe shielding of it from direct human gaze, a reading with enormous importance for later Western Christian 'negative theology'.[3] Hence this exegetical

---

[2] Except, as we shall examine later, by gnostic sources (which liked to speculate about cosmological 'veils'); and by one other minority strand of Christian tradition which softened Paul's supersessionism by reading Moses's veil as a *secrecy* motif throughout the entire Old Testament dispensation, awaiting its goal and fulfilment in Christ. For more on this strand in the thought of the sixth century West Syrian author, Jacob of Serugh, see the discussion below, section III. For a possible reading of Paul's text as itself *not* 'negative' towards Moses, see n. 30, below.

[3] Bernard McGinn has argued that there are three *different* variations (not to be understood as necessarily mutually exclusive) on the 'negative theology' theme in the West, termed by him 'Negativity 1' ('the unsaying of God and human'), 'Negativity 2' ('the negativity of detachment'), and 'Negativity 3' ('the experience of

history of Christian readings of clouds and veils surprisingly escapes a *crude* form of supersessionism, thanks to certain inversions of Pauline intent in the apophatic traditions of later Christianity. As in rabbinic thought, Moses remains the primary 'type' of the one who meets God directly, dangerously, intimately, yet to some degree himself uncomprehendingly.

Even to chart the first two dimensions of this story, therefore, is to discover a greater congruence between Jewish and Christian thought on the central theme of revelatory hiddenness than one might initially imagine. Moses stands on the *limen* between what can – and cannot – be known of God, with all the power and ambiguity that position bespeaks. The various traditions of Christian mystical theology which reflected on this power and ambiguity in terms of the cloud metaphor probably owed more to Jewish exegetical forebears, especially Philo, than they were conscious of themselves; and so, *despite* Paul, and despite rampant emerging forms of anti-Judaism in the Western medieval period, this 'divine darkness' tradition in mystical theology kept Moses centre-stage, and to a remarkable extent even thereby avoided competitive stands on christological matters.[4] But there was another, and third, dimension to this story which had been implicit – or so I shall argue – even in Paul's discussions of veils, and became the more explicit in rabbinic reflection on Moses once he

---

dereliction'): see ibid., 'Three Forms of Negativity in Christian Mysticism', in ed. John W. Bowker, *Sciences and Religions: Knowing the Unknowable about God and the Universe* (London: I. B. Taurus, 2009), 99–122. In different ways all three of these variations are influenced by the work of ps.-Dionysius, for whom – following Gregory of Nyssa – the figure of Moses is allegorically central.

[4] Thus Gregory of Nyssa's rendition of Moses in *The Life of Moses* (esp. Bk II, 27, 178, 216) manages to introduce christological themes typologically without a crass concomitant anti-Judaism or triumphant supersessionism (indeed in Bk II, 39, he typologically *identifies* Christianity and 'the pure Israelite race': see tr. Abraham J. Malherbe and Everett Ferguson, *Gregory of Nyssa: The Life of Moses* (New York: Paulist Press, 1978), 63). The status of Christology in the ps.-Dionysian corpus is rather different, and a disputed matter as to its orthodoxy, since some read it as tending to monophysitism (see, e.g., Dionysius the Areopagite, *The Mystical Theology*, ch. 3, in tr. Colm Luibheid, *Pseudo-Dionysius: The Complete Works* (London: S.P.C.K., 1987), 138-139); but again the Christology is not perceived as in any tension with the central theme of 'divine darkness' (ibid., chs. 1–2).

was connected with commentary on the *Song of Songs*. This was the matter of the entanglement of certain themes of 'femininity', and of erotic intimacy, with the key question of divine presence and conceal-ment in the story of Moses. And so the ambivalence we have already noted about direct contact with the divine was mirrored in another, and connected, ambivalence: about gender, about the special place of 'femininity' in such direct contact, and about what this meant not just for the male prophet or sage, but for women themselves. If Moses is veiled, is he not in some sense made 'feminine' to God as the particu-lar human locus of divine presence (thereby rendering 'femininity' newly authoritative)? Or is it, in contrast, that *actual* women do not share in this authority, but instead suffer a different, subordinated, fate in their own veiled status? Strikingly, minority elements in both Jewish and Christian tradition could converge on the first alternative, as we shall attempt to show: Moses is at times 'feminized' by both traditions as a sign of his ambivalent revelatory power. And once we read – as I propose below – Paul on Moses's veil *in connection with* Paul on women's veiling in church (1 Cor 11. 1–16), a concatenation of what we might call 'proto-rabbinic' associations fall out of the Pauline text, with fascinatingly ambiguous implications for the status of Christian women. They are lauded with a new 'authority' by Paul (see 1 Cor 11. 10), equivalent – I shall argue – to the restored 'image' of Israel before the Law; but simultaneously, they are relegated to a posi-tion subordinated to Christian male 'headship'. Thus we see that the veil, in a subtly different history from that of the cloud, can, when explicitly related to gender, connote *both* divinely ordained authority *and* divinely ordained subordination.[5]

A fourth, and concluding, twist in our argument comes when we see how the metaphor of 'feminine veiling' undergoes yet a further transformation (indeed inversion) at the birth of modern Western science, yet not without important remaining echoes of the biblical

---

[5] These two need not even be incompatible if the 'subordination' is read through the figure of the bride in *The Song of Songs*, as we shall shortly discuss. It will be clear as the argument unfolds in this chapter that 'subordination' has a necessarily more complex set of associations, paradoxes and possibilities in the realm of 'mystical the-ology' than it does in modern secular feminism: on this point tackled theoretically see, in more detail, my *Powers and Submissions: Philosophy, Spirituality and Gender* (Oxford: Blackwell, 2002), esp. chs. 1, 5, 9.

heritage. What is now veiled is the 'feminine' Nature that the modern male scientist takes as his 'bride'. (The biblical story of Moses's veil, as we shall see, at this juncture becomes curiously elided with the pagan Greek story of the veil of Artemis.[6]) What was previously God's place to reveal or probe is abrogated by the modern scientific investigator; 'revelation' is now a matter of the *scientific* laying-bare of the secrets of the natural world and the making of 'her' a fruitful bride and loyal wife. Hence the history of clouds and veils reaches here a characteristically modern *dénouement*, with the apparent dispersal of noetic darkness (the cloud), but the maintenance of a remaining 'feminine' mysteriousness in Nature (the veil). Nonetheless, modern and contemporary science has still continued to use the metaphor of cloud with surprising regularity, both to connote scientific nescience and also to make remaining suggestive allusions to divine mystery. In that sense, and paradoxically, the mystical tradition of 'unknowing' still laps at the edges of contemporary scientific sensibility, even as its modernistic confidence claims to have rent the veil of pre-scientific ignorance. And the extent to which ambivalence about gender also continues to attend this nexus of associations is a matter still worthy of reflection, and one to which we shall return in closing.

Such are the four strands of tradition on clouds and veils that this chapter will attempt first to distinguish and elucidate, and then finally to braid together again. Taken cumulatively, these strands show the surprising staying-power of biblical metaphor, even when displaced into the supposedly secular discourses of modern science. But they also show that metaphors for *unspeakable* divine presence, multivalent as they are in their evocations, have the capacity to evade or undercut familiar doctrinal disjunctions both within and between traditions, and even to reconfigure expectations about the supposedly fixed 'binary' of gender. To some of the details of this complex story on clouds and veils we now turn.

---

[6] Pierre Hadot, *The Veil of Isis: An Essay on the History of the Idea of Nature* (Cambridge, MA: Harvard U.P., 2006) traces the history and influence of the Artemis/Isis story, but does not discuss its connection with the veil of Moses. Britt, *Rewriting Moses*, ch. 4, investigates the convergence of these two stories in the Romantic period: see Section III, below.

Cloud and Veil in Exodus and Its Rabbinic Interpretation

The book of Exodus is itself the product of the redaction of several sources, and one of the most puzzling and unresolved theological issues that the Masoretic text bequeaths to the reader concerns the possibility – or otherwise – of direct visual relation to the deity. 'Cloud' and 'veil', in their different ways, seem to indicate the need for God's 'glory' (*kavōd*) to be *protected* from direct human gaze – and *vice versa*;[7] yet in more than one puzzling way, this logic is abrogated in the text as a whole. To a significant degree, the riddle may be solved, in modern source-critical terms, by recognizing that different strands of the text come from different authors and sources.[8] Thus, for instance, there is general scholarly agreement that both the 'cloud' and 'veil' motifs come from the 'Priestly' source ('P'), writing originally sometime in the sixth- to seventh-century BCE. The interests of 'P' in divine 'glory', in ritual exactitude, in priestly Aaronic purity, and in Moses's yet more special status as *alone* worthy of unique and direct intercourse with God in the giving of the Law (see Exodus 24. 15–18), all cohere with the concern for the 'covering' of the divine 'glory' which is a persistent motif of the Priestly compiler.[9] However, to allocate to 'P' the crucial passages on clouds and veil does not, in and of itself, solve all the inherent theological problems that arise in the text of Exodus about the ambivalent power of divine presence, even in 'P'

---

[7] See, e.g., Exod 16. 6–7,10; 24. 15b–18a; 34. 29–35; 40. 33–38; Lev 9. 22–24; Num 9. 15–23; 10. 11–12, 33–34.

[8] Thus we note that a couple of stories in Genesis that come from the 'J' source (see Gen 16. 13; 32. 30) do have extraordinarily direct encounters claimed between mortals (Hagar and Jacob) and Yahweh; and Exod 33. 11, which probably comes from 'E', claims that Moses regularly talked to God 'face to face'.

[9] Since the pioneering source-critical work of Julius Wellhausen (1844–1918), the 'P' source in the Pentateuch has been seen as that strand of compilation with special interest in ritual and ceremonial enactment. Thus the whole of Exod 25–40 is attributed to it (along with all of Leviticus and much of Numbers). The interest in the necessary 'covering' of divine 'glory' extends from the motifs of 'cloud' and 'veil' into a ritual concern for the 'covering' (*kaporeth*) over the ark of the covenant throughout the latter portion of Exodus.

alone.[10] To probe these problems, as the rabbis also did (with characteristic ingenuity and richness of imagination), is to be forced to acknowledge that cloud and veil, although ostensibly parallel motifs, are neither *consistently* operative in the protection of divine mystery, nor is their status as coverings of divine 'glory' completely *egal*. Two features of the Exodus text are particularly worthy of critical attention for our purposes.

Firstly, although Exodus 24 contains at least two, and probably three, strands of tradition artfully woven together to suggest a *gradation* of ascents up Mt Sinai,[11] the cloud motif characteristic of 'P' that ends the chapter really does not fit easily alongside what has just preceded it. For there is the extraordinary statement in the (apparently ancient[12]) fragment of tradition preserved in Exodus 24. 9–11, that 'Moses and Aaron, Nadab and Abihu' ascended the mountain, and '*saw the God of Israel*,' and '... *beheld God, and ate and drank;*[13] and this is in obvious contrast to the 'P' tradition that follows it at the end of the chapter (Exodus 24. 15b—18), which not only gives to Moses alone the honour of ascending the mountain, but insists that he does this *in 'cloud'*. Since elsewhere in Exodus (e.g., 19. 21; 33. 18, 20) and Leviticus (16. 1–2), we learn of the mortal dangers of confronting God face to face, Exodus 24. 9–11 represents a certain theological surd that demands a special explanation, not least in relation to the 'P' cloud tradition: are

---

[10] See the nuanced treatment of this portion of the narrative in relation to this problem in R. W. L. Moberly, *At the Mountain of God: Story and Theology in Exodus 32–34* (Sheffield: JSOT Press, 1983), 177–180.

[11] This is the view (to my mind convincingly) propounded by Brevard S. Childs, *The Book of Exodus* (Philadelphia: Westminster Press, 1974), 505, after acknowledging the ongoing disagreements amongst scholars about the number of sources and redactors evidenced in ch. 24 (see ibid., 499–502).

[12] So Ernest W. Nicholson, *God and His People: Covenant and Theology in the Old Testament* (Oxford: Clarendon Press, 1986), ch. 5, esp. 129–130, who in this monograph is mainly concerned to see these verses as the narrative of an ancient and *sui generis* 'theophany', rather than as the first testimony to a 'covenant' meal. Although these verses are often attributed to 'J', we should note that the daring quality of the revelation here in some respects exceeds those 'J' passages noted in n. 8, above; for this is a *direct* describable vision, shared by a whole delegation.

[13] My emphasis. Various attempts have been made to re-read 'ate and drank': see Nicholson, *God and His People*, 130–132.

we to see Moses here also in *direct* contact with the divine, or not? And if so, who is being protected from what by the cloud (is Moses also shrouded protectively *within* the cloud, or is it only the other Israelites who need distance, whilst Moses attains an otherwise unheard of, even 'god-like', intimacy with the divine[14])?

Secondly, the tradition of Moses's veil (Exodus 34. 29–35), also from 'P', is equally perplexing in relation to our key question about divine revelation and hiddenness; for on close inspection, it is not entirely clear what the veil is meant to achieve, either. It is not that Moses veils himself to speak directly to God,[15] nor – on the other hand – to protect the people at all times from the radiance of his mediatorship. Rather, the veil is simply put on *in between times* of communication with God and Israel (when he is 'off duty', as a colleague at the Hebrew University has charmingly put it[16]), such that why Moses veils himself, and on behalf of whom, remains somewhat opaque. So the questions that press are these: How are we to understand the apparent inconsistency about direct divine contact in Exodus 24, in particular as it relates to the theme of Moses in the cloud? What sort of contact does Moses have with God even *in* the cloud? And what exact purpose is performed, later in Exodus 34, by the veil of Moses, if it (seemingly) does not protect or hide him in relation to God or the Israelites?

---

[14] This was indeed the conclusion drawn by some later exegetes on the basis of the Exodus tradition that Moses alone was capable of *unmediated* access to the divine: see Wayne A. Meeks, 'Moses as God and King' in ed. Jacob Neusner, *Religions in Antiquity* (Leiden: Brill, 1968), 354–371, for a cluster of unrelated Jewish texts which attribute a heavenly enthronement to Moses, or even call him 'god' (Philo).

[15] This is why the comparisons with other priestly 'masks' worn in the Near East is misleading: these would have been put on precisely for ritual duty, the opposite of what the text tells us here. For the problem of the meaning of the Hebrew root *q-r-n* in vss. 29, 30, 35 ('shine', or 'horned', or possibly 'scarred'?), see Childs, *Exodus*, 109–110, and Moberly, *At the Mountain of God*, 108–109. Childs and most modern interpreters opt for 'shine'; but Moberly attempts to make the case for a daring supplantation by Moses of the golden calf with his own 'horns'.

[16] Moshe Halbertal; the phrase is also used by Britt, *Rewriting Moses*, 86. He additionally cites Nahum Sarna, *Exodus* (Philadelphia: Jewish Publication Society of America, 1991), 221, who speaks of Moses operating under the veil 'in his capacity as a private individual'.

The rabbis were to manifest a variety of somewhat puzzled responses to these intriguing and problematic dimensions of the text.[17] Whilst in general they tend to heighten the unique status of Moses before God, they recoil from the dangerously idolatrous suggestion of any direct *perception* of God.[18] The targums, for instance, all baulk at the astonishing Exodus 24.10: it cannot be, for them, that all four men '*saw the God of Israel*'; but rather (*Targum Onqelos*) that 'they saw the *glory* of the God of Israel',[19] or (*Targum Neophyti*) 'they saw the glory of the *Shekhinah* of the Lord',[20] or (*Targum Pseudo-Jonathan*) 'Nadab and Abihu lifted up their eyes and saw the glory of the God of Israel'.[21] Even the Septuagint had already resorted to periphrasis, translating Exodus 24. 10 as 'they saw *the place* where the God of Israel stands'[22] (an evasion that was later to be taken over in a similar phrase in the pseudo-Dionysius[23]).

---

[17] Linda L. Belleville, *Reflections of Glory: Paul's Polemical Use of the Moses-Doxa Tradition in 2 Corinthians 3. 1–18* (Sheffield: JSOT Press, 1991), ch. 12, provides a succinct survey of rabbinic responses to the veil of Moses, and also contrasts the rather different Samaritan readings (ch. 8), which see the veil as *intensifying* the motif of divine glory. She divides the rabbinical readings according to various different motivations for Moses's covering his face; but none very obviously confronts the *meaning* of the 'veil' (*masweh*) itself.

[18] Nicholson, *God and His People*, 127–130, gives a useful account of the discomfort caused to the rabbis by this claim to direct perception, some of whom draw attention to the later death of Nadab and Abihu (Num 3. 4) as a presumed punishment (see n. 24, below). Maimonides was later to get around the perception problem by suggesting that this was a mental (not visual) perception: *Guide to the Perplexed* I. 4, as discussed in Childs, *Exodus*, 506.

[19] This quotation from *Targum Onqelos* (approximate date, 1st or early 2nd CE), and from the two other targumim that follow, are conveniently found in tr. M. Rosenbaum and A. M. Silberman with A. Blashki and L. Joseph, *Pentateuch with Targum Onqelos, Haphtaroth and Prayers for Sabbath and Rashi's Commentary* (London: Shapiro, Valentine & Co., 1946), vol. 1, 197.

[20] Ibid. Opinions differ on the dating of *Targum Neophyti*. Its compilation dates from somewhere between the late 1st century to (at the latest) the early fourth century CE.

[21] Ibid. *Targum Pseudo-Jonathan* was compiled in the late seventh century CE, but contains much earlier material.

[22] Exod 24. 10, LXX: *kai eidon ton topon hou eistēkei ho theos tou Israēl*.

[23] Dionysius the Areopagite, *The Mystical Theology*, ch. 1.3, in tr. Luibheid, *Pseudo-Dionysius*, 137: 'And yet [Moses] does not meet God himself, but contemplates, not him who is invisible, but rather where he dwells'.

Not that such one-(or two-)step removals from direct divine contact could thereby eliminate danger, as later rabbinic commentaries indicate. Leviticus Rabbah (XX. 10, *ad* Lev. 16.1, on the death of Aaron's sons) explains that Moses only himself escaped death, despite Exodus 24.10 and the dangerous direct contact there with the *Shekhinah*, because he had earlier 'hid[den] his face' (see Exodus 3. 6) when confronted with God's presence at the burning bush.[24] Numbers Rabbah (XI. 3, *ad* Num 6. 23) explains, in contrast, that, before Israel sinned in worshipping the golden calf, they *could* look on the 'glory of the Lord ... like devouring fire on the top of the mount' (Exodus 24.17) 'undaunted and undismayed'; but after their sin, 'they could not even look at the face of the intermediary [i.e., Moses, without a veil]'.[25] This last interpretation directly links – at least by implication – the theological significance of cloud and veil: both shield Israel from too-dangerous direct contact with their God. Yet that leaves Moses, of course, in a unique mediatorial position, commented upon in the *Pesikta Rabbati* (Piska 10) in the following way that is one of the only extended and convincing rabbinic attempts to explicate the mysterious function of his 'veil'. Here (in Exodus 34. 33), it says, the veil is put on because Moses's original human 'glory' has been *restored* before God, and 'even as a man cannot look at the sun as it rises, so no man could look at Moses, until Moses put a veil on his face'. But this caused resentment, Piska 10 goes on, because the rest of Israel was in disgrace; it caused Moses to go back to 'the Holy One' and plead that the 'head' and 'glory' of all Israel would also be 'lifted up'. Then 'The Holy One, blessed be He, replied: "Go, lift up their heads." '[26]

---

[24] Tr. J. Israelstam and Judah J. Slotki, *Midrash Rabbah: Leviticus* (London: The Soncino Press, 1983), 261–262. This commentary is dated to the fourth-sixth century CE.

[25] Tr. Judah J. Slotki, *Midrash Rabbah: Numbers* (London: The Soncino Press, 1983), 419. This is a considerably later, twelfth century CE, compilation.

[26] Tr. William G. Braude, *Pesikta Rabbati: Discourses for Feasts, Fasts, and Special Sabbaths* (New Haven: Yale U.P., 1968), vol. 1, 180–181. (This text is variously dated, from the sixth to eighth century CE.) It has to be said that the more ramified and 'convincing' (my word) nature of the explanation given here for the veil is achieved only by twisting the reading of the biblical text so that the Israelites commune with Moses when his veil is *on* (as also in the later *Numbers Rabbah*: see above). In the third section of this chapter, below, we shall explore the potential relevance of this text to an understanding of 1 Cor 11.

Even this small, selective smattering of rabbinic commentary indicates the strong remaining ambivalence, even outright recoil, created in rabbinic discussion by the idea of direct human contact with the divine: huge *moral* danger is evoked by such temerity. That Moses is a special case thus requires equally special treatment: the power he evinces tilts dangerously towards idolatry,[27] even as he bears the almost 'incarnational' responsibility for re-ordering the status of Israel's 'headship' after the primal sin of the golden calf incident.[28] Although the precise ways in which the cloud or veil do, or do not, protect Moses himself from direct contact with the divine remain obscure in the text, the responsibility of Moses to bear the full weight of this ambivalence – of seemingly embodied divine presence, yet of stark moral judgement on the shame of idolatry – is hauntingly evoked by the narrative and by its puzzled rabbinic interpreters.[29]

Paul and the Superseded Veil: The Christian Disjunction between Veil and Cloud

We can hardly be surprised that early Christianity was to tackle this Mosaic ambivalence christologically. Coming to Paul (and his supersessionist reading of Exodus 34 in 2 Cor 3. 7–18), after a quick immersion in the rabbinic material, makes one newly aware of the daring nature of Paul's moves, but also of the striking coincidence

---

[27] Note that in this paper I am using the term 'idolatry' in the wide, generic, sense, of the sinful misplacing of worship of God alone by any other intense focus of interest or reverence. This sense includes the making of actual idols (such the golden calf), but is not restricted to it.

[28] As we have noted above, Moses could even be called 'god' in Philo (drawing on Exodus 7. 1): see again Meeks, 'Moses as God and King' (n. 13). Awareness of this backcloth makes Paul's moves in 2 Cor 3 the more pointed.

[29] Britt's insightful reading of this 'ambivalence' (*Rewriting Moses*, ch. 4) is however one I would dispute in some details: he psychoanalyses distractingly, it seems to me, in attributing exegetical 'avoidance of the veil' to '*anxiety* before the veil' (ibid., 84; see 115); or in suggesting that the 'veil has been an unappealing puzzle because it *alienates and silences* Moses' (ibid., 87), my emphases.

of much of the technical *language* of Paul and the later rabbinic traditions. We have noted how the rabbis were to be both puzzled, yet almost wholly literal, in their reading of the Exodus texts. Paul, in contrast, reads Moses's veil allegorically and negatively, as hiding in Moses 'the end of the glory' of the old covenant that was being 'set aside' (vs. 13),[30] and also more broadly as continuing to occlude truth from the minds of *all* Jews who fail to 'turn to the Lord' (vs. 14–15). In the next chapter (2 Cor 4. 3–4), he extends the 'veiling' metaphor to include even non-Jews who refuse to respond to the gospel. Yet despite this daring shift from positive to negative 'veiling', Paul here – and indeed too in 1 Cor 11. 1–16 (to which we shall shortly return) – maintains a repetitive interest in the question of 'glory' and of 'image', to which – in 1 Cor 11 – he also adds the connected matter of 'headship' (which we have just seen discussed in the later *Pesikta Rabbati*). Thus even as Paul reverses the meaning of 'veiling' from that of divine presence to that of significant divine absence, he still insistently tackles the issue of where – in the natural and human world – we are to find the true 'image' and 'glory' of God, and indeed, from that, the right forms of 'headship' in the community. The answer for him, of course, is that Christ, not Moses, now provides such a focus, since 'only in Christ is [the veil] set aside' (2 Cor 3. 14); and 'all of us, with unveiled faces, seeing the glory of the Lord as though reflected

---

[30] Richard B. Hays, in *Echoes of Scripture in the Letters of Paul* (New Haven: Yale U.P., 1989), 136, has made a fascinating case for reading the Greek of 2 Cor 3. 13 somewhat differently, rendering *telos* not 'end' but 'goal'/'aim', thus: 'Moses put a veil on his face in order that the sons of Israel might not perceive the true aim (*telos*) of the transitory covenant (*tou katargoumenou*)'. It is perfectly true, as we shall explore in the third section of this chapter, that one strand in Christian exegesis went on to read Paul in this way (e.g., Theodoret: see ibid., 219, n. 49), and – by implication – Jacob of Serugh (see our discussion below). But Hays does not provide any extensive evidence for his claim (ibid., 137) that 'patristic interpreters unanimously' understood *telos* to mean 'goal', and the negative force of the verb *katargeo* (to annul) cannot really be gainsaid by a rendering such as 'transitory'. Paul is in any case not the only exegete of Exodus 34.34 to suggest that Moses's *doxa* was less than perfectly sustained. Some rabbinic sources also suggest an *inconsistency* in the splendour (see Belleville, *Reflections of Glory*, 67); and the later *Zohar*, interestingly, does speak of a serious deterioration, attributing this to the apostasy of Israel with the golden calf (see ibid., 75, and *Zohar* III, 58a).

in a mirror, are being transformed into the same image from one degree of glory to another' (vs. 18).[31]

If Paul's reading of Moses's veil apparently left little room for its later Christian redemption, we shall see shortly that a minority Syriac tradition of Christian exegesis, at least, was able to rescue the motif of the veil in a subtly different way, such that the 'secret' it enshrined was not perceived as something atrophying, let alone being 'annulled', but merely awaiting its fulfilment.[32] Still, Paul's influence on later Christianity was of course almost all-consuming; and what he provided by way of biblical exegesis was in one way all the more emphasized in later iconographic elaboration: it was the image of the veiled (feminized) '*synagoga*', often alongside the contrasted, and triumphant, Christian '*ecclesia*', that was to become the standard Christian visual representation of superseded Israel.[33] Yet the much rarer representations of a veiled male Moses almost never, interestingly, concealed his face completely – as if the classic ambivalence about his status remained: part respected prophet, pointing forward to Christ's revelation, part upstaged representative of the old dispensation, as Paul had taught.[34]

---

[31] Belleville, *Images of Glory*, ch. 23, provides an exacting exegesis of this climax verse, drawing critically on earlier exegetical attempts and showing that the verse is itself a 'phrase-by-phrase commentary on Exod 34. 35' (ibid., 275).

[32] See the discussion of Jacob of Serugh in the next section; some of the later iconographic representation also interestingly escapes Paul's 'annulment' motif and seems to glorify Moses (as, e.g., in the ninth-century Vivian Bible depiction): see Britt, *Rewriting Moses*, 91–92. Even these two counter-instances show how subtle can be the variants on 'supersessionism', some of them – I would argue – *not* falling into the 'anti-Jewish' category. See also the discussion of Gregory of Nyssa on this issue, below.

[33] Wolfgang S. Seiferth, *Synagogue and Church in the Middle Ages: Two Symbols in Art and Literature* (New York: Ugar Publishing Co., 1970) traces the development of this double motif in detail. Also see Britt, *Rewriting Moses*, 98–103. From the twelfth century *Synagoga* is regularly represented with a blindfold, a broken staff, and the tablets of the Law (often broken or slipping away). With this may be compared the image on the front cover of this volume, from the French Noyon Missal, thirteenth century, in which the blindfolded *Synagoga* lances Christ, and *Ecclesia* catches the blood in a chalice.

[34] See Britt, *Rewriting Moses*, 91–98, for a description of the (scant) number of Christian iconographic representations of Moses's veil, specifically. Almost never is Moses' head completely covered, interestingly (it is either partially covered, or being unveiled by Christ).

But if the image of a veiled Israel or Moses was most commonly negative in its Christian associations, given Pauline influence, this did not prove the case, interestingly, for Moses's *cloud*. The reverse-supersessionism (or moderated supersessionism) in the case of the cloud might seem wholly remarkable were it not for the mediating influence of Philo, who assuredly lies behind the use of Moses himself, and the cloud in particular, as types and symbols of the 'contemplative' advance *through darkness*, which is also emulated in slightly later Christian exegesis. It is Philo who, reading Moses as the supreme 'prophet', sees him as removed from all passion – including sexual passion[35] – and, so prepared, as able to enter 'into the darkness where God was, that is into the unseen, invisible, incorporeal and archetypal essence of existing things'.[36] So here the particular darkness of the cloud first becomes explicitly theologically *positive*, in Philo's eclectic marriage of Judaism and middle-Platonism.

However, this ascription of cloudy darkness as positive was not immediately shared by the first Christian writer to fasten, similarly, on the figure of Moses as contemplative 'type'. For Clement of Alexandria, in striking contrast to Philo, the 'darkness' motif of the cloud was something to be *overcome* – manifesting, in fact, the ignorance of the multitude rather than the advance of Moses's theological consciousness.[37] Thus it was not until Gregory of Nyssa's *Life of Moses*, in the late fourth century, that the *positive* revelatory significance of Moses' 'dark cloud' was brought over into Christian tradition from Philo, and now with a notable new twist of epistemological precision. Here the Platonic *nous* was seen to meet its limits, and to pass even beyond 'contemplation' to an intimacy with the divine that involved its own dethronement. This matter is worth pausing to explicate, given its

---

[35] Philo, *de vita Mosis* II, 68 (alluding to Exod 19. 15), in tr. F. H. Colson, *Philo* (Cambridge, MA: Harvard U.P., 1935), vol. VI.

[36] Ibid., I, 158. In the same passage Philo makes the claim that Moses was 'named god and king of the whole nation'.

[37] Clement of Alexandria, *The Miscellanies*, Bk V, 12, in tr. William Wilson, *The Writings of Clement of Alexandria*, vol. II (*The Ante-Nicene Christian Library*) (Edinburgh: T. & T. Clark, 1869), 267: 'And when the Scripture says, "Moses entered into thick darkness where God was", this shows to those capable of understanding, that God is invisible and beyond expression by words. And "the darkness" – which, is in truth, the unbelief and ignorance of the multitude – obstructs the gleam of the truth'.

interesting – indeed extreme – contrast with the 'modern' scientific epistemological lens with which this chapter will conclude.

For Gregory, Moses's 'ascent' to God starts with the clarification and light of the revelation in the 'burning bush' (identified by him with the 'light' of the incarnation), where noetic clarity is still to be achieved.[38] But when Moses begins his ascent of Mt Sinai, he moves through a light cloud to the 'thick darkness' at the height of the mountain. It is here that he realizes that, 'This is the true knowledge of what is sought; this is the seeing that consists in not seeing, because that which is sought transcends all knowledge, being separated on all sides by incomprehensibility as by a kind of darkness.'[39] Only in his other great commentary of this period, *On the Song of Songs*, does Gregory fill out more completely what it means for the mind thereby to reach its limits; here we see that the use of the 'spiritual senses' (spiritually transformed versions of the 'lower' capacities of taste, feel and touch) have to compensate, in darkness, for the loss of sight and hearing, and simultaneously invoke a form of gender-reformation. Now the soul is not so much the woo-er of 'Wisdom' but more the 'feminine' bride of the Logos.[40] This point is one to which we shall have reason to return; it represents, one might say, the very antithesis of the 'modern' scientific epistemological attitude to 'Nature's' 'feminine' secrets.

It is not obvious that the same could be said of Gregory's more famous successor in the tradition of 'mystical' darkness, the late fifth-century pseudo-Dionysius the Areopagite. Moses is again the 'hero' here, in Dionysius's 'Mystical Theology'; yet it is not so much that the intellect for Dionysius is superseded by some *other* faculty or capacity. Rather, the mind knows 'beyond the mind' in an *ekstasis* of fleeting 'union': 'Here, renouncing all that the mind may conceive ... [Moses] belongs completely to him who is beyond everything'.[41] This is a

---

[38] *The Life of Moses*, Bk I, 20 ; Bk II, 19–27, in tr. Malherbe and Ferguson, *The Life of Moses*, 34–35; 59–61.

[39] Bk II, 163, in ibid., 95.

[40] Verna Harrison usefully explores this theme in Nyssen's *Commentary on the Song of Songs* in her article, 'A Gender Reversal in Gregory of Nyssa's *First Homily on the Song of Songs*', *Studia Patristica* 27 (1993), 34–38. See also Coakley, *Powers and Submissions*, 161–167.

[41] *Mystical Theology*, 1, 3, tr. Luibheid, *Pseudo-Dionysius*, 137. For the *ekstasis* of fleeting union (*henōsis*), see ibid., I, 1 (*Pseudo-Dionusius*, 135).

'dazzling darkness', to be sure, but one completely impenetrable by normal rational thought (even by the 'negations of negations' enjoined on the 'mystical theologian'). God, for Dionysius, is not capable of being brought into some other kind of closeness, except by the *mind's* own capacity for ecstatic self-transcendence.[42] This position contrasts not only with that of Gregory of Nyssa, but also with the much later (fourteenth-century) Western *Cloud of Unknowing*, which – while appealing to 'Denys' and claiming to teach exactly as he does – actually departs from him dramatically, most notably in the insistence that 'to the intellect, God ... is forever unknowable, but *to* .... *love he is completely knowable*' (ch. 4).[43] Moses is still the contemplative hero, 'who for all his climbing and effort on the mountain was seldom able to see it';[44] yet now a *choice* between 'intellect' and 'will' has been introduced (under the influence of Thomas Gallus's translation and interpretation of Denys)[45] such that the 'affective' dimension has become the favoured locus of divine interaction, and the intellect and its activities shrouded altogether in a 'cloud of forgetting', which it is the contemplative's job to place between himself and 'all creation'.[46] Here, in 'dark contemplation', is Mary's choosing of the 'best part', one which declares the intellect contemplatively barren, but 'will', 'love' and 'feeling', in

---

[42] It is the mind (*nous*) that goes beyond itself (*hyper noun*) in union, not some other faculty: see again ibid., I, 1(*Pseudo-Dionysius,* 135).

[43] Tr. Clifton Wolters, *The Cloud of Unknowing* (London: Penguin, 1961), 55, my emphasis. In ch. 70 (ibid., 137), *The Cloud* author claims that 'anyone who will read Dionysius's [Denys's] works will find that he clearly endorses all I have said ...'; but this is in fact highly misleading.

[44] Ibid., 140 (ch. 73). Interestingly, although Moses remains the hero of *The Cloud* author in representing the one who struggles for contemplation in darkness, he is perceived – in contrast to the representation of him in Nyssen or ps.-Dionysius – as ultimately spiritually *inferior* to Aaron: 'Aaron symbolizes all those ... who by their spiritual wisdom and assisted by grace may achieve perfect contemplation whenever they like' (ibid, 139 (ch. 71)).

[45] For a new assessment of the important influence of the Victorine Thomas Gallus on *The Cloud's* reading of Dionysius, see Boyd Coolman, 'The Medieval Affective Dionysian Tradition', in eds. Sarah Coakley and Charles M. Stang, *Re-Thinking Dionysius the Areopagite* (Oxford: Blackwell, 2009), 85–102.

[46] *The Cloud*, ch. 5, in tr. Wolters, 58–59.

contrast, the place of divine grace and presence in the 'cloud of unknowing'.[47]

This last, 'affective', reading of Moses's cloud was not to prove overall the dominating one in Western mystical theology,[48] but its memorable title indicates the honour which the cloud metaphor had accrued to itself in the Christian contemplative tradition by the later medieval period. Thus, as we have now shown in this second section, 'cloud' was positively embraced by those in the Christian mystical traditions, whereas Moses's veil was treated, at best, with deep ambivalence, at worst with outright scorn. Although medieval art, especially art with mystical or hermetic interests, had a great fascination with veils in general (veils, for instance, that shrouded the inner mystery of the Trinity[49]), the veil of Moses seemingly presented too many ambiguous and competing meaning-sets to allow it to become a central, repetitive, or positive theme in the stock armoury of theological metaphors applied to the élite realm of 'mystical theology'.

And the link to 'femininity' was surely a crucial part of that ambiguity, as we shall now explore.

The 'Femininized' Veil: Erotic Intimacy with the Divine, or Gendered Subordination?

By this time, we have seen many hints that the topics of Moses, divine darkness and 'femininity' could not be completely disentangled in the symbolic excess of meanings released by Jewish and Christian exegesis of the Exodus narrative. Whether in the visual representations of Moses as the female superseded/subordinated *synagoga*, bearing her tablets of the Law; or – rather differently – as the 'feminized' contemplative

---

[47] Ibid., ch. 21, in tr. Wolters, 79–81.

[48] Bernard McGinn, 'Love, Knowledge and Mystical Union in Western Christianity: Twelfth to Sixteenth Centuries', *Church History* 56 (1987), 7–24, supplies a succinct and illuminating account of how the Dionysian tradition was variously incorporated into late medieval Western thought. See also my *Powers and Submissions*, ch. 4, for a comparison of 'East' and 'West' on the disjunction of intellect and will at this period.

[49] See, for instance, the fascinating volume by Jeffrey F. Hamburger, *The Rothschild Canticles: Art and Mysticism in Flanders circa 1300* (New Haven: Yale U.P., 1990) for many examples of such iconographic veils.

soul/Moses in Gregory of Nyssa's *Life of Moses*; or — by another associative extension — by the linking of the contemplative Mary of the New Testament with Moses's cloud of the Old in *The Cloud of Unknowing*: all these cases indicate something of the paradox we must now confront explicitly. Although, as we have shown, Moses' veil was for the most part a negative feature in Christian exegesis, and a somewhat embarrassing or elusive mystery in rabbinic thought,[50] it could nonetheless become, in some minority traditions in both religious traditions, positively interpreted — *precisely qua 'feminine'*. The symbolic 'femininity' that in one context associated Moses with subordination and supersession, could, in another, render his veil a mark of special erotic intimacy with the divine. Just as Moses in Exodus straddles, as both traditions saw, the ambivalence between divine presence and dangerous idolatry, so he also occupies — as a few commentators were to intuit — a place in this other, correlative, ambivalence: the double-meaning of the 'feminine'.[51]

Where then, other than in starkly supersessionist Christian iconography, was Moses' veil read as a woman's veil, or Moses otherwise 'feminized'? Two fascinating examples, one Christian, one Jewish, must suffice here as further indicators of this symbolic nexus of association.

---

[50] Rashi, late eleventh century, is the first to attempt a close, *semantic* explanation of the mysterious *hapax legomenon, masweh*, hoping to probe back behind earlier rabbinic discussions to a clear meaning of the word (since it is not one of the other words used elsewhere in the Hebrew Bible for a veil or covering). He connects the word *masweh* back to two uses of the same root in the Babylonian Talmud (*Kethubot* 60a, 62b), which indicate that the verb-form means to 'look, or gaze'. He thus takes Moses's veil to be a 'cloth that was put in front of the face and of the region of the eyes' ... 'out of reverence for the "rays of glory"' — that not everybody should feast on them' (Rashi *ad* Exodus 34.33, in tr. Rosenbaum, Silbermann *et al*, *Pentateuch*, vol. 1, 197). Interestingly, the two examples of the use of the root given from the Talmud both involve women and 'seeing', leading some scholars (†Joseph Dan, private correspondence) to conclude that Rashi is implying — by association — a connection with women's veils. This is not however the stated point of Rashi's analysis, which is purely semantic. It is a further interesting detail that the Western visual depiction of Moses/*Synagōgē* starts to represent the 'veil' as a blindfold some time after the writing of Rashi's commentary (see Britt, *Rewriting Moses*, 99).

[51] Here, either eroticized and elevated superiority; or socially subordinated inferiority.

Taken together, they will then lead us back to Paul on veils with new eyes for gendered cross-connections in his text.[52]

The great poetic Syrian Orthodox bishop of the early sixth century, Jacob of Serugh, was to interpret Moses's veil in a way fascinatingly different from Paul, even though – in so doing – he simultaneously appealed with force to the Pauline corpus, both to Paul on Moses's veil and to (deutero-) Paul on the 'great mystery' of marriage (Ephesians 5. 22–33). In his unique poetic homily on the veil of Moses, Jacob presents a vision of *true* doctrine as irreducibly enshrined in the poetic, the prophetic and the 'secret'.[53] Only Christ unlocks the secret to his followers, and even then, not in crass propositional form open to the 'world's' understanding.[54] The 'great Moses' was thus veiled by God *not* as a sign of his inferiority, argues Jacob, but as an indication of the necessarily veiled nature of all prophecy until Christ was to fulfil it.[55] Moses's veil, according to Jacob, is thus akin to the veiled virginity of the Church as it awaits its bridegroom, Jesus; what 'Moses' (in Genesis 2. 24) spoke of in terms of God's blessing on

---

[52] It must be freely admitted that the making of these connections involve chronological leaps in relation to biblical, patristic and rabbinic materials. However, we do already know that nexuses of thought found in Paul have echoes in much later rabbinic writings, and it is not at all impossible (albeit somewhat speculative on particular points of detail), to see those later writings as enshrining much earlier oral tradition. Hence the deliberate reversal of chronology in this section.

[53] For Jacob, these matters are coterminous. Sebastian Brock supplies a translation and discussion of Jacob's *Homily* 79 on the veil of Moses in 'Jacob of Serugh on the Veil of Moses', *Sobornost* 3 (1981), 70–85. Brock underscores that Jacob is writing in a period of hot contestation of the Chalcedonian heritage, and thus appealing back to an Ephrem-style poetic approach to doctrine as a counter-move against the pressure for greater precision in the reading of the Chalcedonian Definition: '[The Father] wanted to reveal [his Son] to the world in symbolic terms' (ibid., 72)…. 'Thus he cries out in the prophet, "I have a secret"… so that the world might be aware that the prophecy contained secrets hidden in symbolic language' (ibid.).

[54] Thus even Christ remains 'veiled' to the 'sight of spectators' (ibid., 73) – a seeming contradiction with Paul. Yet compare ibid., 75, following Paul on the unveiling in Christ: 'That great beauty that had been veiled has now come out into the open'.

[55] A striking inversion of Paul is found here: 'The radiance of Moses was in fact Christ shining in him' (ibid., 73). As with Gregory of Nyssa, Jacob manages to effect a christological supersessionism which *nests within* an assumption of Moses's full prophetic greatness, rather than denying it.

physical marriage, is now fulfilled though the Church receiving its bridegroom in the sacraments of the Church.[56]

Jacob's chaste 'eroticization' of Moses's veil thus effects a remarkable remodelling of the Pauline notion of the 'glory being set aside' in 2 Cor 3,[57] even as Jacob continues to cite 'the great Paul' with full apparent approbation. This *positive* 'feminization' of Moses finds a certain remarkable Jewish parallel, not so long afterwards, in the rabbinic commentary, *Song of Songs Rabbah*, but with a significant difference of detail. Here, commentating on *Song* 4. 5 ('Thy two breasts'), the author develops an extensive analogy between the female lover's breasts in the *Song*, and Moses and Aaron: 'Just as the breasts are the beauty and the ornament of a woman, so Moses and Aaron were the beauty and ornament of Israel. Just as the breasts are the charm of a woman, so Moses and Aaron were the charm of Israel...'[58] Interestingly, however, the commentator does not make a connection between Moses's *veil* and the 'veil' in the *Song* text just before this (*Song* 4. 1, 3);[59] and one cannot help wondering whether there may be some deliberate repression of that possibility on account of the well-known Christian polemic against Moses's veil: on this matter we can only speculate, but it does not seem a wild supposition to suspect such an avoidance.

Yet once we see this later connection, in both Jewish and Christian contexts, of a Moses 'feminized' by his 'erotic' intimacy with God, an intriguing possibility thereby presents itself, by back-formation: is it that Paul's contentious discussion of women's veiling in 1 Cor 11. 1–16 may also have had his arguments about *Moses's* veiling hovering in the background? To be sure, it would be a highly implicit 'hovering', since nowhere in this passage in 1 Cor 11 does Paul explicitly invoke Moses. Yet certain hints are present that strongly suggest a connection to 2 Cor 3, in addition to the obviously shared theme of

---

[56] Ibid., 74–75.

[57] The 'remodelling' would of course be less dramatic if one were fully persuaded by all the details of Richard Hays's re-reading of 2 Cor 3: see again n. 30, above.

[58] Tr. Maurice Simon, *Midrash Rabbah Song of Songs* (London: The Soncino Press, 1983), 198.

[59] The Hebrew for 'veil' here in *The Song* (4. 1,3; 6. 7: from the Hebrew root *ts-m-m*) has no *etymological* connection to the *masweh* of Exod 34; but – as we have just seen – that does not prevent Jacob of Serugh from making an elision.

'veiling'. In particular, there is the repeated language of 'image', 'glory' and (as discussed above) 'headship', all of which are thematic points of discussion in relation to Moses and his veil in Jewish exegesis, and signs that Paul has a collocation of pre-connected ideas at work in both contexts. In other words, if the idea of Moses as a veiled figure lies in the background of Paul's exposition in this (admittedly tortured and far from consistent[60]) passage in 1 Cor 11, then his argument for women's covering their heads at worship might, implicitly, involve the following logic: man is to woman as (uncovered head of) Christian is to (veiled head of) Jew [*qua* Moses]. Where would this line of thought lead us?

Perhaps particularly suggestive of this putative connection is the verse whose meaning has always effectively defeated the New Testament commentators (1 Cor 11. 10): 'For this reason a woman ought to have authority (*exousia*) on her head, for the sake of [*or, according to: dia*] the angels'.[61] This verse has, to say the least, caused rather desperate exegetical attempts at explication from the very start; and already from the time of Tertullian 'the angels' here were interpreted, negatively, as the 'angels' of Gen. 6 who transgressively mated with human women.[62] In other words, the 'angels' have been seen as

---

[60] I would not be the first to admit that this difficult passage has several, inconsistently related, trains of thought. In particular, one major set of considerations seems to relate to head-coverings, another to hair-styles; and most modern commentators have tried to resolve the meaning of the passage in one of these directions or the other. In addition, the subordinate/dominant relations of 'glory' in vss. 6–8 also seem not completely to cohere with the arguments for equality and mutuality in vss. 11–12. However once we admit that Paul is combining various (somewhat inconsistently related) trains of thought together here, in what I earlier called 'proto-rabbinic' style, then the urgent quest for total consistency falls away.

[61] Because I think that Paul has a covert train of thought here out of his Jewish exegetical inheritance in connection with Moses's veil, I am happy to follow Gerhard Kittel's suggestion, made long ago (*Rabbinica*, ARGU, 1, 3 (Leipzig: Hinrichs, 1920), 17–31), that 'authority' (*exousia*) in this verse involves an Aramaic pun on the root *sh-l-t* ('to exercise power'), which also appears in plural noun form in *p.Shab.* 6, 8b, 48, meaning something like 'head-band' or 'veil'.

[62] See Gen 6. 1–4. Tertullian's rendition ('On the Apparel of Women', 1.2; 2.10; 'On the Veiling of Virgins', 1. 7), is discussed and supported by Dale B. Martin, *The Corinthian Body* (New Haven: Yale U.P., 1995), 244–249. Joseph A. Fitzmyer ('A Feature of Qumran Angelology and the New Testament', *New Testament Studies 4*

what women should *guard themselves against*, prophylactically, in wear-ing a head-covering, and that to protect their sexual modesty.

However, if we make the proposed link to the Moses story, it is possible that the rich nexus of associations we have already unearthed can help us finally understand this elusive verse, which seemingly forms some sort of climax to Paul's argument in 1 Cor 11. Two possibilities in fact present themselves, and in the manner of 'proto-rabbinic' argument (operating characteristically by means of multi-layered and sometime chaotic bombardments of symbolic allusion) the two may not necessarily need to be taken as mutually exclusive.

The first possibility works backwards from a suggestive connection in a much later Jewish source, the *Midrash ha-Gadol*[63] on Exodus 34. 34. In the *Midrash ha-Gadol*, Moses is compared favourably to the angels on account of being able to approach God *without* covering his face,[64] whilst (it is said) even the angels must cover their faces with their wings (as in the vision in the temple in Isaiah 6. 2). This text may well in fact be a latter-day Jewish riposte to the Pauline supersessionist

---

(1957–1958), 48–58, suggests a slight variant of this understanding of the angels, drawing on material from Qumran: the angels could be seen as a sort of police force, potentially offended by unveiled women in the place of worship.

[63] Compiled in the thirteenth century, but almost certainly containing much earlier strands of tradition. The modern Hebrew edition is ed. M. Marguiles, *Midrash ha-Gadol on the Pentateuch: Exodus* (Jerusalem: Mosad ha-Rav Kook, 1967). My thanks to Moshe Halbertal for his original suggestion to me that this text might throw retrospective light on 1 Cor 11/2 Cor 3, when read together. Belleville, *Reflections of Glory*, 69–70, discusses the *Midrash ha-Gadol* exegesis briefly, but not as a proposal to link 2 Cor 3 with 1 Cor 11.

[64] This may in fact be a deliberate Jewish riposte to Paul: it is stressed afresh that Moses is the one who precisely does *not* need to cover his face, even though the angels do: ' "Whenever Moses went in before the Lord to speak with Him, he would take the veil off" (Exod 34. 34). Come and see the greatness [*gedullah, viz.,* distinc-tion, dignity, high office] of Moses which the Holy One (blessed be He!) gave to him – more greatness than the ministering angels. Ministering angels cover their faces opposite the *Shekhinah* whenever they give praise before the Lord – for it is said, "With two [wings] he covered his face" (Isa 6.2). But Moses, our teacher, does not [do] so. He uncovers his face [when] he stands before the *Shekhinah*, for it is said, "He would not take the veil off, until he came out" (Exod 34. 34)', ed. Marguilies, *Midrash ha-Gadol, Ki tissa'*, 34. 34.

claim that reserves for Christ alone the prerogative of approaching God 'unveiled'. But if indeed the figure of Moses is symbolically lurking behind 1 Cor 11, then Paul (as supersessionist), must – unlike the later Midrashic commentor – here be implicitly aligning the status of Moses with the *covered* 'feminine' head, which *is* veiled like the 'angels' in Isaiah 6, and whose particular 'glory' lies in its subordinate – though in some sense complementary – relation to the uncovered head of the (Christian) man. This would 'feminize' Moses, to be sure, but at the same time accord him, and veiled women with him, a certain particular complementary status of 'glory' before God – a status indeed equivalent to the angels furling their wings over their heads before the throne of the Lord. Could it not be, then, that this is what Paul has in mind for veiled women: giving to them most significantly, with one hand, a high status and 'authority' normally reserved for the angels,[65] but taking away, with another, any sense of *straightforward* equality with Christian men? The ambiguity of 'femininity' is fully evident here, but it is now implicitly yoked, most fascinatingly, with the Jewish/Christian ambiguity. As with Paul's notoriously rich and complex understanding of the relation of Judaism and Christianity in Romans 9–11, so here, in parallel, an equally rich and complex understanding of the relation of woman to man is implied: mutually necessary to one another, mutually implied by one another, but not straightforwardly 'equal' in power or 'headship'.

One further – and more commonly known – allusion to head-coverings in relation to the Moses story could also be in background play in 1 Cor 11 as well, and would certainly support the general train of our argument. In Exodus 33. 5–6, Moses is instructed by God to tell the Israelites to strip themselves of their 'ornaments', as a gesture of penitence and fear before the Lord, after their apostasy; and so they do. (This interaction occurs, interestingly, just before Moses requests that he, and he alone, be allowed to see the 'glory' of the Lord directly: Exodus 33. 18.) In the Babylonian Talmud, much is made of this moment of Israel's tragic divestment.[66] It is read as a removal of double

---

[65] Recall Ps. 8. 5: 'a little lower than *elōhim*' is variously translated 'a little lower than the angels', or 'a little lower than God'.

[66] See *b. Shabbat* 88a, tr. H. Freedman, *Hebrew-English Edition of the Babylonian Talmud. Shabbath*, vol. II (London: The Soncino Press, 1972).

'crowns' said to have been put upon the (male) Israelites at the moment of their covenantal acceptance of the Law (Exodus 24. 7); and just as the Talmud sees 'angels' as responsible for the initial crowning, so it also sees an even larger band of 'destroying angels' as undertaking the subsequent removal.[67] If we read 1 Cor 11. 10 in the light of this narrative association (which may well have had some circulation even at the time of Paul), we once again get a revealing clarification: the head-coverings given originally to *male* Israelites by the angels as a sign precisely of their newly redeemed status, their 'authority' and renewed 'headship',[68] is now in Paul's argument on offer to Christian *women*. To ask them to don head-coverings whilst praying or prophesizing, therefore, is in one sense to elevate them to the status of Moses and male Israel, even as they are also required to acknowledge their 'submission' in the christological hierarchy of Christian marriage.[69] In both these implied renditions of 1 Cor 11. 1–10, then, the woman is enjoined to veil herself in order to represent the 'authority' of a derivative and yet status-endowed posture of 'glory' before the Lord, in

---

[67] Ibid.: 'R. Simai lectured: When the Israelites gave precedence to '*we will do*' over '*we will hearken*' [Exod 24. 7], six hundred thousand ministering angels came and set two crowns upon each man of Israel, one as a reward for … '*we will do*', and the other as a reward for '*we will hearken*'. But as soon as Israel sinned [through the Golden Calf], one million two hundred thousand destroying angels descended and removed them, as it is said, '*And the children of Israel stripped themselves of their ornaments from Mt. Horeb* [Exod 33. 6]. R. Hama son of R. Hanina said: At Horeb they put them on and at Horeb they put them off.… . R. Johanan observed: And Moses was privileged and received them all, for in proximity thereto it is stated, *And Moses took the tent* [Exod 33. 7]. Resh Lakish said: [Yet] the Holy One, blessed be He, will return them to us in the future, for it is said, *and the ransomed of the Lord shall return, and come with singing unto Zion; and everlasting joy shall be upon their heads* [Isa 35. 10]; the joy from of old shall be upon their heads'. (Rashi *ad* Exodus 33.5, in tr. Rosenbaum, Silbermann *et al.*, *Pentateuch*, vol. 1, 187, also takes up this theme.)

[68] We recall here the same themes as later discussed in the *Pesikta Rabbati*, see n. 26, above.

[69] 1 Cor 11, 1 Cor 7, and Eph 5, if taken together, present a complex picture of 'mutual submission' between the sexes which is nonetheless also mandated female subordination of a sort. It is however certainly not a *straightforward* 'top-down' hierarchy. The parallels with Ro 9–11 and Paul's treatment of the problem of Israel's relation to Christianity are potentially very revealing, but cannot be further pursued in this chapter.

complementarity to that of the male. This posture is akin to the posture of Israel when their heads were 'lifted up' again before the Lord, causing them almost to attain the status of angels, indeed even to occasion the possibility of jealous *resentment* from the angels.[70]

By now we are seeing more clearly, in this account of clouds and veils, how fascinating are the double-messages of 'feminine' gender in their implications for the topic of 'knowing the unknowable' in God. To be 'feminine' before God may, in some circumstances, to be found in a specially favoured, indeed 'erotic', intimacy with the divine – one uniquely suitable for such an 'impossible' form of knowledge; yet even in this position of special intimacy, there may be a new insistence on actual, *female* subordination of some particular sort. Both Jewish and Christian minority traditions, as we have seen, walk this tightrope of gender ambiguity. And it may well be that, in the failure of Paul, and most of his subsequent interpreters, *explicitly* to link the Mosaic veil discussion of 2 Cor 3 with the 'feminine' veil discussion of 1 Cor 11, we are dealing with a certain double repression in both traditions in relation to this nexus of associations. Not only, as we have seen, did Jewish commentators become remarkably coy – probably under the impact of the Pauline critique – about exegeting the precise significance of Moses's donning of an ostensibly 'feminine' adornment, but mainstream Christianity for the most part kept up a firm *exegetical* disjunction between 'feminine' veils in 1 Cor 11 (about real women

---

[70] This explains why the reference to angels here can remain double-sided: women both attain an equivalent status to them, and simultaneously potentially jostle with them for a superior status, as did Moses at Sinai. (Yet a further variation of the latter is the possibility that the head covering is to keep the angels from being frightened or *disturbed* by the new status of the women: see Belleville, *Reflections of Glory*, 70, for a discussion of this idea *re* Moses's veil and the ministering angels in *Mishnath Rab Eliezer*, 150–151). For a detailed account of the theme of angelic rivalry with Moses, see Joseph P. Schultz, 'Angelic Opposition to the Ascension of Moses and the Revelation of the Law', *Jewish Quarterly Review* 61 (1971), 282–307. The final implication of my suggested reading of 1 Cor 11. 10 in the light of the Moses traditions, is to understand it thus: 'Therefore [*sc.* because of the derivative glory of the woman from the man: vss. 8–9] the woman ought to wear *her* authority [pun: head-covering] on her head [*sc.* as Moses did], for the sake of the angels [*sc.* to indicate that in the hierarchy she is at least as high as them, and indeed higher – paralleling the force of the *dia* in vs. 9 – just as Moses was, albeit now superseded by Christ]'.

in church) and the veiling of Moses in 2 Cor 3 (about Israel and Christianity). In earliest Christianity, interestingly, only gnostic sources make the connection between the two Pauline passages explicit;[71] and only early 'mystical' sources within Christianity line up the Pauline veiling of women in 1 Cor 11 with positive 'erotic' intimacy through 'contemplation'.[72]

It is where Jewish and Christian exegetes converge on the *Song*, then, that the 'erotic' form of veiling connotes *special* access to the (unspeakable) divine. Such an erotic reading of 'veils' was also applied at times, in a public ritual context, to the 'veil' of the Jerusalem temple. As recent studies have illuminated,[73] one rather startling set of rabbinic traditions associate the ancient annual pilgrimage to the temple on Mt Zion with an actual 'seeing' of the Lord (highly dangerous as this was), in the form of an exposition of the ark and a lifting of the temple 'curtain' (or veil) before the Cherubim.[74] The Babylonian Talmud *Yoma* 54a records how, to begin with, the pilgrims could only see the two 'staves' of the ark sticking out from behind the curtain, 'protrud[ing] as the two breasts of a woman' (and here *Song of Songs* is once more cited).[75] But then Rabbi Katina is quoted as

---

[71] Irenaeus cites such a gnostic (Valentinian) source in *Adv. Haer.* 1. 8. 2: 'The coming of the Savior with his attendants to Achamoth is declared ... by [Paul] in the same letter, when he says: "A woman ought to have a veil on her head because of the angels" (1 Cor. 11. 10). Now, that Achamoth, when the Savior came to her drew a veil over herself through reverential modesty, Moses rendered manifest when he put a veil on his face'. Cited and commented upon in Belleville, *Reflections of Glory*, 57–58.

[72] Origen makes this connection explicit at one point in Bk III of his *Commentary on the Song of Songs*, when he identifies the bride of the *Song*, the Church, and the veiled one of 1 Cor 11. 10: see ed. R. P. Lawson, *Origen: The Song of Songs – Commentary and Homilies*, ACW 26 (New York: Newman Press, 1956), 253.

[73] See Michael Fishbane, *Biblical Myth and Rabbinic Mythmaking* (Oxford: O.U.P., 2003), 173–177; and Gary A. Anderson, 'Towards a Theology of the Tabernacle and its Furniture', in eds. Ruth Clements and Daniel R. Schwartz, *Text, Thought, and Practice in Qumran and Early Biblical Material* (Leiden: Brill, 2009), 159–194. I am most grateful to Gary Anderson for an extended personal discussion of this material.

[74] See the discussion in Anderson, 'Towards a Theology of the Tabernacle', 175–176.

[75] This time, *Song* 1.13: see BT *Yoma* 54a, cited in Anderson, ibid. The same passage is cited and discussed in Fishbane, *Biblical Myth*, 174–175.

adding that, in fact, 'Whenever Israel came up to the Festival, the curtain *would be removed* for them, and the Cherubim were shown to them, whose bodies were intertwined with one another, and they would be thus addressed: Look! You are beloved before God as the love between man and woman'.[76] This eroticized and 'feminized' understanding of direct contact with the deity through a 'veil'/'curtain' does not in the Talmud rest on any connection with Moses's veil. Yet when we go to the much later 'Kabbalistic' writings of the *Zohar*, we do – in a completely different context – finally find an allegorical link made between Moses's 'veil' and the more cosmological 'spiritual veils' deemed to divide the divine and material realms, and also to lie between the prophet and God Himself.[77] With this Kabbalistic link our story of the connection of veils, 'femininity' and Mosaic revelation, seems to come full circle, and the ambivalence we have charted all along becomes the more clear; for the 'femininity' that is characteristically adulated in the *Zohar*, and associated with the presence of the *Shekhinah* (or with the secret meaning of *Torah* to be assimilated by the sage), is assuredly not the 'femininity' of ordinary women. Rather, as Elliot Wolfson has put it of late, 'The secret feminine in Kabbalah becomes *part of the male* [sage]', through a process of 'mystical' assimilation.[78]

And that is why a final reference back to Christian 'mystical theology' of a similar period may be a revealing point of conclusion to this complex section. So close was the connection from the early Christian patristic period, given the authority of 1 Cor 11, between veils and

---

[76] Again, BT *Yoma* 54a, also cited in Gary A. Anderson, 'Mary in the Old Testament', *Pro Ecclesia* 16 (2007), 33–55, at 44–45.

[77] See, in the Hebrew, *Zohar* III, 163a; in English translation, tr. Harry Sperling and Maurice Simon, *The Zohar* (2nd. ed., London: The Soncino Press, 1984) V, 235–236. I am very grateful to †Joseph Dan for alerting me to this text, which is missed by Belleville, *Reflections of Glory*, 75–76, in her treatment of the theme of Moses' veil in the *Zohar*.

[78] Elliot R. Wolfson, 'Occultation of the Feminine and the Body of Secrecy in Medieval Kabbalah', in ed. ibid., *Rending the Veil: Concealment and Secrecy in the History of Religion* (New York: Seven Bridges Press, 1999), 143, my emphasis. See also his 'Crossing Gender Boundaries in Kabbalistic Ritual and Myth', in ibid., *Circle in the Square: Studies in the Use of Gender in Kabbalistic Symbolism* (Albany: S.U.N.Y. Press, 1995), ch. 4.

women (in their variously construed forms of subordinate status), that – perhaps unsurprisingly – the connections between *women* and the cloud tradition of dark 'mystical theology' seem in comparison to have been very slight.[79] For a woman to claim the particular divine intimacy of the cloud, mandated by classic 'mystical theology', was perhaps doubly transgressive: it was, firstly, to escape from under the subordinated Pauline 'veil' of 1 Cor 11, and then to enter the noetic 'dark cloud' of an élite theological intimacy with God, one of seemingly different lineage from the 'feminine' intimacy of veiled submission in the *Song*. Marguerite Porete is a striking example of such double transgression; her extraordinary (and wholly *sui generis*) re-reading of the binary of gender in allegorical terms is further evidence of her *outrée* thought styles. Hers was not even straightforwardly the nuptial 'femininity' of the *Song*, but rather the dark transgressive nescience of the Philonic and Dionysian heritage. Her fate at the stake (1310) doubtless witnesses to the uniqueness and uncategorizability of her theological stance, her failure to fit within the established symbolic, and gendered, typologies of cloud and veil that we have here outlined.[80]

---

[79] I am not taking the 'essentialist' line here found in, for instance, Grace Jantzen, *Power, Gender, and Christian Mysticism* (Cambridge: C.U.P., 1995), that 'intellectual darkness mysticism' was entirely reserved for educated men, and women therefore consigned to 'affective' and bodily 'mysticism'. (This disjunction ill fits Porete – who may actually have influenced Eckhart – let alone Julian of Norwich, for instance.) But access for women to scholastic training in Dionysian traditions was indeed highly limited at this time. The later medieval period did see a great outburst of 'nuptial' mystical theologians amongst women; but the sixteenth century Spanish Carmelites (Teresa of Ávila and John of the Cross) were amongst those who combined the Dionysian and the *Song* traditions most creatively. For Teresa in the Counter-Reformation era, however, both an access to Dionysian 'mystical theology' (which could only be through her male confessors), and to the *Song* in the vernacular (which was then banned), was difficult and somewhat transgressive.

[80] See tr. Ellen L. Babinsky, *Marguerite Porete: The Mirror of Simple Souls* (New York: Paulist Press, 1993), with the useful Introduction (ibid, 5–48) by Babinsky to the distinctiveness of Porete's thought and the gender subversions implied in it.

Nature's 'Veil', 'Noumenal' Darkness and the Modern Scientist

The contrast between the pre-modern traditions of cloud and veil (with all their emphasis on human vulnerability in the face of divine transcendence and mystery), and early modern understandings of the scientific probing of 'Nature' under her veil, is a striking one, which is our final task to explore. Whereas Gregory of Nyssa – and some others after him in the 'dark cloud' tradition – could stress the final *failure* of mental mastery in the quest for God, and the necessity thereby of utilizing a 'feminine' posture of veiled receptivity to the divine, the confident attempt by early modern science to *dispel* scientific ignorance concerning the natural world caused an inversion of these epistemological traits, and a concomitant transformation in the application of our two key metaphors. Now it was not God who was being directly sought and investigated (as in 'mystical theology'), but rather the created *vestigia* of His handiwork, to be probed afresh, and scientifically, in the law-governed workings of Nature and the cosmos. Our last section in this chapter will thus focus primarily on these dramatic epistemological reversals in the period of modernity, but not without a final musing on a certain continuing mystique of the language and imagery of clouds and veils, even in contemporary science. Whilst early modern science seized afresh on the metaphor of 'feminine' veiling in order to indicate how the newly confident male scientist could lift that veil of Nature's secrets (and simultaneously throw off the heavy mantle of ecclesiastical 'heteronomy'), that was not to say that Nature always disclosed her innermost self without curious modesty or resistance. And even when 'She' did, clouds of *cosmological* mystery were not so easily dispelled, despite strong modernistic ambitions in the direction of that conquest as well. Indeed, as we shall see, a remnant of the Christian 'dark cloud' tradition, with all its élite and transnoetic associations, arguably still hangs around the language of physics today, especially when its exponents know that they are up against the speculative or even the truly 'unknowable'.[81]

---

[81] We must here distinguish between a variety of levels and types of 'unknowing' confronted in modern and contemporary natural science: from matters which are (or were) merely *difficult* to explain; through matters which are (or were) *intractable*

A few salient, but piquant, examples must suffice, at the end of this long chapter, to support these culminating theses. Early evidence of the new epistemological confidence wielded by modern science, and its revealing connection to gendered imagery, comes perhaps most famously in the pioneering work of the Englishman Francis Bacon (1561–1626). In his writings on science, the sexual metaphor is repeatedly used to describe the scientist's necessary subjugation of his mysterious, but somewhat wayward, 'wife', 'Nature'.[82] Yet it is not simply a matter of making her a 'slave' (as Bacon does put it in his early work *The Masculine Birth of Time*),[83] but more truly of having – as the feminist philosopher Genevieve Lloyd has expressed it – 'the *right* male attitude to the feminine: chastity, respect and restraint'.[84] Nature herself has to be approached with 'a certain reverence', says Bacon, but with a determination to find 'truth in natural things', and to ensure (note) a '*hatred of darkness*'[85] in order to 'renew and enlarge the power and empire of mankind … over the universe'.[86] What today might be called the 'hegemonic' ambitions of the modern European scientific enterprise are here writ large, yet not without a remaining, and

---

on the basis of outworn paradigms; to matters which in pragmatic terms simply *could not be known* by humans at any particular time (e.g., how many species of ants there are); to matters that must remain matters of *speculation* and dispute (e.g., the origins of the cosmos). The history of science also obviously teaches us about moments of discovery when an item in one of these categories has been moved to another, i.e., to a *less* impenetrable form of 'unknowing'.

[82] 'Let us establish a chaste and lawful marriage between Mind and Nature', as Bacon puts it in his *The Refutation of Philosophies*, tr. B. Farrington, in *The Philosophy of Francis Bacon: An Essay on its Development from 1603–1609 with New Translations of Fundamental Texts* (Liverpool: Liverpool U. P., 1964), 131.

[83] Published posthumously in 1653; now in Farrington, *The Philosophy of Francis Bacon*, see ibid., 62: the narrator announces, 'I am come in very truth, leading to you Nature with all her children to bind her to your service and make her your slave'.

[84] Genevieve Lloyd, *The Man of Reason: "Male" and "Female" in Western Philosophy* (Minneapolis: U. Minnesota Press, 1984), 17, my emphasis. I am indebted to Lloyd's treatment of gender in Bacon in ibid., ch. 1, and references supplied there.

[85] Francis Bacon, Preface to *The History of the Winds* (1662–1663), in eds. J. Spedding, R. L. Ellis and D. D. Heath, *Francis Bacon: Works* (London: Longman, 1858-), vol. II, 14–15, my emphasis.

[86] Francis Bacon, *Novum Organum*, I (1620), aphorism CXXIX, ed. J. Devey, *The Physical and Metaphysical Works of Lord Bacon* (London: George Bell, 1901), 446.

interesting, sensibility about the moral dangers of a sheer violation of ('feminine') mystery. A similar transference of the religious metaphor of 'feminine veiling' to the mysteries of Nature continues to appear somewhat later, in the period of the European Enlightenment, in the writings of Jean Le Rond d'Alembert (1717–1783), the avid French follower of Newton. Like Bacon, d'Alembert is also aware that even the new scientific mastery comes with certain limits and cautions; and he puts it the more programmatically when he avers, again utilizing the sexual metaphor, that there are mysteries of the natural world which the modern scientist can never hope to explicate completely: they remain inexorably 'behind' the 'veil', he says – a veil, moreover, that 'always hides the workings of its more delicate parts from our view'.[87] A new apophaticism is here announced for the secular realm of modern science, and one indeed even now still current in the scientific limit-language of 'veiled reality'.[88]

At this point, it might be objected that the metaphor of veiling, especially after the great early modern revival of classical study, might more obviously be connected with the Greek story of the unveiling of Artemis than with the more elusive veiling of Moses in the Exodus narrative.[89] After all, the statue which Apollo had unveiled, according to this Greek story, was said to be precisely a representation of the goddess 'Nature', and to have 'emerged from a fusion between the figure of Artemis of Ephesus and that of Isis, who, according to an ancient inscription reported by Plutarch said, "No mortal has raised

---

[87] Cited in John W. Bowker, Templeton Symposium preliminary paper, 2005, 2.

[88] The metaphor of the veil was used memorably and repeatedly by Sir Arthur Eddington (1882–1944): see the relevant selections from his writing in ed. Ken Wilber, *Quantum Questions* (Boston: Shambhala, 1984), ch. 19 ('Beyond the Veil of Physics'); subsequently the French physicist Bernard d'Espagnat has given 'veiled reality' new coinage in his discussions of quantum phenomena: see his *Veiled Reality: An Analysis of Present-Day Quantum Mechanical Concepts* (Reading, MA: Addison-Wesley Publications, 1995).

[89] Hadot, *Veil of Isis* (see n. 6, above), devotes his whole monograph to the modern history of the reception of the Greek story. On the key issue of the inscrutability of 'Nature', he does acknowledge a possible biblical link – already noted by Pascal – to the book of Job (ibid., x); but he does not consider the thematic connection to the veil of Moses.

my veil'".[90] The objection that it must be Artemis in the minds of modern scientists' reflection on 'veiling', rather than Moses, certainly has initial point; but recent studies suggest that – in the fluid manner of so much in the symbolic realm – these two stocks of 'veiling' tradition were once again grafted onto one another at some point in the early nineteenth century.[91] The Mosaic tradition of revelatory truth, and the Heraclitan interest in the hiddenness of Nature, converged in the texts of Romanticism and in the concurrent fascination with Egyptology and Isis worship; 'veiling' became a newly fascinating topic, not only for the scientist, but for the classical philologist, the poet, and the theologian.

But what, in contrast, of clouds and their parallel modern transformations? As the quotations from Bacon already intimate, we cannot here separate the metaphor of cloudy darkness, or indeed any sort of unclarity, from the exactly inverse ambitions of the 'Enlightenment' for science and philosophy. And yet even here, there is a paradox, a *limit* to the lifting of darkness and of the dispelling of obscurity so characteristic of the period, and one which is particularly apparent in the philosophy of Kant. The very fact that an epistemology wrenched from the false dependence on theological authority had to appeal to 'noumenal' darkness as the *condition* of its chastened, non-speculative knowledge, is an indication that the cloudy 'mystical' darkness of the Dionysian tradition had not so much been routed but re-designed in new garb. The 'noumenal' now became (depending on one's reading) either an epistemological no-man's land, a place precisely where the

---

[90] Ibid., ix. This story must also be understood 'in the perspective of Heraclitus's aphorism, "Nature loves to hide"' (ibid., viii).

[91] Britt, *Rewriting Moses*, 111–114, following leads in Jan Assmann, *Moses the Egyptian: The Memory of Egypt in Western Monotheism* (Cambridge, MA: Harvard U.P., 1997), shows how the European interest in Egyptology in the late eighteenth century led to an identification of Isis and Yahweh in at least one influential masonic treatise of the period (Karl Reinhold's *Die Hebräische Mysterien oder die älteste religiöse Freymaurere* of 1788); and this was followed by Friedrich Schiller's 1790 lectures, *Die Sendung Moses*, which also made Moses's revelation and Egyptian religion equivalent, in quest of a universal religion and natural law. This identification of Mosaic Law and a law of 'Nature' was in turn taken up by Kant, Goethe, and Beethoven (amongst others); the implicit connection here between two 'veiled' figures – Moses and Isis – is striking, although rarely commented upon.

modern secular know-er could not pass at all, or else (and indeed concomitantly) the wholly mysterious *undergirding* and guarantor of the new secular knowledge.[92] Either way, the remaining trace of 'mystical' darkness was no longer a matter of revelatory 'dazzling', no longer an unspeakable and direct access to the divine, but instead the recognition precisely of the human *limits* of 'reason alone'.

In this regard a final pair of comparative examples of the recent scientific use of the cloud metaphor may prove instructive and revealing. The first comes from the end of the era of late Victorian confidence in scientific progress; the second emerges several decades later from the period of the creation of the atomic bomb, and from the eventual dissatisfaction with Niels Bohr's original model for the movement of electrons around an atomic nucleus. But the shift in the rhetorical utilization of the cloud metaphor even in this short passage of time is deeply revealing. Lord Kelvin's talk of 'clouds' in his famous lecture of 1900, 'Nineteenth Century Clouds over the Dynamical Theory of Heat and Light', was in reference to two seemingly imponderable areas (his 'Clouds 1 and 2') of theoretical difficulty in physics which precisely needed to be *dispelled*, in his view, for scientific advance to be furthered.[93] Clouds, for Lord Kelvin, represented, in classic modern fashion, the sort of mental nescience that science by definition set out to rout. Yet it is a nice irony that the quantum breakthrough that Lord Kelvin himself already intuitively gestured towards brought an almost immediate re-introduction of the cloud metaphor in a more positive – albeit still-mysterious – mode. Thus, through the writing of Richard Feynman and others, the term 'the electron cloud' has become the standard popularized way to describe the movement of electrons around an atomic nucleus – a matter still shrouded in some remaining

---

[92] Alvin Plantinga, *Warranted Christian Belief* (New York: O.U.P, 2000), 9–30, esp. 16–20, comments incisively on this ambiguity in Kant's first Critique. For the relevant section in Kant, see tr. Norman Kemp Smith, *Immanuel Kant's Critique of Pure Reason* (Macmillan: St. Martin's Press, 1970), 'Phenomena and Noumena', 257–275.

[93] William Thomson, first Baron Kelvin, 'Nineteenth Century Clouds over the Dynamical Theory of Heat and Light', an address given at the Royal Institution in London, April 27th, 1900, and discussed by John W. Bowker in *Licensed Insanities* (London: D.L.T., 1987), 46–48. The two 'clouds' here were the two remaining arenas of theoretical *aporia* preventing a complete Newtonian account of the universe.

mystery, but made even more inscrutable on Bohr's original hypothesis, which had continued to cling to the Newtonian analogy of the passage of a planet around the sun. Clouds, then, like veils, have staged a remarkable re-entry in the discourses of contemporary physics. Whilst nescience is still the scientist's enemy, mysterious indeterminacy – cloudy and veiled reality – is precisely what science now realizes it cannot methodologically avoid.

In conclusion, we have ended this succinct, but complex, history of two related metaphors ('cloud' and 'veil'), just as Moses was seemingly abandoned as an epistemological hero in the modern period, and clouds of mental darkness ostensibly dispersed by enlightened secular science and philosophy. Yet the modern male scientist emerged into cognitive light only to find a still-resistant 'feminine' 'veiling' of the Nature that he sought to expose and explicate; and the postmodern scientist went on to find that, given the discovery of the indeterminacy principle and of quantum theory, even 'clouds', also, had a remaining and necessary place in scientific discourse. It is hard to avoid the conclusion that, despite the notable secularism of contemporary science, certain key biblical metaphors for 'knowing the unknowable' continue to exercise the scientific imagination, whether wittingly or no. And one final conclusion, in a story that has involved so many notable symbolic twists and turns, reversals and extensions, is a paradoxical and ironic one. It is as well to remind ourselves that the Nobel Prize medal for Physics and Chemistry is inscribed with *two* 'feminine' allegorical figures – *Scientia* lifting the veil of *Natura*.[94] What we have here called the 'ambiguity of the feminine' could hardly be more powerfully expressed. In an era when the female capacity for high-level scientific thinking remains a matter of heated public debate and controversy,[95] it is important to note that veiling, mystery, clouds and darkness are still strongly implicated in the stuff of science, and

---

[94] *Natura* here is the goddess Isis; according to the official description of the medal (which was designed by Erik Lindberg), 'The veil which covers [Isis's] cold and austere face is held up by the Genius of Science'. The inscription, a quotation from Virgil, *Aeneid* VI, 663, runs: *Inventas vitam juvat excoluisse per artes.*

[95] Only consider the public furore (in 2005) caused by the former President of Harvard Lawrence Summers's remarks about the (supposed) relative ineptitude of women for scientific careers; he was subsequently forced into a retraction and apology to the Harvard Faculty.

that these themes, as it has been one of the burdens of this chapter to display, are themselves inextricably connected to deep normative strands of religious thought about the sexes and their interaction. If 'knowing the unknowable' is a resistant paradox of both religious and scientific thought, as this volume is concerned to argue, then it is a theme keenly, and inextricably, entangled with the problems and paradoxes of gender. The Mosaic heritage, and even more significantly its Pauline response, made clouds and veils – whether overtly or covertly – matters of *gendered* response to inscrutable mystery. In seeking to distinguish, and then re-braid, four different strands in this complex history of a double metaphoric tradition, it has been my aim to show how complex is the entanglement of these various themes, yet how rich and suggestive – even now, not only for contemporary scientific theorizing, but more importantly for Jewish-Christian relations and their christological outcomes – is the stock of religious ideas thus combined.

8

In Defence of Sacrifice: Gender, Selfhood and the Binding of Isaac

Introduction: Where Three Roads Meet

This chapter is positioned where three roads meet.[1] When we speak of three such roads, in Greek mythology, we recall immediately the fateful encounter of Oedipus and his father Laius, whom he was to strike down and kill, in dreadful ignorance that this was his own father whom he assaulted. But the three roads of which I am going to speak in this chapter do not intersect at the place where the son kills the

---

[1] This chapter was originally presented at a conference on the three topics ('three roads') of 'Feminism, Sexuality and the Return of Religion', in Syracuse, NY, chaired by Linda Martín Alcoff and John D. Caputo, in which there was a strong emphasis on post-Derridean, and post-Lacanian, interpretations of these three themes in the French, continental tradition. My own task was to run the three themes afresh through the rich complexity of Jewish, Christian and contemporary renditions of Gen 22; and I argue below that (feminist) 'freedom', 'sexuality' and 'God' are necessarily here those 'three roads' which meet in this text, according to my suggested, albeit novel, interpretation.

The Broken Body: Israel, Christ and Fragmentation, First Edition. Sarah Coakley.
© 2024 John Wiley & Sons Ltd. Published 2024 by John Wiley & Sons Ltd.

Figure 8.1 Rembrandt van Rjin (1635), 'The Sacrifice of Abraham'. Rembrandt / Wikimedia Commons / Public domain.

father, as in the Oedipal myth, but rather at the place where the father (nearly – or perhaps actually) kills the son.[2]

---

[2] During the presentation of this chapter at the original conference in Syracuse, a set of visual images were used as backcloth to the unfolding of the argument. Fig. 8.1 (the familiar Rembrandt van Rjin, *Abraham's Sacrifice*, 1635, etching and drypoint) was projected for the whole of the introduction and the first section of the presentation. Note that according to one strand in rabbinic/haggadic tradition (possibly retro-influenced by Christianity), Abraham does 'actually' carry through the sacrifice of Isaac, but Isaac is then restored dramatically to new life: for the classic modern discussion of these traditions, see Shalom Spiegel, *The Last Trial: On the Legends and Lore of the Command to Abraham to Offer Isaac as a Sacrifice*, with introduction and preface by Judah Goldin (Woodstock, VT: Jewish Lights Publishing, 1993); for a more recent account of how Jewish and Christian traditions inter-related on this theme, see Edward Kessler, *Bound by the Bible* (Cambridge: C.U.P., 2004), esp. ch. 5. I shall return to this theme of Isaac's near-death, or 'death', below.

I refer of course to the biblical narrative of the sacrifice, or 'binding', of Isaac (Genesis 22. 1–14). This was a biblical topic on which Freud himself was entirely, but revealingly (one might say, repressively) silent.[3] And to this Freudian silence we shall return, briefly, later; for arguably this lacuna tells us something significant about another silence – a silence about the *divine* – in Freud's system. Yet it is to the 'binding of Isaac', the *akedath Yizhaak*, that I want to turn our attention in this chapter. This story might initially appear to have nothing whatever to do with the themes of 'feminism, sexuality and the return of religion' – those three contemporary 'roads' that we seek now in some way creatively to re-conjoin. For is not the *akedah* the archetypal *male* myth, the utter inverse of anything feminist? Is it not, after all, precisely the *exclusion* of the 'feminine' that is the distinctive characteristic of the cultic act of sacrifice, an intentional supplanting, perhaps, of the primal 'feminine' sacrificial power of childbirth?[4] Is it not the necessary violence of such sacrifice that condones, justifies and even glorifies the abuse of the powerless (including, of course, women and children)?[5] Is it not precisely the establishment of 'patriarchal'

---

[3] The index of Freud's collected works reveals no sustained discussion of Abraham and Isaac, and nothing at all on Gen 22. It is of course Moses who most vibrantly exercises Freud's imagination, not Abraham: see his *Moses and Monotheism* (London: The Hogarth Press, 1939).

[4] This thesis has been most memorably sustained by Nancy Jay, *Throughout Your Generations for Ever: Sacrifice, Religion and Paternity* (Chicago: Chicago University Press, 1992).

[5] See Carol Delaney, *Abraham on Trial: The Social Legacy of Biblical Myth* (Princeton: Princeton University Press, 1998). Similar presumptions about the violence of sacrifice are to be found in Bruce Chilton's *Abraham's Curse: Child Sacrifice in the Legacies of the West* (New York: Doubleday, 2008); and behind both studies lurks the influential theory of René Girard on sacrifice as 'primary violence': see esp. *Violence and the Sacred* (London: Athlone Press, 1977), and *Things Hidden Since the Foundation of the World* (London: Athlone Press, 1987). Note immediately, however, that it remains a moot point whether sacrifice *is* intrinsically and 'necessarily' violent: such is a specifically modern presumption, as Jon Levenson, *The Death and Resurrection of the Beloved Son* (New Haven, CT: Yale University Press, 1993) is wont to insist, and it enshrines the modern Kantian/Kierkegaardian moral dilemma (moral law vs. its 'suspension') on the assumption that sacrifice cannot be distinguished from 'murder' (Kant's word). Anthropological cross-cultural treatments of sacrifice, in contrast, tend to be more careful to stress the multivalence of sacrifice – its capacity for diverse meanings,

religion that is the *telos* of this story, with its adulation of unthinking male obedience, even unto death and its promise thereby of future generations of sons as yet unborn?[6]

My answer to these classic feminist charges against sacrifice will be both 'Yes' and 'No'. It would be foolhardy to resort to the familiar tactic of denial; the story of the 'binding' of Isaac is as dense and multi-faceted as anyone may care to make it. Such is the irreducible complexity of a founding myth of this sort of power, and I am not in the business of attempting to sanitize it from the historic taints of patriarchal interpretation. Indeed – as I shall shortly show – its very earliest interpretation, already lodged in the biblical text itself, might be called a classically 'patriarchal' one, and its original roots may indeed lie in an all-too-vivid acquaintance with the practice of infanticide.[7] And yet where deep truth lies, the more densely do distractions and perversions from such truth congregate; and it is to such a deeper level of truth in sacrifice that I seek to probe in this chapter.

---

including bloodless gift and moral transformation: on this point see the still-useful collection, eds. M.F.C. Bourdillon and Meyer Fortes, *Sacrifice* (London: Academic Press, 1980); and ed. Jeffrey Carter, *Understanding Religious Sacrifice: A Reader* (London: Continuum, 2003), which provides a fine recent introduction to the plethora of modern and contemporary social science theories of sacrifice. Two monographs that witness to a notable recent turn against the Girardian presumption of sacrifice-as-violence are: Jonathan Klawans, *Purity, Sacrifice, and the Temple: Symbolism and Supersessionism in the Study of Ancient Judaism* (New York: O.U.P., 2006), and Kathryn McClymond, *Beyond Sacred Violence: A Comparative Study of Sacrifice* (Baltimore: Johns Hopkins U.P., 2008).

[6] See Yvonne Sherwood's feminist work on the *akedah*, including: 'Textual Carcasses and Isaac's Scar, or What Jewish Interpretation Makes of the Violence that Almost Takes Place on Mt Moriah', in eds. Jonneke Bekkenkamp and Yvonne Sherwood, *Sanctified Aggression: Legacies of Biblical and Post Biblical Vocabularies of Violence* (Edinburgh: T & T Clark, 2003), 22–43; and eadem, 'Binding-Unbinding: Divided Responses of Judaism, Christianity, and Islam to the "Sacrifice" of Abraham's Beloved Son', *Journal of the American Academy of Religion* 72 (2004), 821–861. Note that in this chapter I shall myself use the term 'patriarchy' in a generic sense to denote any cultural arrangement furthering male authority and hegemony, and thereby implicitly undermining the possibility of women's full flourishing. A particular instance of such patriarchal arrangements is of course the insistence on the greater value of sons (especially eldest sons) over daughters, for the maintenance of patrilineal descent.

[7] See Levenson, *The Death and Resurrection*, for a powerful statement of this thesis, already sketched by Spiegel in *The Last Trial*, 85–88.

At this deeper level of truth, I suggest, our first focus must be not on Abraham, the powerful and obedient one, who has so mightily exercised the modern and post-modern imagination as to whether his action was 'ethical' or beyond it; but rather on Isaac, the ostensibly powerless one, who emerges from his ordeal – I shall argue – strangely unscathed, re-enlivened and utterly transformed.[8] Isaac, in short, is in this chapter the type of the one who triumphs over human powerlessness not by a false, compensatory, will-to-power and further patriarchal violence, but in and through the subtler power of a transformative, divine *interruption*. Here is the surprise, then: for the purposes of my own playful feminist *midrash*,[9] Isaac can be read as gender-labile, the

---

[8] As we shall see further below, this 'positive' rendition of the outcome of Isaac's ordeal is one strand in Jewish tradition on the *akedah* that became intensified during the appalling pogroms of medieval Europe; the primary stress at this time was on the figure of Isaac as the suffering and dying (yet victorious) one, rather than on Abraham: see Spiegel, *The Last Trial*, 17–27. Kessler, *Bound by the Bible*, ch. 5, argues that even from the time of earliest Jewish exegesis of Gen 22, it is Isaac who is the main point of interest, in contrast to Christianity's primary focus on Abraham. Contemporary 'liberal' Jewish preaching tends, in stark contrast to rabbinic interpretation, to take for granted the modern identification of sacrifice with violence or murder, and to read Isaac as rendered psychologically damaged and ineffective as a result of his ordeal (I have this from conversations with a number of North American Conservative and Reform rabbis).

[9] It may be important to stress at the outset of my own account of the *akedah* that the genre I am engaged in here is not a straightforward scholarly retrieval of rabbinic and Christian classical sources (such as I have often employed in my other writings), but a deliberately free and imaginative re-deployment of them for my own 'midrashic' purposes. As such, I intentionally emulate traits in rabbinic hermeneutics itself (though admittedly without some of the florid word-play that is usually characteristic of it). My own *midrash* on the *akedah*, then, whilst clearly both Christian and feminist, enters into conversation with rabbinic interpretation not to supersede but to *attend*: by taking my initial inspiration from elements in that tradition which may seem obscure or tangential, I emulate the simultaneously playful and serious mode of rabbinic exegesis, and also its surprising openness to the new. (As Judah Goldin puts it, '... the story of Abraham and Isaac rises almost spontaneously in the mind of one generation after another ... each generation has its own ... concerns' [Spiegel, *The Last Trial*, xvi].) If to standard modern Christian exegetical eyes my method here seems weird or wilful (as I am sure it will do to some readers), I can only plead that it is itself a kind of ascetical experiment in bringing Jewish and Christian traditions

'type' of feminist selfhood transformed. Isaac's experience, that is, can be the paradoxical test–case for feminist freedom.

So let me then make the bold assertion of my thesis at the outset. I seek to propose that only sacrifice, *rightly understood*, can account for a feminist transformation of the self that is radically 'theonomous', rooted and sustained in God. Only thus is the self rendered authentically 'free', and so propelled both beyond the idolatry of false desire for that–which–is–not–God, and beyond the restrictions of the gender binary that so exercises current secular gender theory, and its reactions to it.

Consider, in this regard, the 'three roads' that I now claim meet at the *akedah*. The first is the modern, feminist road that seeks to empower woman, to endow her with 'freedom', or perhaps now in post-modernity to bestow upon her that more elusive possession of 'agency'. The second road is the road of 'sexuality' (as we have come to call it in modernity), the road that seeks to understand the riddle of psychophysical desire and its final satisfaction. The third road is the road that leads us back to 'good old God', as Jacques Lacan would call him. How shall these three roads meet? My claim is that *the contemporary secular difficulties of the first two roads cannot successfully be traversed without converging on the third*; my more specific thesis is that it is only in the crisis of a divine 'sacrifice' (a term to be defined with care), and an accompanying divine interruption of the normal corrupted human workings of power and violence, that a 'theonomous' self is formed that can overcome the secular feminist *impasses* of the first two roads.

Clearly, these are bold claims. I can only make initial headway with them in the space of one short study of this sort. Yet I shall attempt to instantiate the claims in this chapter by making three basic moves. Firstly, I shall position my argument in the context of the current, post-modern debate about 'sacrifice' and 'gift', a debate that has also educed intriguing new interpretations of the *akedah*. Here I shall argue that the tendency in this debate towards a disjunctive choice between 'gift' and 'sacrifice' has obfuscated the possibility of a deeper, and third, alternative, in which such a disjunctive choice is not demanded; yet the same disjunctive choice has – in these recent debates – simultaneously pressed the language of the 'feminine' into positions either of occluded

---

of depth and perplexity into the kind of mutual, but freeing, submission to God that I advocate in this volume as a whole.

powerlessness, or of eschatological 'excess'. Only a careful re-construal of the inner logic and meaning of 'sacrifice' can address these false dilemmas, and probe to the mysterious level of a divine undergirding of human agency. Secondly, I shall – in the most complex and dense portion of the chapter – return to the Genesis text itself, and to some of the more intriguing details of interpretation discoursed upon in later rabbinic exegesis. On the basis of these rabbinic 'hints and guesses' I shall construct my own feminist *midrash*, in which Isaac becomes the type of feminist selfhood, caught, it initially seems, in a web of patriarchal narcissism and threatened violence, but eluding them precisely by means of consent to divine intervention – a supernatural interruption which resists a *false* sacrificial logic. Thirdly, I shall return in closing to consider what all this may mean for current feminist theory, and for our reconsideration of the first two 'roads' of 'freedom' and 'sexuality'. Here I shall contrast my own theological proposal both with some notable seeming *impasses* in contemporary gender theory, and with one heroic attempt, in the spirit of Freud, to bring the *akedah* into complementary psychoanalytic relation to the undertakings of the Oedipal crisis. I shall conclude, as you may suppose, that 'good old God' is far from dead, but not a mere commodity, either, for any instant amelioration of our current gender-theoretical dilemmas. The 'sacrificial' ordeal of our feminist hero Isaac nonetheless remains on offer; its transformations are undeniably costly, but they are the price of freedom in the richest sense. And oddly, this lesson can at the end even be turned back on Abraham: *his* ordeal, too, though not one of powerlessness, is equally one of purgation and transformation – the giving up of a falsely idolatrous desire in aid of proper detachment, proper submission to God. 'Theonomy', in short, is not a given, but a life-time's undertaking – an ascetical task in response to primary divine gift. It changes everything – not least, as we shall see, the relation of sexual desire to gender.

The Post-modern Problem of Sacrifice

The problem of sacrifice in the modern and post-modern period can scarcely be described simply. Nonetheless, here I shall attempt some broad brush-strokes in order to set up my own alternative for consideration.

It is actually *two* problems in the contemporary discourses of sacrifice that I seek to highlight, although in practice they do interrelate and mutually entangle with one another. The first is the issue that currently dominates the continental discussion of 'the Gift': how is gift-giving possible, if at all, without manipulative intent – *do ut des*? And if such manipulation always lurks in gift-giving, can there be such a thing as 'pure gift', which would somehow escape the supposedly tainted economy of exchange? Since sacrifice, at least according to many of its modern theorizations, falls squarely into the *do ut des* category, 'pure gift' and 'sacrifice' are seemingly disjunct – unless, that is, death itself becomes the means of their intersection. So the problem here is that of the apparent *disjunction* of gift and sacrifice, except in the potentially violent finality of death. Gift is insidiously manipulative, unless also necrophilic.

The second problem[10] is obviously related, but nonetheless distinct. It is the problem of whether sacrifice itself can ever be anything *other* than violent – or, as the backside of this difficulty, whether the well-meaning 'liberal' attempt to sanitize sacrifice into some form of moralism may cause it to lose its power and distinctiveness altogether. Let me say a few words about each of these dilemmas in turn. In doing this, we need also to attend to their gender associations.

It is a notable feature of the debate spawned originally by Marcel Mauss's *The Gift*,[11] that the 'feminine' is seemingly occluded by the

---

[10] Already adumbrated in n. 5, above. The massive underlying influence of René Girard in this regard is undeniable, and I was chided at the conference at which this chapter was originally presented (by Gianni Vattimo and others) for not discussing his work more directly. Whilst it would be a distraction here to advert to a lengthy criticism of Girard's original theory (*viz.*, that sacrifice is an essential and foundational violence against a scapegoat, required for the maintenance of all religion and culture), it should be noted that in his later work Girard makes significant retractions, allowing for the transformative effects of *positive* 'mimetic desire', as well as the negative effects of violent competitive desire (and repenting, e.g., of his earlier denigration of the theology of sacrifice in the epistle to the Hebrews). On these points see the revealing interview with Girard by Rebecca Adams, 'Violence, Difference, Sacrifice: A Conversation with René Girard', *Religion and Literature* 25 (1993), 9–33. For a critique of the effects of Girard's influence on post-modern philosophy of religion, esp. in its interactions with science, see my Cambridge inaugural lecture, 'Sacrifice Regained: Reconsidering the Rationality of Christian Belief' (Cambridge: C.U.P., 2012).

[11] ET London: Routledge, 1990.

'economy of exchange', yet — as more than one feminist has pointed out[12] — it is actually crucial to that economy. In a society glued together by ritualized patterns of barter, the 'bride-price' (or alternatively, the sexual favours of the prostitute), figure large, but they are given little explicit emphasis in Mauss's highly romanticized account of 'primitive' social cohesion. What, then, is the alternative to *do ut des*, or gift as manipulation, which is so easily elided with an equally manipulative 'sacrificial' approach to relations with the divine? In reaction to Mauss's adulation of gift-exchange, Derrida famously reasserts the remaining possibility of a 'pure gift' that escapes the economy of exchange, but which by definition can only be offered by the 'absolute other' (the *tout autre*).[13] Reading the story of the *akedah* in this way, in quest for a 'pure gift', Derrida can see Abraham's offering as the one example of sacrifice that *escapes* the taint of exchange, precisely in turning Isaac over to death. For here Abraham 'renounces all sense and all property'[14] in his willingness to kill his son. Death, then, is the one place where 'pure gift' and sacrifice can meet: in 'gift *as sacrifice*'[15] (i.e., in this death-oriented understanding), that is, in the sacrifice of the economy of sacrifice itself. If we ask where 'femininity' resides in *this* account of 'gift', the answer is more elusive than in the case of Mauss's model, but nonetheless still revealing. Whereas Derrida himself remarks on the 'exclusion or sacrifice of woman' in the logic of sacrifice,[16] and leaves the question 'in suspense' whether the inclusion of a woman as a ritual actor would alter that logic, it is striking that

---

[12] See Luce Irigaray, 'Women on the Market', in ed. Alan D. Schrift, *The Logic of the Gift* (London: Routledge, 1997), 174–189; and Hélène Cixous, 'Sorties: Out and Out: Attacks/Ways Out/Forays', in ibid., 148–173.

[13] For the development of this theme in Derrida, see Jacques Derrida, *Given Time: Counterfeit Money* (Chicago: U. Chicago Press, 1992), and idem, *The Gift of Death* (Chicago: U. Chicago Press, 1995). For the theme of the '*tout autre*', see *The Gift of Death*, ch. 4.

[14] *The Gift of Death*, 96.

[15] Ibid., my emphasis.

[16] Ibid., 76: 'Would the logic of sacrificial responsibility, within the implacable universality of the law, of its law, be altered, inflected, attenuated, or displaced, if a woman were to intervene in some consequential manner? Does the system of this sacrificial responsibility and of the double "gift of death" imply at its very basis an exclusion or sacrifice of woman? A woman's sacrifice or a sacrifice of woman, according to one sense of the genitive or the other? Let us leave the question in suspense'.

his own talk of 'excess' or 'pure gift' can itself occasionally garner the
association of the 'feminine', for it stands altogether outside the masculine economy of exchange.[17]

The alternatives, then, seem to be these: *either* gift as manipulation,
in which woman is occluded and subordinate, but an object of barter
necessary to the whole system; *or* sacrifice as the 'gift' of death, from
which any actual woman is ritually excluded, yet 'femininity' vaguely
adulated as a figure for 'pure gift's' 'excess'. The options are scarcely
looking promising from a feminist perspective.[18]

Yet are these really the only alternatives? Before we dare to suggest
an answer to that question, let us superimpose on it the second problem in the contemporary debates on sacrifice: the problem of whether
sacrifice is *intrinsically* violent and thus in need of reduction to the
ethical. We are reminded here of Kant's famous insistence that
Abraham should, from the outset, and on clear ethical grounds, have
resisted the demands of 'God' to 'butcher [ ] and burn[ ]' his son:
'Abraham should have replied', says Kant, 'to this supposedly divine
voice:"That I ought not to kill my good son is quite certain. But that
you, his apparition, are God – of that I am not certain ...'".[19] Yet this
Kantian approach is, of course, most memorably rejected in
Kierkegaard's *Fear and Trembling*, in which Abraham, the 'knight of
faith', finds himself inexorably engaged in a 'teleological suspension of
the ethical'.[20] The seemingly impossible paradoxicality of Kierkegaard's
position is, as Jack Caputo illuminatingly indicates in *The Prayers and
Tears of Jacques Derrida*, remarkably close to the paradoxes of Derrida's
knife-edge account of 'pure gift' in death: both Kierkegaard and
Derrida resist to the end a *transactional* account of faith, and so also
resist reading the *akedah* as straightforwardly restoring the ethical. Yet

---

[17] See, e.g., Derrida, *Given Time*, 4–5, on 'Madame de Maintenon', for whom 'desire
and the desire to give' is the 'same thing', thus achieving the 'impossible'.

[18] I comment on this malaise and further analyse the problem of gift and gender as
it has now been received in Anglophone theology in: 'Why Gift? Gift, Gender and
Trinitarian Relations in Milbank and Tanner', *Scottish Journal of Theology* 16 (2008),
224–235, a re-worked version of which appears in ch. 11, *intra*.

[19] Immanuel Kant, 'The Philosophy Faculty Versus the Theology Faculty', *The
Conflict of the Faculties* (New York: Abaris Books, 1979), 115.

[20] Søren Kierkegaard, *Fear and Trembling, The Sickness Unto Death* (New York:
Doubleday, 1954), see esp. 64–77 ('Problem 1').

if sacrifice is not constrainable in some sense by ethics, is it not merely released into a dangerous realm of non-accountability, in which – as Derrida, ironically, sees more clearly than most – close imitations of sacrificial 'purity' can pass into the opposite and become monstrous instantiations of violence and abuse?[21] In these modern and post-modern stories of sacrifice, then, gift and sacrifice, morality and the suspension of morality, are seemingly set as alternatives; and 'woman', one way or another, is figured out of centre-stage. Is there any other, feminist, way through and beyond these dilemmas, then, which does not simply declare 'sacrifice' a male problem in need of *disposal*?

The chief problem – as Derrida himself indicates – seems to reside in the absence of any feminist presence in the sacrificial site itself. Yet to place a woman in the position of *Abraham* would be to conjure up the spectre of a Medea slaughtering her children, not to transform the fundamental logic of the operation. In contrast, both rabbinical and contemporary feminist exegesis make much of the role of Sarah, whose almost instantaneous death in Genesis chapter 23 is often taken to be the result of maternal shock and grief.[22] Yet her position in the story, excluded as she is from the vital sacrificial action, presents us with little that can be done by way of its inner transformation. It is only Isaac, I submit, who in crucial relation to the interruptive and saving action of the angel, can give us the key to a new feminist reading of the logic of the *akedah*, which maintains the irreducible significance of the sacrificial in relation to the moral, and yet – *without death!* – refuses also the disjunction of divine gift and sacrifice. This refusal of mine to disjoin gift and sacrifice resides in my own Christian theological insistence that *divine* gift (the constant lure and invitation of grace) inevitably presses on us a particular form of 'sacrifice' as it intersects with the timeline of human sin. Under these conditions, divine gift inevitably invites intentional (given) human sacrifice, if it is to draw us more deeply into participation in that gift. More accurately, we should say

---

[21] See John D. Caputo, *The Prayers and Tears of Jacques Derrida: Religion Without Religion* (Bloomington: Indiana U.P., 1997), 220.

[22] See the discussion of *Genesis Rabbah* 58.5 in Sherwood, 'Binding-Unbinding', 852. A rather different, and earlier, feminist interpretation of Sarah's role and significance is to be found in Phyllis Trible, 'Genesis 22: The Sacrifice of Sarah', in eds. Jason P. Rosenblatt and Joseph C. Sitterson, *"Not in Heaven": Coherence and Complexity in Biblical Narrative* (Bloomington: Indiana U.P., 1991), 170–191.

that this divine gift is itself reflexive (a ceaseless interaction between 'God' [the Source] and 'God' [the Spirit], into which humanity is invited as participator, through a purgation that joins her, sacrificially, with the perfect God/Man).[23] *This* 'sacrifice' is neither blind obedience nor condoned assault; nor yet, exactly, is it Derrida's 'gift of death'; for the participation in this reflexivity-in-God involves purgation into life, rather than sacrifice-as-death. Nor again, finally, can this 'sacrifice' be *reduced* to the moral, for it is more truly the mysterious *ground* of the moral – the making of a 'theonomous' self that is authentically free because authentically submitted to God.

My Christian theological commitments are now on the table, and they explain, I hope, my insistence on a 'deeper magic' for sacrifice, beyond the seemingly false alternatives of the current debates. But these Christian theological commitments are also ones with deep rabbinical roots, as we shall now show: the typological connection of Christ with Isaac that is already found in the theology of Paul (Galatians 4. 28–31; Roman 8. 32) indicates the extent of the overlap-to-come. But to this overlap, I now add my own contemporary justification for 'kidnapping' Isaac for feminist reflection. Only Isaac, I suggest, can represent the position of the modern and postmodern feminist woman, who, no longer and inevitably tied to the home (like Sarah), yet thrust into the world of patriarchy in a position of relative powerlessness (under, of course, the superficial guise of a supposed modern 'equality'), is yet further endangered by the false logic of a distorted, *patriarchal* sacrifice. To read Isaac's role thus will be, as we shall see, to select a particular track through myriad and fascinating rabbinical alternatives, and to insist, as did an important strand in that rabbinical tradition, that Isaac was not an innocent and defenceless

---

[23] This 'incorporative' approach to the Christian doctrine of the Trinity, founded in the Pauline logic of prayer in the Spirit drawing one into the life of Christ (see Romans 8. 9–30) has been a feature of much of my recent theological writing. For a more detailed explication of the exegesis of this passage in the early church, and its theological and gendered significance, see my articles: 'Why Three? Some Further Reflections on the Origins of the Doctrine of the Trinity', in eds. Sarah Coakley and David A. Pailin, *The Making and Remaking of Christian Doctrine* (Oxford: O.U.P., 1993), 29–56, and 'Living into the Mystery of the Holy Trinity: Trinity, Prayer and Sexuality', *The Anglican Theological Review* 80 (1998), 223–232. A more sustained discussion is to be found in *God, Sexuality and the Self: An Essay 'On the Trinity'* (Cambridge: C.U.P., 2013).

child, but already a person of maturity and discernment.[24] He was, however, a person whose relationships were about to be 'interrupted'. To Isaac as an 'honorary woman', then, we now turn.

Why Is Isaac a 'Woman'? Rabbinical Exegesis and the Interruption of Patriarchal Violence

So far in this chapter, I have allowed our gaze to be dominated by that most famous of pictorial representations of the *akedah*, Rembrandt's 1635 etching of 'Abraham's Sacrifice'. Yet the more or less subliminal messages of this etching are, it seems to me, significantly different from the oil painting undertaken the very same year by Rembrandt, and on the same theme (Fig. 8.2).

For here, in contrast to the etching, the exposed body of a nearly grown son is curiously hairless – androgynous, we might say, or even 'feminine'; just as the interruptive angel in this painting also appears more 'feminine' than obviously 'masculine', in gender-stereotypical terms. As we pass into this second section of this chapter, then, let us take stock of various chosen textual themes by comparing them with some striking, and unexpected, visual representations, in which gender codings undeniably play an extra part. The combination of textual and iconographic messages undeniably complicates, but also enriches, our quest for exegetical clarification.

My interest in casting Isaac as an 'honorary woman' lies in his perilous negotiation of the line, well known to feminist women in the contemporary workplace, I suggest, between submission to the logic of a *false* patriarchal sacrifice, on the one hand (in which male violence and scapegoating dominate), and the choice of an authentic and discerning 'sacrificial' posture of another sort, on the other hand (in which genuine consent is given to the *divine* call to purge and purify one's own desires in order to align them with God's). These traits involve fine and important distinctions to be made; and there is no

---

[24] Already in Josephus's account, Isaac joyfully and heroically builds the altar himself (*Ant.*, 1.227); in *Genesis Rabbah* (56.8) he asks Abraham to bind him; in *Sifre Deuteronomy* (32, on Deut. 6. 5), the second century CE Rabbi Meir is cited as insisting that Isaac 'bound himself' on the altar; and in the *Pesikta de-Rab Kahana* (ed. Bernard Mandelbaum (New York: Jewish Theological Seminary, 1962), 2.451), Isaac is said to have 'offered himself upon the altar'. See Levenson, *The Death and Resurrection*, 192–199, and Kessler, *Bound by the Bible*, 123–125, for these developments in Jewish exegesis.

Figure 8.2 Rembrandt van Rjin (1635), 'The Sacrifice of Isaac'. Rembrandt / RKD – Netherlands Institute for Art History / Public Domain.

denying the slipperiness with which interpretations of the *akedah* ever threaten to slide back to what I have termed false, patriarchal sacrifice, even as a subtler alternative is displayed and sought. It is striking, however, how certain strands in the rabbinical reflection on the *akedah* regard distinctions of this sort as vitally important. Let us consider a number of rabbinical traces of this kind.[25]

---

[25] Clearly my very brief treatment here of some intriguing rabbinical traditions on the *akedah* is selective, and – some might say – idiosyncratic. See again n. 9, above, for my defence of this hermeneutical procedure and the use of mutually-informing Jewish and Christian traditions on this problematic nexus.

One of the most touching, firstly, is the tradition in the (relatively late: 9th century CE) *Midrash Tanhuma*,[26] that, after his sacrificial ordeal, and his mother's death, Isaac went to look for Hagar, to bring her back for Abraham to marry. What occasions this suggestion in the text is the renewed mention of a place-name (*Beer-Lahai-Roi*)[27] that was earlier linked to Hagar; but implicitly – one might surmise – it involves a striking sense of identification, in the Isaac who has lately come through the ordeal of sacrifice, with the rejected and despised bond-woman, with whom he now apparently seeks some sort of reconciliation.[28] A further rabbinical 'trace' of interest – as already noted – is the emergence, by the third century CE (as evidenced in *Sifre Deuteronomy*) of the tradition that Isaac was himself fully *consenting* to a sacrificial intention, to the extent of even 'binding himself' upon the altar (a move which Jon Levenson describes as a 'sublimation').[29] Here is no instance of child abuse, then, but an adult caught in a nexus of potential violence but fully intentional about his own actions. This exegetical feature is consonant with the tradition enshrined in the fifth-century *Midrash Rabbah*, that Isaac was of a mature mentality (either 26 or 37 years old) at the time of the *akedah*, and therefore could not have been bound without his explicit 'consent'.[30] Whilst later, medieval, traditions about the *akedah*

---

[26] *Midrash Tanhuma*, vol. 1: *Genesis*, tr. John T. Townsend (Hoboken, NJ: Ktav Publishing House, 1989), 143: 5.9 Genesis 25: 1ff., Part III.

[27] See Gen 24. 62 for the mention of this place as the one where Isaac was before he went out to woo Rebekah; but the only earlier mention of the same place is Gen 16. 14, in relation to Hagar's flight into the desert after Sarah's outburst of jealousy. From this point of name-connection the author of the *Midrash Tanhuma* concludes that Isaac, after finding a wife for himself, went to bring Hagar back to Abraham to marry. He thus identifies 'Keturah' (Gen 25. 1) with Hagar (ibid.).

[28] The author of the *Midrash Tanhuma* puts it more laconically, thus: 'It is simply that when Isaac took Rebekah, Isaac said: Let us go and bring a wife to my father' (ibid.).

[29] *Sifre: A Tannaitic Commentary on the Book of Deuteronomy*, ed. Reuven Hammer (New Haven: Yale U.P., 1986), 32 (and see n. 24, above: Levenson, *The Death and Resurrection*, 193, comments that here 'child sacrifice has been sublimated into self-sacrifice').

[30] *Midrash Rabbah Genesis*, vol. 1, tr. H. Freedman (London: Soncino Press, 1983), 497: 'can one bind a man thirty-seven years old (another version: twenty-six years old) without his consent?' These ages are worked out from biblical hints of the

(as Spiegel's *The Last Trial* so memorably traces) tend, paradoxically, to follow the third-century *Mekilta De Rabbi Ishmael* in insisting that Isaac actually *did* have his blood spilt by Abraham[31] (despite all that Genesis says to deny this[32]), what rapidly emerges from this martyrological line of thought is an equal insistence that Isaac then rose again, triumphantly from the ashes. Indeed in some medieval narratives, the *akedah* of Isaac becomes a sort of proof-text for the very possibility of the resurrection of the dead.[33] We have at this point met an important convergence, then, of Jewish and Christian thought about the typological significance of Isaac's ordeal, one that links it to the *purposive* suffering of others, including Christ's; and this is seen as ultimately transformative and life-giving in virtue of the resurrection and of the salvific intentionality Isaac purposefully embraces.[34]

So there is a significant divergence in the available meanings of the *akedah* that we have unearthed at this point, then, which cannot go without further remark. Again, the crucial distinction between a form of sacrifice tending to patriarchal violence and abuse, and a form that

---

length of years between Sarah's bearing of Isaac and her death, on the one hand (37), and from the number of years that Abraham spent in Hebron on the other (26).

[31] *Mekilta De-Rabbi Ishmael*, tr. Jacob Z. Lauterbach (Philadelphia: The Jewish Publication Society of America, 1976), 57.

[32] See Gen. 22. 11–12; yet from the time of the earliest exegetical reflection, there is perplexity that no mention is made of Isaac after the event on Mt. Moriah, for example, in vs. 19: on this problem, see Spiegel, *The Last Trial*, 3–8, who charts the later traditions that Isaac did die and temporarily went to Paradise before returning to life.

[33] See again esp. Spiegel, *The Last Trial*, ch. 3, for the medieval slaughters of Jews which intensified these *haggadic* traditions of death and resurrection. Levenson, *The Death and Resurrection*, 192–199, insightfully discusses the development of the traditions of Isaac's swooning or actual death, burning to ashes, and resurrection.

[34] This convergence and implicit interaction is commented on in Kessler, *Bound to the Bible*, ch. 5, esp. in relation to the theme of the treasury of merits (*zecut avoth*) accrued by Isaac's ordeal. A particularly telling text here is again the *Pesikta de-Rab Kahana*, 2. 451 (see n. 24): 'By the merit of Isaac who offered himself upon the altar, the Holy One (blessed be He) will in the future resurrect the dead, as it is written: [For he looks down from His holy height; the Lord beholds the earth from heaven] "to hear the groans of the prisoner", [to release those condemned to death]' [Ps. 102. 20–21]'.

is voluntarily purgative but aimed at the fullness of life, is what is at
stake here. It would seem that the earliest known interpretation of the
akedah, however, is that enshrined in the Genesis text itself, in ch. 22.
15–18,[35] and it is this that invites quite justifiable feminist suspicion. It
looks in any case like an interpolation, since, rather oddly, it involves
the angel calling to Abraham a *second time*, in order to tell him that his
suitable obedience has earned him the reward of many male descendants: 'Because you have done this, and have not withheld your son,
your only son, I will indeed bless you'…[36]

We are struck here afresh, in this fateful first intra-biblical interpretation, by the ambiguous and suspicious closeness of blind moral obedience, on the one hand, and abusive and violent possibilities, on the
other; which is why it is worth contrasting this, most early, *akedah*
interpretation with that provided, many generations later in the
sixteenth century, by John of the Cross, supplying as he does, in his
own hand, a drawing of Christ's purposive sufferings on the cross
overseen from the perspective of a *loving* Father.[37] When he writes
explicitly of the *akedah* in a letter to a woman directee, Dona Juana de
Pedraza (Letter 11 to Dona Juana de Pedraza, January 28, 1589), his
stress is entirely on the purgation of desire and the placing of the
sacrificial suffering involved in the context of divine love: 'O great

---

[35] See R.W.L. Moberly, 'The Earliest Commentary on the Akedah', *Vetus Testamentum*
38 (1988), 302–323, which analyses this interpolation as a first attempt to make
Abraham's obedience foundational to Israel and somewhat parallel to Moses's significance. Moberly takes up the issue of the existing feminist 'hermeneutic of suspicion'
in relation to Gen 22 in his *The Bible, Theology, and Faith: A Study of Abraham and Jesus*
(Cambridge: C.U.P., 2000), ch. 5, and – in my view rightly – continues to insist that
'*thoroughgoing* suspicion lacks adequate criteria for assessing in what way the story
might be true …' (ibid., 180, my emphasis).

[36] This is, of course, according to my earlier definition a fully 'patriarchal' promise,
about future power and patrilineal descent; whereas the first intervention of the
angel (vss. 11–12) is, quite differently, about the test of Abraham's detachment (even
from the object of his greatest human love), and thus about his primary and overrid-
ing 'fear'/love of God. One might say that this first intervention therefore *breaks*
patriarchal attachment rather than fosters it: see further, below.

[37] John of the Cross, sketch of Christ on the cross (from the perspective of the
Father's gaze), late sixteenth century, reproduced as the frontispiece of John of
the Cross, tr. Kieran Kavanaugh and Otilio Rodriguez, *The Complete Works of John
of the Cross* (Washington, DC: ICS Publications, 1991).

God of love, and Lord!', he writes. 'How many riches do you place in the soul that neither loves nor is satisfied save in you alone, for you give yourself to it and become one with it through love. And consequently you give us its enjoyment and love what it most desires in you and what brings it most profit. But because it behooves us not to go without the cross, just as our Beloved [Christ] did not go without it.... God ordains our sufferings that we may love what we most desire ... But everything is brief, for it lasts only until the knife is raised; and then Isaac remains alive ...'[38] The difference in tone between that earliest Genesis interpretation and this one from John of the Cross is striking and instructive. For John of the Cross, the seeming threat of divine punishment is dissolved in love; moreover, he can pronounce this message of hope to a woman directee, precisely through his insistence that any suffering herewith is merely for her ultimate flourishing through the redirection and purification of desire in God.

But no less instructive is the distinction between the second, and misleading, 'interruption' by the angel, and the first (in which Abraham's hand is stayed and the ram is substituted for Isaac). I spoke earlier of the importance of this *first* angelic 'interruption' in the *akedah* text for the re-thinking of sacrifice and the rendering of it compatible with what I called reflexive, purgative, divine 'gift'. But I now suggest that we might think of this drama of the first angelic intervention at the *akedah* in the light of the earlier, and equally miraculous, angelic appearance in Genesis 18,[39] in which three mysterious angels are entertained by Abraham and Sarah at the Oaks of Mamre, as they come to announce the birth of Isaac and the end of Sarah and Abraham's much-bemoaned childlessness. In both this case and the first angelic intervention of the *akedah*,[40] we might say that a *negative*

---

[38] Ibid., 745.

[39] See Gen 18. 1–5. A fourteenth century iconic representation of this moment in Gen 18 (*The Hospitality of Abraham*, Benaki Museum, Athens), which is particularly suggestive for our themes has both Abraham and Sarah depicted serving the three mysterious angelic visitors.

[40] This interruption is particularly powerfully portrayed in a fifteenth-century French bible illustration in which the angel turns Abraham right around 90 degrees from his concentration on Isaac (who is bound on a stone altar slab), and protectively grabs his drawn sword. Moreover, the angel is seemingly represented here as a 'female'

duality is ambushed and transformed. In the case of Genesis 18, it is the barren sterility of the elderly couple that is fructifyingly interrupted by a mysterious angelic threeness; in the case of the *akedah* (n. 40), it is, we might say, the curious capacity of an intense father/son relationship to tip from mutual narcissism to violence, that is equally, and most decisively, opened up and stopped by an angelic third. For the rabbis, there was a great deal of lore about what sort of angel or angels were involved in this interruption;[41] but the (feminist) point for our purposes here is that an angelic third has decisively broken the spell of an essentially patriarchal duality.

Consider here (in contrast to this *decisive* turning away of Abraham's sword from his prey in the French MS representation of n. 40), the very different effect if the same event is drawn *without* an angel at all (Fig. 8.3).[42] What we observe here, and most poignantly, is a revealing sketch by a disturbed 14-year-old Jewish boy in psychoanalytic treatment in the early 1950s: only a dark cloud hovers above a submissive Isaac, and no angel of salvation is at hand to prevent the threatened violence from the father – only the similarly clouded possibility of the ram's substitution, which is not here effected.

And similarly, I fear, George Segal's memorable sculptured *akedah* behind the chapel at Princeton University leaves us, literally, with violent dagger drawn (Fig. 8.4),[43] as doubtless befits the events in

---

figure: see E. Wellisch, *Isaac and Oedipus: A Study in Biblical Psychology of the Sacrifice of Isaac, The Akedah* (New York: Humanities Press, 1954), facing 96.

[41] See Moshe J. Bernstein, 'Angels at the Aqedah: A Study in the Development of A Midrashic Motif', *Dead Sea Discoveries* 7 (2000), 263–291, for a comprehensive account of differing views of angels which became associated with the *akedah* story over time.

[42] In Wellisch, *Isaac and Oedipus*, facing 97. Wellisch comments: 'In this crayon-drawing of a boy of fourteen, attending a Child Guidance Clinic, Isaac is shown bowing submissively to Abraham's task …'.

[43] George Segal, *Abraham and Isaac*, twentieth-century sculpture (1978–1979), Princeton University, NJ. Here, in contrast to most medieval representations, the figures are directly and shockingly face to face, Isaac kneeling with hands bound, and Abraham's knife drawn in a phallic position as if to stab Isaac directly into his chest. Neither the angel nor the ram are present. Segal has himself acknowledged that he was affected by instances of child abuse and random violence in representing the *akedah* in this way, for he sculpted the representation in the

Figure 8.3   Drawing of the *akedah* by a disturbed boy of 14 years, attending a Child Guidance Clinic. E. Wellisch 1954 / Reproduced with permission from Taylor and Francis group.

American history which Segal wished to commemorate, and which involved no 'interruption' of patriarchal, military, violence whatever. Yet, in contrast, to try to represent the angel as a *mother*, as one early thirteenth-century pulpit relief ostensibly does,[44] is surely not the miraculous psychoanalytic answer that Erich Wellisch, in his fascinating study, *Isaac and Oedipus*, tries to hypothesize. Rightly taking Freud on for his own repression of the *akedah* complex, along with his over-concentration on the Oedipal dilemma, Wellisch seeks to read the *akedah,* with its – in his view – return of the son to harmonious relations with father *and mother*, as the answer to which the

---

wake of the Kent State University massacre of students by the Ohio National Guard on May 4, 1970.

[44] In a relief on the pulpit at Volterra by Bonusamicus, c. 1200, reproduced in Wellisch, *Isaac and Oedipus*, facing 81. Wellisch comments: 'In this rendering of the Sacrifice of Isaac the figures of Abraham, Isaac and the Angel, who has womanly characteristics, appear to form a family. The sculptor has movingly conveyed a depth of feeling and pious simplicity in the group'.

Figure 8.4   Abraham and Isaac, Princeton University, 1978–1979, cast bronze. Oliver Morris / Getty Images.

Oedipus complex is the problem.[45] It is a heroic attempt; but it finally fails, in my view, to do justice to the profoundly *interruptive* force of the staying hand of the angel in the Genesis story, if it is merely figured as the triumphant return of the family power of the Jewish mother to a father–son relationship which has gone astray! No, something more subtle is at stake here – not reducible to the

---

[45] In Wellisch's own words (*Isaac and Oedipus*, 96), stressing the importance of the re-integration of the maternal into the story (reading the angel-as-Sarah): 'The Akedah story itself does not give a clear indication of what follows. One can, however, draw the conclusion that it marked the beginning of a new relationship between father and son which initiated a new era in the family relationships of man. Its realization depends on a situation in which selfish aims are abandoned and real personal love and dedication to God's call are possible. From the phenomenological point of view this new relationship can be described as *a covenant between parent and child* which inaugurated a new era of moral code'.

need for a comforting stereotypical 'feminine' presence merely to *compensate* for potential male violence, nor to resolve the Freudian Oedipal dilemma, as such.

In the third, and last, section of this chapter, then, I now want to draw out the further and subtler implications, as I see them, of this mysterious divine 'interruption' of patriarchal sacrifice, so poignantly expressed in our original Rembrandt representations. I want to relate this interruption more closely to the subtler form of sacrifice – sacrifice suffered as a purgation of desire for the sake of love – which I have already sought to defend and clarify. What can such a form of sacrifice mean for contemporary issues of 'sexuality' and 'gender'? What happens when the mysterious angelic threeness at the Oaks of Mamre renders the barren couple fertile? What happens, again, when an interruptive 'third' complicates and disjoins the close, but tense, duality of a patriarchal father and beloved son? What happens, in short, when divine thirdness interrupts classic human binaries of sexuality and familial descent? Let me close here with a systematic, and *theological*, proposal about the relation of what we now call 'sexuality' and 'gender', and how they might be related to the sacrificial nexus we have here explored.

The Sacrifice of Sexuality and Gender: 'Threeness' Interrupts 'Twoness'

I said at the start of this chapter that I sought to demonstrate that 'only sacrifice, *rightly understood*, can account for a feminist transformation of the self which is radically "theonomous", and thus rendered authentically free, propelled beyond the idolatry of false desire, and beyond the restrictions of the gender binary that so exercises current secular gender theory'. That was a bold claim; but after our engagement with both text and art of the *akedah* we are now in a better position to return to it. We stressed at the outset of this chapter that the modern, Christian, postKantian, interpretation of the *akedah*, largely propelled by the well-known Kierkegaardian dilemmas, is focused almost exclusively on Abraham's ethical dilemma, and primarily concerned with ethics and violence. But we now see that there is another deep vein of Jewish exegesis of the *akedah*, founded in the medieval period but perhaps nowhere better expressed in the modern period than in the work of Rabbi Abraham Kook, that the *akedah* is at base – and under-lying all the fascinating details of exegesis to which we have partially attended – about the problem of *idolatry*.[46] In other words, it is about the primal sin of the false direction of *desire*. Put that way, we see how well Rabbi Kook's insight accords with that of John of the Cross, cited earlier: when I am brought into the reflexive circle of divine desire for me, it is that subtler sacrifice I have sought to describe and defend here – subtler and more profound than the patriarchal sacrifice of violence – that is demanded of me, if I am to unite my desires with God's desires. In that place of true sacrifice, and not without pain and suffering, desires are sorted and idolatry purged: my desires are gradu-ally set in the light of divine desire – a desire *for* life and joy, not for their suppression.[47] In that place of sacrifice, deeper than any *individual* ethical decision, I am also en route to a freedom that is free precisely because it is rooted in God. This is the road back to divine union, to

---

[46] See Rav Kook, '*Olat Re'iyah*, 82–97 for his commentary on the *akedah*. Unfortunately this is not available in an English tr., but commentary may be found in Zvi Yaron, *The Philosophy of Rabbi Kook*, tr. Avner Tomaschoff (Jerusalem: Eliner Library, 1991), ch. 2, esp. 40–43; and in Jerome I. Gellman's 'Poetry of Spirituality', in eds. Lawrence J. Kaplan and David Shatz, *Rabbi Abraham Isaac Kook and Jewish Spirituality* (New York: New York U.P., 1995), ch. 4. The distinctive feature of Rav Kook's rendition of the *akedah* (as beautifully brought out in Gellman's treatment) is that the anti-idolatrous sacrificial urge in Abraham *must* combine both detachment/renunciation and the renewed love of earth, family and relationship. To participate ecstatically in divine love *is* to 'return to the servants and donkeys' (see Yaron, *The Philosophy*, 43); the upwards move of ascent is immediately met with the downwards move of divine compassion and mercy for His creation. Here we meet a striking parallel with Christian mystical doctrines of simultaneous ascent and 'kenotic' descent.

[47] It is surely significant that, in Bk II of the *Dark Night of the Soul* (the terrible 'Night of Spirit'), John of the Cross describes how God draws so painfully and pur-gatively close that is it *felt* as an assault which is also (paradoxically) a seeming aban-donment. In fact, according to John, it is neither; because what is felt as violent is only seemingly such because the soul is not yet used to this level of intimacy with God; in reality it is the lightest and most tender touch of love, inviting the soul into union with Christ. See John of the Cross, *The Complete Works*, *Dark Night* II, esp. chs. 10–13 (414–428).

a perception of what it is for the wellsprings of human agency to flow unhindered in God's own prior agency.[48]

Two important things follow from this line of thought, it seems to me, about our current difficulties on the other two roads, which I claimed at the start meet God at the *akedah*. And with these somewhat bold proposals about 'sexuality' and 'gender' I shall bring this speculative chapter to its close.

Firstly, let me venture a reflection on 'sexuality': if the 'sacrifice' of the purgation of desire draws all desires in its wake, then what we now call our 'sexuality' must be drawn vitally into the divine tether of desire. There is a profound sense, I propose, in which sexuality is, theologically speaking, my most urgent reminder of my creatureliness and my dependence on God. This is not to be confused with a *tantric* approach to sex (there is no direct *identification* of sexual pleasure and our relationship to God I am proposing here); rather, it is about a play within a web of desire which is ultimately God's, and which through sacrifice, rightly understood, draws all my desires more truly into alignment with God's.[49] Hence, and ironically, I can agree most happily with Judith Butler when she says that 'sexuality establishes us as outside of ourselves';[50] yes, I would say, outside of ourselves, and *in God*.

So secondly, and finally, then, there is the vexed matter of gender, understood, I propose, as 'embodied relationship'.[51] What is the relation of this gender to 'sexuality' just discussed, and to the purgative play of divine desire in us? If the logic of 'interruption' in sacrifice that we have examined can be allowed to guide us here, then we shall be forced to conclude that the 'thirdness' of the divine interruption in

---

[48] I have attempted a sustained argument for the *feminist* worth of such a perspective on submission to God in my *Powers and Submissions: Philosophy, Spirituality and Gender* (Oxford: Blackwell, 2002), esp. the Introduction and ch. 1.

[49] See my 'Pleasure Principles: Towards a Contemporary Theology of Desire', *Harvard Divinity Bulletin* Autumn 2005, 20–33 (now republished in Sarah Coakley, *The New Asceticism: Sexuality, Gender and the Quest for God* (London: Bloomsbury, 2015), ch. 1), for a more detailed enunciation of my thesis that this ascetic (*not* repressive) perspective should apply equally to heterosexual and homosexual desire. I do want to stress that my thesis here is not to be confused with the conservative agenda to put homosexuals through reparative therapies.

[50] Judith Butler, *Undoing Gender* (New York: Routledge, 2004), 15.

[51] See Coakley, *God, Sexuality and the Self*, 53.

sacrifice seems to disturb any fixed, or sterile, binary in gender. Divine desire, we might say, is ontologically more fundamental than gender. Gender 'matters', to be sure, for it is our mode of embodied relationship – created, fallen and *en route* to redemption in God. But it is made labile to the workings of divine desire, as twoness is interrupted by the third.[52] Hence, when our three roads, feminism, sexuality and God, meet at the *akedah*, there is a sacrifice, all right. But, unlike patriarchal sacrifice, it is a sacrifice that I have argued feminism cannot do without; for ultimately, it shows us not only where true freedom (from patriarchy and other ills) lies, but also indicates how we might re-think sexuality and gender creatively in God.

Conclusions

In this chapter I have levied an unusual argument for the feminist significance of sacrifice, read through the complex traditions of the *akedah*. In so doing, I have – with the majority Jewish tradition of the pre-modern era – put the spotlight on Isaac, rather than – with the majority Christian tradition of the modern era – on Abraham. I have argued that the Kantian and Kierkegaardian dilemma between the ethical and what 'suspends' it can be sublated by attention to a rendition of sacrifice motivated by the purification and intensification of love for God. As such, the true meaning of such sacrifice – as the passage towards proper ascetical 'detachment' – is ultimately as applicable to the figure of Abraham as it is to Isaac, although for Isaac, it comes through a more painful and dangerous powerlessness, which I have figured as Isaac's symbolic 'femininity' *vis-à-vis* patriarchy. On this picture, sacrifice is the necessary *purgation* of false desire (leading to life, not death) which occurs when the divine gift hits the timeline of human sin and asks of us nothing less than complete and ecstatic commitment to the divine; it progresses ultimately to a 'theonomous' selfhood in which freedom is constituted by right dependence on God, and God alone; and it culminates in re-entry into social and community life, re-charged with divine life and love.

---

[52] Again, I make this argument is made at greater length elsewhere: for the intersection of 'twoness' and 'threeness' in God and in human sexuality, see Coakley, *God, Sexuality and the Self*, ch. 1, esp. 55–58 (at 58).

As such, I have argued, sacrifice is as much a *feminist* mode of trans-formation as it is a death-knell to patriarchy; yet patriarchal sacrifice, its dark mimic, ever hovers as a seductive and demonic alternative, and threatens to obtrude. The one, sacrifice-for-God, brings freedom, union and peace; the other, sacrifice-for-the-world, re-establishes the law of patriarchal violence, possessiveness and abuse. Again, the one, sacrifice-for-God, 'interrupts' the fixed repressive gender binary of patriarchy; the other, sacrifice-for-the-world, re-establishes the vio-lence of mandatory 'heteronormativity' and male dominance. The problem of continuing political vigilance in this area, not to say of intense spiritual discernment, is clearly not to be gainsaid. But the rejection of 'sacrifice', *tout court*, is too high a price to pay for the very freedom that is at stake.

Finally, in the course of this argument, I have brought certain minor-ity strands within Jewish and Christian traditions about the *akedah* into a sort of mutual submission of their own: 'Deep calls to deep', as the Psalmist says; and we may well think thus of the remarkable conflu-ence, in particular, of strands of thought in John of the Cross and Rav Kook. If a founding myth of such ineluctable power and elusiveness as the *akedah* can bring Jew and Christian together once more rather than dividing them, it will indeed be a sign that a transformative spir-itual purgation has occurred – one worthy also, in the best sense, of the name of 'feminism' and the true freedoms it still seeks.

PART 3

The Eucharist, Desire and Fragmentation

9

In Persona Christi: Who, or Where, Is Christ at the Altar?

Introduction

The remaining four chapters of this volume constitute an unfolding, albeit complex, argument and thus should be read together. The ultimate goal is a further, and final, enrichment of the question that has been at the core of this book all along, that is, the quest for the 'identity' of Christ, and where and how to find him.

The heart of what I am seeking to elucidate in this last section of the book runs thus. Let me state it boldly at the outset, for it may cause some discomfort. I aim in the course of these four last chapters to explicate an implicit theology of Christian *desire*[1] that rightly lies, I argue, encoded in any theology of the eucharist once we grasp, and combine, certain pertinent biblical, theological and anthropological

---

[1] This theme, as already explored in my *God, Sexuality and the Self: An Essay 'On the Trinity'* (Cambridge: C.U.P., 2013), esp. 7–11, 51–28, and *The New Asceticism: Sexuality, Gender and the Quest for God* (London: Bloomsbury, 2015), esp. 1–28 and 29–53, is now here extended specifically to the context of eucharistic theology. Brief anticipations of my discussion here are also to be found in the 'Prologue,' and ch. 1, of this volume.

The Broken Body: Israel, Christ and Fragmentation, First Edition. Sarah Coakley.
© 2024 John Wiley & Sons Ltd. Published 2024 by John Wiley & Sons Ltd.

considerations. Firstly, there is the significant contiguity and mutual permeation of key New Testament texts on the sacrificial death of Christ, on the one hand, and on the contested nature of the Christic 'body' in the era of the church, on the other; secondly, there is the implication for our core theme of desire of certain classic scholastic, Reformation and contemporary *magisterial* statements on the eucharist; and thirdly, there are the lessons – more subtle, to be sure – of the bodily liturgical movements of the eucharistic rite itself, and how they in themselves evoke and arouse a sense of Christ's presence, and identity, within the very sacramental act. The point, then, of this investigation is to attempt a distinctive contribution to the remarkable renewal of eucharistic theology that is already in process in the post-modern West, by shifting the focus specifically to questions of desire and gender.[2] But in critical conversation with the literature of this already-existing renewal, I shall seek to develop an accompanying *ascetical* theology of the eucharist that questions and queries the urgent blandishments of the 'commodification of desire' in today's secular culture, daily intensified the more – and imposed most painfully on those in abject poverty – by the advertising wings of the 'Web'. In short, I aim to show how the longing for the efficacious presence of Christ's body and blood in the eucharist is a matter of a *divine* 'economy of desire' that impinges upon us, and chastens us, no less in matters of money and power than in matters of sex and gender; and indeed that these issues are vitally related to one another, once we see the intrinsic connections to the central theme of the 'body of Christ' and our desiring discernment of it.

What is required of the astute commentator here, then, is not only a new attention to the core biblical and historical texts that have informed classic eucharistic theology, both Catholic and Protestant; but also a certain subliminal awareness of the power of the bodily movements of liturgy, of ritual's capacity to evoke and transform

---

[2] As will become clear in this chapter and the ones that follow, I am not alone in recent exploration of these themes in relation to the eucharist; but I attempt here to bring together for the first time, and then adjudicate, treatments of them in modern Roman magisterial documents, French feminisms, continental philosophy of religion, and British post-modern theology. To this task I bring my own, already enunciated, notion of divine and human desire as outlined in *God, Sexuality and the Self*.

unconscious forces, and then – not least – of the relationship between these factors and associations of desire and gender.

So the thesis I aim to explore is that the eucharist is indeed the locus of potentially powerful evocations and transformations of human desire. Such a proposal might immediately meet an objection, especially from a Protestant perspective,[3] that the elucidation of the category of desire has, *prima facie*, little obviously to do with Jesus's initial institution of the eucharist (in Mark 14. 22–25 and parallels), or with the immediate implications of Paul's account of its significance in 1 Cor 11. 23–26.[4] I shall meet these objections a little later. However, any repression of the category of desire in relation to the eucharist would emphatically not be the view of the modern *Roman* magisterium, whose insistence on a *nuptial* vision of the eucharist (founded in Eph 5. 25–33, and in commentary on the *Song of Songs*, and perceived fundamentally as Christ loving the church) forms now the crucial fulcrum of the Roman Catholic rejection of the ordination of women. For Rome, therefore, in recent decades, questions of eroticism and gender have become the *more* central – not the more peripheral – to the official theology of the eucharist.

Rather than sanitizing the issue from the outset, then, I propose to walk boldly, firstly, in this chapter, into the fanned flames of ecumenical debate that this question of women priests enshrines for our theme. It seems the most pertinent, albeit controversial, place to start our investigation. Whereas the usual feminist (and predominantly Protestant) *riposte* to Rome on women's orders has been to *de*-sexualize the eucharist, to stress 'commensality' (eating together) over sacrifice,

---

[3] The most famous modern Lutheran objection to identifying (Platonic) 'desire' with Jesus's teaching on 'love' is of course to be found in Anders Nygren, *Agape and Eros*, tr. Philip S. Watson (London: S.P.C.K., 1953). I respond critically to Nygren in *The New Asceticism*, 45–51.

[4] However, not to be overlooked in this context are the highly evocative words recorded by Luke of Jesus to his disciples at the Last Supper (Luke 22. 15): 'I have eagerly desired (lit., "with desire I have desired") to eat this Passover with you before I suffer', which – if they go back to any accurate memory of Jesus's speech – suggest a desiring intensity of purpose in his institution of the eucharist. And as I have already explored in ch. 7, and will shortly return to again, it is striking that Paul's treatment of the eucharist in 1 Cor 11 is in direct contiguity in this same chapter with contentious issues of gender, sexuality and wealth.

and to declare eroticism and gender irrelevant to eucharistic celebration, I shall here take the opposite tack. Starting from this hotly contested base, I shall seek in this chapter to provide a new response to the issue of what it is for the priest or minister to act *in persona Christi*. True to my focus on the category of desire, I shall argue that both Rome and the Orthodox are entirely right to seek the Christic clue to eroticism and gender *in* the eucharist; but that Rome's particular attempt to debar women from the altar and to 'freeze' the gender binary back into mandated roles finally fails in its very articulation.

In order to sustain this thesis I shall turn first to the contemporary Roman treatment of the classical Thomistic theme of the priest's role as '*in persona Christi*'. What I shall trace briefly here is the particular way that the 1976 magisterial document '*Inter Insigniores*' interprets Thomas on this topic, and – more crucially – how it is forced at points to depart from Thomas. Then I shall note how one conservative defender of the Roman position (Sara Butler), and one liberal Catholic detractor (Dennis Ferrara) have extended – and bifurcated – the debate on the reading of Thomas; and how – hovering behind and between these readings – lies the now-massive influence of Hans Urs von Balthasar, with his significantly greater emphasis than these other writers on the *Marian* role of the priest. This Marian priestly theme is one strangely suppressed in '*Inter Insigniores*', but entirely congruent with late-medieval sensibilities, and indeed with Thomas's own insistence that the priest is *medius* between divinity and humanity – *in persona Christi* but no less *in persona Ecclesiae*, for whom Mary is the ultimate prototype. But once this *duality* of the priest's role is recaptured, I shall argue, the central argument of both the magisterium and of von Balthasar himself begins to unravel. Finally, and in the light of this exposition, I shall state my own view: that precisely in the light of the Christ/church nuptial model of the eucharist, a static or fixed gender binary becomes impossible. For in fact the priest is in an inherently complex gender role as representative of *both* Christ and church, strategically summoning the *stereotypical* gender associations of each, but always destabilizing the attempt to be 'held' in one or the other. Thus, a significant part of the undeniably 'erotic' tug of the priest's position at the altar lies in this very destabilization: a gesturing towards a *divine* 'order' of union and communion beyond any tidy human attempts at gender characterization and binary division.

I *'Inter Insigniores'* (1976) and the Use of Thomas Aquinas's Theme of *'In Persona Christi'*

But this is by way of forecast. Let me now begin with *'Inter Insigniores'*. The document starts – positively – with an acknowledgement of the changed and improved status of woman in the modern world, and a valorization of the theological leadership of certain women religious in the history of the Church (St. Catherine of Siena and St. Teresa of Avila, *par excellence*, as 'doctors' of the church); but it immediately presents the issue of the ordination of women as an 'ecumenical problem'.[5] There are in fact two major prongs to the argument against the ordination of women presented in this document. The first is simply the argument from tradition: Jesus and the early church did not ordain women, it says (barring what it sees as some gnostic aberrations in the second century), and the unchanging tradition is therefore against it. The second prong of the argument, however, is the one that interests us here and on which much weight is made to hang. Citing Thomas Aquinas, first from the *Summa Theologiae*, and then from the commentary on the *Sentences*, the crucial argument of the priest's status *'in persona Christi'* is invoked. A woman cannot be a priest, it is said, because in the eucharist the priest acts 'not only by the power conferred by Christ in ordination', but *'in persona Christi*, taking the *role* of Christ, to the point of being his very *image*, when he pronounces the words of consecration'.[6] But what exactly does this mean? *'Inter Insigniores'* does not mention that this matter remains somewhat elusive in the *Summa* treatment at this point, in which Thomas does not expatiate on the impediment of gender, although he considers a whole range of other possible difficulties, such as senility, or living in sin, or blindness, or leprosy-infested limbs. But in the *Sentence* commentary, to which *Inter Insigniores* next appeals, Thomas ostensibly fills in a gap here: 'Sacramental signs', he says, 'represent what they signify

---

[5] Congregation for the Doctrine of the Faith, *From 'Inter Insigniores' to 'Ordinatio Sacerdotalis': Documents and Commentaries* (Washington, DC: United States Catholic Conference, 1996), 23.

[6] *'Inter Insigniores'*, 41 (my emphasis), citing *ST* III. 83, art. 1, ad 3: 'the priest … enacts the image of Christ …'

by *natural resemblance*';[7] and '*Inter Insigniores*' – by a certain sleight of hand – uses this principle to drive home its point of the necessity of male priesthood. However, it actually tacitly departs from Thomas's own line of argument in *three* significant ways.

Firstly, '*Inter Insigniores*' does not argue, as Thomas does in *In IV Sent.*, that what clinches the argument against the ordination of women is: (a) a Scriptural warrant against female teaching authority over men (1 Tim 2. 12); and (b) the supposed inherent inferiority of woman as 'in the state of subjection' (based on an Aristotelian biology of sex and reproduction, now acknowledged to be defunct). Both these particular appeals are seemingly now an embarrassment to the magisterium, and are passed over. Secondly, '*Inter Insigniores*' signally fails to mention, as Thomas does not fail to do: (a) that 'the power of Orders is founded in the soul', which would apparently make sex indifferent to the reception of orders; and (b) that the office of prophecy has been exercised by women to great effect in the tradition, and that – ostensibly – the 'office of prophet is greater than the office of priest', which should surely affect our approach to female ordination. Both these points are honestly raised by Thomas, and then trumped by his Aristotelian biological argument; but since '*Inter Insigniores*' has now tacitly abandoned that biological line of approach, these other points arguably still have to be faced. Thirdly, then, '*Inter Insigniores*' has to fill in the gap left by the embarrassing and now-defunct biological argument in new ways (and this it does with great haste and stealth, in one short paragraph[8]). It argues, in fact, that the 'natural resemblance' that must adhere between Christ and the priest is not now based in supposed greater male authority and superiority, but rather in physiological resemblance; and that without this resemblance, *qua* male, it would be 'difficult' (not, note, impossible) 'to see in the minister the image of Christ'. It then adds, quickly, 'For Christ himself was, *and remains*, a man.'[9]

Now neither of these last points, as far as I know, is ever wielded by Thomas himself against the ordination of women; and the question of

---

[7] '*Inter Insigniores*', 43, citing *In IV Sent.*, dist. 25, q. 2, quaestiuncula 1 ad 4 (my emphasis).

[8] At '*Inter Insigniores*', 43.

[9] '*Inter Insigniores*', 43, my emphasis.

Christ's physiological/genital maleness, *qua* risen body, might well continue to be a matter of dispute between Eastern and Western Christian traditions: the insistence on it is a *novum*, and might, on one understanding, appear to compromise the soteriological principle that 'the unassumed is the unhealed' where women's very salvation is concerned. Be that as it may, the crucial dimensions of the Thomistic appeal in the magisterial document have now been dissected. But what we should also note, finally, is that *'Inter Insigniores'* then goes on, in clear distinction from the Thomistic appeal, to expand at some length the nuptial theme of Ephesians 5 beloved both of Hans Urs von Balthasar and of the then-Pope (John Paul II); it is this which purportedly, and finally, clinches the argument.

Now as Kari Elisabeth Børresen demonstrated long ago, in her classic feminist account of Augustine and Thomas on the status of women, Thomas himself interestingly makes little of, indeed generally eschews, discussion of the marriage metaphor for Christ and the church, although it had been dear to Augustine;[10] and so this appeal plays no part in his argument on women's supposed incapacity for ordination. Not so *'Inter Insigniores'*. It is actually the supposed 'deep' mystery of sexual 'difference',[11] as enunciated in the eucharist, and in no way 'suppressed in the glorified state',[12] that here renders a female *unable* to be a priest. The priest, *qua* eucharistic, Christic bridegroom, 'must be [it is said] … a man'.[13] There is an ostensibly awkward moment, at the end of this section of the document, when it is admitted that the priest does also act *'in persona Ecclesiae'* – 'in the name of the whole Church and in order to represent her' – as well as *'in persona Christi'*.[14] But no mention, interestingly, is made of this other posture as inherently 'feminine' or 'Marian' – even though the logic of the nuptial argument implicitly demands it; and the immediate conclusion is drawn that, 'It is true that the priest represents the Church, which is the body of Christ. But if he does so, it is precisely because

---

[10] Kari Elisabeth Børresen, *Subordination and Equivalence: The Nature and Role of Woman in Augustine and Thomas Aquinas* (Washington, DC: University Press of America, 1981), 234.

[11] *'Inter Insigniores'*, 45.

[12] *'Inter Insigniores'*, 46.

[13] *'Inter Insigniores'*, 45.

[14] *'Inter Insigniores'*, 47.

he *first* represents Christ himself, who is the head and shepherd of the Church'.[15] No argument is given for this final move, although – as we shall shortly see – much hangs on it.

II Disputing the Thomistic Reading: Dennis Ferrara and Sara Butler

Unsurprisingly, the appeal to Thomas in *'Inter Insigniores'* did not go long unchallenged within the Roman Catholic world of scholarship. A significant dispute ensued, mostly in the pages of the journal *Theological Studies*, between Dennis Ferrara and Sara Butler;[16] but the Benedictine scholar Guy Mansini later added his further corrections to Ferrara in *The Thomist*.[17] Not all the details of this complicated exegetical debate need detain us here, for we have already sketched some of the ways that *'Inter Insigniores'* significantly departs from Thomas's own intentions. The crucial dividing issue for our own purposes lies in Ferrara's well-intentioned, but ultimately misleading, attempt to read Thomas on *'in persona Christi'* 'apophatically', as he puts it, rather than 'representationally'. What is evidently motivating him here (and is worthy of note, because it is a classic 'liberal' ploy that I explicitly wish to eschew in my own argument), is a desire to make eroticism and gender entirely *irrelevant* to the matter of priesthood. Thus, according to Ferrara, Thomas does not intend by speaking of the priest acting *'in persona Christi'* a personal, let alone, gendered, 'representation' of Christ. Rather, says Ferrara, he is inviting the priest merely to 'quote' Christ, and so to 'give way visibly to the *persona* of

---

[15] *'Inter Insigniores'*, 47, my emphasis.

[16] See Dennis Michael Ferrara, 'Representation or Self-Effacement? The Axiom *In Persona Christi* in St. Thomas and the Magisterium', *Theological Studies* 55 (1994), 195–224; idem, 'The Ordination of Women: Tradition and Meaning', *Theological Studies* 55 (1994), 706–719; Sara Butler, M.S.B.T., '*Quaestio Disputata*: *'In Persona Christi'* – A Response to Dennis M. Ferrara,' *Theological Studies* 55 (1994), 61–80; Dennis Michael Ferrara, 'A Reply to Sara Butler', *Theological Studies* 56 (1995), 81–91; and idem, 'In Persona Christi: Towards a Second Naiveté', *Theological Studies* 57 (1996), 65–88.

[17] Guy Mansini, O.S.B., 'Representation and Agency in the Eucharist', *The Thomist* 62 (1998), 499–517.

Christ'.[18] On this (so-called) 'apophatic' reading of the elusive '*in persona Christi*' theme, Ferrara can claim that gender has nothing to do with priesthood, once Thomas's erroneous Aristotelian biology is jettisoned.

To this argument Butler rightly replies, in my view (and some of her points are echoed in the subsequent article by Mansini) that Ferrara on this particular issue of '*in persona Christi*' has utterly misconstrued Thomas — or rather, flattened the elusive subtlety of his position. Thomas intends the priest to be both *sign* and *instrument* in the sacrament of the altar: it is therefore not enough for the priest simply to 'quote' Christ in order to consecrate the elements. If that were all that was involved, there would be a mere memorial, but not a *bona fide* 'sacramental representation'. Thomas argues in the *Sentence* commentary, points out Butler, that Christ uses not just the words, but the minister too, as 'instruments' in the form of the sacrament (*In IV Sent.* d. 8, q. 2, a. 3, sol. 9); and thus it must be that the *person* of the priest 'gives sacramental visibility to Christ whose minister and instrument he is'.[19] Were this not so, there would be no reason for Thomas to reject the ordination of women at all. Ferrara's spuriously 'apophatic' reading of Thomas therefore abstracts — gnostically we might say — from the essential bodiliness of the sacramental representation; and this is an ironic position to arrive at given that Ferrara wishes to make a *feminist* commitment to the ordination of women. But Butler is surely right to insist that Thomas intends the minister neither to be physically insignificant, nor merely to 'play act' Christ: as she puts it, the sacramental mode of representation in Thomas is '*sui generis*',[20] and that is doubtless why it is so hard to describe or encapsulate clearly. It is neither a complete self-effacement nor yet a *dramatic* representation. Both those analogues are misleading.

There are two remaining points, however, on which Butler has to admit a certain defeat where the limits of Thomas's argument are concerned. One issue finds her in agreement with '*Inter Insigniores*', the other in implicit criticism of it. Like the authors of '*Inter Insigniores*', firstly, she has to acknowledge her modern disavowal of the faulty

---

[18] Ferrara, 'Representation or Self-Effacement?', 213.

[19] Butler, 'Quaestio Disputata', 73.

[20] Butler, 'Quaestio Disputata', 74.

biological argument that finally undergirds Thomas's rejection of the ordination of women; women are *not* naturally subordinate to men, and this means, she admits, that some different – and, as she puts it, 'complementary' – view of the sexes[21] will have to be brought in to sustain the magisterial rejection of women's ordination. (Butler does not acknowledge at this juncture in her argument that the modern rendition of the sexes as 'complementary' or, more pointedly, as 'opposite', is a particular invention of the Romantic era – but to this point I shall shortly return in discussing von Balthasar.) Secondly, Butler helpfully clarifies that there is an apparent sleight of hand in *'Inter Insigniores'* in suggesting – albeit briefly – that it is Thomas who makes the argument for the necessary likeness to Christ in the priest's male *body* or *visage*. On the contrary, notes Butler, the fittingness of the male representation in Thomas resides in the man's supposed natural superiority (back to the faulty biology again), not in his physiological impression; it is in fact a strand in *Bonaventure*'s sacramental theology that is being drawn upon here, she rightly points out, not Thomas's; and it is this that is needed to fill the gap in the argument as to the relevance of the 'male sex to the signification of Christ the Mediator, who became incarnate as a male'.[22] It is Bonaventure, then, who – in commenting on the same point in the *Sentences* that Thomas also responds to – insists that only a man can 'signify' the Mediator, not because the male is superior, but simply because Christ *was* a man: 'quoniam mediator solum in virili sexu fuit et per virilem sexum potest significari' (*In IV Sent.* d. 25, a 2, q. 1 concl.).

But where does all this leave us? Let me gather the strands of the argument so far so that we can see where we are going.

What the complex technical debate over Thomas's account of '*in persona Christi*' shows us, it seems to me, is three things. Firstly, there is something irreducible about the *bodiliness* of the priest's representational function at the altar – and not just of the recitation of words – that cannot be magicked away; but the question of how that bodiliness relates to Christ as a *man* remains obscure once Thomas's Aristotelian biology is questioned. Secondly, if Thomas's faulty gender theory is to be replaced by a specifically Romantic view of the so-called

---

21 Butler, 'Quaestio Disputata', 80.
22 Butler, 'Quaestio Disputata', 67.

'complementarity' or 'oppositeness' of the sexes – as Butler proposes –
then this has to be made explicit. It is here that we shall find
von Balthasar's example peculiarly revealing; but at the same time it
must be acknowledged, as '*Inter Insigniores*' does not acknowledge,
that the notion of woman as the 'opposite sex' – as Thomas Lacqueur
and others have controversially explored of late[23] – was a product of a
particular period of Western medical and cultural history, precisely
replacing the 'subordinate sameness' theory that Thomas Aquinas and
the whole Aristotelian tradition had long taken for granted. It is in no
way obviously mandated by Bible or earlier Christian tradition.
Thirdly, when *Inter Insigniores* covertly slides away from Thomas to
invoke a Bonaventuran principle of necessarily male representation at
the altar, the issue of the priest's representation of the *laity* becomes
obscured. Yet as Thomas himself rightly insists, it must be that the
priest is representative *both* of Christ and of the people.

In the remainder of this chapter I shall now make a brief analysis of
the telling gender arguments of von Balthasar – which themselves lap
at the edges of '*Inter Insigniores*', given von Balthasar's role as an official
commentator on the document – and are, I believe, credible extensions
and clarifications of the official Roman position. All three of the issues
just highlighted come explicitly to the fore in von Balthasar's treatment; but all three – as I shall argue – reach a certain point of logical
crisis. From our treatment of von Balthasar, we shall then be able to
conclude with a reading of the '*in persona Christi*' theme that chooses
neither the falsely 'apophatic' route of Ferrara nor the Bonaventuran
argument of Butler. Instead I shall plot a third way through the dilemma
and argue that the very nature of the priest's role *destabilizes* the fixed
gender binary: precisely the bodily and gendered significance of priesthood, and especially the nuptial and erotic overtones of the eucharist,
make the 'freezing' of the gender binary impossible.

But firstly, to von Balthasar.

---

[23] See Thomas Lacqueur, *Making Sex: Body and Gender from the Greeks to Freud*
(Cambridge, MA: Harvard U.P., 1990). The historical details of Lacqueur's account
have not gone unchallenged; but the shift from the Aristotelian vision of the woman
as inferior replica of the man, both physiologically and psychically, to an 'opposi-
tional' or 'complementary' account of gendered characteristics in the early modern
and modern period, is hard to debunk altogether.

III   Hans Urs von Balthasar (1905–1988) on the Eucharist and Gender

The extraordinary richness and complexity of Balthasar's theory of gender has in recent years received increasing attention, both critical and appreciative.[24] To read, say, von Balthasar's short *Mysterium Paschale* (alone), as many in the English-speaking world do, is to miss completely the gender evocations with which his kenotic trinitarian theology of the cross is larded elsewhere (most notably in his *Theodramatik*).[25] Gender is so profoundly woven into his deepest theological themes (Trinity, Christology, ecclesiology, Mariology), and so surprisingly and counter-intuitively in some of its twists and turns, that I cannot possibly do full justice to its entanglement with the issue of priestly status in this brief treatment. I shall simply fasten for these present purposes on three central points of analysis, which roughly correlate with the three issues for further discussion which I have just raised: together these will provide us with a fulcrum for critical discussion. I shall turn, firstly, to the central issue of his rejection of the ordination of women, and his ostensible reasons for it; then, secondly,

---

[24] A doctoral dissertation written at the Gregorian in Rome gives an exhaustive, but entirely adulatory, account of von Balthasar's views on gender and the priesthood: see Robert A. Pesarchick, *The Trinitarian Foundation of Human Sexuality As Revealed by Christ According to Hans Urs von Balthasar: The Revelatory Significance of the Male Christ and the Male Ministerial Priesthood* (Rome: Editrice Pontificia Università Gregoriana, 2000). With this should be compared, amongst a burgeoning and continuing secondary literature: eds. Lucy Gardner, David Moss, Ben Quash and Graham Ward, *Balthasar at the End of Modernity* (Edinburgh: T & T Clark, 1999); the essays by Rowan Williams, 'Balthasar and the Trinity', and Corinne Crammer, 'One sex or two? Balthasar's theology of the sexes', in eds. Edward T. Oakes, S.J., and David Moss, *The Cambridge Companion to Hans Urs von Balthasar* (Cambridge: C.U.P., 2004), 37–50 and 93–112; and Karen Kilby, *Balthasar: A (Very) Critical Introduction* (Grand Rapids, MI: Eerdmans, 2012), which is particularly discerning in its critique of von Balthasar's gendered account of the internal relations of the trinitarian 'persons'.
[25] Compare Hans Urs von Balthasar, *Mysterium Pascale* (Edinburgh: T & T Clark, 1990) – a text originally written at speed for an encyclopaedia volume, and strikingly devoid of gender allusions – with idem, *Theo-drama* (San Francisco: Ignatius Press, 1988–1998), esp. vols. 3 (1992) and 4 (1994), which are replete with gender themes.

to his accompanying Mariology, as the crucial extra focus for his reflection on the church as 'feminine'; and then, finally, to the complexity of his gender-theorizing on the Trinity, a place where – I shall argue – the influence on his work of the patristic writer Gregory of Nyssa shines through, with its strong hint of a possibility of gender transformation as a continuing condition of the life of incorporation into God.[26] To anticipate: what I find here is a stern argument for the cosmological *impossibility* of women's priestly sacramental ministry, paradoxically *combined with* the very potential for that argument's undoing. To these three tasks I go briefly in turn, then.

At the heart, firstly, of Balthasar's explicit rejection of the ordination of women is a key paradox, which simultaneously reveals a capacity for 'fluid' thinking about gender *vis-à-vis* men, and yet a means of 'fixing' womanhood outside the bounds of priesthood. It is well expressed in the essay he wrote as commentary on the publication of '*Inter Insigniores*', entitled, 'The Uninterrupted Tradition of the Church', and also in a later essay on 'Women Priests?' in *New Elucidations*. On the one hand, men and women are 'equal', and nowhere is this clearer than in the person of Christ: as Balthasar puts it in the latter essay, 'One can say that Christ, inasmuch as he represents the God of the universe in the world, is likewise the origin of both feminine and masculine principles in the church ...'[27] Yet this equality does not suppress a 'difference' which is even more fundamental: 'the Catholic Church is perhaps humanity's last bulwark of genuine appreciation of the *difference* of the sexes', he writes, and of 'the extreme oppositeness of their functions ...'[28] It is actually the 'feminine', which for Balthasar is seen as primary for the church, and pedestalized as the 'comprehensive feminine, the Marian', unsullied and actively 'fruitful', that is 'already *superior* to that of the man'[29]; and yet it is the man, 'consecrated into [his] office' who alone can represent the 'specifically masculine function – the transmission of a vital

---

[26] See Hans Urs von Balthasar, *Presence and Thought: An Essay on the Religious Philosophy of Gregory of Nyssa* (San Francisco: Ignatius Press, 1995). The original French edition was published in 1988.

[27] Hans Urs von Balthasar, 'Women Priests?', in *New Elucidations* (San Francisco: Ignatius Press, 1986), 187–198, at 193.

[28] Ibid., 195.

[29] Ibid., 193, 192.

force that originates outside itself and leads beyond itself'.[30] As Balthasar puts it in a much-quoted remark in another essay in the collection *Elucidations*: 'What else is his Eucharist but, at a higher level, an endless act of fruitful outpouring of his whole flesh, such as a man can only achieve for a moment with a limited organ of his body?'[31]

So here we confront the essential gender double-think at the heart of Balthasar's system: the priest *must* be physiologically male, although also 'feminine' *qua* transmitter of an ecclesial vital force that is more fundamentally that of the 'perfect feminine Church'.[32] Women, however, are always and *only* 'feminine', expressing their 'natural fruitfulness', which is 'already superior to that of the man':[33] 'equal' but 'different', 'equal' but *superior* (even), but 'equal' and inherently and physiologically incapable of the priesthood. As Balthasar puts it triumphantly in 'The Uninterrupted Tradition', alluding to Eph 5, 'The redemptive mystery "Christ-Church" is the superabundant fulfilment of the mystery of creation between man and woman ... The natural difference is charged, *as* difference, with a supernatural emphasis ...' Only this nuptial model can reflect the 'decisive light about the real reciprocity between the man and woman.'[34] Thus if a woman aspires to be a priest, she is disordered, breaking the rules of her own primary 'fruitfulness'.

This central paradox – all are 'equal', but men are more equal than women (to adapt a well-known phrase of George Orwell) – is reduplicated, secondly, in the Marian fundament that explicitly sustains it. For whilst the 'feminine' here, as Mary, is the *sine qua non* of the church (as Balthasar puts it, 'The Church begins with the Yes of the Virgin of Nazareth'[35]), this 'feminine' tips over into Petrine 'masculinity' *where men are concerned*: 'What Peter will receive as "infallibility" for his office of governing will be a partial share in the total flawlessness of the feminine, Marian church,' he writes.[36] Thus a fluidity from and

---

[30] Ibid., 193.

[31] Hans Urs von Balthasar, *Elucidations* (London: S.P.C.K., 1975), 150.

[32] Balthasar, 'Women Priests?', 193.

[33] Ibid., 192.

[34] Hans Urs von Balthasar, 'The Uninterrupted Tradition of the Church', in *From 'Inter Insigniores' to 'Ordinatio Sacerdotalis'*, 101.

[35] Balthasar, 'Women Priests?', 192.

[36] Ibid., 193.

between 'femininity' and 'masculinity' is the lot of the man, whilst, in contrast, woman is only and solely the 'feminine', a conclusion that Balthasar however roundly denies signifies a 'precedence' for the man: 'Who has precedence in the end? The man bearing office, inasmuch as he represents Christ in and before the community, or the woman, in whom the nature of the church is embodied – so much so that every member of the Church, *even the priest*, must maintain a feminine receptivity to the Lord of the Church? This question is completely idle, for the difference ought only to serve the mutual love of all the members in a circulation over which God alone remains sublimely supreme.'[37]

If we ask, thirdly and finally, how this (selective, male) potential for gender fluidity finds its counterpart in Balthasar's thought about God-as–Trinity, we confront even more fascinating, labile, but questionable assertions. As a careful reading of the *Theodramatik* in particular shows, Balthasar can re-apply his theory of 'femininity' and 'masculinity' at this higher level of theological reflection to arrive at the following conundrum: that the Son is 'feminine' in relation to the Father's 'masculinity', yet Father *and* Son are 'masculine' in jointly spirating the (initially 'feminine') Spirit; and yet again that the Father too can be said to be 'feminine' in receiving the processions back into himself from the other two.[38] All the persons, in other words, are *both* 'masculine' and 'feminine' (with the possible exception of the Spirit?); and by extension, it must be again that the Christ/Word/priest who 'pours himself out' as seed at the altar is *also* 'feminine', receptive, as representing the capacity of the church so to be fructified.

And so we arrive at what I suggest is the internal undoing of Balthasar's own recitation of Romantic gender binaries. For while the woman is fixed normatively as 'feminine', both pedestalized and subordinated (though not in rhetoric, as we have seen), the male in contrast has this infinite capacity for reversal and internal reciprocity, just as God's 'persons' do in the Trinity. And indeed his priesthood vitally depends on this fluidity. Is it possible that an influence on Balthasar from Gregory of Nyssa's own malleable theory of gender, so fascinatingly expressed in Gregory's ascetic works and in his commentary on

---

[37] Ibid., 197–198.

[38] See Balthasar, *Theodrama* 3, 283, and *Theodrama* 5, 91.

the *Song of Songs*, and alluded to by von Balthasar himself in his own monograph on Gregory, *Presence and Thought*, is here in the ascendancy.[39] Yet it meets, and is stopped short *in the woman's case*, by Balthasar's equally immovable German romanticism, his seeming adulation of the notion of *das ewig Weibliche*. It is an odd, fascinating and altogether uncomfortable mix, as I hope these brief foci for examination have shown. But it is a mix concocted, however strangely, from two quite different inheritances of the primary symbolism of the nuptial metaphor. For Gregory of Nyssa's treatment of this metaphor (as I have tried to show in my own work of late) precisely *cannot* be constrained into such an immovable binary. For Gregory, gender is always being recast, renegotiated, the closer one gets to intimacy with Christ.[40]

Let us now consider finally, then, what this all might mean for our contemporary consideration of gender and eucharistic priestly enactment, its continuing connection with that erotic metaphor, and the implications for the presence of Christ himself in the eucharist.

IV   The Woman at the Altar: The Cosmological Disturbance of the Incarnation

I said at the start of this chapter that I was set on demonstrating that 'the priest is in an inherently complex gender role as representative of *both* Christ and church, strategically summoning the stereotypical gender associations of each, but always destabilizing the attempt to be

---

[39] See von Balthasar's own discussion of these themes in Balthasar, *Presence and Thought*, 153–161.

[40] For my earlier treatments of these themes in Nyssen, see esp. Coakley, *Powers and Submissions: Spirituality, Philosophy and Gender* (Oxford: Blackwell, 2002), 153–167, and Coakley, *God, Sexuality and the Self*, 281–288. I have adjusted and corrected some elements of my account in my more recent article, 'Gregory of Nyssa on Spiritual Ascent and Trinitarian Orthodoxy: A Reconsideration of the Relation between Doctrine and Ascesis', in eds. Giulio Maspero, Miguel Brugarolas and Ilaria Vigorelli, *Gregory of Nyssa: In Canticum Canticorum* (Leiden: Brill, 2018), 360–375, esp. 366–369. In this latest work I am much influenced by the excellent discussion of Nyssen's various changes of mind about 'gender' during the course of his theological career, in Raphael A. Cadenhead, *The Body and Desire: Gregory of Nyssa's Ascetical Theology* (Oakland, CA: University of California Press, 2018).

"held" in one or the other'. Perhaps we are now in a better position, after our interlocutions with Thomas Aquinas, '*Inter Insigniores*', and especially with von Balthasar, to argue this more fully in closing. However, I shall need to summon at this point, in addition to the complex historical and textual material materials we have already been surveying, certain considerations from ritual and anthropological theory, as well other points of contrast with secular feminist and gender theory.

Again, I can gather my argument under three main headings.

Firstly, what the short excursus into von Balthasar's thought reveals, surely, is that – once the Thomistic appeal to the inherent inferiority of womanhood is debunked – some developed theory of nuptial reciprocity is required if the argument against women's ordination is to be sustained. But once the crucial role of the priest as *medius* between the divine and the human is fully spelled out – the priest '*in persona Christi*' precisely because also '*in persona Ecclesiae*' or '*in persona Mariae*' – then the implicit gender fluidity of the ministerial role becomes apparent. It is precisely the priest's ritual undertaking – '*in persona Christi*' – to stand at the boundary of the divine and the human, and indeed *transgressively* to cross it, just as the very act of incarnation also made that transgressive crossing – once for all. Even outside Christianity, anyone familiar with the anthropological literature of ritual will know of a certain parallel *typos*: as Victor Turner put it classically in *The Ritual Process*,[41] the *shaman* or ritual enactor, whose unique job it is to stand on the 'limen' between the known and the unknown and to mediate across it, is often credited with 'threshold' capacities or traits such as bisexuality, dispossession or strange humility. Likewise, Catherine Bell's now-classic study, *Ritual Theory, Ritual Practice,* attempts, with the aid of the insights of the cultural theory of Pierre Bourdieu, to explicate how ritual practice mediates certain cultural 'oppositions' in a way that *creates* particular sorts of bodies, bodies that could not be so made simply by taking thought.[42] I do not of course intend, by these allusions to anthropological and ritual theory, to imply that the Christian eucharist is merely a manifestation of a recurring 'structural'

---

[41] Victor W. Turner, *The Ritual Process: Structure and Anti-Structure* (London: Routledge and Kegan Paul, 1969) 95–97.

[42] Catherine Bell, *Ritual Theory, Ritual Practice* (New York: O.U.P., 1992), esp. ch. 5.

type of human ritual; but I do intend to draw attention, beyond the mere words of the Christian rite, to powerful effects that are wrought more subliminally by the physical enactment of it, and in this area anthropologists and psychologists can well provide insight.

And so secondly, we are surely forced, after what has been revealed in von Balthasar's example and argument, to re-consider the theological *dangers* of the now-fixed West-facing position of most liturgies – both Protestant and Catholic – in the post-Vatican II era in the West. This might be seen as an odd line of argument for a feminist author to take, since it is often presumed – over-hastily – that the 'anti-hierarchical' opposition to the Eastern-facing position is precisely what should cohere with a feminist liturgical agenda. But as Kallistos Ware remarks in an important essay on Orthodox attitudes to the ordination of women, the Catholic Western-facing 'stuck' position has new dangers of *male* idolatry, and unnecessarily intensifies the facially iconic dimension of the priest's role as being '*in persona Christi*';[43] in fact it emphasizes the *sexed* representation of Christ in a way that (as we now see) even Bonaventure would not have envisaged, given that for him the East-facing celebration would have been normative. The problem may then arise for the congregation *either* of an unconscious male idolatry of the priest's person ('everyone is in love with Fr. X'), *or* of a false – but gnawing – sense of incongruity at the particular appearance of the priest (old, ugly, fat, bespectacled, spotty, etc.). This problem, note, is in no way improved by substituting a woman priest; indeed, the symbolic evocations may ultimately be the more theologically worrying if the eucharist is at the same time perceived, or taught to be, merely a 'family' meal: here, we might say, is all the danger of a West-facing 'Julia Child' posture,[44] with the woman priest and her female assistants deftly whipping up the Sunday lunch.

My point – to return to Aquinas – is that the liturgical circumstances that he could assume as ritual backcloth for his subtle theory of '*in persona Christi*' were those of an East-facing celebration, in

---

[43] Kallistos Ware, 'Man, Woman and the Priesthood of Christ', in ed. Thomas Hopko, *Women and the Priesthood* (Crestwood, NY: St. Vladimir's University Press, 1999), 47–49.

[44] Or in England, perhaps Fanny Craddock or Delia Smith, depending on one's culinary generation.

which much of the symbolic significance of the rite lay in the priest's movements back and forth across the boundary line between representing Christ and his church. As Uwe Michael Lang has argued in his important monograph, *Turning Towards the Lord*, the long tradition of lining up prayer and eucharistic worship towards the East (and so towards Christ's resurrection) is one that is not abandoned without huge symbolic loss.[45] Lang, I need hardly say, does not draw the conclusions that I propose *re* women priests and gender theory; but he is fully aware of the labile symbolic significance of the priestly eucharistic movements in an East-facing celebration.

So finally, and thirdly, what *is* the gender theory that I suppose emerges from these accumulated considerations about '*in persona Christi*', both textual and liturgical? My precise speculation here is one that I find tends almost always to be misheard as something more familiar, and perhaps more feared; so let me be careful, in closing, to distinguish it from certain brands of secular gender theory that I believe it casts under what we might call 'Christic judgment'. What I wish to suggest, firstly, is that the fundamentally 'erotic', or 'nuptial', nature of the eucharist might more properly be called 'proto-erotic': it is, in fact, the gift of Christ's body to the church by a *desiring* God who longs for our desiring, participatory response. But such desire-in-God, of course, does not in God's case signal *lack* − it is, as the Pseudo-Dionysius puts it in a memorable passage from the *Divine Names*, IV, that Thomas was later to comment upon − a divine '*ecstasis*' that ceaselessly seeks and yearns for a responsive human '*ecstasis*'.[46] If it is an 'economy of divine desire' into which we enter in the eucharist, then, we might rightly say that *this* desire is more fundamental than human gender; the priest, acting '*in persona Christi*' but no less '*in persona Ecclesiae*', and moving between them, cannot be 'fixed' in one gender pole or the other in her response to the dictates of this desire (*pace* the masculinist *fiat* in '*Inter Insigniores*' at this point in the argument). Neither the movements of the rite, nor the theological propulsions of the text, can 'freeze' the priestly figure into either pole of the erotic gender play, as von Balthasar too acknowledges.

---

[45] Uwe Michael Lang, *Turning Towards the Lord: Orientation in Liturgical Prayer* (San Francisco: Ignatius Press, 2004).

[46] See the discussion of this theme in Coakley, *God, Sexuality and the Self*, 311–317.

But it is *not*, note, that the priest – male or female – has obliterated the endless differences in 'gender' because, according to some liberal ideology, this is *irrelevant* to the undertakings of the priesthood; *nor* is s/he performing a form of outmoded liberal 'androgyny' that leaves Romantic gender stereotypes untouched whilst conjoining them (like 'John Wayne and Brigitte Bardot scotch-taped together', as Mary Daly once caustically put it)[47]; *nor* again – *à la* the post-modern pragmatist feminism of Judith Butler – is it that the priest is performatively conducting a 'queer protest' that will condone certain previously banned forms of sexual pleasure;[48] and nor finally, as in certain forms of 'third-wave' American feminism (intelligently discussed of late by Astrid Henry) is it that heterosexual binaries have become transgressively *chic* once more precisely amongst those who label themselves as 'queer'.[49] No: it is none of these successively fashionable forms of secular gender theory, any more than it is the fixed Romantic binary that the magisterium has belatedly come to favour; and doubtless this is why this Christic alternative is so hard to 'grasp'. It is rather that the flow of 'divine desire' is what liturgically refuses to allow the human gender binary to settle and 'freeze', let alone to be summed up in some triumphant secular ideology. For the fundamental 'difference' to be negotiated here is *not* 'male' and 'female', let alone the Romantic 'masculine' and 'feminine', but rather the ultimate difference between God and humanity; and this, we might say, only Christ

---

[47] Mary Daly, 'the qualitative leap beyond patriarchal religion', *Quest* 1 (1975), 30.

[48] See the now-classic Judith Butler, *Gender Trouble: Feminism and the Subversion of Identity* (New York: Routledge, 1990). I have given an appreciative, but critical, account of Butler's earlier gender theory from a specifically Christian theological perspective in *Powers and Submissions*, 153–167. It may be clear that the view of gender that accompanies (and indeed arises from) the theology of the eucharist, as proposed in this essay, does not easily fit into *either* side of the theoretical battle-lines in secular gender theory that were mustered at the end of the twentieth century (between the supposedly physiological 'essentialisms' of the French feminists and the pragmatic gender de-stabilizations of American 'queer theory'). That it escapes through the horns of this particular dilemma is arguably a sign of its specifically Christian and incarnational provenance: the transformation of gender is a *divine* – but also an embodied – event, according to this view.

[49] See Astrid Henry, *Not My Mother's Sister: Generational Conflict and Third-Wave Feminism* (Bloomington, IN: Indiana U. P., 2004).

has 'negotiated'. *This* crossing of difference is indeed a 'cosmological disturbance' of unrepeatable status. What happens in the eucharist, then, happens on the *limen* between the divine and the human, where the miracle of divine enfleshment challenges and undercuts even the most ingenious secular theorizing about the order of this world.

If we are to return in closing, then, to the wider question of 'Who, or Where, is Christ at the Altar?' it must be acknowledged that the current fixation on whether the centrally important locus is the priestly *persona* (male or female) is a curious new development in the history of Christian eucharistic theology. If, as I have suggested in contrast, desire for the 'body of Christ' brings even gender-fixity into uncertainty, what conclusions are to be drawn for the current ecclesiastical ructions on matters of sex and gender? The line of argument I have begun to develop here, in conversation with pre-modern sources, urges not that this issue is irrelevant, but that the eucharistic enactment of the logic of 'divine desire' should in contrast be the *primary* point of reference – the primary 'orientation', we might say – both ethical and theological. It is through entering spiritually and ritually into this logic, finally, that one may come to glimpse where, or who, or what, 'Christ' is, whether evocatively symbolized in the body of the celebrant, or densely present in the host, or located more widely in the gathered community, or indeed beyond that in the down-trodden of the earth – for those, that is, who have eyes to see.[50] We might conclude, then, that the attempt to contain or constrain the glory of the presence of Christ has been but one curious attendant feature of the contemporary resistance to the ordination of women.

---

[50] See again, ch. 1, for my initial attempt to capture something of the complexity of the issue of locating Christ's presence and identity, not only in the resurrection and the eucharist but in the faces of the poor.

10

Sacrifice Re-visited:
Blood and Gender

Introduction: Review and Forecast

In Chapter 9, I presented an argument about a distinctive and specifically *theological* view of desire and gender that may arise from reflection on the eucharist and the particular ritual position of the priest as *medius/media* between Christ and people. Adjudicating between different readings of Thomas Aquinas's account of the priestly role of '*in persona Christi*', I argued that the contemporary *magisterial* interpretation departs significantly – if covertly – from Thomas's own account, and that the Roman attempt now to replace Thomas's Aristotelian perspective on the inherent inferiority of woman with a Romantic view of gender as 'complementarity' or 'opposition' is as question-begging as what it replaced. Indeed – especially in the contemporary context of a fixedly West-facing celebration – the effect is of promoting a priestly *male* idolatry perhaps more insidious than the church has previously known. In contrast, I began to adumbrate a theory of gender arising *not* from a base outside Christian theology (whether Aristotelian biology or Romanticism's view of the so-called 'opposite' sex), but rather from the very notion of incarnation, and especially from the labile symbolic bodily movements of the priest – as

The Broken Body: Israel, Christ and Fragmentation, First Edition. Sarah Coakley.
© 2024 John Wiley & Sons Ltd. Published 2024 by John Wiley & Sons Ltd.

representative of both laity and Christ – in the eucharist itself. I argued that, from this perspective, we might speak of a circle of 'desire' – divine desire for us and us for the divine – as more *fundamental* than 'gender', but not as obliterative of the endless play of 'difference' that is indeed strongly – but *fluidly* – evoked by the bodily movements of the eucharist and by its nuptial overtones. In short, von Balthasar is right to see the themes of insemination and fructification as part of the dense symbolic *melisma* of the eucharist, but wrong to 'fix' the priest in only one of these poles – the 'masculine' one (as he terms it). A final, and radical, implication of what I argued in Chapter 9 is that the 'cosmological disturbance' claimed by conservatives to be the effect of a woman at the altar is *indeed precisely that*, a making explicit of the transgressive and world-changing effects of the incarnation which intrinsically refuses the fixed order of worldly 'patriarchy'. And precisely on this point the argument will now be extended into the equally contested eucharistic arena of *sacrifice*.

Let me once again enunciate my core thesis for this chapter in anticipation (for it is a complex one), before I turn to its detailed explication.

The overall aim of the chapter is to establish the vital *positive* christological importance of placing the woman in the eucharist in the role of offering sacrifice. The argument is, once more, seemingly counter-intuitive – and profoundly so. Indeed I shall start by tracing the aetiology of a powerful pincer-argument – that from the side of Catholic theological conservatism, on the one hand, and from the side of modern liberal feminism, on the other – that from both sides, albeit ironically, finds the very idea of a female sacrificer abhorrent. This remarkable consensus has indeed been a recurrent theme historically, even despite – and through – the profound *divisions* ecumenically since the Reformation on whether the eucharist should be thought of as a 'sacrifice' at all, or whether more properly as a 'gift'. And the matter has been further complicated – or perhaps more truly over-simplified – by a range of beguiling modern theories that have vied in their ambition to reduce the matter of sacrifice into *one* primal meaning, a tactic that I shall stoutly resist. Probing back then to the New Testament origins of the institution of the eucharist, we shall at this point start to fill in some of biblical background to our general thesis on 'desire' that I promised in Chapter 9: I shall argue here, following some creative New Testament scholarship on this topic, that Jesus did indeed intend the eucharist as a rite commemorating his sacrificial death, one that replaced the cult of the temple (and of animal sacrifice) with his own body and blood, and thus implicitly challenging established notions of ritual pollution. I shall then return to contemporary, post-modern, discussions of eucharist and sacrifice, and bring some recent papal statements about the role of Mary in the eucharistic sacrifice into critical interaction with the psychoanalytical account of sacrifice and *motherhood* offered by the French feminists Julia Kristeva and Luce Irigaray. By exploring the range of possible – and indeed thoroughly disturbing – symbolic overtones created by placing the woman in the place of sacrificer, I shall eventually conclude that this 'disturbance' is again a disguised blessing, one that signals the new ordering of 'desire' in Christ and ultimately a profound *displacement* of patriarchal violence. Finally, throughout this exposition I shall be drawing attention – as only hinted in Chapter 9 in our brief appeal to ritual theory – to the ways in which an analysis of liturgically enacted theological truth fails to be accounted for *simply* by the straightforward analysis of texts or rational theological arguments; and how, therefore, the French feminists' attention to the mediation of the 'unconscious' becomes a crucial – albeit infinitely contestable – dimension of the argument here presented.

Sacrifice Contested: The Meaning(s) of 'Sacrifice'

I start, then, by clarifying what made sacrifice theologically contentious at the Reformation, and what makes it newly contentious today. As is well known, Luther's assault on the Mass as a 'sacrifice' was at the heart of his initial cry for Reform and a crucial part of his attack on the whole mechanism of indulgences. In the famous reforming tract 'The Babylonian Captivity of the Church' (1521),[1] Luther excoriated the notion of the Mass as sacrifice as the 'third captivity' (along with – firstly – the reservation of the cup to the clergy alone, and – secondly – the theory of transubstantiation), but as 'by far the most wicked of all'. This was because it encapsulated for

---

[1] See Martin Luther, 'The Babylonian Captivity of the Church', tr. A. T. W. Steinhäuser, in *Three Treatises* (Philadelphia: Fortress Press, 1959), 119–245.

Luther the manipulative, or – what would now be termed by anthropologists *apotropaic* – attitude to the deity that his entire renewal of
a Pauline theology of grace and justification sought to reject as
'works righteousness'. Luther was therefore the first to say, in the
'Babylonian Captivity', that the Mass is a 'gift' (or a 'testament') *rather
than* a 'sacrifice' – to set up a disjunct which, as we shall see, still exercises the contemporary philosophical imagination. According to
Luther, what is 'given' us in the eucharist is received, passively, rather
than gained; as he puts it starkly in the 'Babylonian Captivity', 'the
same thing cannot be received and offered at the same time, nor can
it be both given and accepted by the same person'[2] – a remainingly
contentious point to which we shall have reason to return in our
discussion of 'gift' in Chapter 11. As William T. Cavanaugh remarks in
an illuminating article on the *political* implications of Luther's move
here, 'This kind of zero-sum logic is essential to Luther's attempts to
safe-guard our absolute dependence on God for our justification';[3]
yet, as Cavanaugh goes on to hypothesize, this move may itself represent the theological seed-bed for a modern, Lockean, contractual
individualism, in which an 'impassible breach' (as he puts it) is set up
between 'free [or "pure"] gift' on the one hand and the contractual,
self-serving business of enlightened, cooperative 'individuals' on
the other.[4] Be that as it may (and I am not myself convinced that
Cavanaugh is entirely fair to Luther's theology in its fulness here), the
defensive *riposte* of the Council of Trent is well known: the Mass was
a 'true and proper' (*verum et proprium*) sacrifice', offered 'once to God
the Father on the altar of the cross' (here the Epistle to the Hebrews
is cited, just as the Reformers cited it in defence of *their* position), but
still 'performed in the mass ... and offered in bloodless manner', such
that 'the very same Christ is contained and offered' and '*we receive
mercy and find grace to help in time of need*'.[5] In short, the Mass both was

---

[2] Ibid., 172.

[3] William T. Cavanaugh, 'Eucharistic Sacrifice and the Social Imagination in Early
Modern Europe', *Journal of Medieval and Early Modern Studies* 31 (2001), 585–615, at
587.

[4] Ibid., 593.

[5] See ed. Norman P. Tanner, S.J., *Decrees of the Ecumenical Councils*, Vol. 2: *Trent to
Vatican II* (London and Washington, DC: Georgetown University Press, 1990),
Session 22, 17 Sep 1562, chs. 1 and 2, 732–733, my emphasis.

and is a sacrifice, Christ's atoning work daily being 're-presented' to the Father for our ongoing good.

If what was contentious in the sixteenth century about 'sacrifice' was primarily an issue of grace and the presumed locus of its benefits, then, what is disputed today is arguably yet more complex, and now explicitly and fascinatingly entangled with issues of worldly power, wealth and gender – whereby hangs much of this chapter's tale. Despite the remarkable success of *ARCIC*,[6] in producing in 1971 a theological report in which Roman Catholics and Anglicans could ostensibly now agree on the eucharist as the once-for-all sacrifice of Christ 'effectually' made present to those who would 'participate in [his] benefits and enter into the movement of his self-offering',[7] the very period of *ARCIC's* report production was simultaneously a moment of new friction and excitement in the *religious studies* theorizing of 'sacrifice', and one that – we might say – condensed into it over a century of anthropological and psychoanalytic 'over-determination' of the category. At the risk of over-simplification, I would like to suggest that the debate on sacrifice has now, more than 50 years after *ARCIC's* report on the eucharist, *three* signal points of contention, only one of which – the first – is a freshly wrought variation on the Reformation dispute about grace and works. The others are new, but equally revealing for this chapter's topic. Let me explain.[8]

This first area of contention, which I shall discuss at greater length in Chapter 11, concerns the contemporary debate about 'gift' and economic relations, which was originated by Marcel Mauss in 1925,[9] and is fascinatingly related to Mauss and Hubert's equally famous thesis about 'sacrifice' (published originally in 1898) as 'communication' with the sacred.[10] It has since spawned a lengthy *theological* excursus

---

[6] The *Anglican-Roman Catholic International* Commission was established by the Archbishop of Canterbury Michael Ramsey and Pope Paul VI in 1967.

[7] Ed. Julian W. Charley, *The Anglican-Roman Catholic Agreement on the Eucharist* (Bramcote, Nottingham: Grove Books, 1971), 11.

[8] What follows should be read in connection with my earlier discussion of the sacrifice of Isaac in ch. 8, and of gift in ch. 11.

[9] Marcel Mauss, *The Gift: The Form and Reason for Exchange in Archaic Societies* (orig. 1925, London: Routledge, 1990).

[10] Henri Hubert and Marcel Mauss, *Sacrifice: Its Nature and Function* (orig. 1898, Chicago: University of Chicago Press, 1964).

from various quarters – both European and North American – about the possibility of the talk of divine 'gift', participatory 'exchange' and its implications for global capitalism. What I wish to point out only anticipatorily in this chapter about this debate is that it has created a renewed atmosphere of polemical *choice* between the metaphors of 'gift' and 'sacrifice', subtly reminiscent of the Reformation divide, but actually occluding an additional set of overtones about gender, which we shall also examine in this chapter and the next. In short, what this debate does is to galvanize our thought-forms about 'sacrifice' and 'gift' into a new set of reflections, and choices, about economic relations and sexual relations – and their intrinsic connections. So already gender is brought into the picture of 'sacrifice'. But more of this in Chapter 11.

The second point of debate is specifically about 'sacrifice' and *violence*, another issue where gender-relations lurk in the shadows. The constellating figure here is undoubtedly René Girard,[11] whose Freudian-influenced account of 'sacrifice' has led to one of the most pessimistic accounts of human 'desire' on offer today, and one that I shall explicitly contest. Girard's thinking about 'sacrifice' is in one sense determinedly negative, precisely because it is founded in violence. 'Sacrifice' comes about as a result of the outworkings of the 'scape-goat mechanism', which in turn is the effect of competitive and so-called 'mimetic' desire: what you desire, I want too, and in order to sublate endless and impossible competitive jostlings, we purge our violence on a chosen scapegoat, who is 'sacrificed' in order to ensure at least a comparative degree of social harmony. Jesus, according to Girard, called a stop to this endless cycle of violence; but – as many critics have noted – Girard's analysis of the possibility of that *fiat* of transformation seems curiously less convincing than his chilling account of the endless cycle of sin and violence. According to John

[11] See esp. René Girard, *Violence and the Sacred* (Baltimore, MD: Johns Hopkins University Press, 1977), and idem, *Things Hidden Since the Foundation of the Earth* (Stanford, CA: Stanford University Press, 1987). The very brief sketch I give here of Girard's views on sacrifice is admittedly inadequate to their complexity and to the changes of mind that Girard himself underwent in his lifetime on the subject. For a more subtle and detailed analysis, see my forthcoming volume, *Sacrifice: Defunct or Desired?* (Charlottesville, VA: University of Virginia Press), based on my Richard Lectures of 2016 at the University of Virginia.

Milbank's particularly unsympathetic rendition of Girard, indeed, it is but a pale 'liberal Protestant' ideological ethicalism, a thin veneer on the pessimistic Freudianism of the underlying theory of 'desire'.[12] Be that as it may, the important point to note here is that – according to at least one prominent contemporary theory of 'sacrifice' – the very notion is tainted with the idea of ritualized, and mandated, violence, seemingly required as the very condition for the possibility of community, but never convincingly getting to the root of what might be said to be appropriately, or *theologically*, desirable.

Doubtless unsurprising, therefore, is our third – and related – *feminist* critique of the sacrificial system, posited in its most sophisticated form in the work of the late Nancy Jay.[13] For Jay, the essence of 'sacrifice' lies in its attempt to supplant and trump the power of maternality. As Jay puts it, sacrifice (especially *expiatory* sacrifice, in contrast to the sacrifice of *commensality*, intended to bind a community in a shared meal) is 'childbirth done better', a ritualized form of the establishment of patriarchal power. This, she argues – utilizing materials from eight sacrificial traditions,[14] but with a particularly significant focus on the Israelite – explains the way that in these traditions, there are characteristically 'logical oppositions between the purifying power of sacrifice and the pollution of childbirth and menstruation'.[15] *Female* blood and the logic of sacrifice are seemingly incommensurable. Women do not belong in the act of sacrifice, precisely because the whole object of sacrifice is to supplant them. Completely unsurprising to Jay, therefore, is the impassioned resistance of Roman Catholic traditionalists to the ordination of women, and indeed even to the inclusion of women amongst the ranks of acolytes at Mass. So here, indeed, conservative Roman attitudes and Jay's feminist analysis converge: women not only do not, but should not (in their right minds) *want to* take part in the expiatory rites of 'sacrifice'. To do so would be to collude in the very rites that marginalize them, and culturally repress even further the significance and power of their fecundity. Similarly, Jill Robbins's essay on 'Sacrifice' for the influential volume *Critical Terms for Religious*

---

[12] John Milbank, *Theology and Social Theory* (Oxford: Blackwell, 1990), 392–398.

[13] Nancy Jay, *Throughout Your Generations for Ever: Sacrifice, Religion and Paternity* (Chicago: University of Chicago Press, 1992).

[14] See ibid., xxvi.

[15] Ibid., xxiii.

Studies in some ways echoes Jay's position, but greatly intensifies the language of feminist repulsion towards it: 'Sacrifice', she writes, citing as demonstrative the *Aqedah*, the 'sacrifice' of Isaac, is ' ... *impossible* in ethical terms, insofar as it is abhorrent ...'[16]

When we survey the cumulative impact of these three, mutually interactive, debates on sacrifice, which continue today to rumble, if not occasionally to erupt, we begin to see why it is that 'sacrifice' has become yet again such an emotive – but contradiction-laden – topic in contemporary Western culture, and one now *essentially entangled with questions of gender*. But when we dare to breathe the question, 'Well, what *is* sacrifice, then, at base?', we find ourselves immediately confronted – as John Milbank has illuminatingly discussed in his article, 'Stories of Sacrifice'[17]– with a plethora of classic grand narratives from the nineteenth and twentieth centuries that arguably witness more to the moral or political commitments of their exponents, than they do to ethnographic realities: from Wellhausen to Girard, via Robertson Smith, Frazer, and Hubert and Mauss, each had a 'meta-narrative' to tell us about what sacrifice was 'really' about – whether pointless priestly scrupulosity (Wellhausen), or totemism (Robertson Smith), or primitive science (Frazer), or communication with the divine (Hubert and Mauss), or – as we have seen in Girard – the destructive outworkings of 'mimetic desire'. But these classic theories now begin to look – to the jaded eye of the post-modern commentator – distinctively 'modern' and *hubristic* attempts to control multifarious phenomena under *one* constellating idea; and perhaps this is part of the reason that the three hot debating points I have just outlined are fraught with so much passion.

Much better surely to admit, theoretically, with the social anthropologist Michael Bourdillon,[18] that 'sacrifice' is an umbrella term

---

[16] Jill Robbins, 'Sacrifice', in ed. Mark C. Taylor, *Critical Terms for Religious Studies* (Chicago: University of Chicago Press, 1998), 285–297, at 296, my emphasis.
[17] John Milbank, 'Stories of Sacrifice: From Wellhausen to Girard', *Theory, Culture and Society* 12 (1995), 15–46. A very useful teaching adjunct to Milbank's suggestive article is ed. Jeffrey Carter, *Understanding Religious Sacrifice: A Reader* (London and New York: Continuum, 2003), which contains excerpts from many of the relevant theoreticians of sacrifice discussed by Milbank, and more recent ones in addition.
[18] See eds. M.F.C. Bourdillon and Meyer Fortes, *Sacrifice* (London: Academic Press, 1980), esp. Bourdillon's 'Introduction', ibid., 1–28.

under which various, 'family resemblance', ideas cluster (offering, destruction, division, substitution, commensality, apotropaism, 'control of death', moral self-giving) but which are by no means all present in any one cultural or religious context of sacrifice, nor necessarily with the same set of symbolic overtones. Once this has been admitted, as I believe it must be, then the crucial job is to explicate with as much precision as is possible the *particular* sacrificial system one seeks to clarify, and its accompanying 'official' theoretic base, but always with the honest acknowledgement that an effusion of additional, and highly *emotive*, overtones will most likely be being set off amongst one's audience or ritual collaborators which are hard, frankly, completely to predict or control. That is the 'name of the game', in my view, and a crucial feature even of 'sacrifice's' *current* symbolic power and density, if my analysis is correct.

However, it has been a notable *theological* effect of our current theoretical confusion and contestation, I now want to note – and especially of the fashionable exposure of the overtones of capitalist manipulation, violence, or patriarchal bids for power – to back away from, or *sanitize*, the notion of 'sacrifice' in relation to the Christian eucharist; and this defensive strategy I also wish to query, since I seriously doubt that such a sanitization can be achieved by mere mental *fiat*. As I see it, this defensive strategy has recently taken three different, but characteristic, forms. Either it says (echoing, but modifying, Luther) that Christian sacrifice is *really* divine 'gift' alone;[19] or it says that the divine gift of incarnation in Christ tragically ran into perniciously violent responses to it, which should in no way be *positively* 'baptized' as 'sacrifice';[20] or, finally, it argues that Christian thinking needs to be purged of nasty infiltrations from 'religious studies' views of sacrifice, with their emphasis on violence, and instead concentrate on the distinctive *moral* effects of the eucharistic rite. Perhaps the most revealing and important example of this last line of approach can be found in

---

[19] This line of thinking can be seen, perhaps a little surprisingly, in Rowan Williams's early Grove Booklet on 'sacrifice', written perhaps partly to placate Calvinist Anglicans: see Rowan Williams, *The Eucharistic Sacrifice: The Roots of a Metaphor* (Bramcote, Nottingham: Grove Books, 1982).

[20] This is Kathryn Tanner's feminist ploy of avoidance: see Kathryn Tanner, 'Incarnation, Cross and Sacrifice: A Feminist-Inspired Reappraisal', *Anglican Theological Review* 86 (2004), 35–56.

the work of the Jesuit Robert Daly, who has devoted most of his research life to the topic of Jewish and Christian 'sacrifice'.[21] In an article in *Theological Studies* (2003), which sums up his whole, complex, research endeavour over some decades, he nonetheless attempts – in truly 'Protestant' manner, as he admits – to prune away all the overtones of the 'destruction of a victim' in the Christian notion of 'sacrifice'.[22] Citing Girard, interestingly, but approving more of his theory of Jesus's *overcoming* of violence than of Girard's distinctive analysis of the roots of 'sacrifice', Daly goes on to insist that the whole 'religious studies' approach to sacrifice is a mistake; and – to the extent that the Council of Trent appeared to mandate some dimensions of the idea of a repeated currying of divine favour through pointing to the 'destruction of a victim' – it too was 'starting from the wrong end'.[23] Indeed 'the Christ event *did away* with sacrifice in the history-of-religions sense' altogether, according to Daly,[24] to replace it with a liturgically enacted, and trinitarianly understood, perception of the 'free and self-giving *love*' of God,[25] which can be duly found in the late-patristic rites before the so-called perversions of medievalism and of Trent set in. Thus what we need to do pastorally, Daly concludes, is to purge our understanding of 'sacrifice' of the morbid emphasis on suffering and violence that rightly fills us with so much horror and repulsion, and concentrate instead on the moral self-offering that naturally flows from *love*. Such an approach, he ends, 'enable[s] us to put the suffering and negativity that characteristically accompanies sacrifice in its proper perspective'.[26]

---

[21] See esp. Robert Daly, S.J., *Christian Sacrifice: The Judaeo-Christian Background Before Origen* (Washington DC: Catholic University Press of America, 1978); idem, *The Origins of the Christian Doctrine of Sacrifice* (Philadelphia: Fortress Press, 1978); idem, *Sacrifice Unveiled: The True Meaning of Christian Sacrifice* (London: Bloomsbury, 2009); and, more recently, idem, *Sacrifice in Pagan and Christian Antiquity* (London: Bloomsbury, 2019).

[22] Robert J. Daly, S.J., 'Sacrifice Unveiled or Sacrifice Revisited: Trinitarian and Liturgical Perspectives', *Theological Studies* 64 (2003), 24–42.

[23] Ibid., 25.

[24] Ibid., 26, my emphasis.

[25] Ibid., 41.

[26] Ibid.

Why do all three of these defensive ploys not completely convince me? I think I have said enough by now to indicate why. Firstly, we *cannot* completely control, by mere theoretical or intentional decree, what the word 'sacrifice' will connote culturally, and especially in the context of an embodied ritual; if evocations of power, violence and especially sexuality are abroad, then it is better to acknowledge and own them than to deny their force. In fact – as I shall go on to argue – we should aim to *do* something with the power of that 'force' – and transformatively. But secondly, and this leads us now to our next section, the final reduction of 'sacrifice' to a moral principle of self-giving (as ostensibly in Daly) looks suspiciously like one of our earlier, nineteenth-century, rationalist 'over-determinations'. After all, Jesus did bequeath to his followers an inevitably multivalent *rite*, not a mere moral dictum; and to a necessarily brief examination of this crucial point of origin, we now turn.

Jesus and Sacrifice

I can only attempt a very brief treatment of the relevant New Testament materials in the context of this chapter, and on issues that are necessarily hermeneutically contentious.[27] Hence I shall be bold, for the sake of clarity, if not for the gaining of a ready consensus of agreement. Bruce Chilton's rich and extensive work on Jesus and the temple, and Jesus and the eucharist (published mainly in the 1990s),[28]

---

[27] Again, I point to my forthcoming volume (see n.11, above), *Sacrifice: Defunct or Desired?* for a more extensive analysis. But I should also underscore here (see the arguments of the 'Prologue') that my appeal in this Section to a reconstructed view of the 'earthly Jesus', and his intentions in his founding of his 'eucharist', should be read in the light of my earlier discussion of the (carefully circumscribed) significance of both 'positive' and 'negative' uses of 'historical Jesus' research for Christology as a whole.

[28] In what follows I draw esp. on Bruce D. Chilton, *The Temple of Jesus: His Sacrificial Program Within a Cultural History of Sacrifice* (University Park, PA: State University of Pennsylvania Press, 1992). Chilton's sensitive but critical exchange with the sacrificial theories of Girard, and with other classic 'religious studies' interpretations of sacrifice, makes this an outstanding and unusual book from a New Testament scholar. Also relevant to my brief analysis here are: idem, *A Feast of Meanings: Eucharistic*

has, to be sure, some dimensions and details which I consider less than fully convincing; but the broad outline of his theory is not only theologically suggestive, but deeply probing and original, and this outline I shall rehearse here (glossing it slightly with small *addita* of my own). His views on Jesus and sacrifice are also supported, and developed, by Bernhard Lang,[29] whose work I am additionally drawing upon, although again not without some extension and critique.

Chilton's fundamental thesis rests on a hypothesis, firstly, about Jesus's own intentions in the institution of the eucharist; and then on a complexification, one might say, of Hans Lietzmann's famous theory that the earliest church dealt with *two* kinds of meal: 'Mass and Lord's Supper'.[30] Chilton, in contrast, sees *several* layers of different interpretations of Jesus's meal active in the New Testament, and this bespeaks for him the inevitable multivalence, in a first-century Jewish context, of the fundamental symbolic actions that Jesus gave his followers – the breaking and sharing of bread, and the passing of the cup.

Chilton first draws attention to the features of Jesus's meals that were characteristic of his teaching and person *before* the Last Supper. In my view he is right to gather this evidence into the orbit of his reflection on the eucharist. For what seemingly made Jesus stand out during the period of his ministry was his willingness, indeed eagerness, to eat with 'tax collectors and sinners'; to ignore certain aspects at least of *halakhic* law about cleanliness, the Sabbath, and purity, including – in his healing ministry – touching women who were unclean by reason of blood; and to be unafraid of being cast as a 'glutton and a wine-bibber'. Also, if we include the stories of the feeding of the 4,000 and the 5,000 in the Synoptic Gospels, and the rich theological reflection on 'bread in the wilderness' in John ch. 6, we

---

Theology from Jesus Through Johannine Circles (Leiden: Brill, 1994); the more popular volume, idem, *Jesus' Prayer and Jesus' Eucharist* (Valley Forge, PA: Trinity Press International, 1997); and idem, 'Eucharist: Surrogate, Metaphor, Sacrament of Sacrifice', in ed. Albert I. Baumgarten, *Sacrifice in Religious Experience* (Leiden: Brill, 2002), 175–188.

[29] See Bernhard Lang, 'This is my Body: Sacrificial Presentation at the Origins of Christian Ritual', in ed. Baumgarten, *Sacrifice in Religious Experience*, 189–205.

[30] Hans Lietzmann, *Mass and Lord's Supper: A Study in the History of Liturgy* (orig. 1926; Leiden: Brill, 1953).

can see that Jesus himself (and/or the earliest church) thought of at least some of his sharing of bread in his earthly ministry as explicitly recapitulating the satisfaction of the Israelite 'craving'/'desire' for bread in the wilderness (see Psalm 78. 29), this time properly and happily enacted, though not without remaining eschatological suggestions for its final fulfilment (given the 'breaking' and re-gathering of 'fragments' necessary for this end).

At a second level of symbolic evocation, however, there are the events of the institution of the eucharist itself,[31] at a meal which may – or may not – have been an official Passover *seder* (Chilton thinks not), but certainly was at the general *time* of Passover. Here Chilton goes somewhat beyond what I regard as strongly established evidence, and argues that Jesus instituted the eucharist immediately after a 'riot' (*sic*) in the Temple,[32] in which he had symbolically enacted his *rejection* of the sacrificial Temple cult, *tout court*. Even if we think that this hypothesis is uncertain (as I do), we may nonetheless be drawn to Chilton's suggestion that the words with which Jesus gave bread and wine to his disciples *suggested* not merely a *berakhah* or fellowship meal (which it also was), or even first and foremost the overtones of the Passover, but a deliberate *replacement* of the animal-sacrifice system of the Temple cult (his blood 'poured out') with his own 'sacrificial' body. Especially if we also take seriously the Johannine strand of reflection on Jesus's 'body' as a replacement/cipher for the Temple, we may legitimately understand Jesus's sharing of bread and wine as a consciously sacrificial act, and moreover, a daring and again implicitly transgressive one, since it involved the actual *drinking* of the life-blood of Jesus – which was not of course allowed in the case of animal sacrifice in the Temple.

---

[31] It is revealing that N.T. Wright, *Jesus and the Victory of God* (Minneapolis, MN: Fortress Press, 1996), 554–559, draws quite heavily and appreciatively on Chilton's work in discussing the Last Supper, only quibbling over a point of emphasis: 'The intended contrast is not so much between the Temple-system and the regular celebration of a meal instituted by Jesus, so much as between the Temple-system *and Jesus himself* ...' (ibid., 558). For Wright, that is, the ritual meal is not the central focus but rather the entire teaching of Jesus on the kingdom and his representational standing as Israel, leading to his death.

[32] Here Chilton draws selectively, but by no means uncritically, on the controversial work of S.G.F. Brandon, *Jesus and the Zealots: A Study of the Political Factor in Primitive Christianity* (Manchester: Manchester University Press, 1967).

(Chilton here cites a saying from the *Mishnah* – *m. Para* 4.3 – and opines that this regards a priest's intention to consume such blood as the most heinous priestly crime imaginable.)

Chilton then goes on from here to suggest that we have evidence in the New Testament for a considerable variety of different attempts at interpreting Jesus's ritualized, eucharistic action *after* his death and resurrection. Amongst these was an early 'back-sliding' interpretation, as Chilton puts it, which he dubs the 'Petrine', and which we note occurring in the early chapters of the book of Acts. Here, the Temple is still being used as a place of worship (one evidence of 'back-sliding', as Chilton sees it), but also, and correlatively, the focus is on the 'breaking of bread' rather than on the more telling drinking of the *blood* of the 'new covenant'. Another level of interpretation, however, comes of course in both the Synoptics and Paul, and this reads the meal now *also* as a clear identification of Jesus's body with the Passover lamb, and thus with a subtly different set of symbolic associations from that of the identification with a Temple sacrificial animal. And yet a further spiral of symbolic evocations – I would myself add – is to be discovered once we explore the full range of associations of Paul's rich theology of the 'body', once it is correlated, in 1 Cor 11. 23–6, to the institution narrative itself. As I would myself want to argue here – and this thought was already implicit in Chapter 9 – it is not a *coincidence* that the re-telling of the institution narrative in Paul comes in close contiguity to the contentious debate about women's roles, women's behaviour and dress at worship (also in 1 Cor 11. 3–16), and to the whole panoply of arguments in 1 Corinthians about how issues of gender and sexuality and class and food and money have all been affected by entry into the ecclesial 'body' of Christ through baptism. For these are issues of somatic *integrity* – the integrity of the ecclesial *and* individual body – which indeed align all these themes, and demand that we rightly *order* our desires; so that when Paul warns of the dangers of eating and drinking the eucharist to one's damnation (1 Cor 11. 32), he is I believe merely recapitulating all the themes of the Christic body's integrity that this difficult letter has spawned. And likewise, when he (or his source) tells us at the end of the institution narrative 'to proclaim the Lord's death until he comes' (1 Cor 11. 26), this is not I think merely the instruction for a liturgical refrain, but a recapitulation for Paul of his whole, densely symbolic, theology of baptism *into* the 'death and resurrection' of Christ's body, with all that signifies for ongoing ethical and spiritual transformation.[33] Perhaps then we might call this Pauline line of thought – as I suggested in the last chapter – the requisite, and repeated, need for the reformulation of our bodily 'desires' according to the pattern of Christ's *original* 'sacrifice', his own bodily passage into death and resurrection transformation.

And if, as I have now briefly argued, Jesus's own special ritual meal was intentionally redolent of Temple 'sacrifice', yet equally designed to challenge and sublate it, and to transgress the rules of priestly purity in a number of distinctly polluting ways, we now have a natural point of transition to our contemporary context of discussion. How, if at all, can we think of *women* as priestly enactors of 'sacrifice' today, and how does this issue relate to that problematic nexus of death, desire, pollution, and the transgression of ritual purity laws, which we now see was also endemic to Jesus's original institution of the eucharist?

The Woman Sacrificer: Patriarchalism Disturbed

It is here that I propose a brief, but I trust revealing, interaction with the psychoanalytic feminist work of the well-known contemporary 'French feminists', Julia Kristeva and Luce Irigaray. Both have written illuminatingly on 'sacrifice', but their different lines of thought should not be carelessly conflated. Indeed, their conclusions about the meaning of the Christian sacrificial rite of the eucharist are strikingly divergent, as we shall now see. Both bring, however, the particular insights of post-Lacanian psychoanalysis to the table of our discussion of ritual. They take it as read, then – as I myself also began to argue in Chapter 9 – that ritual is one of the distinctive forms of human activity in which the unconscious may be creatively, if disturbingly, released; and that the so-called 'semiotic' (the form of the unconscious in Lacanian terms especially associated with the memory of identification with the maternal, but – according to the same theory – repressed at the stage of entry into language) is especially important in the negotiation of *feminist* transformation, and the release of what Lacanian theorists call *jouissance* – 'feminine' joy or ecstasy. For one of them,

---

[33] See Romans 6. 5–11. On this same cluster of themes see the illuminating article by Beverley Gaventa, "'You Proclaim the Lord's Death': 1 Corinthians 11. 26 and Paul's Understanding of Worship', *Review and Expositor* 80 (1983), 377–387.

however (Irigaray), 'sacrifice' in its usual, 'male', form (especially in the Christian eucharist) is associated precisely with the *repression* of such 'joy', and the imposition of the dead hand of the male realm of order and linguistic clarification; whereas for the other (Kristeva), a way is glimpsed to bring the power of fecundity and motherhood, of female blood and milk, *positively* into the orbit of 'sacrifice'. By examining the divergent nature of their arguments, we shall be forced to face the huge feminist *risk* that is taken by allowing this full symbolic range of possibilities to accrue liturgically and to come to clear consciousness. But then I have been arguing all along that this messiness must be *faced* rather than sanitized away. In finally favouring Kristeva's insights, however, we shall indicate how the very idea of a female sacrificer can become a creative new source of symbolic *disturbance*, precisely redolent of Jesus's own rupture of the Temple system of animal sacrifice, and thus of the fundamental destabilization of the 'world's' order implied by the incarnation.

The divergence between Irigaray and Kristeva on sacrifice may be expressed, albeit oversimplifyingly, in the following terms. Irigaray's argument is somewhat reminiscent of Nancy Jay's,[34] and indeed was developed independently at about the same time. Whereas Jay uses the insights of anthropology, however, Irigaray comes at sacrifice as a Lacanian psychoanalyst. In her essay 'Women, the Sacred, Money',[35] she argues that 'Most societies have been built on sacrifice', but that – more often than not – woman has been the hidden victim in the system. Sacrifice, then, at least in the dominant Western sense, is a code for men asserting their power – often violently – over women; whereas underlyingly another 'feminine' sacrifice is always going on – '*the sacrifice of natural fertility*' – without which the male version would not even be able to exist. However, the dominance of the 'male' system of sacrifice ensures that women and children are regarded as *unpaid* 'commodities' of barter, and that violence against them can be justified, along with the 'unconsidered destruction of the products of the earth'. This analysis leaves Irigaray highly ambivalent towards the Christian eucharist, understood as a 'sacrifice'. She can only see its

---

[34] See n. 13, above.

[35] Luce Irigaray, 'Women, the Sacred, Money', in eadem, *Sexes and Genealogies* (New York: Columbia University Press, 1993), 73–88.

overtones as positive for women if it can be cleansed altogether (here comes the sanitizing move, of which I have already warned) *away* from any association with male violence and aggression, and re-thought as an enjoyment of 'the fruits of the earth',[36] already of course a conventionally 'feminine' realm. This goes along with another sanitizing suggestion — reminiscent of the (American) feminist ploy of Kathryn Tanner, already cited — that one should look at Jesus's own death as an unfortunate 'accident': 'The cross is accepted by Christ', Irigaray writes, 'but it forms no part of his message that the flesh has been divinely redeemed by the flesh of Mary'.[37] Fleshliness and fruitfulness need to be celebrated by women, then, but it is not clear that Irigaray has in any way *shifted* the gender binary she began with; although she points to a 'female' sacrifice underlying the male order, which needs now to be elevated and properly acknowledged, it is not clear how classic 'male', Girardian violence (and Irigaray explicitly refers, with *approval*, to Girard) will in any way by changed by this, or indeed how it *was* changed — if at all — by the incarnation itself. We are seemingly left, then, in the classic Girardian bind, further intensified by the gender dualisms of Lacanian theory; and although Irigary does not explicitly state this, it seems that, for her, were woman to step into the male sacrificial system, she might merely emulate the worst of its phallic potential for violence.

The comparison then with Kristeva's treatment of sacrifice is strik-ing and noteworthy, especially given that both authors work out of the same Lacanian school of psychoanalysis. Kristeva in fact writes of Christian sacrifice in two contexts, which are worthy of bringing together here for theological reflection. In *Powers of Horror*,[38] firstly, her brief analysis of the Christian eucharist is part of a much longer treatment of the subject of what she calls 'abjection'. 'Abjection' is the term in Kristeva for a state of horror and disgust that she hypothesizes always hangs around the mother/child relationship, a sort of 'primitive terror of maternal engulfment and devouring that threatens the boundaries of the self almost before they come into being' — as one

---

[36] Ibid., 78.
[37] Ibid.
[38] Julia Kristeva, *Powers of Horror: An Essay on Abjection* (New York: Columbia University Press, 1982).

acute commentator on Kristeva, Cleo Kearns, has put it.[39] Kristeva describes the state of abjection variously, but often as 'clammy' or 'nauseous'.[40] Once the child has entered into the realm of language and of male 'order', this memory still lurks (of being held safely, but engulfingly, in the arms of the mother); and it is peculiarly the place of religion – or in secular society, of psychoanalysis or poetry or art – to attend to its difficulties. This is where the Christian eucharist comes in, as far as Kristeva is concerned; it is precisely its genius to bring the abject/maternal and the linguistic/paternal into newly creative *relation*, into a sort of crossing-over of gender roles in which the linguistic is rendered bodily or semiotic, and *vice versa*. 'To eat and drink the flesh of Christ means' she says ' ... to *transgress* symbolically the Levitical prohibitions' [notice the contrast with Irigaray here], 'to be symbolically satiated as at the fount of a good mother ... [On the other hand] by the very gesture ... that corporalizes or incarnates speech, all corporeality is elevated, spiritualized ...'[41] In other words, rather than re-instantiating the order of male violence, according to Kristeva, the eucharist precisely confuses and undoes it – re-directing us back to the realm of maternal feeding, but doing so in a way that does not threaten re-engulfment, but rather gives bodily 'substance' to *speech* (see Fig. 10.1).

This subtle psychoanalytic account of the eucharist's possibilities then should be read, I suggest, alongside Kristeva's justly celebrated 'semiotic' essay, 'Stabat Mater'.[42] Here it is that Kristeva argues that egalitarian, and especially North American, feminism has fatally repressed the 'maternal'. In the efforts of this brand of feminism to allow women equal rights in the workplace, she argues, there has been a dreadful cost. The significance of the bodiliness of maternality has been pushed out of sight and mind; and hence both the sacrifice and the joy of birthing have been repressed: 'Silence weighs heavily ... on the corporeal and psychological suffering of childbirth', she writes,

---

[39] Cleo McNelly Kearns, 'Kristeva and Feminist Theology', in eds. C. W. Maggie Kim, Susan M. St. Ville, and Susan M. Simonitis, *Transfigurations: Theology and the French Feminists* (Minneapolis, MN: Fortress Press), 1993, 49–79, at 58.

[40] Kristeva, *Powers of Horror*, 6.

[41] Ibid., 119–120, my emphasis.

[42] Julia Kristeva, 'Stabat Mater', in ed. Toril Moi, *The Kristeva Reader* (New York: Columbia University Press, 1986).

Figure 10.1 Northwest German Master, 'Eucharistic Man of Sorrows with the Allegorical Figure of *Caritas*', c. 1470. Christ feeds the faithful from his breast/ wounds, and so disposes the powerful presence of Love.

'and especially the self-sacrifice involved … A suffering lined with jubilation [*jouissance*]'.[43] Using the Virgin Mary as her focus for reflection on the ambivalences of the construction of motherhood in the West, she notes in the figure of the *Pietà* a 'wrenching between desire for the masculine corpse and negation of death';[44] but she ends with

---

[43] Ibid., 183.
[44] Ibid., 175.

Figure 10.2 Giovanna Bellini, 'Pietà Donà delle Rose', c. 1505: Mary cradles the dead Christ, as she did at his nativity. Giovanni Bellini / Wikimedia Commons / Public domain.

an insistence that contemporary feminism must return to the subject of motherhood to construct a newly creative ethics (a 'her-ethics') that looks birth, death and sacrificial suffering full in the face. Otherwise, she says, motherhood 'will be left without a discourse' (Fig. 10.2).[45]

Perhaps it will be clear by now why I think it is Kristeva who can best help us – from the perspective of her particular post-Freudian psychoanalytic theory – with the apparent symbolic *aporia* of the woman in the place of sacrificer. According to her, all the *power* of womanhood (the 'sacrifice' of birthing, the intimacy of suckling and – at the other end of the life-span – the so-called 'feminine' attention to death and dying) can implicitly be brought into the realm of the eucharist, and in such a way as to challenge and undercut the violence of 'patriarchal' sacrifice. Such at any rate are the potential lessons of this excursus into the world of post-modern French feminisms.

---

45 Ibid., 184.

But before I draw the strands of this complex chapter into some sort of systematic conclusion, I must point to yet one other view on the Virgin and sacrifice that was explicitly favoured by Pope John Paul II,[46] but that should be clearly distinguished from Kristeva's very subtle rendition of Marian motherhood and sacrifice. And this influential papal interpretation I find distinctly worrisome. Whereas Kristeva points to the possibility of a *transformation* and supplanting of violent, 'male' sacrifice by the mutual infection of the so-called 'symbolic' and 'semiotic' realms, John Paul II's understanding of Mary's role in Christ's sacrifice remains firmly circumscribed in the role of 'feminine' observer and supporter. At the same time, however, it *ostensibly* elevates her 'femininity' to an extraordinary degree, whilst ruling out the possibility of her actually taking the institutional priestly role: the double-think paradoxes of von Balthasar's view of Marian 'femininity', as discussed in Chapter 9, are again apparent (see Fig. 10.3).

As John Paul II himself declared, on the solemnity of Corpus Christi, June 5, 1983: 'Christ offered on the Cross the one perfect Sacrifice which every Mass in an unbloody manner, renews and makes present. In that one Sacrifice, Mary ... the Mother of the Church, had an *active part*. She stood near the Crucified, suffering deeply with her Firstborn; with a motherly heart she *consented to his immolation* ....; she offered him and she offered herself to the Father'.[47] Whilst this statement appears to approach dangerously close to giving Mary priestly status, it stops just short; and somehow, as Cleo McNelly Kearns has commented,[48] this maternal *consenting* to a son's sacrificial death makes one 'queasy': is she therefore in the role of female *voyeuse*, neither institutionally priest, nor – as in Kristeva's 'Stabat Mater' – a *protesting* and anguished mother? Is not this poised 'consent' somehow just as

---

[46] John Paul II, 'At the root of the Eucharist is the virginal and maternal life of Mary', *L'Osservatore Romano* N. 24 (788), 13 June, 1983, 2 [weekly edition in English].
[47] Ibid., my emphasis.
[48] Cleo McNelly Kearns, 'Mary and the Eucharist in the Sacrificial Discourse of the Roman Catholic Church', *Maria* 3 (2003), 255–274. See also McNelly Kearns's more systematic and extended discussion of these themes of Mariology, eucharist, and sacrifice in eadem, *The Virgin Mary, Monotheism and Sacrifice* (Cambridge: C.U.P., 2008).

Figure 10.3 Jean Auguste Dominique Ingres, 'Madonna and the Consecrated Wafer', 1865. Gift of Lila and Herman Shickman, 2005 / The Metropolitan Museum of Art / Public Domain.

worrying, morally, as the threat of a destructive, phallic mother merely emulating the worst 'male' violence?

Conclusions

Let me now conclude this chapter, but at the same time pave the way into the next, and closely related, one on the topic of 'gift'. I have gone to some lengths in this chapter to probe the complex sets of association with the metaphor of 'sacrifice', and have argued that in the contemporary setting, especially, themes of gender, sexuality and power lap at the edges of a debate on 'sacrifice' that was differently encoded at the Reformation, and then thoroughly over-determined in a variety of ways in its modernistic theorization. When one ventures further back to Jesus himself and to the original institution of the eucharist, I have hypothesized that the theme of 'sacrifice' was powerfully there all along, and taken up into the new Christian rite in which Jesus intentionally collapsed the notion of 'priest' and 'victim' into himself and substituted his own body and blood for the animal sacrificial system of the Temple. As the theme of the 'body of Christ' then became a constellating one for Pauline theology, it served to straddle and constellate not only the idea of the ingested eucharistic bread and Christic presence in the rite of communion, but also issues of sexual and moral integrity in the church at large. Finally, it follows from all this, as I have tried to illustrate graphically, that today's priestly 'woman at the altar' must necessarily run the gauntlet of a range of competing symbolic associations between sacrifice, gender, power, pollution, intimacy and violence, not all of which can be conveniently sanitized in favour of a merely *alimentary* understanding of the woman's role. If Kristeva is right, however, there is a profound, and creative, symbolic destabilization of the old male order of sacrifice provided by the very presence of the maternal body at the altar, and the transgression thereby of traditional views of pollution and male hegemony; this is not after all *patriarchal* 'birth done better', as Nancy Jay was wont to put it, but more truly a joyous opening-up of the appropriate 'disturbances' of Christian incarnation. As such, the woman priest – in the tradition of the Epistle to the Hebrews, one might urge[49] – rightly 're-presents' Christ as bringing the order of repeated male blood sacrifice to an end, and thereby banishing the fear of ritual contamination and pollution.

But what then does this mean for the disputed *relation* of divine 'gift' and 'sacrifice' – still unsettled, it seems, since the Reformation? To that issue we shall duly turn in Chapter 11.

---

[49] See esp. Hebrews 7. 26–28.

11

Gift Re-told: Spirals of Grace

Introduction: Review and Forecast

So far in these last two chapters, we have been examining the ways in which the themes of desire and gender are woven deeply into two of the most disputed current topics in eucharistic theology – the issue of the priest's status as '*in persona Christi*', and the ecumenically contested topic of the eucharist as a 'sacrifice'. A cumulative argument has been mounting, however, in these last chapters: firstly, that divine desire for *us* – held out to us eucharistically in the form of Christ's body and blood – involves an invitation to responsive transformation that cannot leave the world's gender binary as it is: it 'queers', if you will – disrupts or renders labile – the fixity of gender as rigid binary; and, secondly, that the particular form of 'sacrifice' bequeathed to us by Jesus refuses, either, to be fixed in the forms of the mandated violence of patriarchalism. A certain *fluidity* of gender is created, I have argued, in stepping eucharistically into the circle of divine desire, just as is also a concomitant release of joyousness – a permeability to the workings of divine longing. And it will be clear by now, I trust, that the notion of 'desire' with which I am operating has a lineage quite distinct from the pessimistic Freudianism of Girard's theory of mimetic rivalry. Here is not the endlessly violent

The Broken Body: Israel, Christ and Fragmentation, First Edition. Sarah Coakley.
© 2024 John Wiley & Sons Ltd. Published 2024 by John Wiley & Sons Ltd.

jostling of competitive *mimesis*, but rather the one focus of desire that is fully and *ontologically* appropriate – a progressive 'orientation' precisely to the body of Christ, the incarnate life of God.

In taking up now our third contested topic in eucharistic theology, that of the meaning of divine 'gift', we shall seek to extend and clarify our argument in a number of ways. We shall return, firstly, to the issue already opened up in the last chapter, of whether the eucharistic metaphor of 'gift' should be regarded – as Luther urged in 'The Babylonian Captivity' – as a *disjunctive* alternative to that of 'sacrifice'. Our own answer will doubtless already be clear (no, we shall argue; we need *both* metaphors, suitably parsed); but in the course of this chapter, we shall not only give an aetiological account of the extraordinary contemporary *obsession* with the category of 'gift' (so interesting a contrast to the equally extraordinary *revulsion* towards the category of 'sacrifice', discussed in Chapter 10), but also end with a clarification of the relation of the two, especially as mediated liturgically by the person of the Christian priest. On the way, as we unfurl some of the main stages in the current 'gift' debate, we shall demonstrate how it has rightly brought *economic* issues of wealth and distribution to the centre of theological discussion, in a way that I shall argue has intrinsic connections to our eucharistic theme of submission to 'divine desire' – to *divine* 'gift'. As I have already hinted in my analysis in the last chapter of the Pauline theme of the 'body', issues of sexual integrity and economic integrity *hang together* under the aegis of the Christic body, given to us eucharistically. But now, at the end of this current chapter, we shall develop the argument that mere *donation* to the poor is too weak an ethical response to the workings of the 'divine economy', and that the more radical gospel idea that the poor give Christ to *us*, is an implication of Jesus's teaching that demands proper integration into our eucharistic theology of 'gift'. For 'gift' is a circle, and it is God who enables it. Finally, as we investigate the gender undertow of the current theology of 'gift', we shall be pressed to clarify the specifically *trinitarian* dimensions of the notion of a circle of divine 'desire', and the particular, *epicletic*, role of the Spirit in the transformations of desire that response to divine 'gift' entail. Here, finally, and as a lead into our final chapter in this volume, we shall be forced to indicate how our desire is 'broken' and purified in the eucharist, as much – if not more – as it is joyously released; and how this particular breakage (the 'sacrifice of a broken heart', as the psalmist calls its[1]) can be crucially distinguished from the destructive *violence* of Girardian, patriarchal sacrifice.

But firstly, and now, we must embark on a brief explanation of the contemporary obsession, both philosophically and theologically, with the category of 'gift'. It is a complicated story, but one that I shall attempt to clarify in what follows.

Why Gift? The Evolution of a Post-modern Theological Debate

Why 'gift'?[2] Since discussion of the term 'gift' has become almost mantric in its repetition in continental and North American theology in recent years, it is worth reminding ourselves at the outset why this is, and whether it *ought* to be so. This preliminary matter, indeed, will exercise me in this first, expository, section of this chapter, in order to provide an explanatory backdrop within the Anglo-phone literature to the fascinating work of John Milbank and Kathryn Tanner on the

---

[1] Psalm 51. 17, a theme that was to be taken up by the Reformers, especially within 'Anglican' eucharistic theology.

[2] A presentation on this theme was originally given at the November 2003 Annual Meeting of the *American Academy of Religion*, at Atlanta, GA, USA, and was responded to in the same session in person by John Milbank and Kathryn Tanner. I have lightly edited this published version of my part of the session, preserving as much as possible the tone of the original exchange, but at the same time adding updates both on philosophical substance and on bibliography (especially some brief comments on more recent, relevant, writings by Milbank and Tanner). The opening section here is intended as an accessible account, for a general audience, of a highly complicated debate about 'gift' which stretches back several decades now: I have here risked over-simplification for the sake of clarity. Further details of this ongoing debate may be pursued in the secondary literature cited below; but useful introductory materials that have stood the test of time can be found in: ed. Allan D. Schrift, *The Logic of the Gift: Toward an Ethic of Generosity* (New York: Routledge, 1997); eds. John D. Caputo and Michael J. Scanlon, *God, the Gift, and Postmodernism* (Bloomington, IN: Indiana University Press, 1999); and Robyn Horner, *Rethinking God as Gift: Marion, Derrida, and the Limits of Phenomenology* (New York: Fordham University Press, 2001).

'gift',[3] the *gender* implications of whose work I shall then move to explore and critique. In short, I shall be taking us to a point where we can – once again – glimpse the covert gender dimensions of a theological debate that is intrinsically, and importantly, related to the eucharist. I shall start, then, by providing a reminder of *why* it is that this particular obsession with 'gift' has grabbed the post-modern theological imagination, and how it has evolved from its continental roots in anthropology and philosophy into the sharp current theological debate in North America (in which John Milbank and Kathryn Tanner have become key players) about the relation of trinitarian theology to economics and politics.

Then, in my second section, I shall turn more closely again to Milbank and Tanner in turn, seeking to expose in each case a different weakness or theological *lacuna*, as I see it, about the way that trinitarian relations are understood in their thought under this guiding category of 'gift'. My operating hypothesis here, in a theological debate that so far has been markedly silent about gender issues (*why*? I shall ask), is that problems of difference and sameness – both human and divine – are strongly latent in the debate, and *necessarily* entangled with the economic questions of difference (differences of rich and poor), which seem now to be the main backdrop for the current Anglo-American discussion. Here I shall pick up on Milbank's own revealing foray into gender theory in the last chapter of his important book *Being Reconciled* (2003),[4] and probe from there how what he, and Tanner, say about divine, trinitarian 'gift' could relate to these intuitions about the gender binary.

So much by way of initial overview. Now to our brief historical survey of the 'gift' debate.

---

[3] The chief materials from these authors to be discussed are: John Milbank, 'Can a Gift be Given?', *Modern Theology* 11 (1995), 119–161; idem, 'The Ethics of Self-Sacrifice', *First Things* 91 (1999), 33–38; idem, *Being Reconciled: Ontology and Pardon* (London: Routledge, 2003); and, more recently, John Milbank and Adrian Pabst, *The Politics of Virtue: Post-Liberalism and the Human Future* (London: Rowman and Littlefield, 2016). For Kathryn Tanner, see her *Jesus, Humanity and the Trinity* (Minneapolis: Fortress Press, 2001); eadem, *Economy of Grace* (Minneapolis, MN: Augsburg Fortress, 2005); and again, more recently, her 2017 Gifford Lectures, *Christianity and the New Spirit of Capitalism* (New Haven, CT: Yale University Press, 2019).

[4] See Milbank, *Being Reconciled*, ch. 10: 'Culture: The Gospel of Affinity', 187–211.

The origin of this discussion (stage 1, let me call it), as is well known, lies in Marcel Mauss's influential anthropological mono-graph, *The Gift* (1925),[5] which attempted, in an era of French politi-cal utilitarianism, to resurrect a utopian vision of (supposedly) 'primitive' gift-exchange in which the competitive individualism of modern capitalism was *not* the assumed *status quo*, but rather a com-plex system of codified interactions, which together combined, according to Mauss, to create a society of remarkable cohesiveness and harmony. The principle of *do ut des* was not, in other words, here regarded as manipulative or cynical, but an integral part of a society in which supposedly everyone was implicated in responsible relations with each other. More a utopian *social* and *political* recommendation than an accurate ethnography of Polynesia, Mauss's neo-Durkheimian vision was then later responded to, and criticized, by Jacques Derrida with a completely different set of interests in mind (stage 2), this time philosophical and theological. Indeed, we could say that at this point in the 'gift' genealogy, the continental discussion turned into an *apol-ogetic* one about the possibility of keeping the notion of the 'divine' afloat at all in post-Heideggerian continental philosophy.[6] Joined, then, to the backcloth of the Maussian anthropological debate, were the elusive remarks that Heidegger had made at the beginning of his *Sein und Zeit* on a form of 'giving' supposedly more fundamental than 'Being', a possible response to the problem of 'onto-theology', of false reification of the divine: 'To think Being', Heidegger had written, in one of his more gnomic sentences, 'explicitly requires us to relinquish Being (*Sein*) as the ground of beings (*des Seinden*) in favour of the giving which prevails concealed in unconcealment, that is, in favour of the It gives (*Es Gibt*). As the gift of this It gives, Being belongs to giving'.[7] In Jacques Derrida's reading, however, this elusive

---

[5] Marcel Mauss, *The Gift: The Form and Reason for Exchange in Archaic Societies* (London: Routledge, 1990). The 1st edition of the monograph appeared originally in French in 1924, as *Essai sur le Don, Forme et Raison de l'Echange dans les Sociétés archaïques* (*L'année sociologique*, 1923–1924; subsequently Paris: Alcan, 1925).

[6] See Jacques Derrida, *Given Time: 1. Counterfeit Money* (Chicago: Chicago University Press, 1992), and *The Gift of Death* (Chicago: Chicago University Press, 1995).

[7] This quotation is from *Time and Being* (New York: Harper and Row, 1972), 6. Heidegger's repeated remarks about a fundamental 'givenness' that lies even beyond 'Being' hover in the background of the discussion taken up by Derrida here.

Heideggerian idea of a fundamental givenness beyond 'Being' becomes what Derrida calls '*pure* gift' – something impossible by definition in Mauss's system of repetitive exchange – but a code now for Derrida of *divine* excess, and thus, in his own programme of 'deconstruction', a favoured expression for the purported 'apophaticism' of endlessly deferred meaning. No gift that hits the timeline, so to speak, can – according to Derrida – fail to be corrupted by the manipulations of Maussian exchange; thus it can only be a *final* gift – in human terms the unspeakable gift of death – that escapes such beschirchment. 'Pure' gift here becomes ineffable, elusive, death-obsessed, eschatological, but nonetheless endlessly alluring, a remaining token or trace of the 'divine'.

Jean-Luc Marion's important adjustment and critique of Derrida, which has gone through various stages,[8] challenges and recasts Derrida's puzzling – even impossible – notion of '*pure* gift', replacing it with the idea of the 'saturated phenomenon', in which revelation occurs not so much by 'apophatic' elusiveness but by epistemic overload: the given 'intuition' in the saturated phenomenon far exceeds what can be conceptualized, and so re-summons the divine. We shall see in our last chapter, below, how this re-conceiving of 'God Without Being' as a revelatory *gift* in Marion's work is crucially implicated too in his eucharistic theology. So we might say

---

[8] Marion's work is animated less by response to Mauss (or even primarily by response to Derrida) than by an interest in Husserlian phenomenology and its possibilities for a *theological* renaissance. Relevant writings of Marion on 'gift', Husserlian 'givenness', and Heidegger's *es gibt*, which show the development of his thoughts on these matters, are: *God Without Being* (Chicago: Chicago University Press, 1991); *Reduction and Givenness: Investigations of Husserl, Heidegger and Phenomenology* (Evanston, IL: Northwestern University Press, 1998); 'The Saturated Phenomenon', in eds. Dominique Jaricaud *et al.*, *Phenomenology and the 'Theological Turn': The French Debate* (New York: Fordham University Press, 2000), 176–216; 'Sketch of a Phenomenological Concept of Gift', in ed. Merold Westphal, *Postmodern Philosophy and Christian Thought* (Bloomington, IN: Indiana University Press, 1999), 122–143; *Being Given: Toward a Phenomenology of Givenness* (Stanford, CA: Stanford University Press, 2002); and Marion's Gifford Lectures of 2014, *Givenness and Revelation* (Oxford: O.U.P., 2016). The last volume, in particular, can be recommended for providing both a broad but incisive sweep of Marion's philosophical thinking as a whole.

that it is the very category of *revelation* that is at stake at this complex stage 2 of the 'gift' saga, the possibility that post-modernity – and continental phenomenology – still hides in its pocket the capacity for the recognition of the divine presence, whilst avoiding the pitfalls of so-called 'onto-theology'.

With all this we must compare what I shall call stage 3 of the 'gift' debate, at which point enters John Milbank's robustly theological notion of '*purified* gift exchange', originally introduced in his 1995 *Modern Theology* essay, 'Can a Gift be Given?'[9] Here the interest ostensibly shifts back to Mauss, but now to the possibility of re-adjusting 'gift-exchange' *not* as self-interested or agonistic manipulation between human parties, but as a circle of delayed, but appropriately human, response to the ultimate, divine gift ('asymmetrical reciprocity and non-identical repetition', as Milbank's tag becomes). Derrida's 'pure gift' is declared by Milbank a chimera, a will-o'-the wisp of 'modernity'; and (with whatever justification – that I believe could be disputed), Marion's alternative is also seen by Milbank as too exercised with the same false binary of ineffable purity and tainted manipulation.[10] For Milbank, the ethical ideal of a 'pure gift', a self-sacrifice even unto death, is a modernistic perversion that is wholly exercised with the nihilistic thought of death, and cut off from all hope of resurrection.[11] In contrast, the *divine* self-gift as Milbank construes it is now unashamedly *asserted* in doctrinal, trinitarian terms and human response dubbed 'participation' in it: the primary anxiety about getting theistic discourse off the ground at all – which was certainly the main concern at stage 2 of the debate – falls away as if by *fiat*. If we ask what now *drives* the debate at this third stage, it is – to be sure – partly Milbank's sheer theological polemicism against his continental interlocutors. But more significant, I surmise, is the urgent *economic* backdrop of global capitalism, and Milbank's ambitious new plans to write a full systematics (of which his book *Being Reconciled* was originally conceived as the first part), under what he auspiciously calls the

---

[9] Milbank, 'Can A Gift be Given?' (His much shorter essay, 'The Ethics of Self-Sacrifice', is also relevant to my exposition here.)

[10] See 'Can A Gift be Given', 133–144; also compare *Being Reconciled,* 156.

[11] See 'The Ethics of Self-Sacrifice', *passim.*

'transcendental category' of gift, in order to demonstrate the remaining possibility of an alternative Christian *socialism*.[12]

Now if I am right in this analysis of focal themes in the different stages of the 'gift' debate, then Kathryn Tanner's project on *Economies of Grace* (along with her earlier monograph *Jesus, Humanity and the Trinity*, and her subsequent Gifford Lectures, *Christianity and the New Spirit of Capitalism*), also fit neatly into the same stage 3, in which current world economic travails also dominate the imagination, but in Tanner's case with a very different theological response. Or at least it *seems* very different from Milbank's.

Rather than adjusting and 'purifying' Mauss's exchange, Tanner declares the whole Maussian analysis, and Milbank's theological reworking of it, as just as much implicated in individualistic agonism and contractualism as is contemporary global capitalism. So what is left as an alternative? Interestingly, Tanner – strongly influenced by a *selective* reading of John Calvin at this point – happily embraces the notion of divine 'unilateralism' that Milbank rejects as the false, 'modern' idea of 'pure gift'.[13] In sum, whereas Milbank's theological vision is of a *circle* of divine gift and human, participatory response – thereby creating an alternative social reality to that of capitalism – Tanner's vision is of a '*unilateral*' and absolutely '*unconditional*' divine gift by what she dubs the non-competitive 'persons' of the Trinity, which, if duly welcomed, issue forth in a 'reflected' human 'horizontal' generosity of wealth to those in need: 'The good is distributed by God, and is to be distributed by us, in imitation of God'.[14]

---

[12] This developed undertaking is now to be found in Milbank and Pabst, *The Politics of Virtue*, in which a very rich and complex new argument is mounted against modern 'liberalism' (both philosophical and economic) and its discontents, in favour of a 'politics of virtue', which moves even beyond good-hearted 'communitarianism' to a reconsideration of 'the good', *tout court* (see ibid., 1–9, for the outline of the argument of the book as a whole).

[13] I say a 'selective' reading of Calvin, because a closer reading of his corpus reveals a complex relation of divine providential ordering and human *participatory* response – which renders the idea of divine 'unilateralism' somewhat questionable. On this theme see J. Todd Billings, *Calvin, Participation and the Gift* (Oxford: O.U.P., 2007), esp. chs. 1, 3.

[14] Kathryn Tanner, 'What does Grace have to Do with Money?', *Harvard Divinity Bulletin* (Spring 2002), 9a; see now her *Economy of Grace*, 25: 'The good is distributed

If this somewhat breathless account of the 'gift' debate so far is roughly correct, then I immediately have the following queries about Milbank's and Tanner's treatment of it, answers to which will also inform our own alternative perspective. As we have seen, they appear to adopt quite different strategies for combating the ills of competitive capitalism, and for both this *is* the fundamental economic problem to be addressed. Both also utilize patristic models of trinitarianism (without feeling any apparent need to woo the sceptic into theism by preliminary philosophical routes); both speak of 'participation' in the Trinity, rather than social imitation of it – though Tanner's 'reflection' model seems very close to *mimesis* here, as we have just seen (since she sometimes *does* continue to use the language of 'imitation'). And both deny what is classically called a 'substantial' notion of evil – Milbank powerfully re-expressing the *privatio boni* tradition, and Tanner vehemently rejecting the need for any idea of divine 'punishment' or Christic 'sacrifice'. The result in both cases is a vision of the world radically and ontologically disposed to reflect the glory of God; we *can* block the flow of divine 'gift', to be sure, but true cooperation and 'participation' in this Gift would seemingly produce inexorably a changed world, economically and politically. There is huge optimism here, note, about the power of pure theological *ideas* to change political and economic structures, an optimism I would personally question, unless a *ritually* mediated transformation of minds and bodies that must attend such a change is fully accounted for.

But from this brief comparison of the two authors, I am also led to ask: Are the rhetorical differences between Milbank and Tanner (between 'purified gift exchange' on the one hand and 'unilateral' gift on the other) in *some* respects more apparent than real? Is Tanner's rather sharp critique of Milbank's 'purified' gift exchange thus a misfire? And, more probingly, what is achieved, other than a rhetorical flourish in the direction of Mauss and his French detractors, by elevating the category of 'gift' over more traditional loci such as 'grace', 'Trinity', 'faith', 'sanctification', etc., not to speak of 'sacrifice'

---

by God and it is to be distributed by us in imitation of God, in an indiscriminate, profligate fashion that fails to reflect the differences in worthiness and status that rules the arrangements of a sinful world. The purpose of the giving is elevation, without limit, so as to bring all recipients to the level of the giver, ultimately God. ... The good is distributed without the giver suffering any loss thereby'.

(of which both Milbank and Tanner are notably suspicious)? Once its interesting philosophical and apologetic capacity to sustain the language of theism (stage 2) has ostensibly been pushed to one side by Milbank and Tanner, has 'gift' become a mantra that has, after all, lost its own meaning in repetition, and is in danger of flattening doctrinal subtleties that these older categories protected?

Finally – and this point will act as a bridge into my next section – we should be *surprised*, I submit, at Milbank's and Tanner's relative lack of attention to the gender evocations of 'gift'. Mauss, in contrast (stage 1) was actually quite clear about this: women, and more specifically, their sexual favours, are at the heart of an economy of barter and return; whether *women* achieve actual agency on a par with men in such societies, however, is highly questionable. The point is that *economics and gender relations are inextricably entwined*, as Mauss himself acknowledges quite patently;[15] yet English-speaking exponents of gift theology have been strangely coy or slow to admit this deep sexual subtext to the very origins of the 'gift' debate. In contrast, both Luce Irigaray and Hélène Cixous (notable feminist contributors to the French debate on 'gift') have responded to Mauss in the sharpest terms: it is a 'phallocentric' society that Mauss adulates, they say, in which women are the assumed objects of barter, not 'subjects' themselves in the male system of exchange; thus arguably only love *between* women could escape the trap of subordinate chatteldom that Mauss holds out to us in his adulated 'primitive' society.[16]

Even Derrida, we note, is somewhat aware of gender in his own system (stage 2), in a completely different way: his supposedly 'apophatic' 'pure gift' is notably figured as 'feminine'/excess at various points in his discourse.[17] What was bartered ('woman') in Mauss's exchange thus becomes the eschatological key to the divine (the 'excess' of 'femininity') in Derrida's – a nice transference. So what

---

[15] See, e.g., Mauss, *The Gift*, 8–20.

[16] See Hélène Cixous, 'Sorties: Out and Out: Attacks/Ways Out/Forays'; and Luce Irigaray, 'Women on the Market', in Schrift, *Logic of the Gift*, 148–173, 174–189.

[17] This connection is, as far as I know, never made explicit by Derrida himself, but may be readily intuited from such passages as Jacques Derrida, *Spurs Nietzsche's Styles* (Chicago: Chicago University Press, 1979), 56–59, 63, cf. 108–109, read in relation to Derrida, *Given Time: 1*, 4–5 (the discussion of Mme de Maintenon's 'feminine' desire).

then *is* happening to gender (*vis-à-vis* the economy, both divine and human) at what I have called stage 3 of the debate? Why has this issue so far been occluded? And what can we learn from its exposure, in explicating how economics and gender hang together in this debate? Let us look briefly and critically at this issue in relation to the writing of Milbank and Tanner in turn, because here *real* difference between their views is exposed, in a way that can help our own eucharistic project forward.

Gift and Trinitarian 'Desire': Economics and Gender

To be fair, this gender nexus has *not* completely escaped John Milbank's attention (what does?), although his remarks on the matter are somewhat fleeting and occasional. As early as his important essay, 'The Second Difference' (reprinted in *The Word Made Strange* [1997]), Milbank suggests in a footnote that, 'If sexual difference is taken to be an equal but asymmetric difference ...' [then we may see] 'Trinitarian difference as the *ground* of sexual difference'.[18] We are immediately reminded here of this same line of thought in von Balthasar (as discussed in ch. 9). Here, albeit briefly, Milbank explains that this is why he feels free to follow the early Syriac tradition and refer to the Spirit as 'feminine' in this essay; although, as he puts it, 'This does not, *of course*, mean that I think she is essentially feminine, any more than the Son and Father are essentially masculine'.[19] The meaning of the terms '*essentially* feminine/masculine' is something on which we might want greater clarity from Milbank, especially when we come to the more explicit discussion of gender in the slightly later book, *Being Reconciled*. Here, in the final chapter, we are told, with reference to the thought of Luce Irigaray on the significance of bodily difference, that 'certain ... inherited generalizations do hold [about gender] ...: men are more nomadic, direct, abstractive and forceful, women are more settled, subtle, particularizing and

---

[18] John Milbank, 'The Second Difference', in *The Word Made Strange: Theology, Language, Culture* (Oxford: Blackwell, 1997), 171–193, at 190, n. 3, my emphasis.
[19] Ibid., my emphasis.

beautiful …'[20] Moving back from here to the crucial opening remarks
in *Being Reconciled* about the divine, trinitarian 'ground' of gender
'difference', we find that, as in *The Word Made Strange*, the Spirit is
said to be 'complementary' to the Son as Word;[21] she — if it is still
'she' — is also 'listener' to the Word, and in a sense buttress against, or
overflow from, 'the closed communion of a dyad',[22] a 'feminine' Giver
who seemingly complements the prior masculine Word. One may
readily see, I think, why I suspect Milbank of a continuing fascination with either a Romantic view of the 'opposite' sex, so-called, or
with Freudian/Lacanian gender dualisms such as Irigary presumes
(and which we discussed in the last chapter). Are they by Milbank
here smuggled into the trinitarian economy and made the divine
'ground' of a particular view of sexual difference in the human
'economy' of gift, shoring up expectations of silent self-giving from
the woman? And if so, we might press, is the Maussian system then
really improved upon after all?

If a covert subordination of the 'feminine' is indeed going on in
Milbank in this volume, then I am suspicious also of the divergence
from Augustine's *trinitarian* economy of 'gift' that has occurred by a
kind of sleight of hand even as his authority is invoked by Milbank.[23]
No longer is 'gift', *donum*, precisely that which indicates the relational
'difference' (within equality) of the *Spirit* — so Augustine; instead 'Gift'
has been — seemingly — arrogated to the whole Trinity. If we probe
what 'difference' *this* makes, and especially in relation to gender, is it
not implicitly to deflate the important *hypostatic* differentiation of
'Gift' *as Spirit*, and thus to cast the Spirit either as a subordinated
'feminine' adjunct to the Father and Son, or as a sort of divine 'excess'
(the false alternatives of 'femininity' in stage 1 and 2 of our gift saga,
note)? Whereas, and in contrast, for Augustine in Bk 15 of the *de
Trinitate* — as I read him — the *Spirit* is specifically and hypostatically
Gift and Love — the absolutely non-negotiable point of entry for us
humans into the divine life;[24] and, as such, the Spirit is the irreducible

---

[20] Milbank, *Being Reconciled*, 207.

[21] Ibid., ix.

[22] Ibid., x.

[23] See ibid., x.

[24] The crucial relevant section is *De Trin.* 15. 27–37; tr. Stephen McKenna, C.S.S.R.,
Saint Augustine: The Trinity (*The Fathers of the Church,* 45) (Washington, DC: Catholic

donum that does not merely *conjoin*, but breaks open, and keeps open, we might say, the dyad of Father/Son – which could otherwise become, symbolically, the very image of narcissistic patriarchalism. Here, in the *donum* of the Holy Spirit, however, is no mere 'feminine' adjunct to an established 'masculine' household, but the very *possibility* and guarantee of love as non-narcissistic. At the beginning of *Being Reconciled* Milbank explicitly confronts this very issue, but then backs away from its apparently radical implications; the 'closed perfection of the dyad *is* the *ground* [of the Spirit]', he repeats; let there be no 'figure of amorous promiscuity here'.[25] In other words, and if I read him aright, Milbank again tames ('feminizes' and domesticates) the 'difference' of the powerful Spirit, constrains the blowing of its wind where it wills, its implicit capacity to upend the settled gender binaries of patriarchalism.[26]

Lest these questions seem far from the dominating crises of global capitalism, let us just remind ourselves, firstly, that the *female* poor are invariably doubly subjected. When we gender the persons of the Trinity, however subtly, and implicitly valorize such difference within *God* (as 'ground'), we cannot avoid creating a texture of assent to human analogues. How then might the gifting God *transform* the manifest inequalities of the human gender binary, for Milbank, and so present an image of a truly *equal* as well as 'asymmetric' difference – just as that gifting God also supposedly transforms the inequalities of

---

University of America Press, 1963), 491–504. The specificity of the Spirit for Augustine as loving gift is not only founded in Scripture (in particular, in Rom 5. 5), but is intimately bound up with Augustine's understanding of the Spirit's 'procession' from both Father and Son: 'it is not without reason that in this Trinity only the Son is called the Word of God, and that only the Holy Spirit is the Gift of God, and that only He, of whom the Son was begotten, and from whom the Holy Spirit principally proceeds, is God the Father ... [The Father] so begot [the Son], therefore, that the common Gift should also proceed from Him, and that the Holy Spirit should be the Spirit of both' (*De Trin.* 15. 27, 493).

[25] See again Milbank, *Being Reconciled*, x, my emphasis.

[26] I am admittedly going beyond what Augustine explicitly argues here in *De Trin.* 15, in connecting what he says about the specificity of the Spirit as *donum* to questions of gender; but he does elsewhere in the *De Trin.* consciously consider, and reject, the idea of making the Trinity the prototype of the nuclear family: *De Trin.* 12. 5–8 (*Fathers of the Church* tr.), 346–351.

rich and poor?[27] Only, I shall be arguing at the end of this chapter, if 'gift' is correctly seen *in relation to* 'sacrifice', and if the Spirit in the *Trinity* is rightly perceived as the transformative point of entry into a circle of divine desire that 'breaks' the orderings of the 'world'.

But it is here, too, that some parallel comments and questions about Tanner's alternative theological strategies may also rightly fit. For in strong contrast to Milbank's attempt to ground gender difference in God, Tanner's trinitarianism is notably *sanitizing* of difference of any sort, let alone the presumed difference of gender. Her emphasis is on what she calls 'trinitarian non-competitiveness' and the attendant, Calvinist-inspired, notion of a divine 'unilateral gift'. The primary model for the Trinity, for Tanner, then, is that of 'non-competition'; there is no hint of *kenotic* reflexivity in God — a theme that Milbank seemingly picks up from von Balthasar — nor of any mutual relations of submission and response that might subliminally summon gender associations. Indeed, this erasure might cause Milbank to riposte that

---

[27] In this connection it is fascinating to follow what Milbank (and Pabst) more recently have had to say about gender in *The Politics of Virtue* (see esp. ibid., 270–276; but also see important passing remarks at 16, 27, 77, 199, 266, 277, 281, including strongly affirmative appeals to Ivan Illich and Luce Irigaray). As we might expect from his earlier writing, Milbank's chief *nemesis* is modern 'liberalism', *tout court,* including its commitment to an 'egalitarian', and therefore seemingly gender-*erasing*, politics and economics of the self. In this short, but highly revealing passage in the book (270–276), various negative elements of so-called 'liberal' gender traits are identified: the 'separation of sex from procreation'; the 'sexual permissiveness' that becomes a political 'opiate' to the 'loss of other freedoms'; the 'tyranny' of 'unisexual-ity'; the '*abolition* of gender difference'; the 'dissolution of gender difference [which] helps to give rise to a new liberal economic subject'; the 'breaking of reciprocity'; 'a supposedly basic, asexual humanity [based] implicity upon the model of the male sex' (which then merely re-subordinates women). Up to here in his tirade Milbank is largely following Ivan Illich. But he then concludes (ibid., 273, my emphasis): 'The more than difficult task before us is to imagine how men and women could share all roles that admitted of an *enigmatic complementarity* ... This alone would allow any true possibility of gender equality'. If these various remarks seem remarkably non-cognizant of recent, rather different, developments in 'queer' and 'non-binary' views of gender, we may conclude from (e.g.), ibid., 16, that 'absolute identities' based on 'race ... gender, sexuality', etc., are *also* tainted features of 'liberalism' and its 'endless discontents'. Or, 'Where all free choices are validated in the name of negative liberty, then infantile options go unrebuked' (ibid. 17).

here we have in Tanner an instance of what he provocatively calls 'transcendental homosexuality' – some supposed kind of 'non-narcissistic' unity *beyond* gender difference of which Milbank is duly suspicious.[28] Strangely, he thinks such a move gives human homosexuality a sort of status as emulating the 'angels'; but he defensively denies that this can be as 'sacramentally' significant as 'the unity in difference of the man and woman', which coupling he argues sustains 'the place of the non-angelic within the cosmic and erotic order'.[29] Be that as it may, for Tanner herself, in order to purge not only gender evocations from God but also all taint of 'gift exchange' (and by now we see how these hang together), it is necessary to insist that the non-competitive 'community' of the Trinity gives nothing 'away' *even to each other*: in God, she says, nothing is 'transferred' and nothing 'lost'.[30] But the 'unilateral' and 'unconditional' gift of divine grace to us *should* result – not in a 'return' of any sort – but in an extension of similar linear giving to the poor, in 'solidarity'. Such giving, says Tanner, should *not* involve 'sacrifice' or inordinate loss (just as Jesus's death was not a 'punishment', and therefore not a 'sacrifice', according to Tanner[31]), but rather an *appropriate* redistribution of the gifts of creation: 'giving should not be at odds with one's continuing to have'.[32]

---

[28] See Milbank, *Being Reconciled*, 207–208.

[29] Ibid., 208.

[30] Tanner, *Economy of Grace*, 77: 'Nothing is transferred, as if these gifts involved the moving of material goods from one site to another, and therefore one can retain full possession of one's own property in giving to others'.

[31] See Kathryn Tanner, 'Incarnation, Cross and Sacrifice Revisited: A Feminist-Inspired Reappraisal', *Anglican Theological Review* 86 (2004), 35–56, for an earlier account of Tanner's resistance to the themes of sacrifice and punishment in her account of Christian soteriology.

[32] Tanner, *Economy of Grace*, 84; and see ibid., 'What one gives remains one's property and possession and that is why giving does not come at one's own expense; one isn't giving by a giving away that might leave one bereft'. Tanner's more recent *Christianity and the New Spirit of Capitalism* (2019) apparently does not roll back on this perception; but what it does provide is a much more extensive, and rich, analysis of contemporary 'finance capitalism' and its ills: the way it chains people in repetitive debt, and therefore in a depressive constriction of their imagination of the future; the way it leads to a presumption of guilt and failure if its presumed 'competitive individualism' does not lead to immediate economic success; the way it thus reifies and justifies inequalities in the social fabric of society. All this is apparently quite reminiscent of

Now if this strikes one as an essentially bourgeois solution to the dilemmas of global capitalism, I fear that this may be the result of the determined erasure of the motif of 'exchange' in Tanner's work, and thus of the effective obliteration of distinguishing 'differences' of *relation* both in God (*qua* persons of the Trinity) and in us (*qua* even-ing out difference of resources out of 'our' plenitude). But where, in Tanner's system, one might ask, is the radical gospel *dispossession* demanded of the rich young man, or commended in the widow's mite given precisely 'out of poverty'?[33] Where is the perception – beloved, as we have already seen in this volume, of the fourth-century Cappadocian Fathers – that our whole life is actually 'indebted' to God from the outset, and that in giving financially – and to our limit – we receive back far more from the 'poor' than we ourselves have given?[34] The obliteration of the idea of divine/divine or divine/human 'exchange' comes, it now appears, with theological cost in Tanner's system. It seemingly erodes not only Milbank's possibility of 'asymmetrical reciprocity', but even more so the more complex sorts of 'spirals' of grace and revelation to which the Cappadocian theology of donation points. For all, then, that I have earlier emphasized the *commonalities* of interest and theological themes in Milbank's and Tanner's concepts of the 'gift', it is in the area of *difference* – hypostatic

---

Milbank's 'socialist' analysis, and critique of 'modernity', in *one* sense, but quite different in another: for again, Tanner's 'non-competitive' analysis seems neither to present a vibrant, let along *practical*, vision of how God's 'economy of grace' might seriously interrupt and *change* this economic state of affairs ('there is simply no direct relationship between the successful pursuit of mundane projects and successful pursuit of devotion to God as one's life project', ibid., 95), and nor, interestingly, does differentiated gender feature in any significant sense in her analysis of economic and divine 'relations'. For some astute discussion of this important and challenging book, see the 'book symposium' on Tanner's volume in *Modern Theology* 36 (2019), 358–419.

[33] See Mark 10. 21, 12. 44. (It is striking that Tanner explicitly *disavows* the idea of 'giving out of poverty': see again, *Economy of Grace*, 84: 'we are to give to others not out of our poverty but out of our own fullness'). A comparison with Paul's discussion of alms-giving in 2 Cor 8 may be instructive here. At best, Tanner's position seems to approach Paul's compromise, second-best, option for the more recalcitrant Corinthians (see 2 Cor 8. 10–15), who are only willing to even up to some extent the difference between the haves and the have-nots; whereas it is clear that the more exalted option for Paul is a truly sacrificial one (see 2 Cor 8. 1–7).

[34] See ch. 1, above, esp. n. 33.

differentiation, gender and strategies for the alleviation of the 'differences' of rich and poor – that Milbank and Tanner most strikingly diverge. And for all that I have criticized the *particular* gender differentiation in Milbank's solution, I find myself finally more committed to a critical re-enunciation of his intuition that the *differences* of gender, Trinity and 'gift' must be worked out together, than to the flattening strategies of non-competitive 'sameness' that seemingly reside at the heart of Tanner's proposal.

For what I myself have argued systematically – not only in this volume but in earlier work[35] – is that 'gender' in God, *if we can so speak at all*,[36] cannot be a simple replication of human sexual difference (for God, *qua* God, has no sexualized body), and therefore is emphatically not a straightforward justification or 'ground' of the world's gender binary; for the specific gift of the Spirit, to emphasize this point once more, cracks open the human heart to the breaking of that binary, making 'gender' ultimately fluid to the priority of divine *desire*. Far from being a 'feminine' adjunct to a more fundamental 'masculine' dyad (as, seemingly, in the earlier work of Milbank), the Gift of the Spirit exposes the idolatry of a Father/Son dyad *perceived as justification for patriarchal narcissism*. In this sense, the Spirit refuses patriarchy just

---

[35] Sarah Coakley, *God, Sexuality and the Self: An Essay 'On the Trinity'* (Cambridge: C.U.P., 2013), esp. 52–65 and 322–327.

[36] The question *in what sense* gender can be 'grounded' in God is a complex one, which Milbank does not explicate in detail. It seems to me that we confront an irreducible paradox here: on the one hand there is clearly *not* gender in God, since God-qua-God has no body; but on the other hand, if the authority of revelation is accepted, there are *two* ways in which we seemingly have to speak (in some sense) of gender in relation to God: (i) on account of the inner-trinitarian 'Fatherhood' being *analogously*, though mysteriously, related to human fatherhood (I follow Aquinas here in distinguishing carefully between 'Fatherhood' as applied to God analogously when trinitarian, on the one hand, and metaphorically of the generic divine, on the other); and (ii) on account of the incarnation of the Second Person in a male human body. In the latter case, it is by no means obvious that this results in 'masculinity' *in* God. For we would then have to discuss the implications for gender-in-God of different construals of the *communicatio idiomatum* (and only if it were two-way would human maleness affect the divinity); we would also need to debate the relationship of Jesus's earthly, human body to his *risen* human body, since the tradition has tended to avoid dogmatism about the maleness of the risen Christ given the importance of the soteriological principle: 'The unassumed is the unhealed'.

as it refuses its own 'feminized' subordination to the Father and Son. And that, significantly, is why 'difference' in God is and always must be a difference of *three*. Part of John Milbank's argument, it must be admitted, already pushes in this direction.[37] But by arrogating 'Gift' to all three persons of the Trinity, both Milbank and Tanner in *different* ways occlude this vital specificity of the Spirit (both ontologically and economically): one – Milbank – by reining in the Spirit and so implicitly restabilizing the unequal human gender binary; the other – Tanner – by seemingly erasing differences of mutuality from the trinitarian picture altogether.

Spirals of Grace: The Divine Economy and Christ in 'the Poor'

Difference or sameness, exchange or unilateralism – whether in God, between God and us, between the sexes, or between rich and poor: these finally are the core issues in the current and ongoing 'gift' debate, and a decision in the one affects all the others – or so I have argued so far in this chapter. But I want now to clarify further, albeit very briefly, what I meant by speaking of '*spirals* of grace', in indicating how I departed from Kathryn Tanner's proposal about the *levelling* of the economy between rich and poor; for this in turn will specify how I also differ from John Milbank on questions of poverty as well as on questions of gender, and indeed in ways that are in some sense analogous to one another. From here, and in closing, we shall be able to arrive at a point where we can finally clarify the relation of 'sacrifice' and 'gift' with greater precision, and explain their mutual significance for the eucharistic ritual.

It is the patristic example, and preaching, of Basil of Caesarea, Gregory of Nazianzus and Gregory of Nyssa on donation to the poor that I believe to be of special interest, once again, at this point in our reflection on 'gift' and its putative connection to eucharistic sacramentality.[38] Daring in their time for their theories of monastic – and thereby social – transformation in Christ, the 'Cappadocian Fathers'

---

[37] See again Milbank, *Being Reconciled*, x.

[38] As already discussed in the context of the issue of Christ's 'identity' in ch. 1, above.

enunciated in a variety of texts and sermons a vision of 'gift' in Christ that upended and de-stabilized the normal presumptions about economic benevolence. Returning to the 'hard sayings' of the gospel about wealth,[39] but particularly also to the intriguing paradoxes of the parable of the sheep and the goats in Matt 25. 31–46, they put forward the idea that mere financial gifts of the 'rich' to the 'poor' (Tanner's 'levelling', if you like) were not enough, significant as they indeed were. But no, the whole perception of 'gift' had to be extended, or rather turned inside out, so that the *primary Gift* of divine life and grace to us could first render us *all* sensible of our own eternal 'debt'; and then – perhaps more paradoxically still – that the burden of wealth amongst the privileged be not lifted by mere benevolent donation, but turned back to reveal, that even in gifts to the 'poor', it is actually the donee who *gives* – gives back 'Christ', indeed, in his own person, to the one who has 'emptied' himself of his wealth. 'And you, whatever fruits of beneficence you do yield, you gather up for yourself', writes Basil: 'for the grace of good works and their reward is returned to the giver. Have you given something to a person in need; what you have given becomes yours, and is returned to you *with an increase*'.[40] Or Gregory of Nyssa: 'The money-lender labors without shame in order to double his capital while God freely bestows a hundred-fold to the person who does not afflict his brother'.[41] Or even more passionately, Gregory Nazianzus: 'O servants of Christ, … while there is opportunity, let us visit Christ, let us heal Christ, let us feed Christ, let us clothe Christ, let us gather up Christ, let us honour Christ, … Let us offer him this through the needy, who today are cast on the ground, so that when we have departed from here, they may receive us into the eternal dwellings, in Christ himself our Lord …'[42]

It is this set of *radical* thoughts about gift and reception that cause me to talk about 'spirals of grace' rather than merely (as with John

---

[39] E.g., Mark 6. 24, Mark 10. 23, Matt 6. 19–21.

[40] Basil of Caesarea, 'Homily 6: I Will Tear Down My Barns', in tr. M. F. Toal, *Sunday Sermons of the Great Fathers*, vol. 3 (Chicago: Regnery, 1959), 325–332, at 327.

[41] Gregory of Nyssa, 'Against Those Who Practice Usury', tr. C. McCambley, *Greek Orthodox Theological Review* 36 (1991), 287–302, at 297.

[42] Gregory Nazianzus, 'On the Love of the Poor and Those Afflicted with Leprosy', in tr. M. F. Toal, *Sunday Sermons of the Great Fathers*, vol. 4 (Chicago: Regnery, 1963), 43–64, at 63.

Milbank) of an 'asymmetric reciprocity' between *two* parties. For there is more here in this Cappadocian vision than a mere two-way relationship – however importantly 'asymmetric' – between the divine and the human. Rather, if the Cappadocians have read aright the disturbing demands of the gospel about matters of money and financial obligations, there is a sort of *breakage* of the normal sense of dual, reciprocal response – a reaching out beyond that model to a most surprising *inversion* of the expected sense of return. It is, we might say, a *pneumatological* interruption of a sort analogous to the 'breakage' of the gender binary we have already discussed: I seek to respond, albeit asymmetrically, to what I owe God, but instead of finding a way to negotiate that binary in a simple act of giving back, I am instead thrust out to a third – the beggar at the gate, the madwoman in the street – who, whilst s/he does indeed need my earnest financial benevolence, is more importantly waiting precisely to give *me* back *Christ*, the source of all my true longings. In calling this a 'spiral' of grace, I am thus drawing attention to a complexity in divine gift and human response that is precisely trinitarian, by a form of ecstatic analogy. For it cannot do without the 'third'; in fact it cannot even *start* without the 'third'; it cannot happen without the Spirit's breakage of even my very best intentions as a human moral quester and even 'sacrificial' giver. Only thus am I *given back* what I most desire – precisely the body of Christ. In eucharistic and sacramental terms, then, one may dare to say that this is an effect of the *epiclesis*: the calling in of the Spirit not only to make Christ present, but to break our hearts open *to* the Spirit's divine presence in the most unexpected places.

Conclusion: The Eucharist as the 'Breaking' of Desire

And so we can now arrive, finally, at a point where the various complex strands of this chapter, and indeed of the last one, can be re-threaded. We started the last chapter on 'sacrifice' with a reminder that Luther opened the continental Reformation with a rhetorical insistence, in the 'Babylonian Captivity', that the eucharist is *not* a 'sacrifice' but a 'gift'. Although, as we have seen with Milbank and Tanner in this current chapter, the same disjunction has again become a temptation in a contemporary era of fascination with 'gift', and revulsion against (self)-'sacrifice', it has been the burden of these last two chapters, and especially of our complex excavation of the gender and economic associations of both 'sacrifice' and 'gift', to insist that these two classic metaphors for the eucharist must at all costs be *held together*. The very integrity of the notion of the 'body of Christ', if I am right, depends on it. Thus it is not, as we explored at length in the last chapter, that we thereby *valorize* patriarchal violence or atavistic desire or the continuation of blood sacrifice; but rather – as we can now clarify with greater theological precision – that the demanding effects of the reception of divine, trinitarian Gift, *while sin still reigns in the order of the 'world'*, are *inevitably* 'sacrificial', both morally and spiritually. As the Spirit breaks open the heart to these realities, so we are changed, purged: 'the sacrifice of a broken heart thou wilt not despise', as we again recall the witness of the psalmist (Psalm 51. 17).

Yet we should continue to be careful, with Milbank, in clarifying that *this* breakage is not the patriarchal destruction of Girardian violence, and nor does it lead to a final, irrevocable horizon of 'death' beyond which there is *no life*, no hope: it is precisely that purportedly 'modernistic' founding of ethics on 'death', without any hope of return, which Milbank has so brilliantly exposed and rebuked.[43] On the contrary, the vision of 'gift' we have developed in this chapter involves a stepping into the *life* of the Trinity, a step which is demandingly purgative to be sure – more purgative than I think either Milbank or Tanner allow in their rhetorical resistance to 'sacrifice' – and painfully destabilizing of things we may have long taken for granted; but it is neither punitive nor *annihilating*. For this is a re-forming of the self *in* God rather than a shattering of an uneasy ego *in* death. And this last distinction is particularly important from a feminist perspective (a point not noted by Milbank), in that women may rightly wonder, in an era of deconstructive post-modern philosophy, whether they are being asked to resign a sense of 'self', that they never even fully achieved at the Enlightenment, and is now once more in question. Yet the model to which we gesture is of course a model of selfhood much older than the Enlightenment, in which divine 'power' and human 'submission' are not mutually antithetical, and moreover – in the traditions of 'mystical theology' – gender is strangely fluid; in short, it is a view of the person in which the self is most truly established *in God*.

---

43 See Milbank, 'The Ethics of Self-Sacrifice', 33–34.

Perhaps nowhere is this vision of the self more beautifully expressed in 'mystical theology' – and precisely as divine Gift, sacrificially and transformatively received – than in John of the Cross's last descriptions of union in 'The Living Flame of Love' (1585-1586). Here is the soul, after long purgation of its desires, *established* within the very heart of the Trinity: 'Therefore', says John, 'even as God is giving Himself to the soul with free and gracious will, even so likewise the soul, having a will that is freer and more generous in proportion as it has a greater degree of union with God, is giving God in God to God Himself, and thus the gift of the soul to God is true and entire'.[44]

'Giving God in God to God Himself': if it is *this* that the priest prospectively and symbolically does eucharistically, on behalf of and for the people, and 'in' the person of Christ, then it must be – as we have explored in this chapter – that s/he does it through the *epicletic* breakage of the Spirit; and she does it not to offer a 'sacrifice' that changes *God's* mind, but to mediate an often disturbing change of the *human* mind (and body) – through confession and absolution, prayer and praise – that is demanded by the very presence of the 'true body' of Christ.

But how we can – or should, or fail to – speak of that 'presence', and how to explicate its (often devastating, if mysterious) 'absence', we shall explore in our final chapter.

---

[44] John of the Cross, 'Living Flame of Love', *Stanza* III, 78, tr. E. Allison Peers, *The Complete Works of Saint John of the Cross, Doctor of the Church*, Three Volumes in One (London: Burns and Oates, 1964), vol. III, 184. (In the case of this particular passage the Peers translation is to be preferred over that of Kieran Kavanagh, O.C.D. and Otilio Rodriguez, O.C.D., *The Collected Works of St John of the Cross* (Washington, DC: ICS Publications, 1991), at 706.) I refer the reader back here to my opening comments in the 'Prologue', on John of the Cross's christological 'apophaticism' as genuinely combining 'dazzling revelation' with 'dark mystery'.

12

Real Presence, Real Absence: The Eucharist and the 'Apophatic' Christ

Introduction: Review and Forecast

Let me start the final chapter of this book with a brief vignette, which may perhaps throw some unexpected side-light on the distinctive feature of eucharistic celebration that we have been exploring intensively up to now — that of its capacity to become the means of a bodily and psychic transformation of 'desire'.

The story is told of the great Afro-American jazz pianist and composer, Thomas 'Fats' Waller (1904–1943), that he was once approached by a 'dewy-eyed' white admirer (so says *Time* magazine for August 9, 1943), who earnestly inquired of him if he could explain in his own words what 'swing' was — 'swing *to auto*', one might say, in Platonist mode; to which 'Fats' instantly, and cuttingly, replied, 'Lady, if you have to ask me what swing is, *you ain't got it*'.[1] I mention this (ostensibly unconnected, but nonetheless *à propos*) remark here for a reason — and that before starting in this last chapter on what might be said to be *the* most intensely cerebral and doctrinally disputed topic of the four I have tackled in this last section of the book, that of the nature and

---

[1] As reported in 'Thomas Waller', *Time Magazine*, August 9, 1943.

The Broken Body: Israel, Christ and Fragmentation, First Edition. Sarah Coakley.

explanation of Christ's personal eucharistic 'presence'. For Waller's remark draws attention to a crucial, indeed irreducible, dimension of liturgy that it also shares with jazz, and that cannot be gainsaid in any account of it:[2] that of the peculiar coincidence of given text and established tradition, bodily gesture, rule-governed but nonetheless improvisational 'play', and release and transformation of emotion and affect, which – in an important sense – if you don't understand, you '*ain't got*'. And in the course of these last chapters, we have more than once issued a reminder that mere explication of theological or liturgical *texts* will not, alone and *per se*, do justice to the *embodied* force and impact of theological truths ritually and physically conveyed. We are now about to apply this insight to the problem of 'real presence'.

The cumulative force of what I have argued so far in these last chapters, then – about desire, gender, affect, will, and about the implicit eucharistic pressure towards the economic redistribution of wealth – relies in good part on these more evocative, but thereby transformational, dimensions of ritual activity; these features are no mere dispensable 'accompaniments' devised only secondarily or derivatively from a text, or from the 'official' ecclesiastical theology of the liturgy, but are part and parcel of the nature of 'sacrament' itself. And if so, we shall have to take care to pay insistent attention – as perhaps anthropologists and psychologists and feminists can best now remind us – to the matter of *bodies*, not just Christ's but our own, as we attempt here to do some real theological justice to the implications of the notion of Christic 'real presence'. For if it be thought that *this* arcane topic, surely, has nothing to do with 'desire' or gender, then again some surprises are in store.

In this context, in particular, Victor Turner's work[3] as a psychological anthropologist still has relevance – although it now lies under the inevitable shadow of post-modern critique for its misguided attempts to encapsulate a generic 'essence' of ritual. Yet Turner's insights about the capacity of ritual to summon the energy of our most basic bodily passions and preoccupations (what he calls the 'orectic' pole of

---

[2] For a judicious academic account of how 'jazz' has now become a disputed territory musically and ethnically, see the special issue of *Daedalus*, Spring 2019, with its introduction by Gerald Lyn Early and Ingrid T. Manson ('Why Jazz Still Matters'), ibid., 5–12.

[3] See esp. Victor Turner, *The Forest of Symbols: Aspects of Ndembu Ritual* (Ithaca, NY: Cornell University Press, 1967).

symbolic meanings: the desire for food, for sex, for power, or for revenge), and in the course of the ritual to purify, or re-channel, those energies towards the 'moral' pole of symbolic meanings (in re-building the *communal* 'body' of the life of ritual actors) has, I think, remaining explanatory force, despite its undertow of Freudian 'sublimation'-theory (which I should want to treat with some critical caution). Yet undeniably, in Turner's analysis, the rite is more – much more – than the sum of its *textual* parts or 'official' explanations; and it is this point that I shall be wishing now to emphasize, as we tackle the admittedly intractable Thomistic theory of 'transubstantiation'. We shall also find recurring echoes in this last chapter, as indeed in the preceding ones, of Mary Douglas's insistence[4] that the 'body' (so fundamental a metaphor of the Christian eucharistic rite itself) is *the* 'medium of expression' – and so the key site of personal inscription – of any culturally negotiated meaning-system relating self, society and cosmos. We should watch, therefore, what is happening – or signally failing to happen – to the ritualized individual *bodies* of those who claim to eat the 'body of Christ': in theological terms, questions of sacramental 'validity' and ethical 'efficacy' *must* hang together. Or again, finally, as Catherine Bell has put it, 'ritual mastery' (her term) involves the negotiation of intractables, the mediation of oppositions – such as life and death, rich and poor, male and female – which *only* ritual (or, as Christians would prefer to put it, 'sacraments') can effect; and these oppositions, according to Bell, are 'mediated' or re-negotiated ritually in *bodily* form in a way that is by definition partly 'blind' or 'ambiguous' to the liturgical actors. If it were not so, she underscores, we would not be doing the distinctive raids on the unconscious – both creative and disturbing – that ritual is designed to effect.[5] That, too, is a lesson for the theologian who may find embodied truths ritually conveyed not *easily* reduced to coherent propositional statements, as we shall again observe in what follows.

Given these methodological preambles to this chapter's reflection on eucharistic 'presence', we shall now attempt *three* distinct tasks, each of which will bring our reading of 'presence' (via a fresh analysis

---

[4] See Mary Douglas, *Natural Symbols: Explorations in Cosmology* (1st edition, New York: Pantheon, 1970).

[5] Catherine Bell, *Ritual Theory, Ritual Practice* (New York: O.U.P., 1992).

of Thomas's classic doctrine of transubstantiation) into clear relation to our central thesis about the eucharist as the primary locus of trans-formed 'desire', and thus of what I have called the *Christic* 'orientation' of erotic meaning.

Firstly, and in the lengthiest two sections of this chapter, we shall turn back to the medieval discussion of 'transubstantiation' – the despised 'second captivity' of the church, as Luther saw it[6] – and argue, following a train of excellent recent scholarship on the matter, that no consistent explication of this doctrine could be achieved in the medi-eval period following the supposed mandating of it by the fourth Lateran council (1215), and that Thomas's own account of it should therefore be read in some important sense (to be defined) *apophatically*, and in explicit correlation with his equally mysterious christological account of the 'hypostatic union' in the *Tertia Pars* of the *Summa*. From here, and more briefly, we shall throw into contrast two intriguing and creative contemporary re-interpretations of the Thomistic doctrine of transubstantiation in the work of Jean-Luc Marion and Catherine Pickstock, but argue that, in their different ways, Marion and Pickstock have so far failed to give a fully convincing account of the *embodied* transformations that eucharistic presence, *if efficacious*, should bring about. Here we shall press, in our account of eucharistic presence, not only to re-raise issues of desire and gender, but to bring questions of sacramental *validity* and *efficacy* much more closely together than is customary, and thus gesture towards a possible route of *rapprochement* in ecumenical divides on eucharistic theology that go back to the Reformation. Finally, we shall return at last to the matter of *epicletic* 'breaking' in the Spirit discussed in the last chapter, and place the sym-bolic import of the eucharistic 'fraction' into our explicitly *trinitarian* account of the ascetical refusal of idolatry that we are claiming should occur in the eucharist. In this final chapter, then, which – as we shall see – densely recapitulates the other eucharistic themes we have treated (priest 'in persona Christi', 'sacrifice' and 'gift'), we shall again underscore how what is disclosed in the eucharist *should* involve disconcerting ruptures of human expectation, and bring merely secular sexual or political programmes under judgement.

---

[6] See again Martin Luther, 'The Babylonian Captivity of the Church' (1520), tr. A. T. W. Steinhaüser, *Three Treatises* (Philadelphia: Fortress Press, 1959), 119–245.

Medieval Diversity and the Thomistic 'Theory' of Transubstantiation

Any attempt to understand the goals of Thomas's 'theory of transubstantiation' must take some account of Thomas's own context, and of his particular motivations for proposing the account as theoretically normative. Three preparatory points should perhaps be stressed here initially, for these may still startle those brought up on an earlier historiography of doctrinal development.

Firstly, it is certainly not the case that the specific, technical doctrine of transubstantiation (the theory that the 'substance' of bread and wine is *turned into* the body and blood of Christ) was regarded as a necessary 'article of faith' after the condemnation of Berengar of Tours at the Synod of Rome (1059), when a mere 'symbolic' reading of eucharistic transformation was firmly ruled out; nor even – more surprisingly – after the anti-Albigensian decrees of the Fourth Lateran Council (1215), in which the very word 'transsubstantiatio' was first used with official favour. Well after 1215, as James McCue showed in a justly famous article,[7] a variety of theories of eucharistic presence were for a while well-tolerated in the West (most especially so-called 'consubstantiation', the theory that the true body and blood are present *along with* the unchanged substance of bread and wine[8]). It is only *with* Thomas, then, that an insistence on transubstantiation as the sole acceptable explanation was pressed; only *after* him that alternative theories were retroactively rejected as 'heretical' by appeal to the Fourth Lateran Council; and only from the later time of Duns Scotus that the Council was (re-) interpreted as 'a *formal definition* of transubstantiation over against cons[substantiation]'.[9] So there is more looseness and fluidity in the history of development of this doctrine than is still sometimes supposed. And especially in the earlier period before the Lateran Council began to exercise repressive influence, there was an extremely rich diversity of

---

[7] James F. McCue, 'The Doctrine of Transubstantiation from Berengar through Trent: The Point at Issue', *Harvard Theological Review* 61 (1968), 385–430.

[8] And this despite the fact that influential thinkers other than Thomas also implied or stated their rejection of it as contrary to the Catholic faith, for example, Alexander of Hales, Albert the Great, and Bonaventure. 'Consubstantiation' was, of course, to become Luther's preferred eucharistic theory.

[9] McCue, 'The Doctrine of Transubstantiation', 392, my emphasis.

eucharistic theologies, which do not, as Gary Macy's work reminds us,[10] 'represent a ... harmonious development',[11] and should not be con-strained, falsely and teleologically, towards the disjunctive eucharistic alternatives of 'the great prism of the Reformation'.[12]

Secondly, even when the theory of transubstantiation did become normative, it remained hotly contested and debated because of the inevitable philosophical *aporiai* it appeared to involve, especially where the problem of the application of the Aristotelian notion of 'substance' was concerned. Since, in Aristotle's philosophy, 'substance' is that which *endures* through change, the idea – at the heart of the various renditions of transubstantiation – that it is the 'substance' of the bread/wine that *turns into* that of Christ's body/blood, whilst leaving the 'accidents' (the visible features) of the bread and wine unchanged, is seemingly entirely counter-intuitive in Aristotelian terms.

Yet this problem has itself spawned different trajectories of his-torical explanation in contemporary scholarship. On the one hand, as an important monograph by David Burr,[13] and an elegant article by Marilyn Adams,[14] have argued in detail, there is the critical view that the philosophical desperation – or ingenuity – thereby induced in theologians devoted to 'Aristotelian' metaphysics and physics in the later medieval period necessarily involved questionable special pleading of various sorts; and Thomas's particular ploys here – shortly to be discussed – thus have to be seen against this wider backcloth of other, and subsequent, alternatives. On Adams's rendition, then, the Aristotelian 'bind' led authors as diverse as Thomas himself, Bonaventure, Giles of Rome, Henry of Ghent, Duns Scotus, and

---

[10] Gary Macy, *Theologies of the Eucharist in the Early Scholastic Period: A Study of the Salvific Function of the Sacrament according to the Theologians c. 1080–c.1220* (Oxford: Clarendon Press, 1984).

[11] Ibid., 137.

[12] Ibid., 4.

[13] David Burr, *Eucharistic Presence and Conversion in Late Thirteenth-Century Franciscan Thought: Transactions of the American Philosophical Society*, V. 74, Pt. 3 (Philadelphia: American Philosophical Society, 1984).

[14] Marilyn McCord Adams, 'Aristotle and the Sacrament of the Altar: A Crisis in Medieval Aristotelianism', in eds. Richard Bosley and Martin Tweedale, *Aristotle And His Medieval Interpreters, Canadian Journal of Philosophy*, supplementary vol. 17 (1991), 195–249.

Ockham, to have to make *different* sorts of final appeal (to *sui generis* infusions of divine grace, to multiple miracles, or finally to the mere institutional authority of Lateran IV), to attempt to get over the explanatory problem. In short, a diversity of interpretations of transubstantiation is not a thing of the past after Thomas – on the contrary. Adams would argue that it led to multifarious and somewhat desperate re-thinkings of Aristotelian notions of space and change, especially, to accommodate even 'miraculous' possibilities for the doctrine's philosophical coherence.[15] The troubling *uniqueness* of the eucharistic presence demanded this re-thinking.

A somewhat different contemporary scholarly rendition of Thomas's contextualized approach, however, would not question this acknowledgement of eucharistic uniqueness, nor would it deny the difference of varieties of rendition of 'Aristotelianism' on offer in Thomas's lifetime and after. But what it would stress (in *riposte both* to the standard sceptical modern charge of a classic 'Aristotelianism' meeting its inevitable *dénouement* in transubstantiation, *and* to Adams's account of a multifaceted philosophical desperation over this doctrine in particular), is the narrative of a consistent re-appropriation by Thomas, even from the time of his *Sentence Commentary*, of crucial influences from the variant 'Aristotelian' metaphysics of the great Islamic philosopher, Avicenna.[16] According to this alternative narrative, Thomas's assimilation of Avicennan metaphysics caused him significantly to *modify* the historical 'Aristotelian' accounts of 'substance' and 'accidents', 'form' and 'matter', and from there to do creative and coherent new business with some of the most paradoxical features of classic Christian doctrine, including that of transubstantiation.[17]

---

[15] See Adams, ibid., esp. 249 for this last point. Note that Adams returned to this topic in greater historical detail in her monograph, *Some Later Medieval Theories of the Eucharist* (Oxford: O.U.P., 2010); and that in her 1998 Gifford Lectures, *Christ and Horrors: The Coherence of Christology* (Cambridge: C.U.P., 2006), ch. 10, she declares in more systematic mode that her own preference is for a theory of 'impanation' over Thomistic 'transubstantiation'.

[16] The classic article by Étienne Gilson on this exegetical point is "Quasi Definitio Substantiae", in ed. Armand Maurer, *St. Thomas Aquinas 1274–1974: Commemorative Studies* vol. 1 (Toronto: Pontifical Institute of Medieval Studies, 1974), 111–129.

[17] For a detailed extension of Gilson's insights on Thomas's critical assimilation of Avicennan views on 'substance' (and the application to transubstantiation amongst

This latter line of approach, then, is much more sanguine than Adams's about Thomas's own metaphysical consistency and coherence – and across a range of doctrinal issues to which Avicenna's metaphysical adjustments were apposite, especially the linked doctrines of 'hypostatic union' and transubstantiation. Whilst this particular exegetical debate about different forms of 'Aristotelianism' and their reception cannot be settled in the brief context of this chapter, the important lesson is that Thomas's account of transubstantiation is necessarily a subtle and indexed one, and was never intended as a straightforward exposition of 'Aristotelian' principles in their original form. Nonetheless, as we shall see, the importance for Aquinas of some account of 'substantial' *continuity* in the process of transubstantiation remained crucial. This principle will remain at the heart of our analysis.

Thirdly, then – and here we approach the systematic nub for our own purposes – we need to admit that whereas modern analytic exponents of Aristotle often regard Thomas's theory of transubstantiation as arrant nonsense, others more sensitive to his context may read it as a sign of his 'apophatic' *subtlety*. But there is a difference between nonsense and mystery here, which we must carefully chart. Despite the undeniable difficulties in expounding Thomas's 'positive' philosophical account of transubstantiation, as already indicated, it may be that its greater wisdom lies finally not so much in what it does say but in what it does *not*.[18] In short, in Thomas's own understanding, *'explanation' in this area has to be a highly chastened form of explanation* – or rather, the delimiting of a space of mystery that mainly focuses on ruling out *errant* explanations rather than providing a complete and definitive positive analysis. This is a classic apophatic strategy, note,[19] that is by no means a *giving up* on theological explication (rather as *The Anglican-Roman Catholic Agreement* disappointingly shrugs off 'transubstantiation'

---

other topics) I am indebted to Daniel De Haan's unpublished MS, *'Ens Per Se Non Est Definitio Substantiae*: Avicenna, Aquinas, and the Aristotelian Doctrine of Substance'.

[18] We might say that this instinct also permeates Thomas's justly-famous eucharistic hymn, *Te adoro*: 'O thou whom now beneath a veil we see'... etc.: it is only in heaven that we shall know and understand Christ's presence fully.

[19] Right from the start of his *Summa* Aquinas regularly reminds his readers that strictly speaking we cannot know what God is, but only what he is *not* (see *Summa Theologiae* I. q3, Prologue).

and relegates it to a mere footnote[20]), let alone a collapse into simple incoherence; instead it is a manifestation of precisely the form of chastened 'desire' (desire to control, to predict, to define 'divine things') that surely should attend any account of the eucharist and its meaning. This is a very important point for my current purposes, because I want to posit here that Thomas, precisely because of his metaphysical subtleties in neo-'Aristotelian' terms, gives us also certain *resistant markers* of how to proceed rightly with the question of eucharistic 'presence'; and if these are ignored, we are led on to graver doctrinal and pastoral difficulties. I say this moreover in the spirit of ecumenical *rapprochement*, because I think these features of his account are important for anyone who wishes to defend a doctrine of 'real presence' (and that would of course include Anglicans, Lutherans, and Orthodox, as well as Roman Catholics), whether or not they wish to encumber themselves with the traditional Catholic bag and baggage of the language of 'transubstantiation'. Let me explain further.

'Resistant Markers' in Thomas's Account of Transubstantiation: In Pursuit of a 'Discerning Apophaticism'

My suggestion is that we posit the following 'resistant markers', so-called, in Thomas's own discussion of transubstantiation in *Summa Theologiae* III. qq. 73–78.[21] Firstly, there is this matter of choosing a *discerning* apophaticism, as I have just called it. Secondly, there is the principle that the operation of this apophaticism must be congruent with the metaphysics of *incarnation* that ultimately sustains it, including the relation of the divine Word and 'fleshliness' that is thereby implied. And thirdly, there is the question of attendant sacramental

---

[20] *The Anglican-Roman Catholic Agreement on the Eucharist* (*ARCIC*), orig. 1971, ed. Julian W. Charley (Bramcote, Nottingham: Grove Books, 1972), 11, n. 2: 'The term [transubstantiation] should be seen as affirming the *fact* of Christ's presence and of the mysterious and radical change which takes place. In contemporary Roman Catholic theology it is not understood as explaining *how* the change takes place'.
[21] All citations are from the Blackfriars edition of the *Summa Theologiae* (vol. 58, ed. William Barden O.P., Cambridge: C.U.P. reprint, orig. 1964).

efficacy, in particular the transformation of what Thomas calls the 'affections', an issue which I shall argue is an intrinsically significant accompaniment to what he discusses under the rubric of 'transubstantiation'. I shall essay a reflection about each of these strands of thought in turn.

It is in the first area, of course – that of the extent of Thomas's capacity to *explain* presence – that all the blood is spilt in assessing the 'success' or otherwise of his theory. As we have already acknowledged at some length, it is not difficult to demonstrate that Thomas's purported attempt to 'explain' Christ's 'transubstantiated' presence in the bread and wine of the eucharist *positively* runs into insuperable difficulties if one simply applies the normal assumptions of classic Aristotelian physics and metaphysics. P.J. Fitzpatrick, for instance, is one commentator who drives this critique home with ferocity when he claims that 'transubstantiation is a eucharistic application of Aristotelian terms which *abuses them to the point of nonsense*'.[22] But a close reading of *ST* III. q. 75 shows Thomas insistently and carefully explaining why it cannot be that *this* change – in transubstantiation – is like any other sort of 'natural' change: Christ's body cannot be in the sacrament in the same way as any other body is in place (*art.* 1); for this body 'begins simultaneously to be in different places' (*art.* 2); the bread cannot be annihilated, according to Thomas, or reduced to 'prime matter' (leaving it with no form at all), so it must be transformed in some divinely *unique* and *sui generis* way (*art.* 3); and hence – the apophatic *coup de grâce* – 'This conversion is *not like any natural change*, but is entirely beyond the powers of nature and is brought about *purely by God's power*' … 'Hence this change is not a formal change, but a substantial one. *It does not belong to the natural kinds of change* (*Nec continetur inter species motus naturalis*)' (*art.* 4). The result is that we cannot be guided by our senses in assessing *this* particular kind of change; we are required to respond in *faith* (*art.* 5), or – as Thomas puts it later (q. 76, art. 7) – with the intellect in its capacity as a '*spiritual* eye'.[23]

---

[22] P. J. Fitzpatrick, *In Breaking of Bread: The Eucharist and Ritual* (Cambridge: C.U.P., 1993), 11, my emphasis.

[23] The 'spiritual senses' doctrine does therefore seem to inhere significantly in *some* way in Thomas's eucharistic thought, *pace* Richard Cross's insistence that Aquinas has no consistent epistemological need for a formal account of such: see Richard Cross,

Although Thomas's ruling out of the 'annihilation' option was to remain contentious,[24] it is obvious that Thomas is playing his 'mystery cards' here with great care and caution; and this is what I mean by a '*chastened* or *discerning* apophaticism'. He is perfectly aware that he can only apply the Aristotelian distinctions in a particular – though not *random*, note, or *irrational* – sense; but he equally does not wish to multiply discrete appeals to the miraculous. His insistence on the substantial change of bread *into* Christ's body, moreover (instead of an extrinsic miracle of annihilation and replacement) seems to me entirely consistent with his general sacramental principle (*ST* III. q. 60, art. 6) that the eucharist must be seen as an *extension* of 'the mystery of the Incarnation', in which 'Word is united to the flesh', and thus our bodies given 'medicine' just as our souls receive the word in 'faith'. Eucharistic change is an unfolding of that fundamental, incarnational transformation of fleshly life, and in continuity with it: were there 'annihilation' rather than *change*, something basic to this incarnational understanding of 'sacrament' would be abrogated.[25] The result, at one climax moment of the discussion of transubstantiation, is a passage with important implications for desire and gender as understood by Thomas: citing Ambrose, Thomas argues that transubstantiation *must* be 'unlike any natural change' since it is the outcome of the original divine impregnation of the Virgin (*ST* III. q. 75, art. 4). It is seemingly therefore a primal, and unique, erotic act crossing the boundary between divine and human that both guarantees and parallels the unique 'change' involved in eucharistic presence.

Once we read the section of the *Tertia Pars* on transubstantiation in close relation to the earlier section on the 'hypostatic union' (*ST* III. qq. 1–6. esp. q. 2), then, the playing of 'mystery cards' that we have already noted in Thomas's discussion of eucharistic presence assumes

---

'Thomas Aquinas', in eds. Paul L. Gavrilyuk and Sarah Coakley, *The Spiritual Senses: Perceiving God in Western Christianity* (Cambridge: C.U.P., 2012), 174–189.

[24] As Marilyn McCord Adams puts it, defending Scotus's later alternative: if you are going to have a *sui generis* divine intervention anyway, why not one involving Christic presence *without* conversion, as such, but simply a new *relation* of presence? (Adams, 'Aristotle and the Sacrament of the Altar', 224).

[25] On this point see also Herbert McCabe, O.P., *God Matters* (London: Geoffrey Chapman, 1987), 154, to whose own account of transubstantiation we shall shortly return.

a structural parallel to the treatment of the equally mysterious *particularity* of Christ's human nature (*ST* III. q. 2, art. 5), in which soul and body are *uniquely* joined together 'in such a way as to be conjoined to another and higher principle [the divine Word]'. *Pace* Richard Cross, who sees this ploy as thoroughly dubious and tending to monophysitism,[26] I am more inclined – as I have argued in detail elsewhere[27] – to read it as a firm stress on the non-negotiable, albeit hypostatically unique, *reality* of Christ's incarnate humanity, a *guarding* of the full integrity of the humanity. It is this marked care over the transfigured capacity of human nature that surely explains Thomas's repeated insistence on the resistant incarnational *fleshliness* of the sacrament of the eucharist and its significance no less as transformative 'food' than as spiritual reality (e.g., q. 73, art 6). Participation in God precisely involves *eating*, ingesting, even though – as Augustine had already said in the *Confessions* – its spiritual nature makes it more like being turned into what one eats (Christ) than turning Him into you (q. 73, art. 3).

One final feature of Thomas's account demands our attention, as I have already hinted. There are several places in Thomas's discussion of the eucharist where he expatiates on the necessarily transformative effects of the rite (if efficacious) on our 'affections', or what we might call the apparatus of our desire.[28] In a moving passage in *ST* III. q. 73, art 5, Thomas first reiterates his point about the incarnational foundation of the eucharist, and explains that Jesus had to give us a 'sacrament of his body and blood' so that the 'body which he had hypostatically united to himself' could still be salvifically available to us.

---

[26] See Richard Cross, *The Metaphysics of the Incarnation* (Oxford: O.U.P., 2002), 51–64.

[27] 'The Person of Christ', in eds. Denys Turner and Philip McCosker, *The Cambridge Companion to the Summa* (Cambridge: C.U.P., 2016), 222–239.

[28] The theme of 'desire' in Aquinas is of far-reaching significance, and performs both a metaphysical and an epistemological role in his thinking. For Aquinas's careful account of human desire as an a 'appetite', and its relation to (rational) will and intellect, see esp. *Summa Theologiae* I. qq 80–83, and I–II. qq 30–31. For one recent study of this topic in Aquinas, which focuses especially on what (in contemporary parlance), is now called 'emotion', and thus links to contemporary analytic philosophy, see Nicholas E. Lombardi, O.P., *The Logic Of Desire: Aquinas and Emotion* (Washington, DC: Catholic University of America Press, 2010).

He goes on – in language that is now rendered particularly evocative for descendants of Newman and the Oxford movement[29] – that 'the parting of friends is the affection of love most sensitive' (*inflammatur affectus ad amicos*), and thus, in Jesus's institution of the eucharist, he transformatively invested his own human affective intensity and sense of impending loss; thus, as Thomas goes on, 'the more our affections are involved, the more things are deeply impressed upon our souls' (q. 73, art. 5). In fact the last supper was Jesus's ritualized way of gathering into *integrity* the affections, memories and bodily dispositions of his disciples so as to rightly relate them to their souls – an authentic 'incarnational' propulsion in ritualized form. However, conversely, if this uniquely integrated form of transformation *fails* to occur, Thomas warns later (q. 79, art. 8), desire is *not* purged and venial sin 'hamper[s] this sacrament's effect'. In that case, the crucial affective dimension of eucharistic presence is blocked. What should be happening, however, he says, quoting John Damascene, is that '*The fire of that desire within us which is kindled by the burning coal,* namely the sacrament, *will consume our sins and enlighten our hearts, so that we shall be enflamed and made god-like*' (ibid., citing John of Damascus, *de Fide Orthodoxa*, VI).

I have taken this much time here on neglected strands in the text of Thomas himself on the theme of transubstantiation in order to emphasize his peculiar significance, even ecumenically, for *any* attempted discussion of 'eucharistic presence'. Whilst it is tempting, with *ARCIC* and other eirenic ecumenical endeavours,[30] to bracket Thomas on transubstantiation as a theological mine-field that can lead only to harmful explosions in the ecumenical realm, I have here been suggesting exactly the opposite case. One should not hastily 'retire hurt' from this crucial ecumenical debate, and either step back away from a metaphysical account to a 'symbolic' theory, or disappear into an *undiscriminating* apophaticism in which 'mystery' is invoked as a blanket that could cover anything. For there is an important alternative, as we have now seen. Thomas has a resistant 'subtext' that is deeply theologically fruitful and regrettably overlooked: firstly, he has an

---

[29] See John Henry Newman, 'The Parting of Friends', in ed. Francis J. McGrath, F.M.S., *The Letters and Diaries of John Henry Newman*, vol. IX: *Littlemore and the Parting of Friends, May 1842–October 1843* (Oxford: O.U.P., 2006), 733–740.

[30] See above, n. 20.

intense interest in philosophical coherence, but an equally sophisticated way of indicating the *limits* of his own positive, explicative powers; secondly, he plays the 'mystery card' in eucharistic presence in precisely the same way as he does christologically (admitting what is non-identifiable with natural changes, and thus to be expressed apophatically, and insisting simultaneously on the transformative, if transgressive, *continuity* between two states of affairs, x following y);[31] thirdly, he sees what happens in the eucharist precisely as an *extension* of the mystery of the annunciation/incarnation, and thus as a bodily matter of insemination/birth; and finally he is correlatively insistent on the significance for the eucharist of bodily ingestion, integrative ritual enactment, and the importance of 'affective' transformation.

Transition to Contemporary Expositions of Transubstantiation

Having presented this textual thesis in succinct detail, I want now to contrast these 'resistant markers' of Thomas's account with some ingenious re-workings of his theory of transubstantiation that are currently on offer in the post-modern philosophical milieu. I shall shortly focus on a brief comparison of the work of Jean-Luc Marion and Catherine Pickstock in this regard, because both are consciously operating in the train of the post-Derridean discussion of 'gift' that has dominated continental philosophy of religion of late (as we saw in ch. 11), and with results that are – in my view – both revealing and concerning, especially where gender and 'bodies' are concerned. However, let me bridge into this comparison with a transitional comment on an influential, but slightly earlier, re-reading of Thomas on transubstantiation by Herbert McCabe, O.P.,[32] since McCabe's approach may already reveal a trend that the other exponents intensify.

On the face of it, McCabe would appear precisely to exemplify the 'discerningly apophatic' approach to transubstantiation I have already proposed, and that is certainly his intention. Yet on closer inspection, we see that he performs this task in a Wittgensteinian mode that troublingly seems to subsume ontology – and even bodies too – *into*

---

[31] See esp. *ST* III. q. 75, art. 8, resp.
[32] McCabe, *God Matters*, 116–129.

language. Thus McCabe will write, intriguingly, that 'Our language has *become* his [Christ's] body';[33] or that 'language itself is transformed [in the eucharist] and becomes the medium of the future, *the language itself becomes the presence*, the *bodily* presence of Christ';[34] ... 'his body is present in the mode of language – rather as meaning is present to a word'.[35] The underlying intuition is, once more, the need to protect a mystery: that we cannot 'explain' transubstantiation in terms of a *secular* philosophical set of presumptions about 'stuff' and change. We have to learn a *new* 'language' – one which only the body of Christ can disclose to us. So far so good. McCabe admits that his approach is 'enigmatic', but then tries to clarify it by saying that, 'What makes a human body *human* is that it is involved in linguistic communication'.[36]

But at this point, I myself baulk at this reduction, precisely as one informed by the insights of Thomas's own example, outlined above. For if bodies are 'really' words, then what we have is a theoretical subsumption of flesh into Word, an incipient gnosticism that also threatens to render 'inhuman' the pre-linguistic baby at the breast, the brain-damaged mute, or the inarticulate groaning of the dying. And this is odd and unexpected from McCabe, who equally wants to stress the necessity of bodiliness for all communication, and – at one point in the same discussion – the special communicative significance of the intimacy of lovers' gestures.[37] Yet at the same time, he is willing rhetorically to reduce bodies to 'language', albeit the new language learnt almost uncomprehendingly in the Mass.

Here is one theological danger, then, that threatens when we try to escape what I have identified as the cumulative lessons of Thomas's 'resistant markers': the possibility of a subsumption of body *into* Word. This lesson may be remainingly important. But for now we turn briefly to two other dangers, equally revealing and instructive. If McCabe attempts, in his re-thinking of transubstantiation, to

---

[33] Ibid., 118, my emphasis.

[34] Ibid., 128, my emphasis.

[35] Ibid., 118.

[36] Ibid., 118, my emphasis.

[37] See ibid., 117. Of course, McCabe might well riposte that, from the Wittgensteinian perspective from which he writes here, there *are* no words without bodies. Yet it remains puzzling that he does not focus more explicitly on the sustaining importance of 'fleshliness' or 'materiality' for any account of eucharistic presence.

re-parse ontology *as language*, with undergirding Wittgensteinian assumptions, then Jean–Luc Marion – as Gerard Loughlin has argued – more truly 'transcribe[s] ... ontology into ... *temporality*';[38] to which we might add: and Catherine Pickstock realigns 'Aristotelian' ontology into neo-Platonic *ecstasy*. With Marion and Pickstock, however, the philosophical conversation-partners are more Heidegger and Derrida than Wittgenstein, as we shall now see. In each of their cases, a new, post-modern, response to 'Aristotle' goes well beyond even the options outlined in our earlier discussion of contextualized, late-medieval alternatives.

Marion's 'Gift' and the Occlusion of Gender: Pickstock's 'Ecstasy' and the Problem of Enfleshment

I am obliged in this context to treat Marion's and Pickstock's intriguing renditions of transubstantiation more briefly – and thus more cavalierly – than I should like in this context. Yet some broad brush-strokes will at least indicate their main points of unity and difference, and also the reasons why I find certain *different* strands of their arguments both positive and problematic, especially in the light of what we have learnt from Thomas himself.

The novelty of Marion's approach to transubstantiation in his renowned early monograph *God Without Being*,[39] firstly, lies in his insistence that here in the eucharist, if anywhere, is what Derrida sought in his notion of a '*pure* gift',[40] and at the same time supposedly the only means of escape from the problem of 'metaphysics' in Heidegger's sense, that is, the problem of the false reification of Being.[41] Coming straight from Thomas, we have to remind ourselves

---

[38] See Gerard Loughlin, 'Transubstantiation: Eucharist as Pure Gift', in eds. David Brown and Ann Loades, *Christ: The Sacramental Word* (London: S.P.C.K., 1996), 123–141, at 136.

[39] Jean-Luc Marion, *God Without Being: Hors-Texte* (Chicago: University of Chicago Press, 1991).

[40] See Jacques Derrida, *Given Time: 1. Counterfeit Money* (Chicago: University of Chicago Press, 1992); idem, *The Gift of Death* (Chicago: University of Chicago Press, 1995).

[41] See Marion, *God Without Being*, 161–182.

that, for Marion, the true God can only be '*without* – or beyond – Being' – an idea that would of course have been completely senseless to Aquinas himself (for whom God *is*, by definition, *esse subsistens*).[42] But for Marion, this extrication from Being (in his Heideggerian sense) is crucial if we are to avoid the taint of *idolatry*. How, then, is such a God available to us at all, if He is *beyond* Being? According to Marion, we do not have to wait for death (as in Derrida) to receive this 'pure gift', since Jesus Christ, who 'exceeds every metaphysic'[43] gives himself to us in the eucharist in a way that transcends, or trumps, the normal way we think about *time*; and precisely this allows us to receive the 'pure gift' now. Instead of time being seen as something controlled by *our* consciousnesses from moment to moment, this eucharistic time is *given* afresh every moment in a way that both gathers up the past and opens us to the future: 'The eucharistic presence comes to us, at each instant, as the gift of that very instant, and, in it, of the body of the Christ in whom one must be incorporated'.[44] Only thus can it be an *icon* – a true window into God – rather than an *idol*.[45] (This is a distinction crucial in Marion's thought as part of his response to Heidegger, though in it we see him reaching – not for the first or last time – into the resources of Greek patristic thought, with echoes of the classic defence of icons at Nicaea II).

Now given Marion's antipathy to classical metaphysics in general, and Aristotle in particular, it would seem highly unlikely that he would want to hang onto the language of 'transubstantiation' at all, since – as Loughlin has rightly commented – it is a new dimension of *temporality* that here seems to be doing the work that was previously done by ontology, almost by a kind of *fiat*. However, there is here another surprising twist: Marion does want to rescue Thomas's account of

---

[42] Note that some time after writing *God Without Being*, Marion acknowledged that he there falsely implicated Aquinas in the Heideggerian problem of Being: see his 'In the Name: How to Avoid Speaking of "Negative Theology"', in eds. John D. Caputo and Michael J. Scanlon, *God, the Gift and Postmodernism* (Bloomington and Indianapolis: Indiana UP, 1999), 20–41; and 'Thomas Aquinas and Onto-the-ology', in eds. Michael Kessler and Christian Sheppard, *Mystics: Presence and Aporia* (Chicago: University of Chicago Press, 2003), 38–74.

[43] *God Without Being*, 163.

[44] Ibid., 175.

[45] See ibid, 7–24.

transubstantiation by reading it in a way that is not just '*discerningly apophatic*' (as I have outlined above, in my own exposition of Thomas's view), but what we might call *thoroughgoingly* or even *obliteratingly* apophatic. For Marion claims that Thomas is here using the language of *substantia* in a way *utterly* divorced from Aristotle;[46] and that only the council of Trent, later, misconstrued Thomas's views in a way that reconstrained the theory of transubstantiation back into a flat-footedly Aristotelian way of thinking about substance, and thus fetishized the host into a controllable object of *our* gaze.[47] For eucharistic presence to continue to take us 'beyond Being', and beyond normal time, says Marion, we must be aware of our *complete lack* of intellectual control of its explanation (such that even the 'resistant markers' I have noted in Thomas apparently evaporate): the presence of the Gift should be reduced neither to an idolatrous object that we can manipulate, nor to a code for a social programme of reform that we approve. The host is raised before us as a reminder of that *lack* of grasp, of *complete* unknowing; hence we must talk as truly of Christ's absence or 'distance' as his presence, until – eschatologically – all is fulfilled in Christ.[48] Meanwhile, 'only [this] distance ... renders communion possible',[49] and we must prepare for this communion with the silence of contemplative prayer, so that it will be really Christ that is given to us, and not some counterfeit we have made in our own image.

If Marion stresses the transformation of *time* in the eucharist, and the necessity of silence in welcoming that time non-idolatrously, Pickstock is, in contrast, surprisingly resistant to Marion's insistence on silence as a preparatory counterpart to the Word. Like McCabe in this regard, she wants the eucharist, and Christ's transubstantiated presence, to signal a *new* language so different from our current one that it subsumes all previous halting attempts at sign and language, rather than throwing us into a realm of silence supposedly *beyond* language.[50] This indeed is a significant part of *her* latter-day riposte to Derrida (and she shares this ambition with Marion): the endlessly

---

[46] See ibid., 163–164.
[47] See ibid., 164.
[48] Ibid., 169.
[49] Ibid.
[50] See Catherine Pickstock, *After Writing: On the Liturgical Consummation of Philosophy* (Oxford: Blackwell, 1998), 262, for this contrast with Marion.

deferred meaning of Derrida's 'deathly' (as she sees it) programme of deconstruction is, she insists, not just brought to completion in the eucharist, but *founded* in it. Hence her striking and celebrated claim, at the climax of *After Writing,* that transubstantiation is the 'condition of the possibility for *all* meaning'.[51]

What is meant by this? Pickstock's contention is that rather than the eucharist somehow requiring us to go *beyond* language (so Marion), it 'situates us more inside language than ever';[52] yet it is a completely new language with seemingly no obvious transition of continuity with our current one. And at this point, Pickstock starts to sound more like McCabe: 'For the resurrected body is a completely *imparted* body, *transmuted into a series of signs*'.[53] Again, then, we note that 'body' in Pickstock's eucharistic theology has a tendency, as in McCabe and Marion, to turn into *something else*, and in Pickstock's case, something intrinsically sign- and word-related. Yet there is another side to her argument, and this differentiates her rhetoric significantly from Marion's (which she criticizes): she does insist in the final paragraphs of her book that she would wish to distinguish her position from any form of Platonism or neo-Platonism in which the body must ultimately be *transcended*;[54] her claim, then, is that the ecstasy of 'desire' in the eucharist (and Pickstock, as an exponent of the Platonist tradition in this regard, significantly does *not* repress the language of desire, but celebrates it), in some sense makes us *more* bodily (in Christ) rather than less.[55]

The trouble for many commentators with this claim is that Pickstock seeks to explain transubstantiation (again, with an intensified apophaticism somewhat reminiscent of Marion) as a veritable neo-Platonic *sublation* of 'Aristotelian' categories in Thomas. Indeed, her stated view is that Thomas himself has given up on *any* rendition of 'substance' *qua* 'Aristotelian', not only in his section in the *Tertia Pars* on transubstantiation, but by extension everywhere else in his

---

[51] Ibid., 261.

[52] Ibid., 262.

[53] Ibid., 266, my emphasis (in the latter part of the sentence).

[54] See ibid., 273.

[55] Ibid., 231. What this means is of course a little obscure in the context of the philosophical discussion already provided by Pickstock here.

Summa as well.[56] He has, she claims, 'disturbed' the ontology of 'substance' and 'accidents' with the neo-Platonic distinction between 'being' and 'essence' (*esse* and *essentia*): 'Hence', she writes, 'every creature is "pulled" by its participation in *esse* beyond its own peculiar essence – it exceeds itself by receiving existence – and no created "substance" is truly substantial, truly self-sufficient, absolutely stable or self-sustaining'.[57] This represents an intriguing but essentially controversial rendition of Thomas's ontology, *tout court*, which has received much critical attention;[58] and the exegetical questions it raises necessarily go beyond the scope of this particular discussion. All I want to stress here again, however, is the insights of our earlier account of the 'resistant markers' in Thomas's text; for these are precisely

---

[56] The more complete picture of this metaphysical vision is found in Pickstock's chapter, 'Truth and Language', in eds. John Milbank and Catherine Pickstock, *Truth in Aquinas* (London: Routledge, 2001), 76–95, which is all the more important in its particular appeals to Aquinas (given the fact that Pickstock cites Thomas himself only very sparingly in her account of transubstantiation in *After Writing*). Pickstock here gives due credence to Aquinas's emphasis on 'desire' in his eucharistic theology, but again refracts his theory of eucharistic 'presence' and simultaneous 'absence' through the lens of a post-modern theory of 'signs'.

[57] *After Writing*, 261. Pickstock does not discuss the historical complications of the *various* renditions of 'Aristotelianism' in Thomas's own lifetime (see our earlier discussion, above). Some of her rhetoric might initially suggest a potential parallel with the 'Avicennan' rendition of 'substance' (see n. 16, *supra*); but in her case the solution is found in a neo-Platonic 'ecstasy', which seemingly entirely *cancels* classic 'Aristotelianism' in any of its forms, according to her rhetoric.

[58] Some of this is merely dismissive: for example, Anthony Kenny, 'Aquinas and the Appearance of Bread', *Times Literary Supplement*, 5th October, 2001, who famously ends his review, 'If this is truth in Aquinas, then there is no truth in Aquinas'. Also see John Marenbon, 'Aquinas, Radical Orthodoxy and the Importance of Truth', in eds. Wayne J. Hankey and Douglas Hedley, *Deconstructing Radical Orthodoxy: Postmodern Theology, Rhetoric and* Truth (Aldershot: Ashgate, 2005), 49–63, who finally avers that, 'The Aquinas of Radical Orthodoxy is a fine monument to the arbitrary power of postmodern hermeneutics: a totem …' (ibid., 62). But see also the penetrating assessment in Bruce D. Marshall, review of *Truth in Aquinas, The Thomist* 66 (2002), 632–637. Perhaps the most patient, sympathetic, but nonetheless painstakingly critical account of Milbank and Pickstock on Aquinas is to be found in Paul J. DeHart, *Aquinas and Radical Orthodoxy: A Critical Inquiry* (London: Routledge, 2012).

intended to respect the mysterious divinely ordered *continuity* between ordinary resistant fleshliness and incarnational transformation.

This brief comparative sketch of Marion and Pickstock is of course unsatisfactorily over-simplified; their suggestive brilliance and originality are undeniable, especially in the complex postKantian, continental, tradition in which they situate themselves;[59] and I have by no means been able to do justice to the full complexity of their positions in this account.[60] But what I think my brief outline shows us is two outcomes to take forward into our conclusions of this chapter, one negative, one positive.

My critical response to Marion and Pickstock, firstly, may be apparent from the way that I earlier set up my 'resistant markers' in Thomas. In both Marion and Pickstock (and despite their mutual disagreements), we confront an apophatic manoeuvre so profound that it threatens any resistant *continuity* between material existence as we now know it and Christic presence as delivered in the host. Indeed, this difference between here and there, or now and then, is profoundly interruptive, established either by an eschatological *fiat* (Marion), or an ecstatic invasion (Pickstock), launching us into a completely new realm and *against all appearances*. The result of this intensified apophaticism is that in both Marion and Pickstock, the *ordinary* fleshliness of the incarnation seems threatened,[61] as does the implicit emphasis on physical feeding and bodiliness in the rite itself. One is eerily reminded of the *destructive* inedia of the medieval saints described so unforgettably by Caroline Walker Bynum in *Holy Feast*

---

[59] Indeed, this is perhaps the most significant philosophical backdrop of what I have been probing here about what I have called their 'extreme apophaticism': is it not ultimately still haunted more by the spectre of Kantian *noumenal* nescience than by the paradoxes of simultaneous revelation–cum–unknowing in the authentic patristic tradition of 'apophatic' theology in the Dionysian tradition? (See again, my 'Prologue', above.)

[60] The more ambitious dimensions of Pickstock's wholesale attack on propositional 'truth' in the Western tradition is to be found in her recent book, *Aspects of Truth: A New Religious Metaphysics* (Cambridge: C.U.P., 2020), a project that goes well beyond her particular, Platonizing, interpretation of Aquinas as enunciated earlier.

[61] And this despite Pickstock's insistence (already noted) that eucharistic presence 'repeats' the incarnation, and renders us *more* bodily (whatever that means), not less.

and Holy Fast,[62] for whom eating *only* the host became an obsession, to the point of women's self-destruction and complete disregard for the ordinary physical body – ecstatic and erotic to be sure, but ultimately 'sacrificial' in the falsely *annihilative* (or punitive) sense. Further, although 'desire' is a Platonic notion greatly accentuated in Pickstock (precisely *qua* 'ecstatic'), it is utilized in a register very different from Thomas's patient insistence on the full integration of bodily affect, memory and understanding in the eucharistic rite over time.[63]

Finally, it is somewhat eerie, in Marion, to have the distinction between 'icon' and 'idol' that is so crucial for his theory of eucharistic presence worked out *specifically* in the language of the so-called 'mirror phase' of Lacan (the point in Jacques Lacan's psychology at which the child begins to repress the memory of pure identification with the mother and to move into the 'male' realm of language and signs[64]). For Marion, this self-regard in the mirror is the *essence* of what he calls 'idolatry', whereas the 'icon' avails itself to us as excess and gift, *without* our capacity for control. It cannot be that Marion is unaware of the way that Lacan himself 'genders' this particular binary – as 'masculine' over against 'feminine' – and equally impossible to believe that Marion has no awareness, in the cultured Parisian circles in which he moves, of the theological and feminist reflection on this binary of the 'mirror phase' developed by Luce Irigaray and Julia Kristeva.[65] Yet not the faintest flicker of acknowledgement of the Lacanian source, nor of its accompaniments, is made: *gendered* bodiliness is indeed completely occluded in Marion's account of eucharistic longing, a feature that perhaps coheres with what I deem the gnostic-veering tendency of his extreme apophaticism. Yet as we have seen above, Thomas's own correlation of virginal conception, incarnational transformation of

---

[62] See Caroline Walker Bynum, *Holy Feast and Holy Fast: The Religious Significance of Food to Medieval Women* (Berkeley, CA: University of California Press, 1988).

[63] It is important therefore to note how this difference of emphasis distinguishes Pickstock's account of divine/human 'desire' from my own, as adumbrated throughout these last four chapters, and earlier in my *God, Sexuality and the Self*.

[64] For this (now-classic) short essay, see Jacques Lacan, 'The mirror stage as formative of the function of the I', in idem, *Écrits: A Selection* (London: Tavistock, 1977), 1–7.

[65] For their reception and feminist critique of Lacan, see Luce Irigaray, *Speculum of the Other Woman* (Ithaca, NY: Cornell University Press, 1974), and Julia Kristeva, *Powers of Horror: An Essay on Abjection* (New York: Columbia University Press, 1980).

physical flesh, and transubstantiated host, is in contrast shot through with implicit gender evocations from the outset: it is precisely through the 'yes' of the Virgin that Christ takes ordinary human flesh and transforms it.

The positive conclusion that I draw from these post-modern theological authors, on the other hand, is that the illuminating emphasis on the eschatological implication of time in the eucharist helps to drive home afresh something also differently hinted at in Thomas: that eucharistic presence in the host is constricted, incomplete, without *efficacious* fulfilment, and therefore that 'presence' and 'absence' are seemingly two sides of the same eucharistic coin as long as historical time endures.[66] This reflection helps us to draw attention away from the danger of the host as a *fetishized* object (as both Marion and Pickstock insightfully remark), and instead look to the transformative presence of Christ disposed into the 'body' of believers *and* in those they seek to serve, as well as densely in the bread and wine themselves, and reflectedly in the person of the priest who celebrates. This conclusion need not, I believe, undermine the continuing significance for many Christians of 'adoration' or 'exposition' of the reserved host itself; but it does chasten it into a continued reflection on the necessary ethical and spiritual *outcomes* of Christ's efficacious presence. This greater *distribution* of the sense of Christic presence, indeed, opens the possibility of a certain renewal of ecumenical understanding, since it was in the tortured controversies of the Reformation *Abendmahlstreit* that false alternatives were set up on eucharistic presence that threw, for instance, presence in the host and presence in the people into a disjunctive ideological choice, which split the church (and the 'body of Christ') at the time.[67]

---

[66] But this does not mean that eschatology should be *collapsed* into the presence/absence dimensions of the daily eucharist itself. For an important critique of this tendency in Pickstock's thinking, see Euan Alexander Grant, 'An Eschatological Critique of Catherine Pickstock's Liturgical Theology', *New Blackfriars* 100 (2019), 493–508.

[67] For a brilliant résumé of the eucharistic divergences of the early Reformers, see David C. Steinmetz, 'The Eucharist and the Identity of Jesus in the Early Reformation', in Beverly Roberts Gaventa and Richard B. Hays, *Seeking the Identity of Jesus: A Pilgrimage* (Grand Rapids, MI: Eerdmans, 2008), 270–284.

Conclusions: Flesh and Blood – The Eucharist, Desire and Affective Transformation

Let me now try to sum up the systematic conclusions to this chapter, but also to this volume as a whole.

I have attempted in this last chapter to re-read Aquinas's account of eucharistic presence as 'transubstantiation' with new attention to his accompanying sub-texts of virginal impregnation, incarnational transformation of the possibilities of human flesh, and eucharistic efficacy as crucially involving affective, bodily outcomes of transformed desire. What these accompanying features of the eucharist drive home afresh is Thomas's absolute insistence on the transformative continuity and congruence of ordinary physicality and divine presence in the eucharistic host, the core instinct that lies at the heart of his understanding of transubstantiation, whatever the particular rendition or reception of 'Aristotle' that sustains it. At the same time, and in *riposte* to outright scoffers at that 'Aristotelian' rendition, I have drawn attention to the careful, indeed discerning, 'apophatic' markers in Aquinas's text, his insistence as to the *limits* of philosophical explanation in this matter, limits which again link to the insistent bodily emphasis of his account. Finally, I have commented briefly, both critically and appreciatively (and by way of contrast to my own rendition), to some important contemporary post-modern accounts of transubstantiation that attempt to modify or dissolve the seemingly problematic links with 'Aristotelianism', and replace those with inspiration from other, more recent, philosophical conversation-partners, or with an appeal to specifically neo-Platonic 'ecstasy'. Their efforts, I have argued, have been only partially successful to the extent that they tend to abstract disarmingly from ordinary physicality or fleshliness, and so to intensify their apophatic strategy as to render the meaning of transformed, efficacious bodiliness puzzling or 'ecstatically' arcane.

Returning finally to Thomas's own accompanying account of sacramental efficacy, then, is a fit focus for any attempt to assess his theory of transubstantiation, more generally. For it has been the burden of the foregoing argument to insist that any proper assessment of that theory, rather than isolating its apparent metaphysical oddities as straightforwardly explanatory of the unique Christic presence in the eucharist, should at the very least *contextualize* it as Aquinas also did: in direct continuity with his sophisticated account of Christ's 'hypostatic union', on the one hand, but no less importantly, in integral connection with his equally sophisticated account of human affective, and *efficacious*, responsiveness to the ingestion of the sacramental meal.

★

Now let me sum up my final conclusions, and also draw attention to the way in which the discussion of the last section of this volume has attempted to contribute to the overall theme of christological method, which has propelled the argument of the book as a whole.

I have been concerned in the last four chapters of this book with the category of 'desire' (specifically in its eucharistic manifestation) – its divine nature, and our human participation in it: the veritable stuff of our salvation. I have tried to show that the rendering of the differences of gender are *not* irrelevant to that salvation, precisely because adumbrated by the crossing of 'difference' that occurred transgressively, and indeed cosmologically, in the incarnation itself; but ultimately therefore they must be rendered subservient, fluid, to the flow of divine incarnational desire that, in the Spirit, 'breaks' human idolatries and restrictive categories and remakes us in Christ. This crossing of difference is founded in the incarnation, manifested symbolically in the priest's body and movements in the eucharist, and is implicit too in the transactions of 'real presence'. This approach to gender, I have tried to show, is a very different one, and in some ways more radical, than that characteristically used by contemporary feminist and queer theologies, where the co-opting of a *secular* view of gender then becomes a sort of blunt instrument for beating the Christian tradition and excoriating it.

Correlatively, I have argued that the ostensibly unconnected 'differences' of rich and poor are curiously aligned with this same logic: here, too, we must be involved in a re-thinking of the distribution of wealth, which proceeds not merely from the well-intentioned *largesse* of the wealthy, but at the same time from another 'breakage' in the Spirit that causes an inversion. It is the down-trodden and the despised who *give us* Christ, and so complete the trinitarian logic of 'gift', 'sacrifice' and 'presence' started at the incarnation, re-instantiated every time bread and wine are shared, but never – I have argued – brought *efficaciously* to completion until that *epicletic* breakage is fulfilled. In an important sense, then, eucharistic 'presence' in the *host* remains

blocked, uncompleted, without the moral transformation and responsiveness to the Spirit's working that is here demanded. In ritual terms,
the *fraction* of the host, Christ's own body broken and distributed,
signals not only that Christ is given to all, but no less the necessity that
all the brokenness of the world be gathered back into Him 'so that
nothing may be lost' (John 6. 12). It is the integrity of the body of
Christ that is finally at stake, as I have argued all along. Further, I have
attempted to show how the disruptive transformations required by
the eucharist in our consciousness – 'our souls and bodies' – cannot
come about *merely* by *taking thought*, important though this is, still less
by a kind of dogmatic, *falsely* 'apophatic' erasure: it is a matter too of
irreducibly *physical* ingestion, and of a willingness to be led into
unconscious realms where the Spirit does its gusty and powerful work,
'blowing where it wills'. I take it that was why Jesus bequeathed us an
almost infinitely multivalent *rite* – something to say, do, eat and drink,
in honour of his body, rather than merely a creed or a theory. And
if you do not understand how rites have the performative capacity
so to mediate contradictions and invert otherwise 'reasonable'
presumptions, then, to return to this chapter's opening, '*you ain't got it*'.

As for the current Anglican and Roman Catholic ructions about
bodies, sex, gender and the priesthood, finally, not to speak of the
probable continuing 'breaking' of the Anglican communion on issues
of gender and sexuality, I hope this volume will have also given some
further food for thought in that area. For it is a characteristically 'liberal' ploy, when confronted with the current *débacles* on homosexuality, to retort: '*Can we talk about something else?* The world's poor are
starving and dying, and we are arguing about *sex?*'; just as it is also a
characteristically 'liberal' ploy, when confronted by the issue of wom-
en's ordination, to deny that gendered bodies have anything whatever
to do with it. If these last chapters have done nothing else, I hope that
they will have given the lie to such rhetorical disjunctions: 'This bread
which we break', I have argued, is the key to the integrity of desire,
of gendered bodies, and of *Christic* 'orientation' – the only orientation, one might dare to say, that finally 'matters'. It is no less the key to
the irreducible *combination* of 'sacrifice' and 'gift' that is required for us
to resist the blandishments of our culture's endless 'commodification
of desire,' and so not only to resist those enticements, ascetically,
creatively and politically, but also – and finally – to receive back Christ
himself from the 'broken'.

Index

The Broken Body: Israel, Christ and Fragmentation, First Edition. Sarah Coakley.
© 2024 John Wiley & Sons Ltd. Published 2024 by John Wiley & Sons Ltd.

Printed and bound by CPI Group (UK) Ltd, Croydon, CR0 4YY

09/12/2024

14607540-0001